# INTERNATIONAL FACULTY IN HIGHER EDUCATION

In an interconnected and globally competitive environment, faculty mobility across countries has become widespread, yet is little understood. Grounded in qualitative methodology, this volume offers a cutting-edge examination of internationally mobile academics today and explores the approaches and strategies that institutions pursue to recruit and integrate international teachers and scholars into local universities. Providing a range of research-based insights from case studies in key countries, this resource offers higher education scholars and administrators a comparative perspective, helping to explain the impact that international faculty have on the local university, as well as issues of retention, promotion, salaries, and the challenges faced by these internationally mobile academics.

**Maria Yudkevich** is Associate Professor of Economics and Vice-Rector of the National Research University Higher School of Economics (HSE) in Moscow, Russia.

**Philip G. Altbach** is Research Professor and Founding Director of the Center for International Higher Education at Boston College, USA.

**Laura E. Rumbley** is Associate Director of the Center for International Higher Education at Boston College, USA.

# INTERNATIONAL FACULTY IN HIGHER EDUCATION

Comparative Perspectives on Recruitment, Integration, and Impact

Edited by Maria Yudkevich, Philip G. Altbach, and Laura E. Rumbley

NEW YORK AND LONDON

First published 2017
by Routledge
711 Third Avenue, New York, NY 10017

and by Routledge
2 Park Square, Milton Park, Abingdon, Oxon, OX14 4RN

*Routledge is an imprint of the Taylor & Francis Group, an informa business*

© 2017 Taylor & Francis

The right of Maria Yudkevich, Philip G. Altbach, and Laura E. Rumbley to be identified as the authors of the editorial material, and of the authors for their individual chapters, has been asserted in accordance with sections 77 and 78 of the Copyright, Designs and Patents Act 1988.

All rights reserved. No part of this book may be reprinted or reproduced or utilised in any form or by any electronic, mechanical, or other means, now known or hereafter invented, including photocopying and recording, or in any information storage or retrieval system, without permission in writing from the publishers.

*Trademark notice*: Product or corporate names may be trademarks or registered trademarks, and are used only for identification and explanation without intent to infringe.

*Library of Congress Cataloging in Publication Data*
Names: Yudkevich, Maria, author. | Altbach, Philip G., author. | Rumbley, Laura, author.
Title: International faculty in higher education : comparative perspectives on recruitment, integration, and impact / by Maria Yudkevich, Philip G. Altbach, Laura E. Rumbley.
Description: New York : Routledge, [2017]
Identifiers: LCCN 2016025322| ISBN 9781138685161 (hbk) | ISBN 9781138685178 (pbk) | ISBN 9781315543437 (ebk) | ISBN 9781134857807 (mobipocket/kindle)
Subjects: LCSH: College teachers, Foreign—Cross-cultural studies.
Classification: LCC LB1778 .Y83 2017 | DDC 378.1/2—dc23
LC record available at https://lccn.loc.gov/2016025322

ISBN: 978-1-138-68516-1 (hbk)
ISBN: 978-1-138-68517-8 (pbk)
ISBN: 978-1-315-54343-7 (ebk)

Typeset in Bembo
by Apex CoVantage, LLC

# CONTENTS

| | |
|---|---:|
| *Preface* | *vii* |
| *Acknowledgments* | *ix* |
| | |
| 1 International Faculty in 21st-Century Universities: Themes and Variations<br>*Philip G. Altbach and Maria Yudkevich* | 1 |
| 2 The Long-Term Mobility of International Faculty: A Literature Review<br>*Georgiana Mihut, Ariane de Gayardon, and Yulia Rudt* | 15 |
| 3 International Faculty in a Brazilian University: International Trajectories in a Nationalized System of Scientific Production<br>*Ana Maria F. Almeida, Mauricio Érnica, Luciano Antonio Digiampietri, and Marcelo Knobel* | 32 |
| 4 International Faculty in Canada: Recruitment and Transition Processes<br>*Diane V. Barbarič and Glen A. Jones* | 51 |
| 5 International Faculty in Two Top-Tier Chinese Universities: One Country, Two Types of Internationals<br>*Gerard A. Postiglione and Xie Ailei* | 76 |

6 Integrating International Academic Staff into the Local Academic Context in Lithuania and Estonia 101
*Anna-Lena Rose and Liudvika Leišytė*

7 Recruitment and Integration of International Faculty at German Universities: The Case of the University of Konstanz 124
*Martin Bruder and C. Giovanni Galizia*

8 International Faculty Recruitment in Kazakhstan: The Case of Nazarbayev University 150
*Alan Ruby, Aliya Kuzhabekova, and Jack T. Lee*

9 Attraction, Integration, and Productivity of International Academics in Mexico 173
*Sylvie Didou Aupetit*

10 International Academic Recruitment in a Turbulent Environment: The Case of the Higher School of Economics in Russia 196
*Valentina Kuskova and Maria Yudkevich*

11 International Faculty in Saudi Arabia's Universities 220
*Mohammad A. AlOhali*

12 International Academics in Africa: The South African Experience 240
*Damtew Teferra*

13 International Faculty in Higher Education: Common Motivations, Disparate Realities, and Many Unknowns 267
*Laura E. Rumbley and Hans de Wit*

*Contributors* 288
*Index* 295

# PREFACE

The idea for this book stems from our conviction that the academic profession is increasingly globalized and internationalized, with dramatically increased mobility worldwide. There are no accurate statistics concerning the numbers of globally mobile academics, and widely accepted definitions for this population do not exist. However, the United Nations Organization for Education, Science and Culture (UNESCO) Institute for Statistics estimates that some 4.1 million students studied internationally in 2013. Although there is no clear correlation between student and faculty mobility, it is easily possible to speculate that there are tens of thousands—perhaps more—internationally mobile faculty on the move globally today.

Our basic concern in this volume is to examine how universities and academic systems in eleven countries attract international faculty and to understand the role international faculty play in the systems and individual universities where they are employed. All of the cases examine the following themes—and many go beyond them:

- National policies relating to the appointment of international faculty
- Regulations and other requirements concerning the hiring, promotion, and contractual arrangements for international faculty
- University interests in hiring internationally
- Comparisons between international and domestic faculty relating to terms and conditions of work, salaries, and other variables
- Opinions of international faculty concerning hiring, salaries, promotions, and other aspects of their work

Not all of the chapters provide a full analysis of all of these themes due to data limitations. However, taken together, they are able to provide a coherent, though diverse, picture of national policies around the world.

The basic methodology of this volume is simple: We have asked experts in eleven countries to write according to a common template and to respond to a consistent set of questions. Of course, the chapters reflect to some extent the available data and the specific interests of the researchers, but all deal with the core considerations framing the research.

This is the sixth book focused on various important aspects of contemporary higher education in comparative perspective co-sponsored by the highly productive collaboration between the Laboratory for Institutional Analysis at the National Research University Higher School of Economics in Moscow and the Center for International Higher Education at Boston College (Altbach, Reisberg, Yudkevich, Androushchak & Pacheco, 2012; Altbach, Androushchak, Kuzminov, Yudkevich & Reisberg, 2013; Yudkevich, Altbach & Rumbley, 2015a; Yudkevich, Altbach & Rumbley, 2015b; Yudkevich, Altbach & Rumbley, 2016).

## References

Altbach, P. G., Androushchak, G., Kuzminov, Y., Yudkevich, M., & Reisberg, L. (Eds.). (2013). *The global future of higher education and the academic profession: The BRICs and the United States*. Houndsmills, Basingstoke, UK: Palgrave Macmillan.

Altbach, P. G., Reisberg, L., Yudkevich, M., Androushchak, G., & Pacheco, I. F. (Eds.). (2012). *Paying the professoriate: A global comparison of compensation and contracts*. New York: Routledge.

Yudkevich, M., Altbach, P. G., & Rumbley, L. E. (Eds.). (2015a). *Academic inbreeding and mobility in higher education*. Houndsmills, Basingstoke, UK: Palgrave Macmillan.

Yudkevich, M., Altbach, P. G., & Rumbley, L. E. (Eds.). (2015b). *Young faculty in the Twenty-first century: International Perspectives*. Albany, NY: State University of New York Press.

Yudkevich, M., Altbach, P. G., & Rumbley, L. E. (Eds.). (2016). *The global rankings game: Changing institutional policy, practice, and academic life*. New York: Routledge.

# ACKNOWLEDGMENTS

This research project was funded largely by the Basic Research Program at the National Research University Higher School of Economics (HSE) in Moscow. It was designed and implemented by the research team of Maria Yudkevich, Philip Altbach, and Laura Rumbley. At HSE, we thank Vera Arbieva and Natalia Denisova for their excellent technical support. At the Center for International Higher Education at Boston College, we thank Hans de Wit for his overall support and constructive input, as well as Salina Kopellas for her technical assistance. Laura Rumbley was principally responsible for coordinating the research and for editing the chapters.

We are, of course, mainly indebted to our co-authors and research colleagues—a number of whom are themselves international faculty, living out academic careers outside of their country of origin—who authored the case study chapters. Their expertise and dedication to this project are at the core of this book.

Maria Yudkevich, Moscow, Russian Federation
Philip G. Altbach and Laura E. Rumbley, Chestnut Hill,
Massachusetts, USA

# 1

# INTERNATIONAL FACULTY IN 21st-CENTURY UNIVERSITIES

## Themes and Variations

*Philip G. Altbach and Maria Yudkevich*

In the era of globalization, it is hardly surprising that growing numbers of academics are working outside of their home countries. Universities are themselves increasingly globalized—they are perhaps the most globalized of all prominent institutions in society. Even though the global percentage of international academics is small—there are no accurate statistics and there are a variety of challenges in defining international academics—this group is quite important. We broadly define international faculty as academics who hold appointments in countries where they were not born and/or where they did not receive their first postsecondary degree. In most cases, they are not citizens of the country in which they hold their academic appointment. They are drivers of international consciousness at universities, they are often top researchers, and in some countries they constitute a large percentage of the academic labor force.

Although there is very little research on this group of academics, they seem to cluster into four broad categories. A small but highly visible group of international faculty holds appointments at top research universities around the world, but especially in the major English-speaking countries—the United States, Canada, Australia, and to some extent the United Kingdom. A second group is employed by mid-range or upper-tier universities in a small number of countries that, as a matter of policy due to their size, geographic location, or specific perceived needs, appoint international faculty—such as Switzerland, Hong Kong, and Singapore. A third group teaches at universities in countries where there is a shortage of local staff—such as Saudi Arabia and other Gulf countries, some African countries, and a few others. Here, international academics are frequently hired to teach lower-level courses and often come from Egypt, South Asia or other regions and frequently from nonprestigious universities. The fourth category, which overlaps the first three, consists of academics who immigrated from one country to another and obtained citizenship in that country—in some ways they may be considered 'pure' international faculty, while in other ways they are not. A final group includes academics who have obtained their doctorates abroad, and perhaps have had a postdoc abroad, and continue on to make their careers abroad as well. Some international faculty can be found in virtually every country in the world.

## Why Hire International Faculty?

The rationales for hiring international academics vary considerably. They are seen as key contributors to university internationalization because they bring experiences of other academic systems and perhaps different paradigms of research and teaching. Hiring 'high-profile' international faculty may be a quick way to boost research productivity because these professors can attach their research profiles to their new institutions and, of course, contribute their work once they are hired. A small number of universities want to be fully international in research and teaching, and therefore have a policy to hire faculty members internationally, as well as to recruit an international student population; these institutions recruit faculty and often students without reference to nationality. International faculty may help foster institutional reform or innovation because of their experiences in other countries. Perhaps the most common reason for hiring international faculty is that they fill gaps in teaching and research at a university. Many countries have severe shortages of local academics and must look outside for needed personnel. Without question, international academics are a central part of the global higher education environment of the 21st century.

## Definitional Dilemmas

Who are international faculty? As noted, we are using the broadest possible definition—individuals who were not born in and/or do not have their first degree from a postsecondary institution in the country where they have their primary academic appointment—and the appointment must be regular, full-time status. There are many other definitions in common use around the world. Many countries use visa or citizenship categories to define international faculty. For example, Saudi Arabia considers anyone who is not a Saudi citizen international faculty, no matter where they may have been educated—and it is very difficult to obtain Saudi citizenship. The United States has a complexity of visa categories and several 'pre-citizenship' categories, but citizenship is relatively easy to obtain—and American citizens are not considered international faculty—thus making it impossible to calculate the true number of international faculty in American universities. Canada defines international faculty as those who have received their advanced degrees in another country and were born outside of Canada because obtaining Canadian citizenship is also relatively easy. Other countries have other ways of defining international faculty. And many simply leave definitions up to individual universities.

There are a variety of academic appointments that, in some countries, are considered faculty level (and therefore potentially occupied by 'international faculty') which fall outside the definition we have endeavored to stick to in this study. For example, in some places, postdoctoral appointments or research fellows have faculty status. In others, lecturers or even graduate fellows working on a doctoral degree are counted. For the purposes of this discussion, these categories are not considered international faculty, although they may bring significant international experience and orientation to the university. Similarly, international master's and doctoral students, who may play a significant internationalization role in universities, are not considered international faculty, although some of them may do some teaching and most (particularly at the doctoral level) are involved in research.

Some countries or universities, especially those eager to internationalize their institutions or increase their status in the rankings, hire international faculty on a part-time basis—these individuals typically hold their main appointment in one country and spend part of the academic year in another country. In some cases, these part-time or occasionally 'honorary' appointments are made specifically to produce better statistics for research or internationalization—thus boosting ranking or other measures. Our definition would not permit such part-timers to be included as international faculty.

## Internationalization and International Faculty

Many countries and institutions see employing non-native academics as a key part of internationalization strategies. Indeed, international faculty are often seen as the 'spearhead' of internationalization. Further, increased numbers of international faculty are seen as a key marker of internationalization by the global rankings and often by ministries and other policy makers within countries.

It is assumed that international faculty will bring new insights to research, teaching, and perhaps to the ethos of the university. But, of course, the effectiveness of the contributions of international faculty depends on the organizational arrangements of the university, the expectations on both sides for contributing to internationalization, and other factors. While there do not seem to be many available data, international faculty are often not effectively integrated into the internationalization programs of many universities. They teach in their subject areas but are asked to do little else for the university. And in many cases, the lack of familiarity of international faculty with the norms and perhaps the politics of the local academic system and institution may limit their participation in governance and other university functions.

International faculty in non–English-speaking environments are often key contributors to increasing the number of English-taught courses and degree programs, and in general essential for boosting the English-language orientation of the university. The use of English for both teaching and research is seen as a key factor in internationalization, and thus international academic staff who have competence in English have an advantage over others in obtaining appointments.

Many countries and universities have increased the number of international faculty as a matter of institutional and sometimes national policy. Government-funded excellence programs or related initiatives often include funding to hire international academics. This is the case in the Russian 5–100 program and in Japan's new "Global 30" effort, among others. In some cases, universities choose cheaper and lower-quality options in terms of recruitment to increase formal indicators of internationalization as much as possible. These programs also include plans to expand the numbers of English-taught courses and degrees, as well as an upgrade in foreign-language competence of professors and students. In other words, in non–English-speaking countries, the expectations for international faculty are higher as they include both increasing excellence in teaching and research, and contributing to the creation of an English-speaking environment for both domestic faculty and students.

At the same time, bringing international faculty into the environment where the local national language (other than English) is dominant creates evident challenges for their successful integration into the academic and social life of the university, and thus affects the future prospects for their careers in the university and the country.

## National Policies Relating to International Faculty

Some countries and universities welcome international faculty, and even implement initiatives to attract them. Others are much less welcoming. Some universities have stated policies encouraging the recruitment of international faculty. Harvard University, among a few others around the world, has a specific goal that each faculty member hired should be the best globally, without regard to citizenship or national origin. Universities in Hong Kong, Switzerland, and Singapore have as a goal to hire about half of their faculty on the international market. A growing list of countries has national—and, in many cases, institutional—policies to hire internationally in an effort to internationalize the academic profession, increase overall English competence and offer degree programs in English, improve research productivity, and—not incidentally—improve placement in the global rankings.

More than a few countries, perhaps surprisingly, place various obstacles in the way of hiring international faculty. Many have extremely complicated and bureaucratic procedures relating to obtaining work permits, procedures concerning security and other issues, and visa regulations, which are sometimes combined with numerical quotas relating to specific job categories, sometimes including academic and research positions. In some cases, bureaucratic and other procedural and legal barriers at the national level are a serious detriment to appointing international academics, and may restrict the number and the kinds of appointments available. Another problematical example is the treatment of spouses or partners when negotiating complex visa categories, work permit arrangements, and the like.

There are also examples of national policies that are aimed against international academic appointments. India, until quite recently, had national regulations that prevented offering permanent academic appointments to noncitizens, and even now only a handful of foreigners can be found in Indian universities. Canada, from time to time, has imposed "Canada first" hiring policies, under which universities have had to painstakingly prove that each individual international appointment was not taking the place of a comparably qualified Canadian. However, in general, Canada has been welcoming to international faculty—and, as mentioned, it is relatively easy to obtain citizenship. It has been noted earlier that Saudi Arabia offers only term contracts to international academics. Although the United States is quite open to hiring international academics, the bureaucratic hurdles of work permits and immigration are generally problematical and sometimes insurmountable (Hutchison, 2016).

While it is certainly true that many countries have opened their borders to highly qualified professionals, including professors, the practical challenges of rules and regulations, as well as nationalistic policies, sometimes make hiring and supporting international academics difficult. Overall, however, national policies, both in terms of bureaucratic arrangements and an orientation toward recognizing the importance of international professors, have moved in a more welcoming direction in recent years, perhaps recognizing the inevitability of globalization. At the same time, as noted earlier, the practicalities, both at the level of government regulations and bureaucracy and in terms of integrating international faculty into local academic life, remain significant almost everywhere.

In some countries or individual universities, the same procedures are used for recruiting both domestic and international faculty. However, in countries with a tendency toward academic inbreeding and/or with weak national academic markets, different procedures for these two streams of faculty emerge. When inbreeding is prevalent due to an inadequate supply of high-quality academics in-country, universities have to set different standards for local faculty and international hires. In these cases, international recruitment is used to foster competition within the university and to contribute to the long-term strategy of eliminating inbreeding (Yudkevich, Altbach & Rumbley, 2015a).

Different conditions often correspond to different contract arrangements, including prominent variations in salaries that often provide significantly better remuneration to international faculty than is provided to local faculty, which in turn may lead to social tensions between these two groups of faculty. Special effort is needed to prevent these tensions and create productive conditions for collaboration between people hired locally and those attracted from the international market.

## Institutional Policy and International Academics

Universities around the world are increasingly committed to hiring international academics. While for many academic institutions hiring foreign academics requires some modification in policy and orientation, there is noticeable movement toward more welcoming policy and practice (Helms, 2015). For some universities, arrangements for appointments, promotion, and career advancement norms were developed for citizens and must be modified for international staff. Further, in some cases, international academics require special treatment—for example, when they hold appointments at universities in their home countries as well as positions in a foreign country.

In some cases, distinguished international academics are treated as super-professors, earning higher salaries and having extra privileges. At times, although beneficial to the top scholars themselves and the hiring institutions, such arrangements can cause resentment among local faculty who do not have such advantages. In other cases, international academics may be treated as second-class academic citizens—without access to standard appointments, barred from academic governance, and often teaching more than domestic faculty.

Hiring international faculty is very expensive in many countries and is associated with some financial issues. Indeed, for universities to offer tenure-track and tenured positions to their faculty, they must be able to keep their long-term monetary commitments to these individuals and have a stable source of funding for this type of hiring arrangement. The inability of a university to find such resources results in practical restrictions in relation to long-term contracts in favor of short-term contracts (Khovanskaya, Sonin & Yudkevich, 2008). This problem is aggravated even more in times of financial crisis and instability of the local national currency. For example, in Russia, whereas local faculty care more about purchasing power parity, international faculty think more about the local currency exchange rate—since many spend their earnings in their home countries—and demand that their salaries be adjusted to levels that are competitive on the global academic market. Again, such financial obligations may be very expensive for a university to meet, and also difficult to predict.

## Teaching, Research, or Service

Although international faculty are hired for different functional purposes, teaching and research are the dominant activities. In some countries and universities, international faculty are considered a source of high-quality teaching and are expected to set properly 'international' (and sometimes innovative) standards with respect to teaching and the curriculum. Many universities seek to provide their students with some international experience and better prepare them for the global job market. A good way to do so for a large number of students is to expose them to teaching in English by international faculty in the core curriculum or in selective parts of the educational program. Evidence shows that such experiences, as well as participating in multicultural classrooms where they face diverse teaching techniques and get their first taste of learning and interacting in a non-native language, may be very important for students (Jones, 2009).

In many countries, international faculty are considered an important and powerful source of improving university research performance, and thus they are recruited mainly to do research. In such cases, universities may even be ready to waive teaching requirements and to offer a prominent international scholar low or even no teaching loads—a highly attractive proposition for scholars who want to concentrate on research. International faculty may improve the university's research performance in several ways. This can be done directly, by adding high-quality publications to the university's publication record in key international journals. In academic systems where faculty are mostly oriented to local journals and outlets, the effect of additional publications beyond the local context can be substantial. In such systems, the international faculty can share their expertise in publishing in international journals and, more broadly, share their research expertise, both as mentors and as collaborators, with local faculty. Since international faculty with some considerable external international experience are more 'visible' and better connected with the broader international community, their work may also become more widely circulated and more prominently cited. Finally, prominent international research faculty often collaborate with local faculty, thus providing valuable mentoring as well as improved international visibility for local professors and researchers.

International faculty may bring important experience in governance and administration to the university; thus, they may provide new ideas and insights into existing routines and suggest innovative ways to tackle administrative problems. Attracting international faculty to administrative duties may be a good idea, especially for academic systems that suffer from inbreeding or a general lack of external experience. However, involving international faculty in administration is not widely practiced due to several limiting factors. These factors include language barriers—it is difficult to take part in administrative processes if all documents and discussions are maintained in the local language—as well as cultural challenges. Whereas in research academics may refer to widely recognized international standards and practices, in administrative services the limited knowledge of local routines and norms may be a problem.

## Push and Pull: Motivations for International Mobility

Individuals have many reasons for choosing an international career path. They may be pushed by circumstances in their home country or university to take a position in another country, or they may be pulled by the attractions of an overseas academic job. Or, quite often, there may be a combination of push and pull factors.

While global data are unavailable, it is likely that a combination of push elements is most important in decision making. Academic salaries may be low in the home country, or working or other conditions of academic life may be unfavorable. In much of the world, academic jobs do not provide an appropriate middle-class lifestyle relevant to the standards of the country (Altbach, Reisberg, Yudkevich, Androushchak & Pacheco, 2012). Thus, many academics may find it difficult to provide adequately for themselves and their families in their home country. In many countries, there may be a shortage of full-time academic positions available, leading many to search for employment abroad. Conditions of academic work may be unfavorable—with high teaching loads, lack of general support, lack of academic freedom, or other negative factors, again pushing some to seek employment elsewhere. Problems of academic freedom; corruption in aspects of academic life; and discrimination based on ethnicity, religion, or other factors may also encourage academics to seek employment elsewhere. In many countries, the job market for academics is limited, and opportunities for career-grade appointments are particularly scarce—in which case, younger academics may look abroad for opportunities. In some countries, compulsory retirement policies may force senior academics to give up their positions before they are ready to retire, and some will seek appointments in other countries (including those associated with administrative posts).

Some countries lack clear career paths for young faculty, thus pushing some to seek more secure career paths elsewhere (Yudkevich, Altbach & Rumbley, 2015b). In other academic systems, promotion to the highest ranks is very difficult, regardless of academic accomplishments; and in many systems, promotion is awarded mainly as a result of seniority, frustrating many talented and ambitious academics. These factors, and others, may be considered push elements.

Pull forces also may encourage academics to seek employment elsewhere. Many are, of course, the mirror images of push elements. Favorable salaries, good working conditions, academic freedom, attractive living environments for the academic and his or her family—and of course the availability of jobs—and other circumstances are obvious attractions. Universities in some countries may be very attractive to young academics by offering them faster progress along the academic career ladder; greater availability of resources for ambitious research projects; and better access to data, equipment, or research assistance. An attraction may also be the possibility of obtaining citizenship—this varies considerably among countries. The chance to work with productive colleagues and to forge links with key scientific communities is also a pull factor. The availability of a stable environment for an academic career, as well as clear contractual arrangements, a system for promotion up the academic ranks, and reasonable security of tenure, are all key attractions. For example, young academics in Germany face a highly complex set of arrangements for promotion, and few can hope to be promoted up the ranks in one university, regardless of performance. This instability contributes to some Germans seeking employment abroad.

Academic culture—governance issues in universities, patterns of academic interaction, a sense of meritocracy, and other factors—may also contribute to the lure of an overseas position. As mentioned previously, in some cases, international faculty are offered contracts with more attractive conditions, such as lower teaching loads and more time and resources (both financial and infrastructural) for their research. For productive young scholars, such benefits may constitute an important pull factor. In any case, many people choose work overseas as an efficient way to improve their market value, develop more social ties, become involved in important research collaborations, and gain more visibility on the international academic market. They realize that their employment prospects in their home country, or elsewhere afterward, will critically improve by having worked at a decent university abroad for a while.

Individuals may also consider other intangible variables. These might include whether taking an overseas position is seen as a permanent or temporary move—and whether re-entering the home job market is a practical possibility. Family considerations—including general quality of life, schooling for children, jobs for spouses or partners—the ability to adjust to an entirely new foreign environment, language barriers, and other factors may enter into the equation too.

Thus, for many, the choices by individuals and families relating to international academic employment are a complex balance of push and pull factors, as well as numerous intangible elements.

## The Stratification of the International Academic Labor Market

The realities of international academic appointments vary substantially. Salaries, working conditions, and other aspects will be different from country to country. Appointments of world-renowned academics from, for example, the United Kingdom, taking jobs in the United States or Canada will differ immensely from jobs offered to a professor from Pakistan working in Saudi Arabia or Oman. The international academic labor market, like academe itself, is highly stratified.

Stratification may be based on many factors. Language is certainly a key element. For example, international mobility in the Spanish-speaking academic world of Latin America and Spain can be seen as a language-specific network. Similarly, Francophone Africa, France, and Quebec constitute another network, as do the countries of the former Soviet Union, where Russian is widely used in higher education. English conforms in part to the language network concept, but has also created its own particular global dynamic because English is the global scientific language and many non–English-speaking universities recruit English-speaking staff. Even in the English-speaking world, there is stratification. For example, there is significant mobility between India and Pakistan and the

Gulf countries of the Middle East, but seldom between those countries and the United States or the United Kingdom. At the same time, there is considerable mobility among the main English-speaking countries—the United States, United Kingdom, Canada, Australia, and a few others.

## Different Forms of Mobility

In a globalizing world, mobility is increasing not only in terms of the numbers of people who move, but also in relation to the forms that mobility can take. Some decades ago a decision to move implied a total move from one country to another and a complete abandoning of one's former university and home country. This may no longer be the case in a growing number of situations. A small number of academics, especially prominent researchers, obtain jobs at universities in other countries and may choose to work in more than one university in more than one country, splitting their time between two (and in some cases even more) institutions. They become 'servants of two masters,' and these 'master' universities must adjust to this new reality as well, taking into account that not all of the time and output of their mobile faculty member will be attributed to their organization.

In the contemporary world, people also collaborate more with people from other countries—the current means of communication (such as Skype, email, or even phones) allow people to work on collaborative projects without even meeting their co-authors in person for months or even years. Technology also allows faculty to teach without actually seeing their students in person—for example, teaching via video conference. This new reality means that there is less pressure to move simply in order to work with someone else. At the same time, such connectivity makes academics more visible and sometimes more attached to groups in other countries. This means that, potentially, they may have more incentives, and possibilities, to move.

Thus, not all forms of mobility require effort from a host university when it comes to the integration of international faculty into university life or help to accommodate to the new culture, routines, and environment. In contrast, some forms of 'partial' mobility allow a university to enjoy many benefits associated with international faculty without the need to cope with the associated problems and costs. However, this strategy may be risky and not provide the full range of longer-term benefits sought by a university with an international faculty recruitment policy, since many of the advantages of hosting international faculty lie not in an increase of formal productivity, an improvement in formal indicators, or the delivery of high-quality teaching, but are rather associated with the routine day-to-day communication between international faculty and domestic colleagues and students.

## International Scholars: Part of a Community or an Isolated Ghetto?

There are many important trade-offs for the universities that consider attracting international faculty. Should these faculty be hired to teach or to do research?

Should their salaries differ from the remuneration received by their local colleagues? Should requirements for their promotion and contract extension be different from those of domestic academics? Should they be forced to learn the national/local language or are they allowed to teach in English?

Among such important questions there is one that is of primary importance for academic life: Should international faculty be deeply integrated into the general university environment (bearing all related costs and enjoying all associated benefits), or should they be placed in a kind of 'international ghetto,' with special conditions where competitive 'international standards' are maintained? In some countries (such as the United States, Canada, or Australia), this question does not arise. In many others, however—such as Russia and Saudi Arabia—this question is of great importance and does not have an obvious answer. Deep integration of international faculty into 'ordinary' university life should contribute toward improving research and teaching culture, exposing the host institution and local academic community to new perspectives, and generally increasing diversity (Jepsen, et al, 2014). At the same time, there may also be risks associated with this process, including the possibility of social tensions between international and local faculty, and low levels of satisfaction among international scholars, due, for example, to nontransparent bureaucratic rules that dominate in many academic systems.

## The Challenging Aspects of Hiring International Professors

While this discussion has largely indicated the positive elements in the appointment of international academics, there are some problems and challenges as well. In many cases, international academics expect competitive international-level salaries—remuneration similar to that offered in such high-salary countries as the United States, Germany, France, the United Kingdom, and others. Recent research has shown that there are quite dramatic variations in academic salaries worldwide, and many of the countries seeking to hire internationally provide low average salaries (Altbach, Reisberg, Yudkevich, Androushchak & Pacheco, 2012). This means that salaries paid to international academics are often significantly higher than those for local faculty members. This may create pressures on local salaries, foster resentment among local faculty members who may be paid less than their foreign colleagues, and lead to a kind of two-tier academic salary hierarchy. At the same time, domestic faculty may feel the competitive pressure from their international colleagues, with whom they now have to compete for limited resources. In particular, in systems with high levels of academic inbreeding, international hires are considered by the local community as a potentially destabilizing factor that may destroy the status quo system that is based on local social ties, favoritism, and paternalism and that also values seniority and long-term organizational commitment. In new international colleagues, local faculty see agents of change that depreciate their specific human capital investments, and therefore such newcomers are met with opposition and distrust. Where these international hires may also be rather young, especially if they are being considered for tenure-track positions, this can contribute to the conflict, adding an intergenerational dimension to the picture.

International hiring also may raise questions of quality and fit among those hired (Grove, 2015). Academics at the pinnacle of their fields may not be willing to leave their home countries or tend to go to the major high-salary and high-prestige academic systems, such as the United States, the United Kingdom, and a small number of others. Thus, international academics available for hiring in most of the world may not be the 'academic stars' that are desired. A related issue is that professors who are well established in their careers and at the peak of their research productivity may find it difficult to be lured away from their home universities. Not only is their academic work well established, but families may be difficult to dislodge.

For universities seeking to hire international academics in large numbers for teaching purposes, there may be difficulties in obtaining accurate information about the individuals being hired. This can be a challenge in countries such as Saudi Arabia, Ethiopia, and others that hire large numbers of expatriates from the Middle East or South Asia.

In general, the issue of a university's ability to organize recruitment procedures in a way that will ensure the effective hiring of appropriate academics is a challenging one. If a university seeks international faculty to improve research and teaching, it also means that it perceives that it has weaknesses that international faculty can help correct. In such cases, it is likely that the institution lacks experience and procedures in recruiting on the international market. Cultivating mechanisms to recruit internationally—as well as to retain top international faculty—requires time and sophistication.

International faculty who are not fluent in the local language often are not able to fully participate in academic life, university committees, and the like. Thus, they may not be full citizens of the academic community, and their involvement with colleagues and students may be limited, even if the language of instruction is English or another international language. Such noninclusiveness is associated with higher risks of turnover, since these academics are not well integrated into university life and they often do not have any long-term commitment to the university. Little participation in academic governance may make people passive and quite critical when problems do arise. Expatriate faculty may tend to create their own subculture and thus cut themselves off to some degree from the mainstream of university life—or seek to transform the university into the image of institutions in their home country.

There may also be a clash of teaching styles, and perhaps also in terms of approaches to research, between local and international academics. For example, it has been noted that in the United States, professors trained in China frequently bring their lecture-oriented and relatively noninteractive teaching styles with them, and thus are at odds with local norms, perhaps necessitating some retraining in teaching philosophies and methods. Although less common, there may also be some conflicts in research cultures as well—including methodological variations and occasionally variations in norms related to author credits, citations, and the like.

Differences in administrative cultures can also add to frustration and miscommunication on both sides. Indeed, since faculty contracts do not describe the entire detailed list of mutual obligations and expectations (e.g., exactly how office hours should be run), but rather provide just a general framework describing the most important obligations and responsibilities (e.g., maximum annual teaching loads), a substantial part of mutual expectations and conditions are left unwritten. In different cultures, the understanding of these conditions may be different, thus creating substantial tensions.

None of these negative aspects necessarily argue against hiring on the international academic market, but they do point out that such hiring may bring problems as well as advantages. These aspects also suggest that substantial effort and commitment are needed to turn international recruitment into an effective mechanism for advancing teaching and research in the university and within the national academic system as a whole. This raises the question of who might be the most appropriate 'agent of change' when local academics themselves are not always supportive of, or positive toward, their international peers. The ability of a university to find the answer to this question and to successfully integrate international faculty into university life—beyond considering them a mere tool for improving formal indicators—becomes critically important for building academic excellence.

## Conclusion

International faculty are an increasingly important part of the global academic environment of the 21st century. Part of both the symbolic and practical aspects of internationalization, international academics constitute a diverse subset of the global academic labor force. At the top, distinguished senior professors are recruited by highly ranked research universities worldwide. Elsewhere, many international faculty are a necessary part of the teaching staff in countries with shortages of local academics. The motivations for institutions—and countries—to recruit international academics vary, as do the reasons that individuals seek positions outside of their home countries. One thing is clear—international faculty are a growing and increasingly important part of the global academic labor force—bringing diversity, new perspectives, and skills wherever they go.

## References

Altbach, P. G., Reisberg, L., Yudkevich, M., Androushchak, G., & Pacheco, I. F. (Eds.). (2012). *Paying the professoriate: A global comparison of compensation and contracts.* New York: Routledge.

Grove, J. (2015, October 8). Fish out of water. *Times Higher Education*, 31–35.
Helms, R. (2015). *Internationalizing the tenure code: Policies to promote a globally focused faculty*. Washington, DC: American Council on Education.
Hutchinson, C. B. (Ed.). (2016). *Experiences of immigrant professors: Cross-cultural differences, challenges, and lessons for success*. New York: Routledge.
Jepsen, D. M., Sun, J. J. M., Budhwar, P. S., Klehe, U. C., Krausert, A., Raghuram, S., & Valcour, M. (2014). International academic careers: Personal reflections. *International Journal of Human Resource Management, 25*(10), 1309–1326.
Jones, E. (Ed.). (2009). *Internationalisation and the student voice: Higher education perspectives*. London: Routledge.
Khovanskaya, I, Sonin, K., & Yudkevich, M. (2008). Budget uncertainty and faculty contracts: A dynamic framework for comparative analysis. *Center for Economic Policy Research*, Working Paper series.
Yudkevich, M., Altbach, P. G., & Rumbley, L. (Eds.). (2015a). *Academic inbreeding and mobility in higher education: Global perspectives*. New York: Palgrave-Macmillan.
Yudkevich, M., Altbach, P. G., & Rumbley, L. (Eds.). (2015b). *Young faculty in the twenty-first century: International perspectives*. Albany, NY: State University of New York Press.

# 2

# THE LONG-TERM MOBILITY OF INTERNATIONAL FACULTY

## A Literature Review

*Georgiana Mihut, Ariane de Gayardon, and Yulia Rudt*

This chapter aims to offer an overview of the scarce academic literature on the long-term mobility of international faculty around the world and attempts to include an institutional perspective on this phenomenon. This task is challenging for four reasons. First, the literature on academic mobility prioritizes discussions about student mobility and, to a large extent, neglects issues connected to the international mobility of faculty. Second, the academic literature on faculty mobility overwhelmingly focuses on aspects related to short-term mobility, as opposed to analyzing the realities related to long-term mobile faculty. Third, when long-term faculty mobility is addressed, the literature uses either the individual perspective of the mobile faculty themselves, in the form of personal narratives, or the system perspective, in the form of describing general push and pull factors causing the mobility of faculty. For the most part, the prioritization of the individual viewpoint and of system-level descriptions has marginalized the perspective of universities as key actors in the faculty mobility phenomenon. Finally, the relevant academic literature disproportionately focuses on 'star' faculty and the surge of international mobility into prestigious institutions, not the mobility of 'worker bee' faculty moving toward demand-driven tertiary education systems. This focus on a minority of the world's internationally mobile faculty is due to the preeminence of discussions about university reputation and the challenges faced by institutions located at the center of the academic world within the relevant literature.

Given the limitations of the existent academic literature, this chapter begins by highlighting the importance of studying international faculty mobility today. It subsequently describes definitions and typologies that have been used in the literature to describe faculty mobility. We then introduce both the rationales for mobility—through the lens of push and pull factors—and its challenges. Finally, policies aimed at attracting international faculty are presented, initially at national and regional levels and then at an institutional level. Unless otherwise noted, this chapter employs the term 'international faculty' to refer to long-term faculty mobility.

## The Increasing Importance of Studying International Faculty

Throughout the ages, and more so today, higher education institutions have been examples of places where individuals of varying nationalities and geographic origins have coexisted productively (Scott, 2015; Welch, 2008). While there are no exact figures, the number of international faculty at universities around the world has increased significantly in recent years. This increase is a product of powerful internationalization trends (Altbach, Reisberg & Rumbley, 2009) in an academic capitalist environment of increased competition for talent (Slaughter & Leslie, 1997) due to push and pull factors (Mahroum, 2000; Teichler & Cavalli, 2015) as well as supply and demand forces (Cantwell & Taylor, 2013). In short, the phenomenon of international faculty mobility is amplifying and will continue to pick up momentum in the coming years.

At the same time, the trends and realities associated with the mobility of faculty and their needs remain insufficiently explored in the academic literature (Balasooriya, Asante, Jayasinha & Razee, 2014; Kim, Twombly & Wolf-Wendel, 2012; Pherali, 2012; Teichler, 2015). For example, although many databases report quite extensively on the international movement of students—for example, the Institute of International Education's annual *Open Doors* data, and the Institute of Statistics (2014)—data about the movement of scholars are harder to come by (Cradden, 2007; Teichler, Ferencz & Wächter, 2011). In fact, there is no international database that appropriately captures faculty mobility trends.

The study of academic mobility has the potential to allow for a better understanding of both its positive and negative consequences at regional, national, and institutional levels. Such knowledge is crucial, as the long-term international mobility of faculty is associated with challenges, such as the perpetuation of systemic inequalities between nations, the difficulty of integrating international faculty in the local context, and doubts about the value and productivity of international faculty.

Academic mobility plays out in a context of inequality and is itself characterized by inequalities. Overall, the global flow of international faculty tends to originate at the periphery of the academic world and be directed toward the academic centers (Altbach et al., 2009; Docquier & Rapoport, 2009; Scott, 2015). Faculty mobility will often translate into brain drain for source countries and brain gain for host countries. This tension begs for close scrutiny of the ways countries at the periphery can take advantage of brain circulation. Three responses are offered by the relevant academic literature.

First, it has been shown that international faculty maintain ties and contribute toward the capacity building of their respective fields in their countries of origin through partnerships and established networks (Docquier & Rapoport, 2009; Fahey & Kenway, 2010; Meyer & Wattiaux, 2006), thus alleviating some of the effects of brain drain. Jacob and Meek (2013) suggest that technological advances as well as networking among overseas and local researchers contribute to the capacity building of countries with modest research capabilities. Attempts to increase networking with the knowledge community in the mobile faculty's home countries have been accompanied by repatriation policies aimed at facilitating the return of overseas faculty (Fontes, Videira & Calapez, 2013). Jowi (2012) argues that developed countries have a responsibility to ensure that collaborations with developing economies are balanced and to enhance the flow of mobility toward Africa. Knobel, Simões, and de Brito Cruz (2013) highlight the importance of intensifying South-South cooperation among faculty.

Second, international faculty are understood to facilitate better knowledge circulation. The knowledge produced by researchers originally from the academic periphery but now working at more internationally recognized institutions receives wider attention and credit (Mahroum, 2000), thus promoting marginalized fields and perspectives. Additionally, knowledge circulation is assured through the transfer of academics from one region to another (Schiller & Diez, 2012). Last, international faculty may be well positioned to support foreign-born students who want to be mentored by scholars with the same cultural background (Corley & Sabharwal, 2007; O'Hara, 2009). While these four arguments are not sufficient to overcome concerns about the consequences of brain drain on developing nations, they offer a positive outlook on long-term international faculty mobility and ways to take advantage of the diaspora.

The international mobility of faculty is not solely grounded in the global search for talent for outright competitive advantage, in which institutions at the center of the academic world have a general advantage. Internationally, mobile faculty also respond to demand factors, as, for example, the flow of academics to higher education systems with an aging academic workforce (Balasooriya et al., 2014; Hugo & Morriss, 2010), as well as to rapidly massified (or massifying) higher education systems in need of qualified labor.

Although their presence in the host country often serves to meet important educational and research needs, international faculty are frequently not well integrated or adjusted to the new local context in which they operate (Kim et al., 2012; Mamiseishvili & Rosser, 2010). Challenges with respect to the integration of international faculty have raised considerable concerns among tertiary education institutions. In response to these concerns, Saltmarsh and Swirski (2010) encourage institutions to create campus cultures better equipped to welcome international faculty. Programs and processes aimed at recruiting, inducting, and supporting the development and retention of international faculty need to be cognizant of the challenges posed by the professional and personal transitions of faculty from one educational system to another and from one cultural context to another. Such programs need to imbed a high level of awareness about cultural differences and not assume that international faculty possess taken-for-granted local knowledge.

Significant attention is given in the academic literature to the debates concerning the productivity of international faculty. While an important section of the academic literature exploring this question argues that international faculty may have increased research productivity compared to domestic researchers (Kim, et al., 2012; Mamiseishvili & Rosser, 2010), some suggest that the link between academic mobility and research productivity is not so straightforward (Hunter, Oswald & Charlton, 2009). The teaching and service productivity of mobile faculty has, however, been found to be lower than that of their local peers (Boice, 1992; Mamiseishvili & Rosser, 2010; Webber, 2012). By better understanding the challenges encountered by international faculty as well as the institutional, national, and regional policies meant to attract and integrate them (and the motivations behind these policies), an increase in productivity among international faculty across all dimensions of their work could be facilitated.

## Definitions and Typologies of International Faculty

The task of defining international faculty is complicated, on one hand, by the simple fact that there is no generally agreed-upon answer to the question what does it mean to be 'international' and, on the other hand, by challenges associated with the diversity of motives, lengths of stay, and modes of mobility among this population. Intrinsically, international faculty are defined in contrast to domestic faculty. This often implies that criteria such as citizenship (Mamiseishvili & Rosser, 2011) or place of birth (Collins, 2008; Webber & Yang, 2014) are used to distinguish between the two. In particular, tertiary education institutions in the United States usually report residency status and define international faculty as individuals who are neither citizens nor permanent residents (Gahungu, 2011). However, defining international faculty in relation to their citizenship or residency status is not sufficient and may lead to underreporting the number of migrant scholars. Additionally, this could create hierarchies between domestic faculty, who benefit from the legal protections of citizenship, and international faculty, who do not. As such, efforts have been undertaken to use other defining criteria. For example, Kim, Twombly and Wolf-Wendel (2012) define international faculty "according to whether they earned their undergraduate degrees" in their home or host country (p. 30).

Understandably, relevant academic literature focuses on offering a general and systemic understanding of the faculty mobility phenomenon as a whole. As such, long-term faculty mobility is viewed as a subcomponent of the broader faculty mobility trend. Consequently, typologies of faculty mobility, rather common in the academic literature, define long-term mobility in contrast to short-term mobility, because the length of stay abroad is one of the easiest ways of categorizing mobility. In this sense, the academic literature distinguishes between the temporary and the permanent mobility of faculty. Temporary mobility is generally referred to through labels such as *short-term exchanges* (Hoffman, 2009) and *temporary expatriation* (IDEA Consult, 2008). The academic literature also discusses cases of faculty who undergo serial periods of short-term mobility—labeled by William Solesbury & Associates (2005) as *intellectual tourists*—and cases of *commuter faculty*, who are individuals living in one country but who travel regularly for academic work to a neighboring country (IDEA Consult, 2008). Permanent or long-term faculty mobility, on the other hand, is captured in the academic literature under labels such as *definite migration* (Cradden, 2007) or *expatriates and exiles* (William, Solesbury & Associates, 2005). For Dervin and Dirba (2008), the intention to return to the home country is a key element in separating short-term and long-term faculty mobility.

Typologies describing faculty mobility use criteria beyond length of stay to fully understand the international flow of academics. Three additional defining criteria are advanced:

1 Whether the mobility is physical or virtual
2 The life stage when migration occurs
3 The anchor between faculty and host institution

First, faculty mobility may be physical or virtual (Hoffman, 2009; IDEA Consult, 2008; William Solesbury & Associates, 2005), as faculty may be physically present at the institution providing the academic appointment or may use information and communication technologies to fulfill their academic obligation from a distance. Second, academic migration can take place at different moments in the life of international faculty. Mobility of international faculty may occur at an early career stage (Cradden, 2007; William Solesbury & Associates, 2005), either before or after obtaining academic credentials. Alternatively, immigration may occur at an even earlier stage as a result of parental immigration during childhood (Hoffman, 2009). Although these classifications offer important conceptual tools to illustrate the heterogeneity among international faculty, they do not have a primary focus on either long-term faculty mobility or the role of universities in attracting or retaining international faculty.

As an exception, Cradden (2007) considers the relationship, or *anchor*, between the mobile faculty and their host institutions, where the contractual arrangement between the two parties is considered a key element. Cradden labels the situation when international faculty occupy nontenured positions at institutions abroad as *import of cheap academic labor* and the situation when international faculty occupy tenured positions as *targeting the international labor market*. The first is associated with the need to attract 'worker bee' faculty to meet a variety of institutional or system needs, and the latter encapsulates the competition between institutions for academic talent. This typology is an important classification of faculty mobility from the perspective of this book, as it actively includes the perspective and/or motivations of individual academic institutions in the equation of defining international faculty.

## Rationales for Faculty Mobility

The academic literature devotes significant attention to understanding the systemic factors contributing to the international mobility of faculty. Two frameworks explaining the global migration of the workforce are generally discussed: demand and supply (Cantwell & Taylor, 2013), and push and pull factors (e.g., Cantwell & Taylor, 2013; Cradden, 2007; Mahroum, 2000). The demand and supply framework focuses strongly on economic rationales and justifications, whereas the push and pull framework provides a broader understanding of the rationales behind faculty mobility, including economic rationales (Cradden, 2007). For this reason, this section will employ the latter framework.

In higher education, push factors are understood as rationales that encourage someone to leave their country of origin, and pull factors are viewed as rationales that entice someone to enter a host country (Cantwell, Luca & Lee, 2009; Lauermann, 2012). These include economic and noneconomic factors. Table 2.1 summarizes some of the frequently referenced push and pull factors in the literature, both for highly skilled workers (Cradden, 2007; Mahroum, 2000) and more specifically for academics (Altbach, 1998; Altbach, 2007a; Cantwell, 2011; Cradden, 2007).

To a significant extent, academics relocate in response to *economic considerations*. More than ever, the global market dictates the direction of the flow of academic talent (Cantwell, 2011). Better income is often cited as a motivation for academic mobility (Altbach, 2012; Janger & Campbell, 2014; Janger & Nowotny, 2013a); therefore, the economic state of a country is a significant factor in academics' decision regarding relocation, as income is directly correlated with national wealth (Androushchak & Yudkevich, 2012). It is thus unsurprising that most elite academics turn to countries with high gross domestic product (GDP) levels (Hunter et al., 2009) and more resources (Cantwell, 2011; Cradden, 2007; Hunter et al., 2009), highlighting the difference between centers and peripheries in higher education (Altbach, 2007b) or between "edges and empires of knowledge" (Fahey & Kenway, 2010).

Janger and Nowotny (2013b) created a competitiveness index for countries based on their ability to attract international faculty. The competitiveness index focused on three categories of indicators: monetary resources and considerations, country characteristics, and working conditions. Based on the results of this study, institutions in the United States, Netherlands, Sweden, Switzerland, and the United Kingdom are among the most competitive systems when it comes to the ability to attract international faculty.

**TABLE 2.1** Commonly Referenced Push and Pull Factors for Highly Skilled Workers and Academics

|  |  | *Highly skilled workers* | *Academics* |
|---|---|---|---|
| Push Factors | Economic | · Low earnings<br>· Poor working conditions<br>· Unemployment, underemployment | · Low public research funding<br>· Low salaries<br>· Lack of career opportunities<br>· Poor facilities |
|  | Noneconomic | · Poor quality of life<br>· Political instability<br>· Lack of opportunity for children | · Lack of academic freedom<br>· Discrimination (racial, religious, ethnic) |
| Pull Factors | Economic | · Higher earnings<br>· Good working conditions<br>· Safe working environment<br>· Greater career opportunities | · High public research funding<br>· Better laboratories and libraries |
|  | Noneconomic | · High quality of life<br>· Political stability<br>· Educational opportunity for children<br>· Family ties | · Being at the center of world science and research<br>· Reputation of the country in the discipline<br>· Prestige of institution<br>· Favorable teaching responsibilities |

Sources: Altbach, 1998; Altbach, 2007a; Cantwell, 2011; Cradden, 2007; Mahroum, 2000.

*Career considerations* are also important motivations related to relocating. Beyond higher salaries, developed economies are more likely to offer favorable conditions for research and teaching than developing economies, thus attracting academics worldwide (Altbach, 1998; Balasooriya et al., 2014; Cradden, 2007). The connection between the academic world and industry can also be a decisive factor for scientists to leave their home country in search of a more commercialized research environment (Cooke, 2001; Cooke et al., 2007; Zucker & Darby, 2007). Scholars who have the opportunity to work with multinational corporations are indeed more motivated to stay in the host country (Schiller and Diez, 2012). The decision to be mobile is linked with the type of contract proposed in the foreign country: positions offering tenure are more likely to entice a scholar to cross borders, as such positions bring job security and higher job satisfaction (Carmichael, 1988; McPherson & Schapiro, 1999; van de Bunt-Kokhuis, 1994; Welch, 1997).

*Institutional characteristics* further influence the choices of faculty to relocate abroad. As mentioned earlier, one institutional characteristic that catalyzes mobility—prestige—receives the most attention in the academic literature. This pull toward the most prestigious institutions is not representative of the bulk of faculty mobility, but it is predominant in the academic literature and deserves some consideration. Often situated in the United States, highly prestigious institutions represent centers of excellence for elite scientists (Laudel, 2005; Mulkay, 1976). As a result, it was estimated that between 1981 and 2004 the United States hosted 62 percent of the world's best scientists (Zucker & Darby, 2007). Mobile scholars also value institutional prestige and excellence in their specific areas of focus, as they tend to choose institutions with "outstanding faculty, colleagues or research teams" and "excellence or prestige of the foreign institution in [their] area of research" (Franzoni, Scellato & Stephan, 2012, p. 9). Conventional short-term visits or sabbaticals are indeed most likely to be decided based on research focus and department prestige (Shimmi, 2014). Institutions are very aware of the importance of reputation for their capacity to attract foreign scholars and have turned to international marketing tools to develop their brand (Boekholt et al., 2001). Beyond prestige, factors like equipment, facilities, research opportunities, and network possibilities play an important role (Altbach, 1998; Cantwell & Taylor, 2013; Schiller & Diez, 2012; Shimmi, 2014).

Mobile scholars also consider *family and personal factors* in choosing to relocate abroad and in determining the length of their stay overseas (Altbach, 1998; McKenna & Richardson, 2007). Scholars with family have been deemed "inflexible academics" (Leeman, 2010) due to the additional hardship created by family ties when relocating—especially for female faculty. Family-related concerns have indeed brought attention to gender inequalities in faculty mobility. Personal and family issues can also be an important factor that leads scholars to move back to their home country (Franzoni, Scellato & Stephan, 2012; van de Bunt-Kokhuis, 1994), thus shortening their stay abroad.

## Challenges Faced by International Faculty

Challenges faced by academics have been widely documented. Testimonies often describe the varying degree of difficulty international faculty face in adapting to the new academic and social environment. Challenges encountered by academics who relocate to a foreign country can broadly fall into one of two categories: temporary logistical and perennial cultural (Pherali, 2012).

First, international faculty members face a set of logistical problems that are not experienced by their domestic peers. Foreign-born faculty have more difficulties finding positions due to visa restrictions (Foote, Li, Monk & Theobald, 2008). Therefore, they have been found to settle for postdoctoral positions because other—and better—academic positions are sometimes not available to them (Corley & Sabharwal, 2007). Once in-country, international faculty can also face instability in relation to their legal and immigration status (Pherali, 2012). Besides immigration challenges, logistical problems encountered by international faculty may include finding accommodation, identifying appropriate schools for children, and limited working opportunities for their partner (Kastberg, 2014).

Second, cultural integration difficulties exacerbate feelings of isolation and marginalization of international faculty and affect their morale and productivity. Foreign-born faculty face challenges in adapting to the new academic culture, including understanding the higher education system of the host country (Gahungu, 2011), as well as adapting to different teaching load expectations, student behaviors, and prospects to advance professionally within the academic career (Jepsen et al., 2014). Such issues are intensified by the lack of institutional support dedicated to nonlocal academics and networking difficulties (Foote et al., 2008). Additionally, students may be prejudiced when it comes to international professors, perceiving them negatively as a result of their minority status or as less intelligent due to their cultural differences and language capacities (Bang, 2015; Manrique & Manrique, 1999). Even when international faculty obtain institutional support, they can still experience significant difficulties integrating into the local community (Foote et al., 2008).

Cultural problems are, however, nonuniform among international faculty: they have been found to be dependent on geography, discipline, and career trajectory or professional advancement. In Europe in particular, non-European international faculty face greater difficulty in the adaptation process (Pherali, 2012). Hoffman (2007), on the other hand, found that migrant scholars' status, needs, and career expectations are highly stratified based on the disciplinary culture, the match between the faculty expertise and their position, and their social network.

Transition difficulties are especially salient for scholars from ethnic and gender minority groups (Welch, 1997). Ethnic and gender differences can be a source of discrimination and cultural pressure in the academic community (Mayuzumi, 2008; Munene, 2014). At the same time, the disparities in gender are an important factor in creating opportunities for the migration of scholars. Male academics are usually more mobile than female academics (Jons, 2011). However, the proportion of men and women in the academic diaspora depends on the demographic situation in the host and home countries (Welch, 1997). In light of these challenges, Leeman (2010) considers that the best-adjusted mobile scientist or academic is still an independent scholar with no family and who can easily adapt to new social conditions.

## Regional and National Policies to Attract International Faculty

Some regions and countries around the world have created policies and designed incentives to attract international faculty. Unfortunately, the academic literature covering these policies is disproportionately focused on the centers of the academic world. The rationales of such policies are diverse. Some countries seek to attract international faculty in an attempt to support the development of the local knowledge-based economy, whereas others need to support an intensely massified higher education system (Horta, 2009).

Regions and countries rarely create specific policies to attract international faculty. Instead, policies aim at attracting talented and highly skilled individuals, regardless of their occupation. Policies relevant to attracting international faculty—such as visa, salary, and hiring policies—indeed often do not explicitly mention academics or scholars. At the same time, financial incentives from governments focus primarily on short-term mobility and outbound mobility of existing faculty.

The creation of regional free trade agreements—such as the European Union (EU), the North American Free Trade Agreement (NAFTA), Mercosur, or the Association of Southeast Asian Nations (ASEAN)—has enhanced the fluid movement of persons across borders. In most cases, highly skilled workers, including faculty members, are the targets of specific arrangements that make their permanent or temporary migration within the region easier (Nielson, 2002).

Europe has the most extensive policies to support the mobility of faculty. Although never its main focus, faculty mobility has been a component of the Erasmus program since its inception in 1987 (de Prado Yepes, 2006). In addition to offering financial incentives for faculty mobility, the European Commission created tools that aim to facilitate the mobility of academics and researchers. Examples of such tools include the creation of EURAXESS, a pan-European job search portal for academics and researchers, and the implementation of the Blue Card Directive supporting the creation of a pan-European work permit. The European Union also promotes high-level policy discussions that endeavor to relax immigration policy for highly skilled workers in the Schengen zone (European Parliament, 2015).

At a national level, agencies such as the Center for International Mobility (CIMO) in Finland, the German Center for Research and Innovation, and the German Academic Exchange Service (DAAD) offer scholarships to young expatriate researchers and university teaching staff to relocate their activities to Finland or Germany, respectively. Not all European countries, however, offer competitive conditions for international faculty. In Portugal, reforms in university hiring processes prompted efforts to attract international faculty. These policies resulted from a government-driven effort to increase international publications of faculty in Portugal and to increase the level of academic qualification of the country's academic staff (Horta, 2009). The success of these reforms has, however, been negatively affected by the low salaries on offer to academics in Portugal and the country's high rate of academic inbreeding (Horta, 2009). Similarly, countries with closed faculty recruitment practices (i.e., where policies and/or practices favor local candidates) in Europe and elsewhere experience difficulties in attracting international faculty (Yudkevich, Altbach & Rumbley, 2015).

Outside of Europe, organizations that aim to facilitate networking and mobility—including faculty mobility—flourish, but funding for faculty mobility is seldom part of their initiatives. Additionally, such initiatives focus on supporting short-term mobility. For example, higher education regional associations—such as the ASEAN University Network, ASEAN 3+, and the Gulf Cooperation Council—include short-term faculty mobility in their main priorities (de Prado Yepes, 2006), but only promote mobility through working groups and advocating for expedited visa applications, among other limited actions. The Consortium for North American Higher Education Collaboration (CONAHEC) in North America is another example of a regional networking organization that does not provide any funding for faculty mobility.

Faculty in Latin America do not typically participate in intraregional mobility as a result of the lack of incentives and openness of Latin American higher education systems and academic labor markets (Rabossi 2015). Instead, faculty prefer to commit to more prestigious destinations outside of the region (de Wit, Jaramillo, Gacel-Avila & Knight, 2005).

In an attempt to become higher education hubs, countries in Southeast Asia, such as Malaysia and Singapore, have provided universities with increased autonomy to improve their quality through measures including the attraction of international faculty (Mok, 2011). In the Singapore Report of the Committee of the Expansion of the University Sector (Ministry of Education Singapore, 2008), the attraction of high-quality international faculty is a strongly articulated objective. Asian countries, particularly China, have managed to attract international faculty using a different strategy: by facilitating the opening of branch campuses of overseas universities within their territory. In addition, China has established a number of bilateral agreements that facilitate the mobility of researchers and academics (Jacob & Meek, 2013).

## Institutional Policies to Attract International Faculty

Relevant institutional-level policies designed to attract and accommodate the needs of international faculty are rarely covered by the academic literature, and examples of specific institutional policies remain vague and rare. Yet again, the existent literature concentrates on the experience of faculty at elite institutions. These host universities, mostly at the center of the academic world, can attract the best and brightest without implementing deliberate international recruitment policies (Boekholt et al., 2001). Many elite institutions draw international faculty by relying heavily on their accumulated reputation. However, for some elite institutions, cultural norms (Jackson & Manderscheid, 2015) and questions of academic freedom (Zha, 2012) might constitute barriers in attracting international faculty. The majority of universities in the world, nevertheless, cannot rely on their global reputation and, if they want to attract international faculty, need to articulate policies and procedures to do so through monetary and nonmonetary incentives.

The literature notes that institutions should take into account a number of factors as they create policies to target international faculty. These factors can be broadly categorized as external and internal. External factors range from national regulations to broad societal considerations and may include such fundamental and technical elements as visa regulations. Internal factors include dynamics between international faculty and local faculty (Laudel, 2005), professional advancement schemes for international hires, integration strategies, and rationales for nonlocal academics (Horta, 2009), as well as financial capacity and cost associated with international faculty recruitment (Richardson et al. 2008; Teichler, 2015).

In a study comparing internationalization policies, Horta (2009) finds that the attractiveness of an institution to international faculty and to international students is correlated with, and dependent upon, the financial capacity of the institution. However, Horta does not describe specific procedures for hiring international faculty or the incentives institutions might design in order to recruit and retain international faculty. As another example, the National University of Singapore promotes the use of partnerships with both reputable foreign institutions and individual researchers as a means to attract international faculty. Its enhancement of postgraduate education is also motivated by an attempt to increase the number of international faculty on campus (Ministry of Education Singapore, 2008).

Institutional policies do not solely cover incentives to attract international faculty, but also incentives to prevent the departure of those who have been recruited from abroad, as well as incentives to increase the short-term mobility of home faculty (van de Bunt-Kokhuis, 1994). Institutions might offer short-term opportunities to their staff in the form of sabbaticals and research leave policies in order to prevent a permanent departure and at the same time promote brain circulation (Shimmi, 2014). Although institutions are increasingly intentional about recruiting international faculty, the literature provides no indications that there are widespread, successfully developed policies to hire international faculty, to accommodate their diverse needs, and to facilitate their adaptation to the local cultural environment (Bang, 2015; Dedoussis, 2007).

## Conclusion

The relevant academic literature on long-term international faculty mobility suggests some key trends, but raises many more questions than it answers. As mentioned previously, there are a significant number of gaps in the relevant academic literature. First, much of the existing work focuses either broadly on the concept of faculty mobility or specifically on short-term faculty mobility. At the same time, the literature analyzes primarily the flow of faculty from peripheries to the center of the academic world, specifically to prestigious institutions. This focus ignores a significant proportion of the world's internationally mobile faculty, that is, 'worker bee' faculty who relocate often in a South-South direction to rapidly massifying higher education systems in need of qualified academic labor. Moreover, where relevant literature exists, the institutional perspective is often overlooked. Given the persistent gaps in the academic literature highlighted throughout this chapter, the current book responds to a significant academic need: to highlight ways in which institutions attract and support long-term international faculty on their campuses.

## References

Altbach, P. G. (1998). *Comparative higher education: Knowledge, the university, and development*. Hong Kong: Comparative Education Research Centre, The University of Hong Kong.

Altbach, P. G. (2007a). Globalization and the university: Realities in an unequal world. In P. G. Altbach (Ed.), *Tradition and transition: The international imperative in higher education* (pp. 23–48). Rotterdam, The Netherlands: Sense Publishers.

Altbach, P. G. (2007b). Peripheries and centers: Research universities in developing countries. In P. G. Altbach (Ed.), *Tradition and transition: The international imperative in higher education* (pp. 85–112). Rotterdam, the Netherlands: Sense Publishers.

Altbach, P. G., Reisberg, L., & Rumbley, L. (2009). Trends in global higher: Tracking an academic revolution. A report prepared for the UNESCO 2009 World Conference on Higher Education. Retrieved from www.uis.unesco.org/Library/Documents/trends-global-higher-education-2009-world-conference-en.pdf

Altbach, P. G., Reisberg, L., Yudkevich, M., Androushchak, G., & Pacheco, I. (2012). *Paying the professoriate: A global comparison of compensation and contracts*. New York: Routledge.

Androushchak, G., & Yudkevich, M. (2012). Quantitative analysis: Looking for commonalities in a sea of differences. In P. G. Altbach, L. Reisberg, M. Yudkevich, G. Androushchak & I. Pacheco (Eds.), *Paying the professoriate: A global comparison of compensation and contracts* (pp. 21–34). New York: Routledge.

Balasooriya, C., Asante, A., Jayasinha, R., & Razee, H. (2014). Academic mobility and migration: Reflections of international academics in Australia. *International Perspectives on Higher Education Research, 11*, 117–135. doi:10.1108/S1479–362820140000011013

Bang, H. (2015). Challenges and self-efficacy of female East Asian-born faculty in American universities. In C. B. Hutchison (Ed.), *Experiences of immigrant professors: Cross-cultural difference, challenges, and lessons for success* (pp. 88–99). New York: Routledge.

Boekholt, P., Arnold, E., Kuusisto, J., Lankhuizen, M., McKibbin, S., & Rammer, A. (2001). *Benchmarking mechanisms and strategies to attract researchers to Ireland: A study for the Expert Group on Future Skills Needs and Forfás*. Brighton, UK: Technopolis-Group.

Boice, R. (1992). *The new faculty member: Supporting and fostering professional development*. San Francisco, CA: Jossey-Bass.

van de Bunt-Kokhuis, S. G. (1994). Determinants of international faculty mobility. *Higher Education in Europe, 19*(2), 94–111.

Cantwell, B. (2011). Transnational mobility and international academic employment: Gatekeeping in an academic competition arena. *Minerva, 49*(4), 425–445.

Cantwell, B., Luca, S. G., & Lee, J. J. (2009). Exploring the orientations of international students in Mexico: Differences by region of origin. *Higher Education, 57*(3), 335–354.

Cantwell, B., & Taylor, B. J. (2013). Internationalization of the postdoctorate in the United States: Analyzing the demand for international postdoc labor. *Higher Education, 66*(5), 551–567.

Carmichael, H. L. (1988). Incentives in academics: Why is there tenure? *The Journal of Political Economy, 96*(3), 453–472.

Collins, J. M. (2008). Coming to America: Challenges for faculty coming to United States' universities. *Journal of Geography in Higher Education, 32*(2), 179–188. doi:10.1080/03098260701731215

Cooke, P. (2001). Biotechnology clusters in the UK: Lessons from localisation in the commercialisation of science. *Small Business Economics, 17*(1–2), 43–59.

Cooke, P., de Laurentis, C., Todtling, F., & Trippl, M. (Eds.). (2007). *Regional knowledge economies: Markets, clusters and innovation.* Glos, UK: Edward Elgar Publishing.

Corley, E. A., & Sabharwal, M. (2007). Foreign-born academic scientists and engineers: producing more and getting less than their US-born peers? *Research in Higher Education, 48*(8), 909–940.

Cradden, C. (2007). *Constructing paths to staff mobility in the European Higher Education Area: From individual to institutional responsibility.* Brussels, Belgium: Education International.

Dedoussis, E. V. (2007). Issues of diversity in academia: Through the eyes of third-country faculty. *Higher Education, 54*(1), 135–156.

Dervin, F., & Dirba, M. (2008). Figures of strangeness: Blending perspectives from mobile academics. In M. Byram & F. Dervin (Eds.), *Students, staff and academic mobility in higher education* (pp. 237–260). Newcastle, UK: Cambridge Scholars Press.

de Wit, H., Jaramillo, I. C., Gacel-Avila, J., & Knight, J. (2005). Educación Superior en América Latina. La dimensión internacional. Retrieved from www.researchgate.net/profile/Jocelyne_Gacel-Avila/publication/267220528_Educacin_Superior_en_Amrica_Latina/links/54fdd7b90cf25eedf74cfc37.pdf

Docquier, F., & Rapoport, H. (2009). Documenting the brain drain of "la crème de la crème": Three case-studies on international migration at the upper tail of the education distribution. *Jahrbücher für Nationalökonomie und Statistik, 229,* 679–705.

European Parliament (2015). The EU blue card directive. Retrieved from www.europarl.europa.eu/RegData/etudes/BRIE/2015/558766/EPRS_BRI(2015)558766_EN.pdf

Fahey, J., & Kenway, J. (2010). Thinking in a 'worldly' way: Mobility, knowledge, power and geography. *Discourse: Studies in the Cultural Politics of Education, 31*(5), 627–640.

Fontes, M., Videira, P., & Calapez, T. (2013). The impact of long-term scientific mobility on the creation of persistent knowledge networks. *Mobilities, 8*(3), 440–465.

Foote, K. E., Li, W., Monk, J., & Theobald, R. (2008). Foreign-born scholars in US universities: Issues, concerns, and strategies. *Journal of Geography in Higher Education, 32*(2), 167–178.

Franzoni, C., Scellato, G., & Stephan, P. (2012). Foreign-born scientists: Mobility patterns for 16 countries. *Nature Biotechnology, 30,* 1250–1253.

Gahungu, A. (2011). Integration of foreign-born faculty in academia: Foreignness as an asset. *International Journal of Educational Leadership Preparation, 6*(1), n1.

Hoffman, D. M. (2007). The career potential of migrant scholars: A multiple case study of long-term academic mobility in Finnish universities. *Higher Education in Europe, 32*(4), 317–331.

Hoffman, D. M. (2009). Changing academic mobility patterns and international migration: What will academic mobility mean in the 21st century? *Journal of Studies in International Education, 13*(3), 347–364.

Horta, H. (2009). Global and national prominent universities: Internationalization, competitiveness and the role of the state. *Higher Education, 58*(3), 387–405.

Hugo, G., & Morriss, A. (2010). *Investigating the Ageing Academic Workforce: Stocktake.* The National Centre for Social Applications of Geographic Information Systems (GISCA). Canberra: University of Adelaide.

Hunter, R. S., Oswald, A. J., & Charlton, B. G. (2009). The elite brain drain. *The Economic Journal, 119*(538), F231–F251.

IDEA Consult (2008). *Evidence on the main factors inhibiting mobility and career development of researchers*. Brussels: European Commission. Retrieved from http://ec.europa.eu/euraxess/pdf/research_policies/rindicate_final_report_2008_11_june_08_v4.pdf

Jackson, D., & Manderscheid, S. V. (2015). A phenomenological study of Western expatriates' adjustment to Saudi Arabia. *Human Resource Development International, 18*(2), 131–152. doi:10.1080/13678868.2015.1026552

Jacob, M., & Meek, V. L. (2013). Scientific mobility and international research networks: Trends and policy tools for promoting research excellence and capacity building. *Studies in Higher Education, 38*(3), 331–344.

Janger, J., & Campbell, D. F. C. (2014). *The performance of different national higher education systems in attracting the best academics*. Paper presented at the EAIR 36th annual forum in Essen, Germany. Retrieved from http://eairaww.websites.xs4all.nl/forum/essen/PDF/1519.pdf

Janger, J., & Nowotny, K. (2013a). Career choices in academia. Retrieved from www.foreurope.eu/fileadmin/documents/pdf/Workingpapers/WWWforEurope_WPS_no036_MS64.pdf

Janger, J., & Nowotny, K. (2013b). Academic careers: A cross-country perspective. Retrieved from www.foreurope.eu/fileadmin/documents/pdf/Workingpapers/WWWforEurope_WPS_no037_MS64.pdf

Jepsen, D. M., Sun, J. J. M., Budhwar, P. S., Klehe, U. C., Krausert, A., Raghuram, S., & Valcour, M. (2014). International academic careers: Personal reflections. *The International Journal of Human Resource Management, 25*(10), 1309–1326.

Jons, H. (2011). Transnational academic mobility and gender. *Globalisation, Societies & Education, 9*(2), 183–209. doi:10.1080/14767724.2011.577199

Jowi, J. O. (2012). African universities in the global knowledge economy: The good and ugly of internationalization. *Journal of Marketing for Higher Education, 22*(1), 153–165.

Kastberg, S. M. (2014). "Sensitive fences": The im/mobility of working-class academics. In N. Maadad & M. Tight (Eds.), *Academic mobility* (pp. 117–136). Bingley, UK: Emerald Group.

Kim, D., Twombly, S., & Wolf-Wendel, L. (2012). International faculty in American universities: Experiences of academic life, productivity, and career mobility. *New Directions for Institutional Research, 155*, 27–46.

Knobel, M., Patricia Simões, T., & Henrique de Brito Cruz, C. (2013). International collaborations between research universities: Experiences and best practices. *Studies in Higher Education, 38*(3), 405–424.

Laudel, G. (2005). Migration currents among the scientific elite. *Minerva, 43*(4), 377–395.

Lauermann, F. (2012). To go or not to go: The decision to pursue higher education abroad. In S. A. Karabenick & T. C. Urdan (Eds.), *Transition across schools and cultures—Advances in motivation and achievement* (pp. 177–204). Bingley, UK: Emerald Group.

Leemann, R. J. (2010). Gender inequalities in transnational academic mobility and the ideal type of academic entrepreneur. *Discourse: Studies in the Cultural Politics of Education, 31*(5), 605–625.

Mahroum, S. (2000). Highly skilled globetrotters: Mapping the international migration of human capital. *R&D Management, 30*(1), 23–32.

Mamiseishvili, K., & Rosser, V. J. (2010). International and citizen faculty in the United States: An examination of their productivity at research universities. *Research in Higher Education, 51*(1), 88–107.

Mamiseishvili, K., & Rosser, V. J. (2011). Examining the relationship between faculty productivity and job satisfaction. *Journal of the Professoriate*, 5(2), 100–132.

Manrique, C. G., & Manrique, G. G. (1999). *The multicultural or immigrant faculty in American society* (Vol. 43). Lewiston, NY: Edwin Mellen Press.

Mayuzumi, K. (2008). 'In-between' Asia and the West: Asian women faculty in the transnational context. *Race, Ethnicity & Education*, 11(2), 167–182. doi:10.1080/13613320802110274

McKenna, S., & Richardson, J. (2007). The increasing complexity of the internationally mobile professional: Issues for research and practice. *Cross Cultural Management: An International Journal*, 14(4), 307–320.

McPherson, M. S., & Schapiro, M. O. (1999). Tenure issues in higher education. *The Journal of Economic Perspectives*, 13(1), 85–98.

Meyer, J. B., & Wattiaux, J. P. (2006). Diaspora knowledge networks: Vanishing doubts and increasing evidence. *International Journal on Multicultural Societies*, 8(1), 4–24.

Ministry of Education Singapore (2008). Report of the committee on the expansion of the university sector: Greater choice, more room to excel. Retrieved from www.moe.gov.sg/media/press/files/2008/08/ceus-final-report-and-exec-summary.pdf

Mok, K. H. (2011). Regional responses to globalization challenges: The assertion of soft power and changing university governance in Singapore, Hong Kong and Malaysia. In R. King, S. Marginson & R. Naidoo (Eds.), *Handbook on globalization and higher education*. Northampton, MA: Edward Elgar.

Mulkay, M. (1976). The mediating role of the scientific elite. *Social Studies of Science*, 6(3/4), 445–470.

Munene, I. I. (2014). Outsiders within: Isolation of international faculty in an American university. *Research in Post-Compulsory Education*, 19(4), 450–467.

Nielson, J. (2002). Current regimes for temporary movement of service providers: Labour mobility in regional trade agreements. Paper presented at the Joint WTO—World Bank Symposium on Movement of Natural Persons (Mode 4) under the GATS, Geneva, Switzerland.

O'Hara, S. (2009). Vital and overlooked: The role of faculty in internationalizing US campuses. *IIE Study Abroad White Paper Series*, 6, 38–45.

Pherali, T. J. (2012). Academic mobility, language, and cultural capital the experience of transnational academics in British higher education institutions. *Journal of Studies in International Education*, 16(4), 313–333.

de Prado Yepes, C. (2006). World regionalization of higher education: Policy proposals for international organizations. *Higher Education Policy*, 19(1), 111–128.

Rabossi, M. (2015). Academic inbreeding in the Argentine university: A systemic and organizational analysis. In M. Yudkevich, P. Altbach, & L. Rumbley (Eds.), *Academic inbreeding and mobility in higher education. Global perspectives* (pp. 45–72). London, UK: Palgrave.

Richardson, J., McBey, K., & McKenna, S. (2008). Integrating realistic job previews and realistic living conditions previews: Realistic recruitment for internationally mobile knowledge workers. *Personnel Review*, 37(5), 490–508.

Saltmarsh, S., & Swirski, T. (2010). Pawns and prawns': International academics' observations on their transition to working in an Australian university. *Journal of Higher Education Policy & Management*, 32(3), 291–301.

Schiller, D., & Diez, J. R. (2012). The impact of academic mobility on the creation of localized intangible assets. *Regional Studies*, 46(10), 1319–1332.

Scott, P. (2015). Dynamics of academic mobility: Hegemonic internationalisation or fluid globalisation. *European Review*, 23(S1), S55–S69.

Shimmi, Y. (2014). *Experiences of Japanese visiting scholars in the United States: An exploration of transition* (Unpublished doctoral dissertation). Boston College, Chestnut Hill, MA.

Slaughter, S., & Leslie, L. L. (1997). *Academic capitalism: Politics, policies, and the entrepreneurial university*. Baltimore: Johns Hopkins University Press.

Teichler, U. (2015). Academic mobility and migration: What we know and what we do not know. *European Review, 23*(S1), S6–S37.

Teichler, U., & Cavalli, A. (2015). The diverse patterns and the diverse causes of migration and mobility in science. *European Review, 23*(S1), S112–S126.

Teichler, U., Ferencz, I., & Wächter, B. (2011). *Mapping mobility in European higher education. Volume I: Overview and trends*. A study produced for the DG EAC of the European Commission.

UNESCO Institute for Statistics (2014). Global flows of tertiary-level students. Retrieved from www.uis.unesco.org/Education/Pages/international-student-flow-viz.aspx

Webber, K. L. (2012). Research productivity of foreign-and US-born faculty: Differences by time on task. *Higher Education, 64*(5), 709–729.

Webber, K. L., & Yang, L. (2014). The increased role of foreign-born academic staff in US higher education. *Journal of Higher Education Policy and Management, 36*(1), 43–61.

Welch, A. (1997). The peripatetic professor: The internationalization of the academic profession. *Higher Education, 34*(3), 323–345.

Welch, A. (2008). Myths and modes of mobility: The changing face of academic mobility in the global era. In M. Byram & F. Dervin (Eds.), *Students, staff and academic mobility in higher education* (pp. 292–311). Newcastle, UK: Cambridge Scholars Pub.

William Solesbury & Associates (2005). *The impact of international mobility on UK academic research*. Higher Education Policy Institute. Available at www.hepi.ac.uk/wp-content/uploads/2014/02/19AcademicMobility_WSAReport.pdf.

Yudkevich, M., Altbach, P., & Rumbley, L. (2015). *Academic inbreeding and mobility in higher education: Global perspectives.* New York: Palgrave Macmillan.

Zha, Q. (2012). Intellectuals, academic freedom, and university autonomy in China. In H. G. Schuetze, W. Bruneau & G. Grosjean (Eds.), *University governance and reform: Policy, fads, and experience in international perspective* (pp. 209–224). New York: Palgrave Macmillan. Retrieved from http://doi.org/10.1057/9781137040107_14

Zucker, L. G., & Darby, M. R. (2007). *Star scientists, innovation and regional and national immigration* (No. w13547). Cambridge, MA: National Bureau of Economic Research.

# 3

# INTERNATIONAL FACULTY IN A BRAZILIAN UNIVERSITY

International Trajectories in a Nationalized System of Scientific Production

Ana Maria F. Almeida, Mauricio Érnica, Luciano Antonio Digiampietri, and Marcelo Knobel

### Introduction

The Brazilian university is a relatively recent phenomenon. Although some professional schools—mainly law, medicine, and engineering—were created in the 19th century in different regions of the country, their evolution into higher education institutions started only in the 1930s. From this period on, the university system has expanded at a rather slow pace, with acceleration in the last 30 years (Schwartzman, 2007). Internationalization has been a key factor in its development. The circulation of European and American scholars through Brazil has played a decisive role in the consolidation of institutions and research fields in different areas, helping to connect these new academic institutions to international research networks.

Although the presence of foreign professors in these processes indicates that scientific leadership and university administrators were committed to the development of fields of study and institutions by means of internationalization, it does not imply that Brazil was engaged in an international market for the purpose of hiring faculty, even in this initial period. On the contrary, the arrival of those scholars was the result of isolated programs facilitated by state or federal governments in specific historical contexts, targeting particular networks and/or institutions. This was the case, for instance, of the French mission that contributed to the creation of University of São Paulo (*Universidade de São Paulo*—USP) in the 1930s (Skidmore, 2003); the participation of the Rockefeller and Kellogg foundations in the development of medical education at the beginning of the 20th century (Cueto, 1997; Stepan, 2011); the role of the United Nations Educational, Scientific and Cultural Organization (UNESCO) in the development of racial studies in the country in the 1950s (Chor Maio, 2011; Telles, 2003); the support of the Ford Foundation for the professionalization of the social sciences starting in 1962 (Canedo, 2009; Miceli, 1993; Trindade, 2005); and a series of partnerships with American universities that contributed to the creation of several institutions and research programs—such as the participation of the Massachusetts Institute of Technology (MIT) in the creation of the Air Force Technology Institute (*Instituto Tecnológico da Aeronáutica*—ITA) in the 1940s (Botelho, 1999).

In addition, the political and/or economic situation of some countries created periodic migratory waves of foreign scientists interested in finding positions in Brazil. This happened, for example, during the military *coups d'état* in Argentina, Chile, and Uruguay during the 1970s; after the fall of the Soviet Union in the late 1980s and beginning of 1990s; and, more recently, during the economic crisis that affected the south of Europe, especially Spain and Portugal. As a result, some Brazilian universities have been able to use this opportunity to hire highly qualified foreign faculty.

As will be explained in more detail later, the lack of any sustained strategy to hire foreign academics, whether at the national, state, or university level, should be understood as the counterpart of the significant and lasting investment made by the Brazilian state in the training of Brazilian graduate students, which provided a constant flow of young academics to the local universities.

This initiative resulted in a steady supply of candidates for faculty positions composed of Brazilians holding Brazilian and foreign PhDs, as well as foreigners holding Brazilian PhDs, decreasing the need for recruiting internationally and contributing, up to a certain degree, to the relative insularity of the Brazilian academic job market.

In addition, some characteristics of Brazilian legislation and bureaucracy have contributed to reinforcing the country's relative isolation from the international academic job market. For example, the constitution passed in 1988, just after the end of the military regime, prevented foreigners from holding permanent positions in the public service sector. Even though universities could rely on special contracts, which could bypass this limitation, they implied additional costs for the permanence of foreigners in the country. This requirement was only annulled in 1998, but foreign candidates are still required to apply for a Brazilian degree equivalency, a process that can take months, or even years, thus delaying the hiring process and increasing the candidate's uncertainty regarding the future.

Another important obstacle relates to the centrality of the Portuguese language in Brazilian society. Fluency in a foreign language is rare among the general population—even among professors and students of prestigious universities—so, very few classes, if any, can be given in other languages.

Finally, another challenge in the attraction of international faculty is the overall image of Brazil abroad, which is usually seen as an underdeveloped country without a research tradition, full of critical social problems, such as inequality and urban violence. Although there are some indications that this image is changing, it has certainly played an important role in the immigration rate of scholars during the second half of the 20th century.

Thus, it is not surprising that the number of foreign faculty members in higher education in Brazil is so small. In 2012, the statistics of the Education Ministry indicated that only 1.5 percent of faculty members were of foreign origin, including naturalized Brazilian citizens (Schwartzman & Schwartzman, 2015, p. 14). When analyzing the curricula of PhD holders in the online platform kept by the federal research agency (the Lattes Platform), just 3.5 percent identified themselves as foreigners in 2013.

Who are these faculty members? What social dynamics explain their presence in Brazil? How did they develop their careers? What challenges did they face in that process? This chapter explores these questions based on a study on the current faculty of the University of Campinas (Unicamp), one of the most important higher education institutions in the country in terms of scientific production and education of highly qualified professionals. The conditions faced by foreign faculty members at Unicamp were studied through three sets of data:

1 The curricula vitae (CVs) available on the Lattes Platform between June and July 2013
2 Unicamp's official data on faculty
3 Data from interviews with a group of Unicamp's international faculty members who have done their doctoral studies abroad

The Lattes Platform is an administrative tool for scientific production that has become central to evaluation dynamics, faculty recruiting, and other Brazilian science and technology policies. It is a public archive of curricula vitae information voluntarily registered by faculty and researchers who each complete a standard form, which collects information related to education, publications, and other professional activities usually included on a standard CV. As the presentation of this information is mandatory when applying for grants, basically all professionally active researchers in Brazil have their curricula registered.

For this analysis, the curricula were gathered using a data-mining tool developed by Luciano Digiampietri et al. (2012), which allowed us to isolate the curricula of researchers who declared themselves foreigners and to identify within this group those who worked more than 20 hours per week at Unicamp. Despite all its richness, the Lattes database has two important limitations. First, it does not allow one to identify retired researchers. Second, as the information is provided by the researchers themselves, there is no quality control over the information provided. Divergences in the interpretation of the form have been noticed as one among multiple reasons for some discrepancies between the information gathered from Lattes and that obtained through other sources (Almeida et al. 2012). As a result, the Lattes information was used mainly to identify general trends.

Altogether, the Lattes Platform and Unicamp information, along with the interview data, allowed us to better understand the international faculty's schooling and professional trajectories from their country of origin and from the countries where they did their doctoral studies, until their arrival in Brazil, and more precisely at Unicamp. Before discussing the results of the analyses, however, the chapter offers a general view of the Brazilian university system. This information helps, first, to clarify the nature of the academic job market and, second, to place Unicamp in the national higher education context.

## The Brazilian Higher Education System

Higher education is still only for a minority elite in Brazil. According to the Organisation for Economic Co-operation and Development (OECD), in 2012, the percentage of the Brazilian population between 25 and 64 years old that finished college was only 11.6 percent, the lowest among the analyzed countries, whereas the average among the member states was 31.5 percent (OECD, 2014). Official data show that, in the same year, just 18.8 percent of the population between 18 and 24 years of age were enrolled in or had finished postsecondary education (INEP, 2014, p. 36).

Besides being rare, a higher education diploma is also much valued in the job market in Brazil. In 2012, the average income of higher education graduates was approximately 160 percent higher than those with just a high school diploma, and 85.7 percent of university graduates were employed, against 77.3 percent of people with just a high school degree (OECD, 2014).

The current shape of Brazilian higher education is a consequence of the broad university reform imposed in the late 1960s, which adapted the university system to the economic development project of the military regime. One of its most important implications was the support given to the growth of private for-profit colleges (Sampaio, 2000). The public university system—maintained by the federal, state, or municipal government—was also expanded, though at a much slower pace, and suffered a significant reorganization.

This expansion must be understood in the context of a highly segmented higher education system, which separates out a select group of institutions with more academic prestige and research capacity from the other institutions in the country. There is a prevalence of faculty members who hold PhD degrees and have stable contracts, tenure, and competitive salaries in the first group, which mainly consists of tuition-free public institutions and a few private, not-for-profit institutions that usually charge high tuition fees. Graduate programs and research-oriented institutions belong to this group. In the second group there are institutions with lower academic prestige, mostly dedicated to professional education and without research capacity. This group mainly consists of private, for-profit institutions. The majority of the faculty members does not hold a PhD and have pay-per-hour contracts without tenure.

According to official data, in 2012 there were 2,416 higher education institutions in the country—2,112 private (87.4 percent) and 304 public ones (12.6 percent) (INEP, 2014). Together, they offered 362,732 positions for academics—150,338 in the public sector and 212,394 in the private sector.[1] PhD holders fill only 31.7 percent of these positions, most of them—67.2 percent—in public institutions (INEP, 2014).

Because of the lasting investment made in academic training by the federal and some state governments, most of the PhD holders found in these positions are locally trained Brazilian nationals and, to a lesser extent, foreign-born scholars. As a result, foreign-born scholars trained abroad fill only a small percentage of the higher education job positions in the country.

One of the main instruments of investment in academic training has been the development of graduate programs in national universities. The first graduate programs appeared in the 1930s and have grown substantively since the 1960s. In the last ten years, on average, around 12,000 students per year were granted a PhD degree in Brazil. In 2014, there were 298,020 graduate students in Brazilian programs, 83.4 percent in the public sector (CAPES, 2014).

In addition to that, public agencies have maintained long-lasting programs to finance international graduate training. The first initiatives of this kind took place in the 1920s. In the 1960s, a more robust program was initiated by the federal government and is still in place today, despite political crisis and economic downturn. Although there are no precise public statistics on the total number of scholarships that have been offered, the estimate is that, on average, around 1,000 Brazilian graduate students were enrolled per year in full-degree programs abroad in the period between 1998 and 2015 (CAPES, 2015; CNPq, 2015). Additionally, another program by the same agencies has distributed scholarships to finance up to one year of study abroad for graduate students enrolled in Brazilian graduate programs (so-called 'sandwich' scholarships). Using official data, it is possible to estimate that, between 1992 and 2012, approximately 24,000 scholarships of this type were distributed nationwide.

Students who are awarded scholarships for graduate studies abroad are, in principle, required to return to Brazil after the end of their sojourn. Most scholarship recipients have, in fact, returned.

Several factors have kept the academic job market attractive to those who hold local PhDs as well as to those who pursued their studies abroad. First, a civil servant faculty career was institutionalized in the public universities, and it is still in place almost without change. It grants tenure to all faculty at the very moment of hiring, along with competitive salaries and, until recently, retirement with full salary after 25 years of work for women and 30 years for men. Second, the university expansion resulted in a rather continuous growth of this kind of position for the last 40 years. Finally, the government investment in the expansion of graduate programs provided stable research funding through the offer of competitive grants, mainly in the science, technology, engineering, and mathematics (STEM) fields (Balbachevsky, 2004; Evans, 1982; Fernandes, 1990), which, in turn, resulted in a constant increase in research capacity. The number of research papers indexed in the Web of Science "increased about three times as fast as the world average from

2003 to 2012 (145 percent vs. 50 percent), resulting in a 1 percent expansion in world share from 1.7 percent to 2.7 percent" (Thomson Reuters, 2014, p. 15).

Simultaneously, there were some special conditions to attract foreign graduate students, mainly from other Latin American countries. The public universities are tuition free at the undergraduate and graduate levels, no matter the student's nationality. In addition to that, the graduate scholarship program established to fund students pursuing degrees could (and still can) be used to support foreign students. For example, at the University of Campinas, 7 percent of graduate students enrolled in 2015 were foreigners, most of them supported by Brazilian government scholarships (Unicamp, 2015). As will be seen later, many of these students remain in Brazil as faculty members after completing their PhDs.

## International Faculty in Brazil

Due to the incentives granted to Brazilian students to pursue graduate studies abroad, the flow of foreign students to Brazilian graduate programs, and the relative insularity of the country in regard to the international academic market, the decision on who should be considered 'international faculty' in Brazil is not a straightforward one. On the one hand, defining the group on the basis of the origin of their PhD degrees would result in the inclusion of a large number of Brazilian scholars who pursued doctoral studies abroad. On the other hand, restricting the group to foreign-born scholars would mean including a sizeable number of foreign scholars who got their PhDs in Brazil. In order to better understand the adjustment processes required from faculty coming from academic traditions different from the Brazilian one, a more restrictive definition of international faculty was put forth in this chapter, one that focused only on foreign scholars who hold a foreign PhD.

This group comprises a small percentage of the Brazilian higher education faculty and displays a distinctive profile in the higher education sector. As mentioned before, they are among the 31.7 percent of the higher education faculty who had completed a PhD as of 2012 (INEP, 2014). Also, a study done in 2007 showed that they were among the 17.3 percent of the holders of foreign PhD degrees in Brazil (Balbachevsky & Schwartzman, 2010; Schwartzman & Schwartzman, 2015, table 7).

As a matter of fact, foreign scholars are only 5,533 out of the total 156,278 PhD holders with a professional address in Brazil registered on the Lattes platform.[2] They are predominantly from Portuguese and Spanish-speaking countries (59.9 percent of the total), with 50.0 percent from Latin America, 7.3 percent from Portugal and Spain, and 1.6 percent from Portuguese-speaking African countries.

More than half of those foreign doctoral degree holders received a Brazilian PhD (n = 2,904 or 52.5 percent of the foreigners). Most of these individuals come from countries with a similar or weaker research tradition than Brazil, usually from Spanish- and Portuguese-speaking systems (82.7 percent). In contrast, foreign

**TABLE 3.1** Origin of PhDs held by Foreign Faculty

| Source of PhD | n | Percentage |
| --- | --- | --- |
| PhD obtained in Brazil | 2,904 | 52.5 |
| PhD obtained abroad | 2,629 | 47.5 |
| Total (N) | 5,533 | 100 |

*Source*: Data tabulated from the Lattes Platform (http://lattes.cnpq.br).

doctoral degree holders who received a foreign PhD (n = 2,629 or 47.5 percent of the foreigners) mostly come from countries with similar or stronger research traditions, including some worldwide hubs—such as the United States, France, Germany, and the United Kingdom—as well as some countries with regional importance, such as Russia and India. These data are summarized in Table 3.1.

Regarding nationality, foreign professors come from a broad number of countries. On the one hand, 77 percent of those who hold a Brazilian PhD come mainly from Latin America, Portugal, and some African Portuguese-speaking countries. On the other hand, 61 percent of those who hold a foreign PhD came mainly from non–Spanish- and non–Portuguese-speaking countries.

Looking just at the group who hold a foreign PhD, one can see a strong concentration regarding the place of graduate education. Although it is possible to count PhD degrees obtained in 66 different countries, 49.7 percent come from just four countries, all considered international centers of research—the United States, Germany, France, and the United Kingdom. Another 20.2 percent did their studies in Spanish- and Portuguese-speaking countries, mainly Argentina and Spain. A smaller proportion received their PhD in India and countries of the former Soviet Union (8.8 percent), most of them in Russia.

These data allow us to identify two patterns of circulation of foreign PhD holders who were working in Brazil in 2013. One is formed by those scholars coming from countries with graduate programs and research traditions less consolidated than Brazil's. They came to Brazil to do their doctoral research and eventually decided to stay in the country. A significant part of them is from Spanish-and Portuguese-speaking countries.

Another pattern is configured by those who did their doctoral studies in countries with similar or more consolidated graduate programs and research than Brazil, including some world research centers. A considerable proportion of them come from countries where Portuguese and Spanish are not spoken.

Foreign PhD holders who work in Brazilian higher education institutions are strongly concentrated in the southeast region of the country; there, we find 79.3 percent of those who got their PhD in Brazil and 68.4 percent of those who completed the PhD abroad. Indeed, this is the region that concentrates the largest number of faculty positions for PhD holders—that is, 50.8 percent (INEP, 2014). It is also where the highest proportion of research is produced in the country and where the graduate programs with the best evaluations by the federal assessment system are located. The University of Campinas (Unicamp) is also located in the southeast region, and it will be the focus of a more detailed analysis.

It is worth emphasizing that much of this discussion relates only to the public universities, which are a minority in the higher education system. Although the private institutions make up the vast majority, most of the faculty in those institutions (except for the few high-quality ones) do not perform any kind of research, and therefore there are no incentives for them to have their CVs in the Lattes database. We could not find any official data on the presence of foreign faculty in the private higher education sector. One can only speculate that their numbers are even smaller than in the public system, considering that they have to teach in Portuguese for a rather long number of hours per week, with salaries that are not very competitive on the national or international market.

## International Faculty at the University of Campinas (Unicamp)

The University of Campinas (*Universidade Estadual de Campinas*—Unicamp) is one of the three universities comprising the state of São Paulo's higher education system, which also includes the University of the State of São Paulo (*Universidade Estadual Paulista*—Unesp) and the University of São Paulo (*Universidade de São Paulo*—USP). Together, faculty members affiliated with these three universities participate in the production of the largest number of research papers among Brazilian universities. Also, Unicamp is one of the most socially and academically selective institutions in the country. In 2015, only 4.3 percent of candidates were admitted (Unicamp, 2015, table 2.7, p. 24), and the average admission rate was around 11 percent for all public universities (INEP, 2015).

Unicamp was founded in 1966 during the military regime. Its creation was guided by the ambition to make it a key factor in the development of São Paulo state and Brazil as a whole (Castilho & Soares, 2008). Its progress owes much to the contribution of many foreign scholars who came to reside in Campinas and who acted decisively to develop a variety of research fields. The university's leadership during its first decade also offered special conditions to welcome experienced Brazilian scholars who had left (or were forced to leave) the country to escape the political persecutions of that period. As a result, the university already counted in its first years on an extremely varied faculty with strong international connections. With the advancement of national graduate programs, however, this scenario started to change. The university today has the same inbreeding pattern seen in other Brazilian public universities, although there is a significant internal differentiation, as certain areas—such as physics and chemistry, for instance—are clearly more internationalized than others.

In 2014, Unicamp enrolled 18,698 undergraduate and 15,918 graduate students (Unicamp, 2015). Its graduate programs have been granting about 800 PhDs and 1,200 master's degrees per year.

As is the case with the other two state universities, Unicamp is fully funded by the state of São Paulo. Since 1989, it has received a fixed share of the net state value added tax (VAT) and has been granted autonomy to define its own budget. The university rector is chosen from among the faculty members and appointed by the state governor following a vote by faculty, staff, and students.

As in other Brazilian public universities, faculty members are hired as civil servants. The academic career is structured by the rather rigid bureaucratic rules that regulate the salary structure and promotions for the whole faculty, without exception. Aspiring new academics must pass a public exam to gain their first position. Full-time faculty are supposed to dedicate 40 hours per week to teaching activities (at undergraduate and graduate levels), research, and outreach/service. Before 2014, tenure was granted from the moment an academic's contract was signed, but new rules have now established that recently hired faculty should go through a three-year probation period, at the end of which tenure may or may not be granted, in a manner quite similar to the faculty promotion system seen in US universities.

The standard academic career is organized across three levels. There is no contract differentiation for individuals who are at the same level. Increases in salary are possible only when there is a promotion or by entering administrative positions. In this case, the salary increase is also standard, that is, it is the same for all who enter that level. Work hours are not negotiable, either. The progression from one level to the next is on the basis of peer evaluation, that is, a committee composed of members of the university and external members.

All faculty members go through periodic evaluations, even if they do not apply for a promotion. Publication record and teaching load are the main axes of this evaluation. University and departmental service, as well as graduate student supervision, are also taken into consideration, although with less emphasis. The ability to attract funding does not play any role in the evaluation. Although valued differently in different areas, one can safely say that internationalization in regard to publication and collaboration is quite valued in most departments, although it does not lead directly to promotion or to remuneration increases. Thus, in such a career path, being a foreigner does not penalize a professor and can even contribute to their career. In all other aspects, foreign professors face the same conditions as local professors in terms of contracts, salary, conditions to apply for internal and external grants, job rights, and obligations.

The majority of the job contracts offered by Unicamp are for higher education faculty positions. There are a smaller number of positions for researchers, language teachers, and vocational high school teachers. Because it is impossible to separate those groups in the data obtained from the Lattes Platform, our analysis looks at all PhD holders who indicated Unicamp as their professional address as faculty.

According to the information collected in the university databases in August 2015, 99 percent of Unicamp's 1,900 faculty held PhD degrees, and 93.4 percent of all PhD holders were hired as full-time faculty. The remaining group held contracts of 20 hours per week. Among all faculty members, 1,710 were Brazilians, 42 were naturalized Brazilians, and 94 were foreigners. The non-Brazilians represent, thus, 5.5 percent of the total (Unicamp, 2015).

These data are reasonably consistent with that obtained in June and July 2013 from the Lattes Platform, which found a total of 109 professors working at Unicamp who self-identified as foreigners, 92.7 percent of whom were hired for 40 hours per week (i.e., on full-time contracts). Since there were 1,759 professors registered in the Lattes Platform in 2013, the international faculty represented 6.2 percent.[3]

Unicamp follows the general pattern in the country concerning the internationalization of its faculty. Even though the presence of foreign faculty members has been important since its foundation, nowadays they represent a small proportion of the professoriate. It is worth noting, however, that the percentage of foreign faculty members at Unicamp is higher than the average in the country, which stood at 3.5 percent in 2013.

The same general pattern also appears in terms of the countries in which the foreign faculty members got their PhD degrees. From the total of analyzed résumés, 55 percent (n = 60) held Brazilian degrees and 45 percent (n = 49) held foreign degrees. The percentage of international faculty who held a foreign PhD working at Unicamp in 2013 was, therefore, 2.7 percent of the total.

Among the 60 foreign faculty members who completed their doctoral degrees in Brazil, 40 are from Latin America and 4 from Portuguese-speaking countries—again, similar to the national-level data. Regarding the Brazilian institutions where Unicamp faculty obtained their PhDs, 44 studied at Unicamp and 11 at USP. Although both universities have a very important role in the graduate system of the state of São Paulo and of Brazil, the numbers suggest a rather high degree of inbreeding (Furtado, Davis, Jr., Gonçalves & de Almeida, 2015; Horta & Yudkevich, 2015). Analyzing the 49 international faculty members who did their PhDs abroad, the same overall trend appears again. In this group, the faculty members from non–Portuguese- or non–Spanish-speaking countries are the vast majority (37 professors, or 75.5 percent). In addition, this group shows a tendency to have studied in countries with a stronger university tradition when compared to Brazil. Those who got their PhD in the United States, France, Germany, and the United Kingdom add up to 30 of the 40 professors (61.2 percent) in this category.

## Perceptions on Building a Career in Brazil

Aiming to collect the impressions of those who had more exposure to other academic environments, the group chosen for interviews was restricted to those who had completed their PhD abroad. Thereby, a larger group of Brazilian doctoral degree holders who did their doctoral studies abroad and the foreign PhD holders who studied in Brazil were not interviewed for the present study. We contacted 21 foreign faculty members, inviting them for an interview for this chapter.

Among these 21, there were only four women.[4] Two professors in the group were foreigners but had come to Brazil when they were young, having completed their undergraduate studies in the country before going abroad to pursue their doctoral studies. They completed their PhDs in foreign institutions, supported by Brazilian scholarships. Eight out of the 21 did not respond, and three declined to be interviewed. Therefore, seven (six active and one retired) faculty members were interviewed. Four of the interviewees came from Europe and three from Latin America. Three arrived at Unicamp during what we call the university consolidation period, between 1979 and 1988. One arrived at the end of the 1990s, and the other two less than five years ago. They work in different areas—engineering, natural and hard sciences, and health—and are actively participating in all aspects of university life: teaching, research, and service.

The interviews shed some light on the complex social dynamics that led to the emigration of each faculty member that eventually resulted in their arrival at Unicamp. The analysis proposed here focuses on three key aspects of their trajectories: the context in which they left their home country with Brazil as a destination, the processes that led them to Unicamp, and their career development while at this university.

Given the lack of a consistent university policy to attract international faculty, what enticed these foreign faculty members to this Brazilian university? Although coming to Brazil and Unicamp was a result of developments in different areas that will be discussed later, the interviewees indicated that the decision to leave their home country was mainly due to the impossibility to develop their careers there because of contexts of decreasing numbers of academic jobs. Having prepared themselves to work in their countries, they were faced with difficulties to find positions they considered 'good' in their specialty areas.

Such difficulties included a lack of networking knowledge or options, or, in one case, a political crisis. A European-born professor, for example, was discouraged from applying for a university position in his Western European home country at the end of the 1980s after finishing his PhD in a North American university. He told us, "[T]he dean of the school [I contacted] said bluntly that they just hired among those who had finished their PhDs in the country." He explained:

> [T]his is because [over there] you become an assistant in order to pursue your PhD. In the end, each professor has under him, I don't know, five, ten assistants, depending on his department. Some of these assistants are doing their PhDs, while some of them have already finished theirs. They are all waiting for the old man to die in order to fight for his place. It is just one position for too many people.

The same problem was faced by another European-born faculty member who decided to emigrate ten years later, after trying for some time to find a position in the job market and coming to the conclusion that a PhD did not give him any advantage. As he recalls, the nonacademic market did not value a PhD, while the academic market did not offer enough positions.

Four of the faculty interviewed came to Brazil immediately after finishing their doctoral studies or right after, with little work experience abroad. One of them, however, had worked for six years as a postdoc in different research groups in his Western European home country before leaving, and another had worked at a different Latin American university for four years before coming to Brazil.

Those with work experience ended up in Brazil while trying to escape other difficult contexts. "The situation was deteriorating fast in all senses—economic, political, social. So we decided, my wife and I . . .—we had one child at that time—to try to leave the country," explained a Latin American–born faculty who found his way to Brazil in 2010 in the wake of a political and economic crisis that reached the other Latin American country where he had pursued his PhD and had begun a promising career.

The arrival of these foreign scholars in Brazil was mediated by different kinds of relationships. In three cases, it was the result of actions developed by the university in Brazil itself in order to recruit international faculty. In the first instance, in the 1970s, a prominent scientist connected to Unicamp visited the laboratory in another Latin American country where the young professor was starting his professional career. Another interviewee was looking for a position outside his country at the end of the 1990s and saw an offer for a postdoc position on an international website published by a research group from Unicamp. The third interviewee in this category came to Unicamp as part of a program to attract international faculty, which lasted during a brief period between 2010 and 2013 (Favaro, 2010).

These three pathways correspond to different moments in the history of faculty hiring at Unicamp: the attraction of foreign scholars in the first years, the building of national knowledge capacity to form new generations of scientists with the consolidation of graduate programs and postdoc positions in the 1990s, and the recent internationalization policies. These policies were, nevertheless, mostly intermittent and the degrees to which they really guided and still guide hiring practices continue to depend on the willingness of specific university administrations.

None of these three professors had previous connections to Brazil or Unicamp. In the case of two of them, the country was not their first destination of choice. Both had tried for brief periods, unsuccessfully, to find jobs in Anglo-Saxon countries.

Another group of faculty members arrived in Brazil due to family ties. Two had married Brazilian colleagues, either during their graduate studies or soon after that. When they did not find job opportunities that they considered acceptable in their countries at the end of the 1980s, they opted to come to Brazil. For different reasons, both did not want to remain in, or go to, Anglo-Saxon countries. Both report that their Brazilian spouses were not happy to return to Brazil. They recognize, however, that they benefited from their spouses' network during the adaptation period to the country, and that this was important to get a position and to develop their careers.

In the first and second groups, the work conditions, salary, and research structure they found in Brazil were important elements in the decision to come and stay in the country. They all consider that they made their decisions based on their interest to "continue in the academic area" or to "continue to do research."

One of them explained that he was "impressed by the [Brazilian academic] dynamism." "Things were not slow as in [his Western European country], they were not cloudy," he added. Also, he continued:

> [T]here was a certain attention to the work, and also recognition. Consequently, you could work. (. . .) Once you get recognition, you have access to research funds. You achieve things. Other colleagues, countrymen [also working in Brazil] say, [the difference is that] if you want to do [research], you can do it.

They affirm, however, that this was not an "obvious" or "natural" decision. Many mentioned that they faced the opposition of their families and even their advisors. This point can be well illustrated by the case of two faculty members who grew up in Brazil and later received scholarships to do their PhD work abroad. Both claim they were not tempted to stay abroad after completing their degrees, as they considered the work conditions in Brazil completely satisfactory. One of them, with a PhD from a very prestigious North American university and after having obtained particularly promising results, was strongly counseled by the foreign advisor—a prominent scientist in the field—not to return to Brazil. He noted that many reasons made him dismiss job offers outside of Brazil, among them the idea that he had an obligation to contribute to the development of his research field in Brazil after having benefitted from the national scholarship program. He also mentioned that he believed he would be capable of building a respectable career in Brazil, as some of his Brazilian professors had while at the same time maintaining a good quality of life.

In addition, some note that they had to adjust their research focus in order to advance their careers in the new environment they encountered in Brazil. One of them, for example, having arrived in the middle of the 1980s, when the Brazilian economic crisis was at its worst moment, told us that he lacked the computers he needed to go on with his work. He explained, though, that

> this handicap became an advantage in the end because soon thereafter a new programming language was launched (. . .) and, since I didn't have an adequate computer to continue with the programming I had been doing before, I had the time to pause and develop a way to adapt the structures I had developed to this new programming paradigm. As a result, I became

a sort of specialist in this new way of developing software in my field and I have [today] a code library more modern than many you can find in other [developed] countries. (. . .)

"This is a research line in which I still work," he added.

This kind of development—one in which a negative situation was seized as an opportunity—is not rare among the group interviewed. The Latin American–born faculty mentioned earlier, for example, although coming from a quite difficult experience, explained that he had a very productive year after arriving in Brazil, even in the period in which he did not have a permanent position "because he was able to concentrate on his research." He explained that the papers he was able to produce in this period were instrumental in putting him in contact with important research groups in Europe and the United States.

After some years residing in Brazil, the interviewees claimed to be "very satisfied" with their decision. They believe that work conditions are good and they receive the research support they would like. Furthermore, they claim that the work environment is relatively calm, "with no great tensions," as one affirms. The large majority declared that they had no problems, or just small difficulties, adapting to the Brazilian university environment. The language barrier seemed to be surpassed rather easily, as they recount having learned enough Portuguese to teach mandatory undergraduate classes or to establish friendly relations with colleagues after a short period of time. In fact, all the interviews were done in Portuguese. Although their accents were quite thick in most of the cases, their command of the language, as well as their familiarity with idiomatic expressions and slang, were evident.

Many of interviewees believe that the success of their adaptation was due to the quality of the welcome they received in Brazil and at Unicamp. One of them only half-jokingly said that he had suffered from "inverse discrimination" for being a foreigner. He explained, "[E]verything I do is considered good. Well, maybe what I do is actually good but . . . leaving it aside, [I believe that] they [his colleagues] see what I do in a positive light."

This feeling seems to extend to their personal interactions, even though one of the more recent arrivals mentioned that he is facing some difficulties making friends.

The careers of these professors show a high level of productivity, comparable to the most productive Brazilian faculty members. They receive prestigious and substantive grants, are part of national and international networks, and publish frequently in international journals. They have all maintained cooperation with research groups in their original countries. Through these contacts, some receive graduate students and have spent periods of time doing research in their countries of origin and/or in other countries. Since this is not very different from what we notice regarding the more productive Brazilian-born and/or Brazilian-educated faculty, it is not easy to evaluate the impact of the foreign-born and foreign-educated faculty on their domestic counterpart without further research.

The interviewees emphasized the positive aspects of their professional trajectories in Brazil; they spoke little about the difficulties they have faced, even when explicitly asked to do so. When talking about disputes inside the university and/or within their field nationally, they tended to play these down, reaffirming that those were "normal disputes" that could happen "anywhere" and were not related to their condition as foreigners. The overall tone of the evaluation was positive, based on the conditions they encountered when developing their scientific careers.

In this regard, they echo their colleagues who were interviewed for the international project The Changing Academic Profession in 2008. Compared to faculty from 18 countries, Brazilian academics were placed in the eighth position in regard to overall job satisfaction, a perception that varied little among academics affiliated with different institutions (Balbachevsky & Schwartzman, 2013).

## Conclusion

The experience of foreign faculty members in a research-intensive university in Brazil such as Unicamp can be better understood when situated in the broader context of international relations created by the Brazilian scientific community.

Some elements are particularly significant. First, the role played by state science and technology policy, such as the massive investments to send Brazilian graduate students to study abroad, meant that the internationalization of the national academic space was essentially the result of Brazilian students' internationalization. The concomitant increase in the capacity of graduate education, as well as the number of academic positions in Brazil, along with the obstacles presented by the need for fluency in the Portuguese language and the restrictions on hiring foreigners, seemed to create a sort of market reserve for Brazilian scientists, at the expense of international faculty.

Still, an important number of foreign scholars who were able to enter this rather closed job market had completed their doctoral work in Brazil. Linguistic proximity, free tuition in public universities, and scholarship offers made the country attractive to many students in Latin America and Portuguese-speaking African countries, where graduate studies were, and still are, less structured than in Brazil.

The longevity and quality of these investments seem to have contributed to turning Brazil into a regional research hub. However, somehow the improvement of Brazilian research and graduate programs has also contributed to isolating the Brazilian academic profession from the rest of the world, as the proportion of faculty members with international experience can be considered rather low, even with the incentives for international experience given by the country's research agencies. Among the faculty of Unicamp who applied for grants from the São Paulo Research Foundation (FAPESP), only 48.3 percent declared in their Lattes profile that they had had an experience of at least one year abroad. Similar figures are found in all universities in the state of São Paulo.

Foreign faculty members educated in developed countries are a minority among Brazilian university faculty. The interviews with international faculty members at Unicamp seem to show that their presence in Brazil owes more to biographical accidents than to organized international mobility dynamics. Although emigration seems to have been forced by obstacles encountered in their home countries or in the countries where they received their PhD degrees, their arrival in Brazil was prompted by singular circumstances and not by institutionalized programs. Some of those without previous ties to Brazil were attracted by intermittent initiatives in different moments of the country's history. Those with previous ties had mainly personal connections.

In all cases, however, the structure for teaching and researching in Brazilian public universities, especially favorable at Unicamp, seems to have played an important role in the process, not only by attracting them at the beginning of their careers but also allowing them to build successful careers thereafter. All faculty members evaluated positively their careers at Unicamp. The frequency of publication, the number of citations received, the number of graduate students, and their capacity to secure competitive grants and to participate in international academic networks are some objective indicators that support their views. Their positive evaluation could also be influenced by some characteristics of the career at Unicamp in particular, and in public higher education institutions in general. After all, they received tenure at the beginning of their careers, and their salary has put them in the top 10 percent of the socioeconomic pyramid (Brasil, 2012). In a country with low per capita income, such as Brazil, this salary allows a standard of living probably higher than those in the middle classes in countries with higher per capita incomes.

Summing up, the science and technology policy still in place in Brazil was developed during the second half of the 20th century. It aimed at building national knowledge capacity to educate a highly qualified academic workforce. International circulation of Brazilian students and faculty has been an integral part of this policy. It helped the country to become a regional academic hub, attracting international students from countries with less consolidated scientific structures, and a few others, who, holding a PhD from important international centers, faced impediments to stay in those countries. Nevertheless, this policy also helped to form a quite closed academic job market, with high levels of inbreeding.

The future of this policy is uncertain, especially in a period when international exchanges are intensifying in a globalized context. Recent initiatives of the federal government, such as the so-called Science Without Borders program, have focused most of the resources mainly on sending undergraduate students for a relatively short period abroad. A very small fraction of the program was designed to attract international scholars, and since it is now compromised by lack of financial resources, its effects may be short lived. Apparently, a more dynamic role in relation to international academic circulation paths is not yet on the radar of the federal government or the main universities. Actually, it is rather safe to state that Brazil pays very little attention to attracting foreign faculty to its universities (perhaps least among the BRIC countries, along with India), something that is also seen in other strategic job sectors in the country. There are not specific policies or programs as observed in other countries, leading to potential consequences in terms of internationalization of the higher education sector, which, in turn, might have an impact on the overall output of Brazilian universities in terms of qualified education of the future workforce, as well as scientific and technological developments.

The rather high degree of isolation of Brazil can be an important drawback in the advancement of knowledge capacity in Brazil, as global integration becomes imperative for the research process. Further research is needed to follow these developments and examine their outcomes.

## Notes

1 It should be noted that one individual can fill more than one position.
2 The way data are presented on the platform did not allow us to include in this group the naturalized foreigners who identify themselves as Brazilians.
3 The small difference between the official data of 2015 and the one from 2013 can be due to an imprecision of Lattes data, as well as a variation in the period.
4 Women are a minority among Unicamp faculty. In 2015, they represented 37.4 percent (n=795) of all professors (N=2,125).

## References

Almeida, A. M. F., Moschkovich, M., & Polaz, K. (2012). Pesquisando os grupos dominantes: Notas de pesquisa sobre acesso às informações. Revista Pós Ciências Sociais, 09, 161–174. Retrieved from www.periodicoseletronicos.ufma.br/index.php/rpcsoc/article/view/994/2735.

Balbachevsky, E. (2004). Graduate Education: Emerging challenges to a successful policy. In C. Brock & S. Schwartzman (Eds.), *The challenges of education in Brazil* (pp. 209–228). Oxford: Symposium Books.

Balbachevsky, E., & Schwartzman, S. (2010). The graduate foundations of research in Brazil. *Higher Education Forum*, 7, 85–100.

Balbachevsky, E., & Schwartzman, S. (2013). Job satisfaction in a diverse institutional environment: The Brazilian experience. In H. Coates, I. R. Dobson, L. Goedegebuure & V. L. Meek (Ed.), *Job satisfaction around the academic world* (pp. 55–58). Dordrecht: Springer.

Botelho, A. J. J. (1999). Da utopia tecnológica aos desafios da política científica e tecnológica: o Instituto Tecnológico de Aeronáutica (1947–1967). *Revista Brasileira de Ciências Sociais*, 14(39), 139–154. Retrieved from www.scielo.br/scielo.php?script=sci_arttext&pid=S0102-69091999000100008&lng=en&tlng=pt. 10.1590/S0102-69091999000100008

Brasil, Secretaria de Assuntos Estratégicos (2012). *Relatório da Comissão para Definição da Classe Média no Brasil*. Retrieved from www.sae.gov.br/wp-content/uploads/Relatório-Definição-da-Classe-Média-no-Brasil1.pdf

Canedo, L. (2009). Les boursiers de la Fondation Ford et la recomposition des sciences sociales brésiliennes, *Cahiers de la recherche sur l'éducation et les savoirs* [En ligne], Hors-série n° 2. Retrieved from http://cres.revues.org/670

CAPES—Coordenação de Aperfeiçoamento de Pessoal de Nível Superior (2015). Geocapes—Sistema de Informações Georeferenciadas. Retrieved from http://geocapes.capes.gov.br/geocapes2/

Castilho, F., & Soares, A. G. T. de (Eds.). (2008). *O conceito de universidade no projeto da Unicamp*. Campinas, SP: Editora da Unicamp.

Chor Maio, M. (2011). Florestan Fernandes, Oracy Nogueira, and the UNESCO Project on Race Relations in São Paulo. *Latin American Perspectives, 38*(03), 136–149. doi:10.1177/0094582X10391070

CNPq—Conselho Nacional de Desenvolvimento Científico e Tecnológico (2015). Séries Históricas. Retrieved from www.cnpq.br/series-historicas

Cueto, M. (1997). Science under Adversity: Latin American Medical Research and American Private Philanthropy, 1920–1960. *Minerva, 38*, 233–245. Retrieved from http://link.springer.com/article/10.1023%2FA%3A1004230000979?LI=true

Digiampietri, L. A., Mena-Chalco, J., Alcazar, J. J. P., Tuesta, E. F., Delgado, K.V., Mugnaini, R., & Silva, G. S. (2012). *Minerando e Caracterizando Dados de Currículos Lattes*. Paper presented at the Brazilian Workshop on Social Analysis and Mining at the Meeting of the Sociedade Brasileira de Computação, Curitiba, Brazil. Retrieved at www.imago.ufpr.br/csbc2012/anais_csbc.

Evans, P. (1982). *A tríplice aliança: As multinacionais, as estatais e o capital nacional no desenvolvimento dependente brasileiro*. Zahar: Rio de Janeiro.

Favaro, T. (2010). Professores são recrutados no exterior. *Jornal da Unicamp, 24*(484). Retrieved from www.unicamp.br/unicamp/unicamp_hoje/ju/dezembro2010/ju484_pag04.php

Fernandes, A. M. (1990). *A construça~o da cie^ncia no Brasil e a SBPC*. Brasília: Editora da UnB.

Furtado, C. A., Davis, C. A., Jr., Gonçalves, M. A., & de Almeida, J. M. (2015). A Spatiotemporal analysis of Brazilian science from the perspective of researchers' career Trajectories. *PLoS ONE, 10*(10), e0141528. doi:10.1371/journal.pone.0141528

Horta, H., & Yudkevich, M. (2015). The role of academic inbreeding in developing higher education systems: Challenges and possible solutions. *Technological Forecasting & Social Change* [online first]. Retrieved from http://dx.doi.org/10.1016/j.techfore.2015.06.039

INEP—Instituto Nacional de Estudos Pedagógicos (2014). Sinopse Estatística da Educação Básica. Retrieved from http://portal.inep.gov.br/basica-censo-escolar-sinopse-sinopse

INEP—Instituto Nacional de Estudos Pedagógicos (2015). Sinopse Estatística da Educação Superior. Retrieved from http://portal.inep.gov.br/superior-censosuperior-sinopse

Miceli, S. (Ed.). (1993). *A Fundação Ford no Brasil*. Sumaré/ FAPESP: São Paulo.

OECD. (2014). *Education at a Glance 2014: OECD Indicators*. Paris, France: OECD Publishing. doi: http://dx.doi.org/10.1787/eag-2014-en

Sampaio, H. (2000). *O Ensino Superior no Brasil—o setor privado*. São Paulo: Hucitec/Fapesp.

Schwartzman, L. F., & Schwartzman, S. (2015). Migrations des personnes hautement qualifiées au Brésil. De l'isolement à l'insertion internationale ? *Brésil(s)*, 147–172. English version: Highly skilled migration in Brazil—from isolation to global integration? Retrieved from https://archive.org/stream/HighlySkilledMigrationInBrazilFromIsolationToGlobalIntegration/bresil_migration#page/n0/mode/2up https://ia801506.us.archive.org/30/items/HighlySkilledMigrationInBrazilFromIsolationToGlobalIntegration/bresil_migration.pdf

Schwartzman, S. (2007). Brazil's leading university: Between intelligentsia, world standards and social inclusion. In P. G. Altbach & J. Balán (Eds.), *World class worldwide: Transforming research universities in Asia and Latin America* (pp. 143–172). Baltimore: The Johns Hopkins University Press.

Skidmore, T. E. (2003). Lévi-Strauss, Braudel and Brazil: A case of mutual influence. *Bulletin of Latin American Research*, *22*(3), 340–349. Retrieved from www.jstor.org/stable/27733587

Stepan, N. L. (2011). The national and the international in public health: Carlos Chagas and the Rockefeller foundation in Brazil, 1917–1930s. *Hispanic American Historical Review*, *91*(3), 469–502.

Telles, E. E. (2003). US foundations and racial reasoning in Brazil. *Theory, Culture & Society*, *20*(04), 31–47.

Thomson Reuters (2014). The research & innovation performance of the G20 and its impact on decisions made by the world's most influential economic leaders. Report. Retrieved from http://sciencewatch.com/sites/sw/files/images/basic/research-innovation-g20.pdf

Trindade, H. (2005). Social sciences in Brazil in perspective: Foundation, consolidation and diversification. *Social Science Information*, *44*(2–3), 283–357. doi:10.1177/0539018405053291

Unicamp—Universidade Estadual de Campinas (2015). Sistema Integrado de Dados Institucionais—Estatísticas de alunos. Retrieved from www.siarh.unicamp.br/indicadores/View.jsf?categoria=PUB_ACAD_MATRICULADOS.

# 4
# INTERNATIONAL FACULTY IN CANADA

Recruitment and Transition Processes

*Diane V. Barbarič and Glen A. Jones*

International faculty have always played an important role in Canadian higher education, with international faculty bringing global perspectives, ways of thinking, and expertise to Canadian campuses. They help in both bringing Canadian institutions into, and promoting them within, international research networks and collaborations, and are an integral component of universities' internationalization strategies. It is estimated that non–Canadian-born university teachers make up approximately 40 percent of the faculty workforce in Canada (Canadian Association of University Teachers, 2014), yet surprisingly little is known about this population. National-level faculty breakdowns by citizenship at the time of recruitment do not exist, and Canada's immigration policies have always tended to favor naturalization of highly skilled immigrants, therefore continually augmenting the number of Canadian faculty members.

On the academic front, there has been little research on the subject of international faculty in Canada outside of its relation to the Canadianization movement of the late 1960s and early 1970s. This movement advocated for increased employment opportunities for Canadians in key social, cultural, and political arenas, such as universities, museums, and government institutions. At the time, concerns had arisen over the large number of non-Canadian professors who had been employed during the postwar expansion of universities, and proponents of Canadianization pressed for both increased Canadian curricular content and increased hiring of domestic faculty over foreign faculty (Cormier, 2004, 2005; Jones, 2009; Mathews & Steele, 1969).

The scarce literature that currently exists on international faculty in Canada has examined the extent to which these faculty members feel that they are contributing to Canadian universities' internationalization efforts and the extent to which they feel their international experience is recognized or rewarded by their university (Richardson, McBey & McKenna, 2009). Other studies have explored such themes as self-initiated expatriation (as opposed to employer-initiated expatriation or transfers), the lived experiences of expatriate academics, and the importance of family support and integration for the success of the foreign faculty member in her or his new environment (Doherty, Richardson & Thorn, 2013; Richardson, 2000, 2006; Richardson & McKenna, 2006). The institutional perspective on international faculty recruitment and the perceptions of individual faculty members have received little attention in the literature.

The objective of this study is to address these two research gaps by focusing on the recruitment and transition processes for international faculty in Canadian universities from both the faculty and administrative perspectives. For the purposes of this study, 'international faculty' were defined as those faculty members working in full-time, tenure-stream positions who were recruited from the international academic market (i.e., from outside of Canada) and who were not Canadian citizens at the time of their recruitment.

We have organized this chapter into three main sections. First, we begin by providing a general introduction to Canada, including its demography and general immigration patterns. Then, we turn our attention to higher education in Canada. Here, we trace the systemic evolution of higher education in the country and analyze various components, such as higher education participation and attainment levels, Canada's first-ever international education strategy, faculty diversity at Canadian universities, immigration policies for recruiting international faculty, and the Canada Research Chairs Program. The third section of the chapter is devoted to our research study. In it, we introduce the University of Toronto, our case study institution, where, since 2008, between half and two-thirds of the new faculty hires have been non-Canadians, with American citizens comprising between 25 percent and 30 percent of the total of new hires per year (Office of the Vice Provost, 2013). We then go on to describe our research design and report on the findings of our empirical study. Based on data obtained through document analysis and in-person, semi-structured interviews with both university administrators and international faculty, we explored the rationales for international recruitment and expatriation and the appointment, transition, and integration processes—including challenges faced by both the administration and these faculty members in their new environment. Finally, we conclude the chapter with a summary of our key findings and discuss some possible avenues for future research into international faculty in Canada.

## Canada

Higher education in Canada is as diverse as the Canadian landscape itself. A federated state with ten provinces and three territories, Canada is the world's second largest country (behind Russia) at almost 10 million square km (3.85 million square miles). It spans six time zones; borders the Atlantic, Pacific, and Arctic oceans, as well as the United States to its south; and has a relatively sparse population of only 35.7 million inhabitants (Statistics Canada, 2015a). Over 70 percent of Canadians live in metropolitan areas (Statistics Canada, 2013a), and Canada is home to people of over 200 ethnic origins. Finally, foreign-born individuals (immigrants) make up just over 20 percent of its total population (Statistics Canada, 2013b).

On this last point, it is important to note that the terms 'foreign-born' and 'immigrant' do not hold the same negative connotation that they do in certain other countries around the world. This is due, in part, to the fact that Canada has always been an immigrant-receiving country. It is also partly due to the fact that Canada has a selective immigration policy that allows the country, by and large, to choose the vast majority of its future citizens. Every year, the country sets an immigration target composed of three distinct admission categories: economic, family reunification, and humanitarian. It then uses a points system to rank the applicants, looking at such factors as educational achievement, language competency, age, and national labor market needs. In 2015, Canada planned to welcome between 260,000 and 285,000 new permanent residents, of which two-thirds (65 percent) are slated to be in the economic immigration class (Citizenship and Immigration Canada, 2015a).

Canada admits temporary foreign workers under a number of programs to fulfill a variety of needs, some diplomatic (like the bilateral youth mobility programs), and some short-term economic (like the seasonal agricultural workers programs). Just over 100,000 temporary foreign workers were in Canada in 2013 (Citizenship and Immigration Canada, 2015b). International academics may be admitted to Canada as economic immigrants or as temporary foreign workers, as we will explain a little later in the chapter.

## Higher Education in Canada

Canada is a federation, and responsibility for higher education rests with the provinces and territories. Given this decentralized authority, higher education in Canada is best understood as thirteen quite different provincial/territorial systems (Jones, 1997). There is no federal ministry for education or higher education and no national higher education policy. Each province has a ministry responsible either in whole or in part for higher education (often defined as postsecondary education) in its jurisdiction.

Canada has approximately 135 colleges and institutes and 97 universities, with these numbers corresponding to the memberships in the two leading pan-Canadian postsecondary education advocacy associations: Colleges and Institutes Canada, and Universities Canada. Most Canadian universities are considered public in that they receive operating support from a provincial government, though most are legally established as private, not-for-profit corporations. There is no national quality assurance mechanism or agency in Canada. Most provinces leave quality assurance in the hands of individual institutions (Weinrib & Jones, 2014), while programs in professional fields are frequently accredited by professional bodies.

Finally, as a bilingual country, efforts have been made nationwide to provide higher education opportunities in English and French. Currently, nine of Canada's ten provinces offer programs in both official languages, and similarly Canada has two distance-only universities: the English-language Athabasca University and the French-language TÉLUQ (Canadian Information Centre for International Credentials, 2015).

## Postsecondary Participation, Enrollment, and Educational Attainment

Since the mid-1990s, Canada has focused its efforts on supporting a burgeoning knowledge economy. From 1995 to 2013, participation in university by 18- to 24-year-olds rose eight percentage points, to 27 percent, whereas college participation over that same time period remained unchanged at 15 percent (Statistics Canada, 2015e). Graduate studies, that is, second- and third-cycle programs or equivalent, made up 16 percent of university enrollments in 2012–2013 (Statistics Canada, 2014a).

In terms of national educational attainment, in 2012, 53 percent of adults aged 25 to 64 had obtained tertiary qualifications, with that number split almost equally between college/vocational tertiary attainment at 25 percent, and university and advanced research degrees at 28 percent (Statistics Canada, 2014b). A breakdown of this latter figure, however, reveals both regional disparities and ongoing equity and access challenges across the country. For example, whereas the average university-level attainment for 25- to 64-year-old non-Aboriginals was 29 percent, that figure plummeted to only 11 percent for Aboriginals in the same age category. That Aboriginal attainment figure has held steady since 2011, whereas non-Aboriginal university attainment has risen 7 percent, or two percentage points, in the same time period, to 29 percent (Statistics Canada, 2015d). Closing this education gap is currently a key issue in Canadian higher education.

## Funding and Institutional Autonomy

As mentioned earlier, the vast majority of colleges and universities in Canada are public institutions insofar as they receive public funding to cover a portion of their expenditures. Once again, the amount and percentage of public funding vary by jurisdiction but, on average, for the 2012–2013 academic year, colleges in Canada received almost two-thirds of their revenue from government (65 percent) whereas that number dropped to just over half (51 percent) for universities (Statistics Canada, 2015b, 2015c). Tuition and other student fees accounted for 23 percent and 24 percent of revenue, respectively, with the remaining portion coming from such sources as donations, investments, and nongovernmental grants and contracts. Federal funding is awarded on a competitive basis through grants from national research councils and federal funding agencies, and each province has developed its own mechanisms for determining operating grant allocations to institutions.

Finally, universities in Canada are autonomous legal entities, and faculty and staff are recruited and paid by the institution that employs them (i.e., they are under contract as employees of the institution). Salaries and benefits account for 59 percent of all university spending (Canadian Association of University Business Officers, 2014).

## International Education

Since 2012, Canada has had its first-ever international education strategy (IES). It was put together for the federal Ministers of Finance and International Trade by an advisory panel made up of six experts from academia and the private sector, and is the result of an extensive pan-Canadian consultative process (Advisory Panel on Canada's International Education Strategy, 2012). In essence, however, more than an international education strategy, this document can be characterized as a 98-page trade policy manifesto in favor of boosting national economic prosperity through the doubling of international student numbers. Although there are token mentions of international research collaboration, partnership building, and overseas experience for Canadian students, the bulk of the document is devoted to recruiting and retaining international students. Trilokekar (2015) rightly argues that Canada's IES visibly fulfills a domestic economic agenda, echoing the earlier position of Trilokekar and Jones (2013) that international education in Canada, at least as it was understood and touted by the former federal government, had indeed become a self-proclaimed pipeline to fill the needs of Canada's domestic labor market.

Of note for this chapter, however, is the absence of any direct mention of recruitment of international faculty as part of Canada's international education strategy. Given that international faculty recruitment is not mentioned in either provincial- or national-level international education strategies, we can only surmise that hiring has remained an institutional prerogative. That is not to say, however, that the provinces or the federal government do not have any influence on how this transpires; rather, their intervention is indirect—namely, through immigration policy.

## Faculty Diversity and International Faculty at Canadian Universities

In 2006 (the most recent year for relevant information), 15 percent of university faculty in Canada belonged to a visible minority (Canadian Association of University Teachers, 2014), which was almost on par with the national average of 16 percent that year (Statistics Canada, 2010). In Canada, "'members of visible minorities' means persons, other than aboriginal peoples, who are non-Caucasian in race or non-white in colour," as defined in Section 3, "Interpretation," of the *Employment Equity Act, 1995* (Department of Justice, 2015). Chinese made up the largest visible minority group of university teachers at 28 percent, followed by South Asian (22 percent), Arab (12 percent), Black (11 percent), West Asian (7 percent), and Latin American (6 percent) faculty. In terms of religious diversity, in 2001 (the last year for which census data were collected for this item), almost two-thirds of faculty members identified themselves as being from one of the three monotheistic religions (Christianity, Islam, Judaism), which is lower than the national average of 80 percent, and 30 percent stated that they had no religion (almost double the national average of 16 percent). The remaining faculty members identified religious affiliation with Buddhism, Hinduism, Sikhism, Paganism, and Native Indian or Inuit beliefs (Canadian Association of University Teachers, 2014; Statistics Canada, 2003).

As for nationality, in 2006, 87 percent of faculty members in Canada were Canadian citizens (Canadian Association of University Teachers, 2014). However, this figure can be misleading because Canada's immigration policies favor naturalization for skilled workers. That same year, non–Canadian-born university teachers made up 41 percent of the faculty workforce, a figure that has remained relatively constant for at least 20 years (Canadian Association of University Teachers, 2014). However, this figure should also be used with caution when talking about international faculty because it includes individuals who immigrated as children, as well as those who came to Canada to pursue an academic career.

## *Immigration Policy for Recruiting International Faculty*

As mentioned earlier, immigration policy plays an important role in international faculty recruitment in Canada. In 2013 and 2014, after a series of highly publicized scandals involving Canadian employers exploiting loopholes in the federal Temporary Foreign Worker Program (TFWP) by replacing seasoned local workers with internationally recruited newcomers, the federal government clamped down on immigration rules for all foreigners. One of the unintended consequences of the new, more stringent, set of international hiring requirements for employers in Canada was the increased difficulty that universities faced in hiring international faculty.

Contrary to what might have been expected, however, these increased difficulties were received with mixed reviews in the university milieu. On the one hand, representatives from Canadian universities predictably worried that the new measures would hamper their ability to recruit the best researchers to their institutions and therefore adversely affect their ability to compete effectively in the global knowledge economy (Chiose, 2014; Tamburri, 2014). The Canadian Association of University Teachers, on the other hand, publicly welcomed the stricter hiring criteria, seeing the new situation as a recruitment opportunity for Canadian citizens and permanent residents already in Canada (Canadian Association of University Teachers, 2015b).

Why would a change in a *temporary* foreign worker program have an impact on recruiting for tenure-track positions? Canada does indeed have several immigration programs for admitting skilled workers seeking permanent residence in Canada for economic reasons, that is, permanent jobs or tenure-track positions in universities; however, the administration of these programs is notoriously slow and the application process extremely cumbersome. The TFWP is, therefore, a more expedient route to use. According to a February 2015 newspaper article, Canadian universities used the "temporary foreign worker program to recruit for approximately a quarter of their new permanent jobs over the last five years" (Chiose, 2015a).

After intense, months-long discussions between the two federal ministries in charge of immigration and domestic labor policies (seeking to protect Canadian jobs), degree-granting postsecondary institutions (aiming to recruit top talent from anywhere in the world), and unions representing Canadian academics (trying to prioritize Canadian or permanent resident academics for university positions), a sector-specific exemption was agreed upon for hiring foreign academics as temporary foreign workers, all within the context of ongoing stricter immigration rules.

As it currently stands, since May 1, 2015, universities that hire foreign academics must still comply with the requisite national advertising criteria, such as advertising vacant positions simultaneously at home and abroad for a reasonable amount of time in order to ensure that Canadians and permanent residents see the offer, and they must also still include the following mandatory statement on all advertisements, "All qualified candidates are encouraged to apply; however Canadians and permanent residents will be given priority." Additionally, they must confirm that wages and working conditions for foreign academics will be identical to those of domestic hires, including all union or collective-bargaining clauses. And finally, they must still pay the new, increased fee of CAD 1,000 per foreign recruit when submitting a Labor Market Impact Assessment. The difference, however, is in the transition requirement. Instead of filling out a plan outlining how the institution will transition to a Canadian workforce and submitting it to Employment and Social Development Canada (the federal ministry in charge of domestic labor laws) after every foreign hire, each university may now send its submission to Universities Canada, which will then, in turn, provide an annual report to the ministry on transition measures being taken by universities across the country (Employment and Social Development Canada, 2015a).

On this last point, we must clarify that "transitioning to a Canadian workforce" does not necessarily mean simply hiring more Canadians or permanent residents; it can also include facilitating the permanent residency process for temporary foreign workers. In this latter case, offering a permanent job is an example of an activity that facilitates the process (Employment and Social Development

Canada, 2015b). Therefore, this new compromise exemption seemingly expedites the arrival of foreign academics on Canadian campuses, allows for sustainable retention measures by including a provision to facilitate the permanent residency of these international academics, and complies with federal directives prioritizing the hiring of qualified Canadian workers. Nevertheless, it has been met with mixed reviews: Universities Canada has lauded the flexibility afforded to universities to continue hiring the best in the world, whereas the Canadian Association of Universities Teachers denounced the "unjustified" exemption (Canadian Association of University Teachers, 2015a; Chiose, 2015b).

Not all foreign scholars are subject to these immigration regulations. Certain categories of international academics are exempt from all Labor Market Impact Assessments (LMIAs), which assess "the likely impact that hiring a temporary foreign worker (TFW) will have on the Canadian labour market" (Employment and Social Development Canada, 2014). International academics exempt from LMIAs and therefore, presumably, easier to hire, include citizens of the United States and Mexico appointed as professors under the university, college, and seminary levels of the North American Free Trade Agreement (NAFTA); citizens of Chile appointed as professors under the Canada Chile Free Trade Agreement (CCFTA); and international academics hired for Canada Research Chairs (CRC) positions (Employment and Social Development Canada, 2015a).

In the year 2000, the federal government created the Canada Research Chairs Program (CRCP), which established 2,000 research professorships at universities across the country. With an annual budget of approximately CAD 265 million, the aim of the program is to "attract and retain some of the world's most accomplished and promising minds" (Canada Research Chairs Program, 2015a) through a combination of new appointments and the appointment of existing faculty as a retention strategy. While not a program geared specifically to international recruitment, and hence not part of the country's international education strategy per se, it is nonetheless a borderless program insofar as institutions may nominate academics or emerging scholars from anywhere in the world for these prestigious chairs; there are no restrictions on nominees with regard to nationality or country of residence. In other words, Canadian-domiciled Canadians or permanent residents, Canadian expatriates, and foreign researchers are all equally eligible to be nominated by institutions and accepted by the peer review committee.

Of the current chair holders in April 2015, 102—or 6 percent—were international (non-Canadian) recruits, and a further 92 were Canadian expatriates lured back to Canada to take up a Canada Research Chair position (Canada Research Chairs Program, 2015b). Given the international prestige attached to these chairs, in addition to the highly facilitated immigration procedures for foreign academics appointed to these positions, the CRCP could arguably be viewed as a recruitment tool for any Canadian university aiming to attract the world's top researchers to its campus. Regrettably, there are no data on the number of international chair holders who later become Canadian citizens or permanent residents.

## Case Study: International Faculty at the University of Toronto

Founded in 1827 as King's College at York, the University of Toronto has grown to become Canada's largest university. In 2014–2015, it had an operating budget of over CAD 2 billion and a total student population numbering almost 85,000. Spread over three campuses in and around Toronto, the student body is composed of approximately 68,000 undergraduate and 16,400 graduate students, of which international students constitute 17 percent and 15 percent respectively. In terms of academic programs, the University of Toronto offers approximately 700 undergraduate and 222 graduate programs, and employs just over 13,200 faculty members in a range of different employment categories.

The University of Toronto is Canada's highest-ranked university in international league tables. In 2015, it was in the Top 20 of the *Times Higher Education* World University Rankings and 25th in the Shanghai Jiao Tong Academic Ranking of World Universities. It also has a long and distinguished record of research and development, including producing ten Nobel laureates since 1923. It is a founding member of U15, a nationwide group of Canada's 15 most research-intensive universities—the equivalent of the Russell Group in the United Kingdom, or the Association of American Universities (AAU) in the United States, of which the University of Toronto is only one of two non-US members.

### *Research Design*

In order to begin to understand both the individual and institutional perspectives on the recruitment and transition processes of international faculty hired by Canadian universities, we conducted a qualitative research study in the summer of 2015, using the University of Toronto as our case study institution. However, as Canada's leading research university, the University of Toronto cannot be considered representative of all Canadian universities, and should not be taken as such. We chose the University of Toronto in order to gain insight into how and why a large, research-intensive university in Canada's most multicultural city recruits faculty members from abroad and what services it provides to them before and after their arrival in Canada. We also wanted to begin to explore the faculty perspective on these services in a context where the processes are well honed.

Data were obtained from documents, websites, and interviews. For the interviews, we used purposeful sampling (Creswell, 2009) in order to focus on our two specific target populations: international faculty members and senior administrators involved in the international faculty recruitment or transition process.

International faculty interviewees had different nationalities, came from a variety of academic disciplines, and included native English speakers as well as individuals for whom English was not their native tongue. Both males and females were interviewed for this study; however, in order to better preserve the confidentiality of our participants, we have chosen to use the pronoun "they" instead of he/she, and the possessive pronoun "their" instead of the gendered his/her in our results section.

We conducted in-person, semi-structured interviews from mid-August to October 2015. Participants in this study were asked open-ended questions about their views on and experiences with international faculty recruitment, appointment, transition, and integration at the University of Toronto. International faculty members were asked to reflect on their experiences as well as the services provided by the university to facilitate these processes for both themselves and their spouses and/or family members; administrators were asked to reflect on the services they provide, their efficacy, and challenges.

Eight senior administrators from central administration were invited to participate in the study. Six accepted the invitation, one did not respond, and one referred us to an already slated interviewee as a replacement. Of the five faculty members we had invited to participate in the study, three accepted and two did not respond. In total, we conducted nine interviews. Each interview lasted approximately one hour and was audio-recorded with the participant's permission.

## *The University Policy Context*

The University of Toronto has an exhaustive Academic Administrative Procedures Manual (AAPM) that outlines processes, policies, and procedures regarding such things as faculty recruitment, promotion, workload, etc. (University of Toronto, n.d.-a). It also links to relevant labor and immigration laws, and provides suggestions for best practices in, for example, hiring new faculty members.

What is most important to note for the purposes of this chapter is that there are no special provisions in the procedures for conducting an *international* faculty search. The search timetable remains generic at both the chair and dean levels, and no mention is made of extra time allotments for international searches. In fact, what is most striking is the absence of any differentiation whatsoever in the recruitment criteria.

To further reinforce this point, in the recruitment section of the AAPM (University of Toronto, n.d.-b), the adjective "international" appears only three times: once when specifying that search committees should advertise in "national and international disciplinary journals," another when discussing spousal appointment requests that would "normally involve senior scholars of international standing," and finally when giving the example of a search committee that had "conducted an international canvass of key department chairs in order to solicit comments on the 'state of the field.'" In none of these instances does "international" refer to candidates, and it is neither a criterion nor a deterrent for faculty recruitment.

Instead of considering the geographic origin of candidates when hiring, the University of Toronto aims more broadly to uphold its core principles of equity, diversity, and excellence and employs a proactive strategy of recruiting members of underrepresented populations. The institution's 1991 *Employment Equity Policy* states the following:

> While remaining alert and sensitive to the issue of fair and equitable treatment for all, the University has a special concern with the participation and advancement of members of four designated groups that have traditionally been disadvantaged in employment: women, visible minorities, aboriginal peoples and persons with disabilities.
> *(University of Toronto Governing Council, 1991)*

In 2000–2001, the university added a fifth designated group to its list: members of sexual minority groups. With the addition of this new group, the University of Toronto went—and continues to go—beyond the workplace equity requirements of the *Federal Contractors Program*, a program established in 1986 by the federal Ministry of Labour to "further the goal of achieving workplace equity for designated groups experiencing discrimination in the Canadian labour market" (Labour Program, 2015). All University of Toronto academic job advertisements must include the following employment equity statement:

> The University of Toronto is strongly committed to diversity within its community and especially welcomes applications from visible minority group members, women, Aboriginal persons, persons with disabilities, members of sexual minority groups, and others who may contribute to the further diversification of ideas.

Given that academic excellence is, of course, a *sine qua non* criterion when assessing faculty applications, and given that no clear distinction, provision, or partiality seems to be made for international applicants at the University of Toronto, where, or how, then, does the foreign origin of candidates come into play in faculty recruitment? It is perhaps within the notion of "diversity" that citizenship, or geographic, cultural, or ethnic considerations may potentially play a role in the hiring process. Indeed, iterations of "diversity" appear almost 50 times in the recruitment section of the AAPM, exceeding any other consideration by far (excellence/excellent is second at 18), the main idea being that diverse faculty members bring diverse ideas to a diverse student body. The notion of diversity is left intentionally vague. An explicit *non-Canadian* component appears only twice in the University of Toronto recruitment documents, and each time it is in response to a federal government legislative requirement.

To begin with, all job advertisements must, by law, contain the following statement: "All qualified candidates are encouraged to apply; however, Canadians and permanent residents will be given priority." This governmental "Canadians first" employment policy harkens back to 1981. It was loosened somewhat in 2001 when two-tiered recruiting was replaced by simultaneous advertising and recruiting in both Canada and abroad, but the overall spirit of the law remains. (Two-tier recruiting entailed advertising in Canada and recruiting Canadians and permanent residents first and then opening up a second round of advertising and recruiting for non-Canadians internationally if a qualified Canadian could not be recruited.)

No mention is made of special considerations for international candidates during the shortlisting and interviewing stages of a faculty search. The question of citizenship returns in the recruitment documents if a non-Canadian is offered and accepts a position at the University of Toronto.

In the case of an international appointment, the university must again conform to government legislation regarding the entry of a non-Canadian into the national labor force, namely by proving that it could not find a Canadian to fulfill its requirements and that employing the foreign worker will not negatively affect the Canadian labor market.

At the institutional policy level, the University of Toronto Governing Council and the University of Toronto Faculty Association have enshrined a policy of nondiscrimination when it comes to faculty matters (University of Toronto Governing Council, 2006, Article 9). Concretely, this means that policies regarding academic appointments and tenure reviews (University of Toronto Governing Council, 2003), salaries (University of Toronto Governing Council, 2006, Article 6), promotion (University of Toronto Governing Council, 1980), and retirement (University of Toronto Governing Council, 2005) make no mention of special provisions for international faculty members, neither positive nor negative. On paper, all faculty members are treated equally.

## Interviews with University Administrators and Faculty

As noted earlier, for this study, we interviewed senior officials in central administration, on both the academic policy development and service provision sides, as well as recently hired international faculty (within the last five years). We divided our findings into four sections: recruiting international faculty, the appointment process, the transition process, and integration. When possible, we tried to give voice to both the institutional and faculty perspectives in each section.

### Recruiting International Faculty

At the outset, we sought to understand *why* the University of Toronto hires international faculty and what draws these faculty members to the institution.

For the institution, it is less a question of hiring international faculty per se than it is of hiring "the best possible faculty member in any particular discipline" (senior administrator). The recognition that the "best" candidate can be anywhere in the world is without a doubt deeply ingrained within central administration. As one interviewee reminded us, citing Friedland (2013), the University of Toronto has been hiring international faculty since before Canada became a nation. Nonetheless, two intertwining motivations appear to underlie international recruitment at the institution: the need to broaden and diversify the applicant pool, and global competition to be a world-class university. Interviewees in senior administrative positions mentioned both Canada's relatively small number of doctoral programs in certain disciplines and the notion of peer institutions in relation to international rankings. Citizenship is neither an influential nor a determining factor when recruiting new faculty. Indeed, nationality is not even a consideration at the senior administrative levels, aside from making sure that all federal labor and immigration laws are being followed for the advertisement and appointment processes: "You're not actually actively looking for a foreign national; you're looking for the best possible person. That 'best possible person' can come in any sort of package" (senior administrator). And further:

> From our perspective, you can only hire *the best qualified* . . . if you actually search worldwide to find *the best* individual out there whose research would then complement, or expand, or strengthen, the exciting strengths that we have in many of our faculties, divisions, departments, which already seem to be of worldwide status.
>
> *(senior administrator)*

Professional motivation was also at the heart of the decision-making process for international faculty. The international faculty members we interviewed for this study chose the University of Toronto because of its reputation, because it was "very good and very relevant to what I do," and because it offered more stability (i.e., tenure-stream appointments) and also more professional diversity (collaborative and interdisciplinary programs) than comparable institutions in their home countries.

However, although the desire and determination to recruit worldwide are evident, appointing a foreign national to a faculty position poses a number of challenges for the university. Every senior administrator with whom we spoke expressed concern over the more stringent immigration rules put in place by the federal government for hiring foreign workers. Some described these rules as "roadblocks," and others spoke of governmental criteria that were completely out of touch with the reality of the academic job market, such as the obligation to advertise academic positions in certain Canadian publications so that—in the government's mind—a maximum number of Canadian applicants have access to job postings, even though top candidates (of any nationality) are reading discipline-specific journals and newsletters, regardless of where they are published. More troubling still, one interviewee pointed to what appeared to be a fundamentally contrasting attitude to the hiring endeavor itself:

> When it comes down to a shortlist, it gets very tricky because universities and the government have a different perspective—I wouldn't say a contradictory perspective—but a different perspective on who should be hired. So, the government's perspective is that if anybody is qualified for the job, sorry, if any *Canadian* or permanent resident of Canada is qualified for the job, we have to offer a job to them before an international candidate. The university's perspective, of course, is that we want the *best* people, not people who *just* meet the bar, but the people who are *best* for the position.
>
> *(senior administrator)*

The "Canadians first" obligation raises a concern that Canada will once again be seen as a parochial and protectionist backwater when, in fact, the institution is going to great lengths to attract the top researchers to its campus:

> We're a bit worried as things become more difficult in the Canadian immigration context. We're a bit worried about the information that's getting out to the international community and maybe scaring people off from applying for jobs in Canada in the first place.
>
> *(senior administrator)*

On the faculty side, in response to a question about whether they felt they had received special treatment (positive or negative) during the recruitment process because they were an international candidate, two faculty members said they did not experience anything that struck them as being out of the ordinary, whereas another spoke overtly of feeling disadvantaged:

> I guess more negative in that, I guess in Canada, you have to, you can't just hire somebody from abroad, you have to show that there is no Canadian who's, like, equally qualified, or qualified to do the job that you're being hired for.
>
> *(faculty member)*

That faculty member also felt disadvantaged in the negotiation process due to the immigration inflexibility around start dates, which only affects foreign nationals.

## Appointment Process

At the University of Toronto, all candidates apply online for positions and the appointment process is public, which is already a radical cultural change for some candidates in whose systems the hiring process is an extremely private affair. During this application process, candidates are introduced to the university's core values regarding the promotion of diversity and equity, factors that do not go unnoticed. One faculty member spoke of being impressed by the university's employment equity statement:

> For me, it was new and interesting, all the parts in the application online about minorities. I found it really serious, and I was, you know, happy and proud that an institution was wondering about this kind of stuff because it's not the case in Europe. Never.
>
> *(faculty member)*

Indeed, as one senior administrator mentioned: "There's an *active* desire to have a more diverse faculty body and range of perspectives that are provided from experiences in other countries and other kinds of backgrounds." The university has acknowledged these values in its senior administrative structure, with the creation in 2001 of a vice-president of human resources and equity who reports directly to the president.

While the online application process did not seem to pose any problems, communication with the department, however, seemed to be a weakness. Faculty members spoke of the anxiety they had felt because of the long periods of silence between each phase of the process: "Those periods of silence were really disconcerting" (faculty member).

Short-listed candidates are invited to come to the University of Toronto for a campus interview. Their stay is organized and paid for by the university. During this time, candidates usually meet students and faculty in the department, give talks and/or teach a class or two within the department, and meet with representatives from various central services whose mission it is to facilitate the transition and integration processes of new appointees. Typically, short-listed candidates will have a confidential 30- to 45-minute meeting with someone from the Faculty Relocation Service. Here, they will be given information about moving to the Toronto area and faculty housing options, the health care system, banking opportunities, and information about other services at the university that may meet their specific needs, for example, the Family Care Office for child or elderly care information, Dual Career Connection for spousal employment options, immigration lawyers for non-Canadians, etc.

None of these services are designated specifically for international faculty; they are open to all faculty, and in some cases students and postdocs as well. In fact, what is most striking when speaking with representatives from these services is the absolute *absence* of the term "international." Administrators, once again, did not distinguish clientele by passport, and the very thought of doing so seemed antithetical to the spirit of the services. Instead, administrators spoke of "prospective faculty," "new faculty," and "faculty." Place of origin was never a consideration, except to know if other services should be discussed, like immigration lawyers, credential recognition for spouses, or work permit conditions for employment insurance. The university is extremely proud of these services and feels that they play an integral role in successfully competing against other world-class universities during the recruitment process:

> It's seen as critical that we provide these services. We're not going to recruit the best people if we can't prove that we care about them. . . . We have to sell ourselves to them. We have to demonstrate to them that we'd be a great place to work, that they'd have great colleagues and a great environment.
> *(senior administrator)*

To what extent were these services important for our international faculty interviewees when deciding whether or not to accept a position at the University of Toronto? According to them, they definitely played a role in the decision-making process, albeit indirectly. One faculty member noted that the services had not been the deciding factor "but the fact that they were there made a big difference" (faculty member). Another faculty member spoke of feeling reassured by their presence:

> The fact that I knew that there were all this bunch of benefits coming with my position, surely this made my, the decision, more appealing because, you know, you thought a little bit before moving so far. You know that you cannot count on the system of support that usually you have when you are in your own country or in countries that you already know. So, the fact of perceiving the university as a place that could really take care of me somehow, this was important in order to make my decision, even though I wasn't able to evaluate the details.
> *(faculty member)*

Additionally, partner/spousal employment options were key considerations for international candidates in a relationship. For some, negotiating as part of the employment package—or having the option of trying to negotiate—an academic term position at the University of Toronto for a partner/spouse who was also an academic was important; for others, the possibility of using the services of Dual Career Connection, which facilitates finding nonacademic work for partners/spouses, was a plus. However, faculty interviewees also felt that communication around academic positions for partners/spouses could have been greatly improved.

## Transition Process

The university has retained the services of immigration lawyers to handle the immigration process for new, non-Canadian faculty hires. The university refers all international appointees to the law firm for all immigration-related questions and issues, and it covers all the expenses related to obtaining the requisite visas and/or work permits for the faculty member and their family, up to and including permanent residency. (Of note, immigration legal counsel may also be available to returning Canadians accompanied by a foreign partner/spouse as well.) This service has been unanimously lauded by international faculty as being extremely useful, with one even going so far as to say: "I'm not sure how we would've managed without the first step, which was the immigration lawyers" (faculty member).

Through the Faculty Relocation Service, the university provides suggestions for moving companies and then covers the faculty's moving expenses up to a maximum amount. It also provides support for the housing search via its Faculty Housing Service. The University of Toronto has a number of properties around campus in downtown Toronto and reserves them for faculty seeking short- and longer-term leases. This is indeed an important service in a city with a 1.5 percent vacancy rate for rentals in the downtown area (Canada Mortgage and Housing Corporation, 2014). For one interviewee, getting faculty housing was the key to a smooth transition and to getting set up in Canada:

> It made the difference in . . . us feeling welcome but also in feeling there's a safety net. But the other thing is that you can't get the infrastructure of your life set up unless you've got an address. You can't even get a mobile phone. So, you can't get a mobile phone, the Internet, a bank account, or anything like that, your OHIP [Ontario Health Insurance Plan] card or your SIN [social insurance] number, unless you have an address. So, for us, that housing thing has been *the most important* transition support that we've had.
>
> *(faculty member)*

There is not enough faculty housing for all who wish to live there, and, once again, it is not reserved exclusively for international faculty; rather, it is open to all faculty relocating from outside the Greater Toronto Area, and it is assigned on a first-come, first-served basis.

The Family Care Office (FCO) provides assistance, services, and resources for all family-related matters. Like every other service, department, and faculty within the university, the FCO uses an inclusive definition of family. The new faculty orientation in August is organized here; staff members run various seminars and workshops on practical matters, such as how to file taxes in Canada if you are a newcomer, and they try to ensure that their support services remain on the departmental radar during the recruitment process by running a training session for administrative staff within the university and also by giving a short presentation to new academic administrators when they are learning about the recruitment process.

The Dual Career Connection (DCC) is the university's service that facilitates job hunting for partners/spouses seeking nonacademic positions in the Greater Toronto Area. Unfortunately, these services comprise only a small portion of a much larger portfolio of career transitions and counseling services and have been met with mixed reviews by faculty members. The DCC runs workshops on writing resumes and cover letters tailored for the Canadian job market, provides access to online resources, and hosts professional development speakers series on such topics as branding and networking. It also provides private, one-on-one career consultations for partners/spouses to discuss such issues as job searches, mid- to late-career transitions, and other needs—for example, case-specific foreign credential recognition. According to senior administrators, the biggest challenge for this service is managing expectations and ensuring that faculty, partners/spouses, and academic units understand that DCC is not a job placement service, but rather that they provide support to partners/spouses, with help "to familiarize them with what a job search looks like in Toronto, begin to help them to network, begin to help them to have the tools that they need" (senior administrator). As with the other services, this one is also offered to all new faculty members, not only foreign nationals. Partners/spouses receive the same service, regardless of country of origin, and can access the service for up to two years after the faculty member has taken up their appointment at the university.

At the more central level, senior administrators noted the challenges associated with navigating the increasingly complex regulations concerning immigration without additional staff resources.

## Integration Process

We asked senior administrators if they felt that there was a tension on campus between Canadian and non-Canadian faculty members. Of those who felt they could respond (i.e., did not feel too distanced from the question), each one said no, adding that they had neither seen nor heard of any such phenomenon. They acknowledged that tensions could arise because of different *cultural values* but, given Canada's highly diverse and multicultural society, these differences were not necessarily linked to passports. On the faculty side, our interviewees who felt they could answer the question likewise did not sense any tension: "I guess I'm not particularly sure about the citizenship of my colleagues. I don't think there's any real separation. I mean, I certainly haven't noticed any, so far" (faculty member).

We also asked international faculty interviewees if they felt integrated both in faculty life and at the University of Toronto in general. Across the board, the answer was "not yet" for the University of Toronto: "U of T is *so* big. It's such a *huge* institution" (faculty member). For one faculty member, institutional identification seemed more manageable at the faculty level: "The principal identification for me would be (my faculty) [faculty name removed to preserve confidentiality], not the U of T" (faculty member), whereas for another, even that level was still too daunting: "The faculty is so huge, I would say no one feels completely integrated. . . . I'm still trying to find my way" (faculty member). All the faculty members did, however, seem to feel that they had their place in their academic unit: "In my little department, I do. . . . I feel like I'm integrated in my field and in my discipline, but not necessarily in the institution" (faculty member).

We were interested in whether international faculty experienced any advantages or disadvantages during the promotion or tenure processes. Although our faculty subjects were too new to the university to have gone through these procedures, senior administrators clearly indicated that there were no differences between international and Canadian faculty. In fact, the mere *idea* of different treatment based on place of origin was treated as an oddity, because promotion and tenure files are brought forth without any indication of citizenship. However, it was noted that there can be issues related to background; for example, faculty with strong accents (regardless of their citizenship) may receive more negative student evaluations of teaching, which could affect a tenure file.

One final issue worth mentioning at the integration stage is the ongoing challenge posed by partner/spousal employment. Some funds are set aside for hiring spouses/partners seeking academic employment at the university, and such appointments are used as recruitment tools for highly sought-after candidates. However, the partners/spouses must themselves meet the university's hiring standards, and funding is only guaranteed for an initial three-year term. "Funding for these appointments is normally a three-way split among the unit hiring the candidate, the unit employing the spouse/partner, and the Provost" (University of Toronto, n.d.-a). As for the services offered by the Dual Career Connection for partners/spouses seeking nonacademic employment, there is a sense among international faculty that their services do not go far enough and do not completely meet the needs of the partners/spouses: one faculty member suggested outsourcing the service to a job placement agency and another suggested providing English-language classes more adapted to the needs of these highly trained job seekers, and not simply referrals to general language classes either on campus or elsewhere. Central administration does seem to be aware of the challenges, but as one senior administrator conceded: "It's kind of an industry problem" (senior administrator).

## Summary and Concluding Observations

The appointment processes at the University of Toronto focus on attracting the best candidate for the position, and no distinction is made between Canadian and non-Canadian candidates in terms of academic policy, recruitment procedures, and faculty services. The basic conditions of employment are the same, regardless of nationality. The university is focused on promoting excellence in research and teaching and on maintaining its world-class standing in international league tables. It seeks to attract the best candidates to further its research and teaching missions and to uphold its core values of equity and diversity. Policies are in place to ensure that throughout the academic career, candidates and faculty members are evaluated on their scholarly contributions and accomplishments, not their passports.

The support services in place to assist new faculty members in the transition and integration processes are well honed and promoted at the highest levels. They have been in place for more than a decade and were championed at the outset by senior academic administrators, who were themselves international faculty when they arrived at the university. Additionally, deeply embedding equity and diversity considerations at the highest echelons of the university governance structure has sent the message that these are core values of the institution, and they are enshrined in both policy and practice. Combined, these two mechanisms seem to be effective retention measures. As one senior administrator told us, the faculty attrition rate at the university is less than 4 percent, and departures were due almost exclusively to external factors, such as better offers that the university could not match or the choice of a different physical environment (e.g., warmer climate, more mountainous region, etc.).

The primary challenge surrounding the recruitment and appointment of international faculty comes from the government of Canada. It is evident that there is an underlying sense of worry and concern within the university administration about the impact that Canada's increasingly stringent labor and immigration policies will have on the university's reputation and its recruitment efforts. Although the number of international faculty hired by the University of Toronto has held steady at approximately 50 percent since 2010 (Office of the Vice Provost, 2013), the current immigration environment is making appointing international faculty more difficult, more time consuming, and more onerous for the university. Internationalization is a priority for the new president of the university, and international faculty members are seen to play an integral role in that process.

International faculty noted ongoing challenges with spousal employment, as well as their own difficulties integrating into such a large university, beyond their local academic unit. They also felt that communication with the institution could have been improved at every stage of the process, from keeping candidates better informed during the recruitment and appointment processes, to offering better-timed orientation sessions upon arrival.

The University of Toronto case study is illustrative of the role of international faculty in Canadian higher education. Canada is a nation that has always relied heavily on immigration, and so have its universities. The number of doctoral graduates emerging from Canadian universities was simply not sufficient to staff the major postwar expansion of the university sector, and many faculty were hired from other countries. As we have noted, there have been periodic tensions over the question of whether universities should or should not prioritize the hiring of Canadian professors, but there have also been concerns about maintaining the capacity of Canadian universities to compete in an increasingly global higher education environment and fears of "brain drain" if Canadian universities are unable to retain their best and brightest (Jones & Weinrib, 2011).

As the University of Toronto case study suggests, the hiring of international faculty is not a major issue in Canadian higher education. Under the current arrangements, institutions strive to hire the very best candidates through search processes that advertise both nationally and internationally. If the best candidate is not a Canadian citizen, steps must be taken to meet government of Canada requirements, but the university is quite willing to provide the administrative and legal support necessary to facilitate the appointment. Recruiting from the international academic labor market is simply a reality for a major research university, and this reality is accepted within the University of Toronto community.

Further research would confirm whether the University of Toronto case is typical of the experience of other Canadian universities, and comparative studies of different Canadian universities would illuminate potential differences in their capacity to attract and/or retain international faculty. It would also be interesting to study the experience of international faculty over time in order to understand the transition and acculturation process and help universities improve the ways in which they support international faculty throughout their careers.

## References

Advisory Panel on Canada's International Education Strategy (2012). *International education: A key driver of Canada's future prosperity*. Ottawa, Canada: Her Majesty the Queen in Right of Canada, represented by the Minister of International Trade. Retrieved from www.international.gc.ca/education/assets/pdfs/ies_report_rapport_sei-eng.pdf

Canada Mortgage and Housing Corporation (2014). *Rental market report: Greater Toronto area*. Retrieved from www.cmhc-schl.gc.ca/odpub/esub/64459/64459_2014_A01.pdf

Canada Research Chairs Program (2015a). *Canada research chairs*. Ottawa, Canada: Canada Research Chairs Program. Retrieved from www.chairs-chaires.gc.ca/home-accueil-eng.aspx

Canada Research Chairs Program (2015b). *Program statistics*. Ottawa, Canada: Canada Research Chairs Program. Retrieved from www.chairs-chaires.gc.ca/about_us-a_notre_sujet/statistics-statistiques-eng.aspx

Canadian Association of University Business Officers (2014). *Financial information of universities and colleges 2012/2013*. Ottawa, Canada: Canadian Association of University Business Officers. Retrieved from www.caubo.ca/sites/137.149.200.5.pilot/files/

CAUBO_2012–2013_FINANCIAL_INFORMATION_OF_UNIVERSITIES_AND_COLLEGES_0.pdf

Canadian Association of University Teachers (2014). *CAUT almanac of post-secondary education in Canada 2013–2014*. Ottawa, Canada: Canadian Association of University Teachers.

Canadian Association of University Teachers (2015a). AUCC should follow the rules on temporary foreign workers program, says CAUT. *CAUT Bulletin, 62*(3). Retrieved from www.cautbulletin.ca/en_article.asp?ArticleID=3982.

Canadian Association of University Teachers (2015b). *CAUT briefing note: Highlights of recent changes to the TFWP (March 2015)*. Ottawa, Canada: Canadian Association of University Teachers. Retrieved from www.caut.ca/resources/briefs-and-reports

Canadian Information Centre for International Credentials (2015). *Directory of educational institutions in Canada*. Toronto, Canada: Council of Ministers of Education, Canada. Retrieved from www.cicic.ca/869/Do-an-advanced-search-in-the-Directory-of-Educational-Institutions-in-Canada/index.canada?

Chiose, S. (2014). Universities say foreign worker crackdown makes recruitment difficult. *The Globe and Mail*. Retrieved from www.theglobeandmail.com/news/national/universities-say-foreign-worker-crackdown-makes-recruitment-difficult/article21549355/

Chiose, S. (2015a). Canadian universities urge Ottawa to relax foreign worker program rules. *The Globe and Mail*. Retrieved from www.theglobeandmail.com/news/politics/canadian-universities-urge-ottawa-to-relax-foreign-worker-program-rules/article22826162/

Chiose, S. (2015b). Ottawa to relax foreign worker rules at universities. *The Globe and Mail*. Retrieved from www.theglobeandmail.com/news/politics/ottawa-to-relax-foreign-worker-rules-for-at-postsecondary-institutions/article23001549/

Citizenship and Immigration Canada (2015a). *Report on plans and priorities 2015–2016*. Ottawa, Canada: Her Majesty the Queen in Right of Canada, represented by the Minister of Citizenship and Immigration. Retrieved from www.cic.gc.ca/english/pdf/pub/rpp-2015–2016.pdf

Citizenship and Immigration Canada (2015b). *Temporary foreign worker program work permit holders by gender, 2004 to 2013* [Data set]. Retrieved from www.cic.gc.ca/english/resources/statistics/facts2013/temporary/1–1.asp

Cormier, J. (2004). *The Canadianization movement: Emergence, survival and success*. Toronto, Canada: University of Toronto Press.

Cormier, J. (2005). The Canadianization movement in context. *The Canadian Journal of Sociology, 30*(3), 351–370. doi:10.1353/cjs.2005.0047

Creswell, J. W. (2009). *Research design: Qualitative, quantitative, and mixed methods approaches* (3rd ed.). Thousand Oaks, CA: Sage.

Department of Justice (2015). *Consolidation of the Employment Equity Act, S.C. 1995, c. 44*. Ottawa, Canada: Minister of Justice. Retrieved from http://laws-lois.justice.gc.ca/eng/acts/e-5.401/

Doherty, N., Richardson, J., & Thorn, K. (2013). Self-initiated expatriation and self-initiated expatriates: Clarification of the research stream. *Career Development International, 18*(1), 97–112. doi:10.1108/13620431311305971

Employment and Social Development Canada (2014). *Labour market impact assessments (LMIA) statistics*. Retrieved from www.esdc.gc.ca/eng/jobs/foreign_workers/lmo_statistics/index.shtml

Employment and Social Development Canada (2015a). *Hiring foreign academics*. Ottawa, Canada: Employment and Social Development Canada. Retrieved from www.esdc.gc.ca/eng/jobs/foreign_workers/higher_skilled/academics//index.shtml

Employment and Social Development Canada (2015b). *Schedule C. Employer transition plan*. Ottawa, Canada: Employment and Social Development Canada.

Friedland, M. L. (2013). *The University of Toronto: A history* (2nd ed.). Toronto, Canada: University of Toronto Press.

Jones, G. A. (1997). A brief introduction to higher education in Canada. In G. A. Jones (Ed.), *Higher education in Canada: Different systems, different perspectives* (pp. 1–7.). New York: Garland Publishing, Inc.

Jones, G. A. (2009). Internationalization and higher education policy in Canada: Three challenges. In R. D. Trilokekar, G. A. Jones & A. Shubert (Eds.), *Canada's universities go global* (pp. 355–369). Toronto, Canada: Lorimer.

Jones, G. A., & Weinrib, J. (2011). Globalization and higher education in Canada. In R. King, S. Marginson, & R. Naidoo (Eds.), *Handbook on globalization and higher education* (pp. 222–240). Cheltenham, UK: Edward Elgar Publishing.

Labour Program (2015). *Federal contractors program*. Retrieved from www.labour.gc.ca/eng/standards_equity/eq/emp/fcp/index.shtml

Mathews, R., & Steele, J. A. (1969). *The struggle for Canadian universities: A dossier* (6th ed.). Toronto, Canada: New Press.

Office of the Vice Provost, Faculty, & Academic Life (2013). *Faculty recruitment report 2012–2013*. Retrieved from www.faculty.utoronto.ca/reports/

Richardson, J. (2000). Expatriate academics in the globalized era: The beginnings of an untold story? *Asia Pacific Business Review, 7*(1), 125–150.

Richardson, J. (2006). Self-directed expatriation: Family matters. *Personnel Review, 35*(4), 469–486. doi:10.1108/00483480610670616

Richardson, J., McBey, K., & McKenna, S. (2009). Internationalizing Canada's universities: Where do international faculty fit in? In R. D. Trilokekar, G. A. Jones & A. Shubert (Eds.), *Canada's universities go global* (pp. 277–296). Toronto, Canada: James Lorimer & Company.

Richardson, J., & McKenna, S. (2006). Exploring relationships with home and host countries: A study of self-directed expatriates. *Cross Cultural Management: An International Journal, 13*(1), 6–22.

Statistics Canada (2003). *2001 census: Analysis series. Religions in Canada* (96F0030XIE2001015). Ottawa, Canada: Minister of Industry. Retrieved from www12.statcan.gc.ca/english/census01/Products/Analytic/companion/rel/contents.cfm

Statistics Canada (2010). *Canada's ethnocultural mosaic, 2006 census: Findings*. Ottawa, Canada: Statistics Canada. Retrieved from www12.statcan.ca/census-recensement/2006/as-sa/97–562/index-eng.cfm?CFID=28529&CFTOKEN=29647354

Statistics Canada (2013a). *Education in Canada: Attainment, field of study and location of study* (99–012-X2011001). Ottawa, Canada: Minister of Industry. Retrieved from www12.statcan.gc.ca/nhs-enm/2011/as-sa/99–012-x/99–012-x2011001-eng.pdf

Statistics Canada (2013b). *Immigration and ethnocultural diversity in Canada* (99–010-X2011001). Ottawa, Canada: Minister of Industry. Retrieved from www12.statcan.gc.ca/nhs-enm/2011/as-sa/99–010-x/99–010-x2011001-eng.pdf

Statistics Canada (2014a). *Postsecondary enrolments by institution type, sex and program groups (Both sexes)* [Data set]. Retrieved from www.statcan.gc.ca/tables-tableaux/sum-som/l01/cst01/educ74a-eng.htm

Statistics Canada (2014b). *Table A.1.1. Distribution of the 25- to 64-year-old population, by highest level of education attained and sex, Canada, provinces and territories, 2012* [Data set]. Retrieved from www.statcan.gc.ca/pub/81-604-x/2014001/t/tbla.1.1-eng.htm

Statistics Canada (2015a). *Quarterly demographic estimates: January to March 2015* (91–002-X). Ottawa, Canada: Minister of Industry. Retrieved from www.statcan.gc.ca/pub/91-002-x/91-002-x2015001-eng.pdf

Statistics Canada (2015b). *Table 477–0060 Financial information of community colleges and vocational schools, revenues by type of fund (Annual)* [Data set]. Retrieved from www5.statcan.gc.ca/cansim/a26?lang=eng&retrLang=eng&id=4770060&paSer=&pattern=&stByVal=1&p1=1&p2=31&tabMode=dataTable&csid=—F2

Statistics Canada (2015c). *Table B.2.12 University revenues, by source, as a percentage of total revenue, Canada and provinces, 2000/2001, 2005/2006, 2010/2011, 2011/2012 and 2012/2013* [Data set]. Retrieved from www.statcan.gc.ca/pub/81-582-x/2015001/tbl/tblb2.12-eng.htm

Statistics Canada (2015d). *Table D.6.3 Educational attainment of the population aged 25 to 64, off-reserve Aboriginal, non-Aboriginal, and total population, Canada, provinces and territories, 2010 to 2013* [Data set]. Retrieved from www.statcan.gc.ca/pub/81-582-x/2015001/tbl/tbld6.3-eng.htm

Statistics Canada (2015e). *Table E.1.2.2 Participation rate in education, population aged 18 to 34, by age group and type of institution attended, Canada, provinces and territories, 1995/1996, 2000/2001, 2005/2006 and 2010/2011 to 2013/2014* [Data set]. Retrieved from www.statcan.gc.ca/pub/81-582-x/2015001/tbl/tble1.2.2-eng.htm

Tamburri, R. (2014). Universities caught up in overhaul of foreign workers program. *University Affairs*. Retrieved from www.universityaffairs.ca/news/news-article/universities-caught-overhaul-foreign-workers-program/

Trilokekar, R. D. (2015). From soft power to economic diplomacy? A comparison of the changing rationales and roles of the U.S. and Canadian federal governments in international education. *Center for Studies in Higher Education, University of California, Berkeley, 2*(15), 1–18.

Trilokekar, R. D., & Jones, G. A. (2013). Finally, an internationalization policy for Canada. *International Higher Education, 71*(Spring 2013), 17–18.

University of Toronto (n.d.-a). Academic administrative procedures manual (AAPM). Retrieved from https://aapm.utoronto.ca/

University of Toronto (n.d.-b). *Recruitment*. Academic administrative procedures manual (AAPM). Retrieved from https://aapm.utoronto.ca/recruitment.

University of Toronto Governing Council (1980). Policy and procedures governing promotions. Retrieved from www.governingcouncil.utoronto.ca/policies/promote.htm

University of Toronto Governing Council (1991). Employment equity policy. Retrieved from www.governingcouncil.utoronto.ca/policies/emequity.htm

University of Toronto Governing Council (2003). *Policy and procedures on academic appointments*. Retrieved from www.aapm.utoronto.ca/appointments

University of Toronto Governing Council (2005). Agreement between the Governing Council of the University of Toronto and the University of Toronto Faculty Association on retirement matters. Retrieved from www.aapm.utoronto.ca/sites/default/files/attachments/_other/Copy of agreement on retirement matters for AAPM website.pdf

University of Toronto Governing Council (2006). *Memorandum of agreement between the Governing Council of the University of Toronto and the University of Toronto Faculty Association*.

Retrieved from www.governingcouncil.utoronto.ca/Assets/Governing+Council+Digital+Assets/Policies/PDF/memoagree.pdf

Weinrib, J., & Jones, G. A. (2014). Largely a matter of degrees: Quality assurance and Canadian universities. *Policy and Society, 33*(3), 225–236. doi:10.1016/j.polsoc.2014.07.002

# 5

# INTERNATIONAL FACULTY IN TWO TOP-TIER CHINESE UNIVERSITIES

One Country, Two Types of Internationals

*Gerard A. Postiglione and Xie Ailei*

The People's Republic of China (PRC) is a country with two systems: the mainland and the special administrative systems. Most universities are located in the Chinese mainland where there has been a rapid expansion of universities, generous funding by government, and an increase in top-tier international universities. Though much smaller, the Hong Kong system, known as the Hong Kong Special Administrative Region of the PRC, has more top-ranked universities than any city in the world. Therefore, this chapter selects one major research university in each system for study and comparison. Both systems espouse the importance of internationalization. The Hong Kong university system, where English dominates as the medium of teaching and research, has a significant number of foreign academics, with most Chinese academics (by both citizenship and ethnicity) having earned their doctorates at overseas institutions. The Chinese mainland system, which leads the world in sending its scholars overseas to earn their doctorates, has seen its universities hiring a substantial increase in returnees, as well as some non-nationals (including returnee ethnic Chinese and other Chinese).

This chapter focuses on two case universities—Shanghai Jiao Tong University (SJTU) and the University of Hong Kong (HKU)—one in each system of the PRC (the Chinese mainland and the Hong Kong Special Administrative Region), though these two are quite similar in many respects. Both are located in world cities (Shanghai and Hong Kong), which are key nodes of the global economic system. Despite espousing internationalization, most of the students in these universities are Chinese—nearly 95 percent at SJTU and 90 percent at HKU. Both universities are among the oldest within their respective systems: SJTU traces its roots to 1896, though its current name dates to 1938, and HKU, established in 1911, is Hong Kong's earliest university. Both universities are among the world's top 100 universities (QS, 2015). Although both espouse internationalization as a priority, these two universities differ significantly in academic culture and governance (Altbach & Postiglione, 2012). Both recruit internationally, but virtually all of SJTU's academic staff are Chinese nationals, whereas more than half of HKU's academic staff are foreign nationals (The University of Hong Kong, 2014). This has much to do with the medium of instruction being English at HKU. SJTU has about 500 academic staff with overseas doctorates (25 percent of the total), and this figure has been increasing, whereas most all of HKU's academic staff have an overseas doctorate.

There are two points at the outset: First, most "internationalized" faculty in the Chinese mainland are Chinese nationals who earned their doctorate overseas, but some may have become foreign nationals before returning to China. Second, most Hong Kong faculty earned their doctorates overseas and a very large proportion are foreign nationals by birth, but an increasing number were born in the Chinese mainland (and thus are also returnees) or Hong Kong. Third, different administrative and cultural dimensions characterize the integration of international faculty, especially nonethnic Chinese speakers, in China's two systems. The chapter begins by providing a context for each university and then includes its role as an international university within the nation, its system, and its higher education system.

## Universities in the Chinese Mainland

Thirty-five years after China launched its economic reform and opened to the outside world, it gradually inches toward becoming the world's largest economy. To maintain its pace of growth is becoming more difficult. Therefore, the government is asking universities to play a bigger role in the nation's economic future. China already has the largest system of higher education with more publications and research and development (R&D) funding than any other country except the United States (Boehler, 2014). Its universities can also recruit from secondary school students in its largest city, where they outperform counterparts in the 60 countries in the Program for International Student Assessment of mathematics and science achievement (Schleicher, 2013).

It is worth remembering that China's universities experienced momentous change since 1949, when the new regime of Mao Zedong and Zhou Enlai nationalized universities. Under influence by the Soviet Union, they separated universities from research institutes and instituted a form of state governance that still exists today. Even after relations with the Soviet Union soured in the late 1950s, most academic exchange continued to occur with the communist bloc nations, and the structure of higher education remained intact. The pace of higher education expansion quickened during the Great Leap Forward period (1958–1960). Not long after that, in May 1966, Mao launched the Cultural Revolution, which threw Chinese higher education into chaos. As China exited the Cultural Revolution, enrollments rapidly shot up again. However, a lack of facilities and qualified teachers reduced enrollments.

When Deng Xiaoping came to power and launched a series of economic reforms, he told universities to emphasize standards and send scholars to universities in the West for training. The official view still rested on a dogmatic critique of universities under capitalism. Yet Deng was adamant about having 1,000 talented Chinese scientists recognized around the world (Deng, 1993). Vogel (2011) recounts the story of a 1978 phone call from China to President Jimmy Carter at 3:00 a.m., Washington time, by his science advisor because Deng Xiaoping wanted approval to send several hundred Chinese immediately to study at American universities, followed by thousands within a few years.

Deng's attraction to American universities was not about liberal arts higher education. It was about science and technology. He knew that China's economic reforms necessitated preparing world-class scientists. Yet, he also knew it was important to gain a deeper understanding of how other societies made their economies grow. Initially, most Chinese went overseas with state financial support to study science and technology. As China's economy grew in the 1990s, the government permitted students to pay their own way as overseas study expanded to encompass other fields, including economics, management science, and many other scientific and professional fields.

The shift away from a centrally planned economy brought unprecedented change to higher education. Western societies with capitalist economies quickly became favored study overseas destinations. This still has deep implications for internationalization in China's top-tier universities, as this chapter will discuss.

China's universities have come to reflect the country's deepening international engagement, global economic rise, and growing leadership in the world. At the same time, the number of international students coming to China has grown. China is now the third largest destination for international students after the United States and the United Kingdom.

By 2015, China's university system became recognizable from its predecessor. However, it struggles to deal with longstanding problems, as well as new challenges, such as graduate employment in the wake of the rapid expansion (Postiglione, 2014). There are about 1.53 million academic staff, including both the regular professoriate and those in research positions. While only about 280,000 (about 18 percent) hold doctorates, the figure is about 90 percent at the most prestigious universities (Ministry of Education, 2015). Academics in Chinese universities earn a lower salary than their Western counterparts or those in Brazil, Russia, or India (Altbach et al., 2012). However, prestigious universities are willing to pay high salaries to a very small number of internationally outstanding academics (Altbach et al., 2012). Recent research suggests that the 10 percent highest-paid professors earn 5.9 times more than the 10 percent lowest-paid professors (Zhang & Zhao, 2014). Academics in the Chinese mainland generally have lower salaries than their counterparts in Hong Kong, which has the highest property prices in the world.

Because China's universities depend heavily on government funding, even as they have become decentralized and more market oriented, public investment is crucial for recruitment of overseas returnees. A number of government schemes help universities recruit international faculty. In 2008, the "Thousand Talents Program" began to recruit overseas scientists and returnees by providing attractive salaries as well as research funding and high-profile research teams. Municipal governments have similar schemes. In 2010, a Shanghai Thousand Talents Program recruited top associate professor–level overseas scientists and returnees. Universities also provide matching salary packages and research funds to those successful applicants of such government schemes. However, as the living costs in first-tier cities continue to rise, overseas returnees are beginning to migrate to second-tier cities. The long-term impact of this flow merits further examination.

Not surprisingly, the flagship universities, where most deans have overseas degrees or have studied overseas, take the lead in innovative practices with world-class universities. Peking University has a Stanford University center that expands its role in global research and a Yuanpei College modeled on Harvard's undergraduate general education curriculum. Tsinghua University's Schwarzman Scholars Program brings future Chinese leaders together with counterparts from all over the world at its home campus. Shanghai Jiao Tong University's joint institute with the University of Michigan has offered joint degrees in engineering for ten years.

Many Chinese universities are engaged with overseas counterparts. There are over 1,000 Sino-foreign joint degree programs on Chinese soil. Tsinghua University and Xiamen University are establishing campuses in the United States and Malaysia, respectively. The number of international students coming to China continues to rise, and the number of Chinese self-funded students leaving for overseas continues to grow. Many who go overseas to study do not return, though the number of returnees is on the rise as China's economy opens up new job opportunities.

The 1,060 approved Sino-foreign joint ventures in higher education enroll 450,000 students (Lin, 2014). Sino-foreign cooperation in higher education comes with a stern warning about risks to Chinese sovereignty, as a minister of education remarked: "Tough tasks lie ahead for China to safeguard its educational sovereignty as it involves our fundamental political, cultural, and economic interests and every sovereign nation must protect them from being harmed" (Chen, 2002). Thus, the debate about the integration of international academic staff is inseparable from the debate about the establishment of universities with Chinese characteristics. The issue remains embedded within an unambiguous paradox, namely the seeming incompatibility of three elements within its university system: internationalization, institutional autonomy, and educational sovereignty.

The 2003 law on educational joint ventures opened the floodgates between Chinese and foreign universities and led to more international academic staff exchanges. Attention is increasingly focused on whether foreign-partnership campuses can have a significant impact on China's current higher education system. These collaborations and partnerships constitute one type of laboratory for the future integration of international academic staff into China's universities. Although the jury remains out on long-term sustainability of cross-border campuses, both host and guest universities will learn a great deal from cooperation in the running of partnered colleges and universities (Wildavsky, 2012).

Sino-foreign campuses and degree programs are popular with middle-class parents because they give their children the cachet of a foreign education without the cost of studying abroad. Some foreign universities have set up full campuses, including Nottingham University in Ningbo, Liverpool University in Suzhou, New York University in Shanghai, and Duke University in Kunshan.

The rise in Sino-foreign joint ventures has led to more discussion about sovereignty in higher education. Pan Maoyuan, an influential scholar, cautioned that permitting foreign entities to hold a majority (more than 51 percent) of institutional ownership can lead to an "infiltration of Western values and cultures at odds with current Chinese circumstances" (Pan, 2009, p. 90). Zhang Minxuan, a vice director of the Shanghai Education Commission, made it clear that a Sino-foreign venture in running an educational institute has to "make sure China's sovereignty and public interests are not harmed" (Zhang, 2009, p. 33). Zhang Li, a Ministry of Education official, pointed out that China's commitment to providing access to its educational market is larger than any other developing country and therefore, "we must safeguard China's educational sovereignty, protect national security, and guide such programs in the right direction" (Zhang, 2009, p. 19). Nevertheless, foreign campuses have had an increased amount of autonomy with less interference from the host campuses since the 2003 law on Sino-foreign cooperation. These examples set the context for the integration of large numbers of internationalized academic staff in China's universities. The case of Shanghai Jiao Tong University is illustrative.

## Shanghai Jiao Tong University (SJTU)

SJTU was established in 1896 and is one of China's oldest universities. It is a 985 university and ranks among China's top five. The 2015 annual QS World University Rankings placed it 5th in China and 24th in Asia. It is one of China's largest public universities with a full-time student population of over 35,000, including over 15,000 undergraduates and 20,000 postgraduates. Although SJTU brands itself as a comprehensive university, over 80 percent of its faculty members are in the fields of natural science and engineering. Among the papers produced by academic staff, nearly 8,000 were published in Science Citation Index Expanded (SCIE)– and Engineering Index (EI)–indexed academic journals. Only 159 were published in Social Sciences Citation Index (SSCI)– and Arts & Humanities Citation Index (A & HCI)–indexed academic journals. Over 40 alumni are fellows of the Chinese Academy of Sciences (CAS) and the Chinese Academy of

Engineering (CAE). This makes it one of the eight universities in China with the largest group of alumni in CAS and CAE. As a public research university, the largest share of SJTU's 2011 income of 7 billion RMB (USD 1.09 billion), about 80 percent, comes from government, and nearly 1.7 billion (USD 0.26 billion) is allocated to research.

## *Policies and Practices Toward an International Professoriate*

The recruitment of "internationalized" faculty is part of SJTU's strategy to build a globally competitive university. Internationalized faculty includes overseas returnees (*haigui*, 海归) and foreign nationals (*waijiao*, 外教). Policy documents do not indicate which types of "internationalized" faculty are a priority, but most of those recruited are overseas returnees (海龟), or senior Chinese researchers who have been working in universities outside of the Chinese mainland for a substantial period and may have become overseas nationals. Among SJTU's professoriate of 2,900, nearly one-sixth hold overseas doctorates. Only about 120, mostly ethnic Chinese, hold foreign passports.

The recruitment procedure has aspects of the old socialist-era system but with an American-style orientation. For example, most professors and administrators are government employees, and each division of the university has centrally determined quota limitations on professorial recruitment. However, decisions are in the hands of school-based search committees, chaired by the dean, instead of by the university personnel office. The search committee discusses the criteria used in selecting potential candidates and reviews the profiles of applicants. Once a candidate is selected, the search committee makes a recommendation to the university personnel office, which usually agrees with the recommendations of the search committee. Naturally, the character of China's universities includes a Communist Party mechanism that operates alongside all administrative appointments and has the power to confirm or veto decisions.

Most contracts are fixed term and renewed every three years. Newly recruited faculty sign a first-term agreement of three years, in which the number of publications they must produce is stated, as well as the number of research grants they must win. Although there is no tenure system comparable with that in the United States, the appointment is virtually lifelong since most faculty get their contracts renewed in a timely fashion. However, faculty members are required to publish a required number of publications before promotions can take place.

The base salary is the same across the university. However, each school also pays faculty an amount depending on available resources and faculty performance. The university also provides faculty with bonuses for outstanding publications and research grants. Faculty may engage in professional practice outside of the university to supplement their pay.

Foreign language ability has come to matter more in recruitment because the university encourages its faculty to write articles in English and publish in international journals. The publication of English-language articles is also an important consideration for promotion. Special funds are available to encourage SJTU faculty to develop English-taught courses. In short, the ability of returnees to teach in English, something that few of their counterparts who earned doctorates in China possess, is highly rewarded. As one of the senior managers interviewed for this study said:

> We have English-taught programs. The aim is to recruit more international students ... To ensure the quality of teaching, we recruit overseas returnees. They will be able to teach (in English).

SJTU aims to increase the number of international publications by recruiting more overseas faculty to a level comparable with other world-class universities. SJTU is well aware of the importance of global comparability as it houses one of the three most influential global university ranking systems, namely the Academic Ranking of World Universities. In a sense, recruitment of overseas returnees is viewed as a shortcut to internationalizing the university. There is even some outside pressure for China's universities to internationalize their research faculty. The president of SJTU pointed to a statement published recently in *Nature*:

> Yet the quality of research, as indicated by citations, lags behind, and technology transfer is sluggish. Ossified practices in evaluation and incentivization—such as rewarding publication quantity over quality— are holding Chinese universities back.
>
> *(Zhang, 2014)*

SJTU policy with regard to international faculty recruitment is reflected in the university's 2007 development plan and recruitment program. SJTU aims to recruit high-profile international faculty at both junior and senior levels. The application requirements for both junior- and senior-level posts are considered to be high. In an associate professor–level scheme, it states that the applicants should be from the world's top 50 universities and the quality of their publications should be outstanding.

About 25 percent of the professoriate hold an overseas degree of some kind: about 8 percent from North America, 6 percent from Europe, and 9 percent from Asian countries (see Table 5.1).

The proportion of overseas returnees is rapidly increasing. In 2013 and 2014, nearly 70 percent of the newly recruited faculty at SJTU held overseas degrees, with 57 percent from North America and 16 percent from Europe (see Table 5.2).

SJTU also has programs that allow overseas professors to work on the campus for several months a year. These part-time positions are usually for collaborative research and teaching purposes.

**TABLE 5.1** Distribution of SJTU Professoriate Staff by Country (Based on Countries in Which the Staff Obtained His/Her Last Degree)

| Country | Headcount | Percent |
| --- | --- | --- |
| Mainland China | 2,253 | 76.9 |
| Other Asian Countries | 249 | 8.5 |
| Australia and New Zealand | 8 | 0.3 |
| European Countries | 176 | 6 |
| North American Countries | 243 | 8.2 |
| Others (e.g., Central and South America, African Countries) | 3 | 0.1 |
| All Countries | 2,932 | 100 |

*Sources*: Compiled data.

**TABLE 5.2** Distribution of Professoriate Staff Who Entered SJTU after 2013 January 1 by Country (Based on Countries in Which the Staff Obtained His/Her Last Degree)

| Country | Headcount | Percent |
| --- | --- | --- |
| Mainland China | 10 | 31 |
| Other Asian Countries | 2 | 6 |
| Australia and New Zealand | 0 | |
| European Countries | 5 | 16 |
| North American Countries | 15 | 57 |
| Others (e.g., Central and South America, African Countries) | 32 | 100 |

*Sources*: Compiled data.

A dual-track recruitment system was established in 2007 with a so-called "Green Passage" system for high-profile international applicants. This provides relatively fast processing of applications. For example, the search committee can meet, discuss, and review the international applications at any time of the year. However, the search committee usually meets only once a year to review the applications from domestic applicants.

The contracts offered to domestic and international faculty differed for many years. For example, international applicants, those at senior levels in particular, could usually get a better salary package. For exceptionally high-profile overseas returnees, leadership positions, such as deanship or department head, could be offered together with the contract. However, with the increase of international applicants, the difference between domestic and international contracts is less apparent. With regard to the terms of service, for example, there is no difference between domestic and international applicants. The salary package for international applicants is usually the same, but is negotiable if the applicants have outstanding achievement in their research area.

Data from a survey carried out in 2013 with representative samples of domestic faculty (117 domestic PhD degree holders) and internationalized faculty

**TABLE 5.3** Crosstab of the Faculty's Satisfaction to University Context in SJTU

| | My current job allows me to fulfill my potential. | I am quite satisfied with current teaching arrangement. | I am satisfied with the school's research management system. | I think my workload is justifiable and reasonable. | I am satisfied with the school's promotion and assessment system. | I am satisfied with the current salary, bonus, and welfare. |
|---|---|---|---|---|---|---|
| Overseas returnees | 3.64+ | 3.73 | 3.22 | 3.58 | 3.35 | 2.81 |
| Domestic faculty | 3.38 | 3.38 | 2.99 | 3.00 | 2.69 | 2.37 |

*Source:* Compiled data.

*Note:* Each of the items is rated on a 4-point scale. The higher the score, the more likely that the participants will agree on the statement.

**TABLE 5.4** Crosstab of the Faculty's Integration into the Local University Context in SJTU

| | I understand school culture and have a sense of belonging. | I can get support and encouragement from a leader. | When I encounter problems or difficulties, I can get the help from faculty (department) leaders. | In terms of teaching, we have a very close team. | In terms of research, we have a very close team. | I can work easily with my colleagues. | I will work for a long time in this school. |
|---|---|---|---|---|---|---|---|
| Overseas returnees | 3.55+ | 3.70 | 3.68 | 3.59 | 3.81 | 4.30 | 3.97 |
| Domestic faculty | 3.21 | 3.35 | 3.20 | 3.40 | 3.77 | 4.20 | 3.79 |

*Source:* Compiled data.

*Note:* Each of the items is rated on a 4-point scale. The higher the score, the more likely that the participants will agree with the statement.

(97 overseas PhD degree holders) suggest that the latter are more satisfied with their current job and are likely to agree that their current job makes them feel able to achieve their full potential. They are more satisfied with the teaching load assigned to them, the research management system, and the promotion and evaluation system. The fact that they are paid more than their domestic counterparts may account in part for their level of satisfaction (Table 5.3).

A 2013 survey indicates the internationalized faculty know more about the university culture and have a stronger sense of commitment to the university. They also show more willingness to remain at the university for a long time. They are also more likely to say that they are able to collaborate happily with their colleagues. They indicate they receive support from the leaders in the university and school (Zhang & Yu, 2014) (Table 5.4).

There are no special programs designed by SJTU to integrate its internationalized faculty into the local university context. All newly recruited members of the university, including Chinese returnees and international faculty, are required to take part in an orientation program. The program usually consists of a week of lectures about the history of SJTU and its policies related to teaching, research and evaluations, training in teaching for junior academic staff, and social activities.

In short, SJTU internationalization of faculty is mainly about attracting Chinese returnees who have international experience. The majority of newly submitted applications for faculty positions at SJTU are from overseas returnees, and the quality of the applicants is said to have become substantially improved. The university is trying to abolish the dual-track system it introduced in 2007 in favor of a single-track system. The basic idea is to have a more flexible recruitment system for all of the applicants—domestic and overseas—and set a higher standard for the applicants. The impact of this on the integration of international faculty merits further examination.

Since there are so many Chinese returnees with doctorates and the ability to teach in English, there is less pressure to recruit non-Chinese nationals. Chinese returnees from overseas are more easily integrated into academic life at SJTU. They have less of a gap with the cultural mainstream. They are also becoming a majority group among new recruits. Naturally, the academic environment in overseas universities has more academic freedom, but this seems to matter less in the main SJTU fields of science and technology.

## The Case of the Hong Kong Special Administrative Region

For most of its history, Hong Kong has been distinguished as a trading port driven by a market economy (Chan & Postiglione, 1996). One English-medium university stood alone for over 50 years until mass schooling led to the establishment of a Chinese-medium university in 1964 (Cunich, 2012, forthcoming). The two universities became elite training grounds for civil servants, professionals, and urban elites. By 1981, only 2 percent of the relevant age group occupied a university place. This grew to 8 percent by 1989, but an outflow of professional talent led to a doubling of university places by 1994. The number of universities increased to eight by 1997 (UGC, 1996). By 2006, 60 percent of the 17 to 20 age cohort was in higher education, a doubling of the 2001 figure. Hong Kong has 12 degree-granting institutions, of which 8 are publicly funded. In 2012, the traditional 5 + 2 + 3 education system was converted to a 3 + 3 + 4 structure (three years of junior and senior secondary education with a four-year university system) (EMB, 2005). Although competition for the best students and for the most research funds among the eight publicly funded institutions of higher education is intense, new incentives were introduced to speed up cross-institutional collaboration as a way of cutting costs and strengthening areas of teaching and research (University Grants Committee, 2002).

As knowledge economics, financial retrenchment, and massification of higher education came to dominate policy discourse at the beginning of the 21st century, Hong Kong executed a rethinking of its tertiary education strategy. A 2004 report by the University Grants Committee of Hong Kong entitled "To Make a Difference: To Move with the Times" stated:

> In short, Hong Kong needs its own higher education system to provide the depth and breadth of people who can participate in making Hong Kong a vibrant, economically powerful, cultured, civilized, and socially active and responsible society. The higher education sector is a key source of impetus for social development. Human capital is the single most important asset of Hong Kong. We need home-grown graduates who have a strong sense of belonging, and a strong sense of identity as being a part of Hong Kong. At the same time it is also important to nurture a core of local faculty who give stability, local character, and cultural and intellectual rootedness to local universities, and engage themselves heavily with the local community. Their social and public role is vital to the development of a civil society and the quality of life.
> 
> *(University Grants Committee, 2004)*

Market competition has long been a sacred part of Hong Kong's way of life (Lau, 1982; Lau et al., 1999). The mainland's transition to a socialist market economy reinforced Hong Kong's economic philosophy and its new effort to link improvements in higher education to the marketplace. As cities like Beijing, Shanghai, and Guangzhou bear down on Hong Kong's position as China's economic powerhouse, university reforms in Hong Kong have taken on a new urgency. It is within this context that the Hong Kong SAR imported a more managerial and entrepreneurial model of higher education (Jao, 2001).

Other drivers that affected Hong Kong included the transfer of manufacturing to the hinterland over the border into mainland China and a transition to a knowledge-based service economy. Moreover, market forces have also made it possible for Hong Kong's universities to recruit top Chinese mainland academic talent via places like the United States, Canada, England, and Australia, where doctorates are earned.

The quarter of a century of reform and opening up of the Chinese mainland significantly affected Hong Kong's long-held position as the key bridging center for China's educational exchange with the West. In order to survive, Hong Kong had to adapt to changes on the Chinese mainland. The earlier role played by Hong Kong left an indelible impression on its historical development and contributed to the impetus for readapting itself from a bridge to China to a window for China (Postiglione, 2005). Hong Kong excelled in this way by capitalizing on its intimate knowledge of China, international links, communication infrastructure, and cultural affinity with the mainland. It remains a key center for interpreting China's reform.

With a scarcity of natural resources and manufacturing industries, Hong Kong is left to rely almost solely upon its human resources. Its higher education system, which has responded to calls from industrialists and civil society alike to encourage more creativity and innovation by intensifying a liberal studies curriculum, continues to place a heavy emphasis on performance measurement and quality indicators (Postiglione & Wang, 2011).

Hong Kong has the highest number of globally ranked research universities in one city, due in part due to its strategic management of knowledge networks (Postiglione, 2011). Yet, this was not the case 30 years ago when Hong Kong was a low-to-mid-level-income economy, surrounded by regional poverty, with only two universities that focused on undergraduate teaching. Hong Kong's rise was accompanied by the expansion of higher education and establishment of research universities.

Research universities in Hong Kong are increasingly expected to take a larger role in economic and social development, including knowledge exchange with society. Several conditions support the development of research universities, including a high degree of internationalism, a highly valued but self-defined Chinese cultural heritage, bilingual and bicultural adaptability, capacity to attract talented scientists, technology that permits a close integration with the global academy, open borders and easy mobility, stern protection of academic freedom, a lively intellectual climate, and the adjacent mainland of China with its policy of economic reforms and opening to the outside world (Altbach & Postiglione 2012; Postiglione, 2006, 2007).

In themselves, these basic conditions constitute an enabling environment fc research universities. They help drive the research output and innovation, b much also depends on the government's macro-steering and the strategic manaʒ ment of specific institutional and organizational circumstances in each univers

Put simply, the government steers higher education but gives universities a high level of autonomy. This is a means for extensive internationalization of the academy. Each institution's research portfolio attracts and manages funds; plans strategic research themes; monitors and evaluates research and publications; disseminates, publicizes, and commercializes research breakthroughs; and provides research teams and their doctoral students with one of the most international academic environments in Asia.

As Hong Kong expanded its universities in the 1990s, it diverged from its regional counterparts. Learning from Japan's success, the governments of the other three tigers (Singapore, South Korea, and Taiwan) supported their high-tech industrial rise. Hong Kong's noninterventionist government and the tendency of investors to think in the short term rather than long term led to an abbreviated vision for high-tech industries. It took a quarter of a century for the government to set up a Bureau of Technology and Innovation. In the meantime, the government focused on infrastructure, which included the establishment of a University of Science and Technology (officially opened in 1991). While Hong Kong University of Science and Technology (HKUST) has become a leading international university, allocation for Hong Kong's R&D was 0.7 percent of gross domestic product (GDP), placing Hong Kong in the 50th position in global rankings for this indicator (Ng & Poon, 2004; World Bank, 2012).

In summary, the government aims to drive internationalization of higher education. The international composition of the University Grants Committee (UGC) and the Research Grants Council symbolizes a commitment to international knowledge network building. The members act as network brokers and conduits between Hong Kong and the rest of the developed world, including top-ranked universities.

UGC members act as fillers of international network holes. Local appointees to the UGC are from the business and industrial community. The local business is internationally connected and acts as amphibious entrepreneurs across a number of sectors, including higher education (Sassen, 2004). As these local stakeholders advocate for excellence, they prefer a heavier reliance on quantification as quality assurance mechanisms. Though Hong Kong's universities subscribe to a culture of assessment, appraisal, and evaluation by international peers, it is limited to an extent by comparisons with counterpart university systems

As Hong Kong's research universities have become more involved in collaboration and cross-border partnerships in research, data from the study make it clear that Hong Kong's research patterns are still closely tied to those in Western countries (Chapman, Cummings & Postiglione, For example, Asian academics from Hong Kong, Indonesia, Malaysia, Philippines, and Vietnam collaborate often with counterparts in the US, Australia, and England. Within Asia, Japan has spent many years trying to build research networks in Southeast Asia. The large size of China and India make them emerging partners for knowledge networks with other Asian partners. Finally, knowledge networks in the natural sciences, medicine, and engineering still predominate. This is the case throughout Asia. However, Hong Kong academics in the humanities and social sciences have a greater outreach, due again to internationalism and academic freedom, to collaborate with counterparts in other parts of the world.

In the final analysis, Hong Kong's research universities are globally collaborative. Recruitment of academic staff is competitive internationally, and institutional management provides opportunities for short- and long-term visits by distinguished international academics involved in collaborative projects. Institutional management facilitates academic productivity by providing advantages for building international knowledge networks and for publishing research findings overseas.

Universities in Hong Kong evolved first within a British colony and then within a Special Administrative Region of China (Chan & Postiglione, 1996; Chan & So, 2002). With a population of seven million, Hong Kong has ten universities, eight of which are funded by the government and four of which are ranked in the world's top 100 (QS, 2015). Under the Basic Law of the Hong Kong Special Administrative Region of China, Hong Kong's universities still enjoy a high degree of autonomy in terms of both government and academic freedom (Altbach & Postiglione, 2012; *University World News*, 2016). This goes a long way to account for why more Hong Kong universities appear in the world rankings than those in any other city in the world, despite a mere 0.7 percent of Hong Kong's GDP going to R&D.

Although long known for its entrepreneurial prowess, competitive business practices, and global trade, Hong Kong has also become a city with world-class universities that recruit and integrate international faculty into their ranks. Its universities have capitalized on the one-country and two-system arrangement by remaining closely integrated with the global academy, while at the same time reaping benefit from the modernization of the Chinese mainland. Although the universities value their bond with the Chinese mainland, they also remain intellectually free to use any teaching and research materials, even those banned on the Chinese mainland. Hong Kong's open borders; official policy of bilingualism; and first-class information technology, media, and communication infrastructure help it attract overseas academics.

The multicultural profile of the academic profession makes it helpful for the translation and interpretation of knowledge between China and the rest of the world. The international professoriate are unencumbered in terms of access to global research networks—a core feature of the role of Hong Kong's universities in anchoring globalization and facilitating brain circulation.

The University of Hong Kong, established in 1911 with the goal of contributing to China's modernization, stood alone for over 50 years until the founding

**TABLE 5.5** Hong Kong Academics, Place of Earned Doctorate—Number of Staff (percent)

| Country | 1992<br>Number (Percent) | 2008<br>Number (Percent) |
| --- | --- | --- |
| Hong Kong | 73 (15.7) | 172 (26.6) |
| United Kingdom | 147 (31.7) | 139 (21.5) |
| United States | 126 (27.2) | 185 (28.6) |
| Canada | 46 (9.9) | 34 (5.3) |
| Australia | 31 (6.7) | 65 (10.1) |
| France | 5 (1.1) | 7 (1.1) |
| China | 4 (0.9) | 15 (2.3) |
| Japan | 4 (0.9) | 6 (0.9) |
| Others | 28 (5.9) | 23 (3.6) |
| Total | 464 (100.0) | 646 (100.0) |

*Source*: First and second international survey of the academic profession.

of the Chinese University of Hong Kong in 1964. By 1981, only 2 percent of the relevant age group (18 to 21 years old) had a university place, a figure that increased to 8 percent by 1989 when a sudden emigration set a further expansion in motion that doubled enrollments. By 1997, admission to bachelor degree places in Hong Kong's seven universities catered to 16 percent of the age cohort. By 2006, access to bachelor degree places reached 18 percent, and the figure for all forms of postsecondary education reached 60 percent.

Hong Kong approached an historic turning point when, in 2012, the length of secondary school was reduced by one year and all universities instituted a foundation year that extended the standard bachelor degree length from three to four years. While the main reason for the change is educational, it nonetheless brought Hong Kong's university system in line with those of its two major trading partners, mainland China and the United States.

According to the latest survey, three-quarters of Hong Kong academics earned their doctorates overseas (Table 5.5).

Hong Kong adheres to a system of laws that ensures hiring depends on merit, without respect to race, sex, ethnicity, or religion. Nevertheless, the profile of the academic staff continues to evolve.

## The University of Hong Kong (HKU)

The president of HKU stated in 2015 that internationalization "is an essential component of enhancing our standing in the world" and within such an atmosphere of internationalization, "the future of global leaders will be born" (Mathieson, 2015). About 90 percent of HKU academics hold overseas doctorates. After the establishment of the university in 1911, early recruitment was mainly from the United Kingdom, but also Canada and Australia. Aside from the Chinese Department, there was only one Chinese full professor, educated in the United Kingdom, appointed before the Second World War. By the end of the 1950s, there were several prominent Chinese professors at HKU, although appointed to lower academic ranks. As the days of the British Empire began to wane, there was recruitment of UK nationals from Africa, South Asia, and British Malaya, especially beginning in the 1960s. Although there was recruitment of local Hong Kong academic staff before the Second World War, this was largely into the ranks of demonstrators and research assistants. By the early 1950s and into the 1960s, local Hong Kong assistant lecturers were recruited, followed by the hiring of locally appointed lecturers in the 1970s (at a time when the academic rank system included lecturer, senior lecturer, reader, and professor) (Cunich, 2012, forthcoming).

By the end of the Cold War, the recruitment net expanded further, including more local Hong Kong academics, most of whom had completed their highest degree in the United Kingdom and other English-speaking countries including Australia, Canada, and the United States. The net has since widened to comprise foreign nationals from a diverse array of countries including Spain, Portugal, Italy, Greece, Serbia, Ukraine, Russia, South Korea, Singapore, etc. (see Figure 5.1). Beginning in the mid-1990s, academics born on the Chinese mainland with doctorates earned overseas became a major source of recruitment, especially in the fields of science, medicine, and engineering.

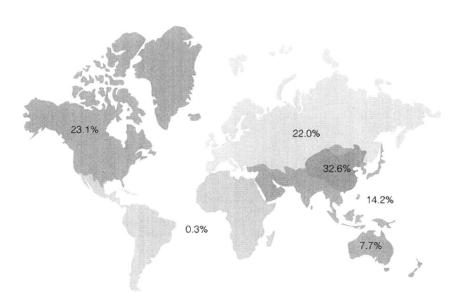

**FIGURE 5.1** Distribution of HKU International Professoriate Staff (Based on Nationality) by Country (Excluding Honorary/Visiting).

*Source*: Management Information Unit, President's Office (2015). QuickStats. Retrieved 16th, May, 2016, from http://www.cpao.hku.hk/qstats/staff-profiles.

92  Gerard A. Postiglione and Xie Ailei

## *Policies and Practices to Sustain an International Professoriate*

HKU attracts huge numbers of applicants from overseas, as well as ethnic Chinese with overseas doctorates and experience. Currently, about 59.2 percent of the HKU professoriate are foreign nationals (see Tables 5.6 and 5.7) (The University of Hong Kong, 2015).

Because more than half of the recruited professoriate are foreign nationals, global knowledge networks remain unencumbered (Saxenian, 2005). The regular full-time professoriate, numbering 1,052 (94 percent with doctorates), ensure HKU's position as a leading institution (UGC, 2014). Within Hong Kong, HKU has the highest number of winning research proposals and the largest amount of research funding. HKU also has the highest number of refereed publications, the highest number of refereed publications per academic, the highest number of refereed journal articles published in journals tracked by Thomson Reuters, and the highest number of citations tracked by Thomson Reuters. One hundred and twenty-five of its professorial staff have been ranked by Thomson Reuters

**TABLE 5.6** HKU Faculty Profile (2014–2015)

| Staff category+ | Male | Female | All | Percent International (Based on Nationality) |
|---|---|---|---|---|
| Professoriate | 808 | 330 | 1,138 | 59.2 |
| Research and Nonprofessoriate Teaching | 1,170 | 1,185 | 2,355 | |
| Administrative and Support | 653 | 1,968 | 2,621 | |
| Technical | 709 | 376 | 1,085 | |
| All | 3,340 | 3,859 | 7,199 | |

*Sources*: www.cpao.hku.hk/qstats/; www.cpao.hku.hk/qstats/staff-profiles.

*Note*: Excluding visiting and honorary staff.

**TABLE 5.7** Distribution of HKU International Professoriate Staff (Based on Nationality) by Country (Excluding Honorary/Visiting)

| Country | Headcount | Percent |
|---|---|---|
| Mainland China | 220 | 32.6 |
| Other Asian Countries | 96 | 14.2 |
| Australia and New Zealand | 52 | 7.7 |
| European Countries | 148 | 22.0 |
| North American Countries | 156 | 23.1 |
| Others (e.g., Central and South America, African Countries) | 2 | 0.3 |
| All Countries | 674 | 100 |

*Sources*: www.cpao.hku.hk/qstats/; www.cpao.hku.hk/qstats/staff-profiles.

as being among the world's top 1 percent of scientists, based on the number of citations recorded for their publications in 2013 (The University of Hong Kong, 2016a, 2016b, 2016c).

HKU seeks out the world's best scholars and scientists through global channels, including advertisements in the *Chronicle of Higher Education*, *Times Higher Education*, and other international publications, as well as through its international networks and amphibious academic administrators—those who have overseas networks by virtue of past study or nationality. Many academic deans regularly attend international conferences and interview candidates from overseas. For senior management posts, advertisements specifically state that knowledge of Chinese is preferred but not required.

There is no specific strategy for hiring local, national, or international faculty. All searches are worldwide. To attract top-quality academic staff, the university provides resources and salaries comparable to other world-class universities, as well as working conditions that scientists and scholars value most—a high degree of academic freedom. In comparison with the Chinese mainland, Hong Kong has no restrictions on Internet access. Information flow is unimpeded, and books and journals are easily accessible. Travel in and out of Hong Kong is also unimpeded. The university is located in China's most international city with open borders. HKU presidents and vice-chancellors are internationally respected scientists and scholars. The university has a high degree of autonomy, values internationalization, and uses English as a medium for most teaching and research. Overseas nationals who reside in Hong Kong for seven years are eligible to become permanent residents and vote in local elections.

A major obstacle to international recruitment is property prices—the highest of any city in the world. Although there are subsidies for living accommodations, it is very difficult, if not impossible, for young academics with families to purchase a home in Hong Kong, which usually means a relatively compact apartment. Academic salaries are competitive with top universities overseas, and tax on earned income is only about 15 percent (though foreign nationals from some countries, including the United States, may be double-taxed on salaries earned in Hong Kong).

For many academics, the rise of Asia is attractive and opens up new opportunities for research. For others, the world-class ranking of HKU or the reputation in specific fields of research is a motivating factor. For those who specialize in the study of Asia, the geopolitical location of HKU is attractive. Other academics with familial roots in the Chinese mainland find it a convenient location for home visits.

HKU academics work within an institutional management format of shared governance. There is a widespread perception among academics that decisions about appointments and the allocation of resources are performance based. Survey data indicate that there are high levels of both work stress and job satisfaction (Postiglione & Wang, 2011). Job satisfaction is helped along by the international reputation of the university, the easy integration of foreign nationals into the structure of shared governance, and the high level of academic freedom (Sharma, 2016).

The main means for the integration of international faculty into the local university context is through the common language medium of English. Although it is common to hear Cantonese used among students and local staff on campus, all academic business is conducted in English, including teaching and research, staff meetings, campuswide announcements, and e-communication. The only exceptions are in the Department of Chinese, the Faculty of Education's division of Chinese language and literature, and selected events on campus that make sense to be presented in Chinese (Cantonese or Putonghua), though translations are usually provided. In many (though not all) cases, English is used in meetings even when all attendees are Chinese speakers.

HKU also ensures inclusion by providing opportunities for overseas hires to take as much of a role as local hires in day-to-day business of the university. University awards and research grants, as well as opportunities to excel in teaching or community service, are open to overseas hires. The staff club, sports facilities, campus restaurants, and other facilities are not segregated. More importantly, international staff may hold an administrative post in the university, though most senior management posts are usually occupied by those from Hong Kong or the United Kingdom, in line with the institutional ethos of HKU's administrative tradition.

It is difficult to distinguish any difference in teaching and research agendas between local and international academic staff. If a difference exists, it is sometimes in the exchange of knowledge with the local Cantonese-speaking community, as well as the visibility of local academic staff in the Chinese press. This is not a hard-and-fast generalization because some overseas academic staff have significant involvement in the local Cantonese-speaking community.

Until the mid-1990s, HKU had few, if any, academics from the Chinese mainland, including those who earned overseas degrees. However, now a large number of mainland academics earn their doctorates overseas at world-class universities. A steady increase in the proportion of academics from the Chinese mainland with overseas doctorates has been especially beneficial to the research profile of the university. The university's annual outstanding researcher awards are often given to academics from the Chinese mainland with overseas doctorates. This has led to the view by some that there is a "mainlandization" of HKU faculty (Macfarlane, 2014).

The template for the exchange of ideas in research and innovation evolves in alignment with policies and practices in the larger global academy. The academic organization and administration of the university are under continual review by outside international specialists. Research quality is assessed through the Research Assessment Exercise, a practice used in the United Kingdom. Part of the university budget supports international initiatives and incentives that aim to strengthen collaborative research, including ways to expand international research networks. The university has five strategic research areas comprising sixteen strategic research themes and five emergent themes that are considered critical to the advancement of Hong Kong, the Chinese mainland, and the rest of the world.

HKU aims to strike a balance in academic collaboration with counterparts on the Chinese mainland and overseas. The high velocity of brain circulation provides the university with the capacity to facilitate cross-border and international research collaborations. The template of institutional arrangements, network agents, and brain circulation for anchoring globalization and national development facilitates a large amount of research collaboration by the professoriate (Table 5.8).

The level of research collaboration has significantly risen in the past two decades according to surveys of the academic profession by the Carnegie Foundation for the Advancement of Teaching and the Changing Academic Profession project (Altbach & Lewis, 1994; ISCAP, 2007; Postiglione, 1997; Postiglione & Wang, 2011).

Most of the professoriate is engaged in international collaborative research. The most productive 20 percent of Hong Kong academics are involved in internationally collaborative research. In fact, the HKU professoriate remains more internationally collaborative in research than most of its Asian counterparts. Research collaboration in the postcolonial era retains the traditional networks of collaboration with Anglo-Western countries, but this has been augmented by newer patterns of collaboration, not only with academics on the Chinese mainland, but also with counterparts in other parts of Asia, especially Taiwan, Singapore, South Korea, Japan, and Malaysia.

In short, the professoriate has a high degree of engagement with regional and international research partners. Institutional management provides the opportunity for short- and long-term visits by distinguished scholars and scientists, including Nobel Laureates and other highly recognized scholars and scientists

**TABLE 5.8** Percent of HK Academics Who Indicate They Collaborate with Foreign Partners in Research

| Country | 1992 Percent | 2007 Percent |
| --- | --- | --- |
| Mexico | 39.9 | 34.6 |
| Brazil | 24.4 | 28.4 |
| Korea | 25.1 | 29.5 |
| Hong Kong, China | 65.0 | 60.2 |
| Australia | 57.0 | 59.3 |
| United Kingdom | 43.1 | 61.4 |
| Japan | 28.5 | 23.8 |
| United States | 39.1 | 33.3 |
| Germany | 55.0 | 50.0 |

*Sources*: Second International Survey of the Academic Profession, for 2007 question D1, and for 1992 question 65a.

from all over the world. The HKU model anchors globalization by capitalizing on its century of heritage with the Western academic model, its strategic position as the leading international university of China, and its ability to attract top students and scholars from all over the world. This model is a product of a long-term process that has required the university to recognize opportunities and take calculated risks in planning and implementation at different phases of its development.

The model rests on an enabling environment of institutional arrangements, deft engagement with international brain circulation, and amphibious stakeholders in the community who have the agility to bridge the wider world of academia, industry, and government (Postiglione, 2013). Above all else, the model is one that places an emphasis on the establishment, protection, and elaboration of internationally collaborative academic knowledge networks and academic freedom. That means a model in which the university takes strategic advantage of its capacity to make globalization work for China's continued rise and growing international leadership in economic development, science, and technology.

Looking ahead, the economy of East Asia will probably continue to be an asset in favor of the integration of international staff as part of a research university in China with a global outreach. That global outreach hinges on a sustained integration of local and international academics.

## Conclusion

The two case studies operate in very different geopolitical systems. They differ significantly in terms of university governance and academic culture. Data from the last international survey of the academic profession point out that internationalization in matters of academic staffing is managed in a top-down manner in the Chinese mainland where there is more concern about the protection of educational sovereignty. For example, when asked who has the primary influence on establishing international linkages, Hong Kong academics generally see influence as ascending (faculty member, faculty committee, academic unit, institutional manager, and government), whereas for mainland China–based academics, the direction is inverted. Yet, surveyed academics on the Chinese mainland do not appear to be as troubled by such a top-down form of university governance.

In the case of the Chinese mainland, the increasing flow of overseas returnees—the so-called internationalized academic staff in Chinese mainland universities—has fostered a more open perspective on academic life and work. This group is well integrated into contemporary academic life in China. It is similar for some of the foreign nationals born in China. The integration of foreign-born academics into university life and academic governance is somewhat different. Their integration depends to some extent on their Chinese language ability and efforts to adapt to the unique political and administrative culture of Chinese universities. In general, foreign nationals, especially those who are nonethnic Chinese, are less integrated into university life. Few choose to continue academic careers in China over the long term because it usually affects their competitiveness in the overseas academic mainstream. That may change as more of China's research universities rise in the international rankings. By contrast, appointment to HKU, for example, is not a drag on remaining integrated into the overseas academic mainstream. A major reason is linguistic. Most foreign nationals, with the exception of some overseas Chinese faculty, are generally not Chinese speakers. Unlike Hong Kong, where both English and Chinese are official languages, the Chinese mainland has one official academic language, and SJTU conducts the business of academic governance in Chinese, whereas HKU conducts it in English.

Another factor of considerable importance is the demography of China's academic profession. SJTU has a younger faculty than HKU, and the Chinese mainland has one of the youngest academic professions in the world. This could mean a higher tolerance in the future for integrating foreign national academics into the Chinese mainland's university system. In fact, the increasing number of Sino-foreign campuses, such as those of New York, Duke, and Nottingham universities, are examples of institutions where foreign nationals are able to integrate into China's higher education system. However, these Sino-foreign campuses are unique and on the periphery of the larger higher education system.

Universities on the Chinese mainland have to manage a delicate balance between the fast-growing aspiration to internationalize academic staff and the concern about protecting the nation's educational sovereignty. While HKU has had no such challenge to date, it also has to manage a balance in recruitment of top talent from Hong Kong, the Chinese mainland, and overseas, while sustaining its international profile and Anglo–Hong Kong Chinese administrative ethos.

*Note*: We acknowledge the support of the Hong Kong Central Policy Unit and the Research Grants Council for project HKU7021-PPR-12.

## References

Altbach, P. G. (Ed.). (1994). *The international academic profession: Portraits of fourteen countries*. Princeton, NJ: Carnegie Foundation for the Advancement of Teaching.
Altbach, P. G., & Lewis, L. S. (1994). The academic profession: An international perspective. In Altbach, P. G. (Ed.), *The international academic profession: Portraits of fourteen countries* (pp. 3–51). Princeton, NJ: Carnegie Foundation for the Advancement of Teaching.
Altbach, P. G., & Postiglione, G. A. (2012). Hong Kong's academic advantage. *International Higher Education, 66*(winter), 22–27.
Altbach, P. G., Yudkevich, M., Reisberg, L., Pacheco, I., & Androushchak, A. (2012). *Paying the professoriate: A global comparison of compensation and contracts*. New York: Routledge.
Boehler, P. (2014). China spending more than Europe on science and technology as GDP percentage, new figures reveal. *South China Morning Post*. Retrieved from www.scmp.com/news/china-insider/article/1410178/china-spending-more-europe-science-and-technology-gdp-percentage

Chan, M. K., & Postiglione, G. A. (1996). *The Hong Kong reader: Passage to Chinese sovereignty*. New York: ME Sharpe.

Chan, M. K., & So, A. Y. (2002). *Crisis and transformation in China's Hong Kong*. New York: ME Sharpe.

Chapman, D. W., Cummings, W. K., & Postiglione, G. A. (Eds.). (2010). *Crossing borders in East Asian higher education*. London: Springer.

Chen, Z. (2002, January 9). WTO, its influences on Chinese education and our strategies (Jiaru WTO dui woguo jiaoyu de yingxiang yu duice yanjiu). *China Education Newspaper*. Retrieved from http://news.xinhuanet.com/zhengfu/2002-01/10/content_232367.htm

Cunich, P. (2012). *A history of the University of Hong Kong: 1911–1945*. Hong Kong: Hong Kong University Press.

Cunich, P. (Forthcoming). *A history of the University of Hong Kong: 1945–*. Hong Kong: Hong Kong University Press.

Deng, X. (1993). *Selected works of Deng Xiaoping (Deng Xiaoping Wenxuan)*. Beijing: People's Publishing House (Renmin chubanshe).

ISCAP. (2007). *International survey of the changing academic profession: Data source from unpublished tabulations of the Hong Kong portion of the data base*.

Jao, Y. C. (2001). *The Asian financial crisis and the ordeal of Hong Kong*. London: Quorum Books.

Lau, S. (1982). *Society and politics in Hong Kong*. Hong Kong: Chinese University of Hong Kong Press.

Lau, S. K., Lee, M-K, Wan, P-S., & Wong, S-L (Eds.). (1999). *Indictors of social development: Hong Kong 1999*. Hong Kong: Hong Kong Institute of Asia-Pacific Studies.

Lin, J. (2014). *Research on quality assurance in Chinese-Foreign cooperation in running schools (Zhongwai hezuo banxue zhiliang jianshe yanjiu)*. Fujian: Xiamen University Press (Xiamen Daxue chubanshe).

Macfarlane, B. (2014). Hong Kong's students ask: If not now, when? Retrieved 15 May 2016, from www.timeshighereducation.com/comment/opinion/hong-kongs-students-ask-if-not-now-when/2016331.article

Mathieson, Peter. (2015, December 17). Our way forward, 2016. The speech of the President and Vice-Chancellor Professor Peter Mathieson to the Court, the University of Hong Kong, Hong Kong.

Ministry of Education (2015). Name list of the national higher education institutions in 2015 (2015nian quanguo gaodeng xuexiao mingdan). Retrieved 18 January 2016, from www.moe.gov.cn/publicfiles/business/htmlfiles/moe/moe_634/201505/xxgk_187754.html

Ng, S. H., & Poon, C.Y.W. (2004). *Business restructuring in Hong Kong: Strengths and limits of post-industrial capitalism in Hong Kong*. New York: Oxford University Press.

Pan, M. (2009). An analytical differentiation of the relationship between education sovereignty and education rights. *Chinese Education & Society*, 42(4), 88–96.

Postiglione, G. A. (1997). The academic profession in Hong Kong higher education within a period of profound change. In P. G. Altbach (Ed.), *The academic profession: Studies from 14 countries* (pp. 193–230). Princeton: Carnegie Foundation for the Advancement of Teaching.

Postiglione, G. A. (2005). China's global bridging: The transformation of university mobility between Hong Kong and the United States. *Journal of Studies in International Education*, 9(1), 5–25.

Postiglione, G. A. (2006). The Hong Kong special administrative region of the people's republic of China. In F. T. Huang (Ed.), *Quality, relevance, and governance in the changing academia: International perspectives* (pp. 97–114). Hiroshima: Research Institute for Higher Education.

Postiglione, G. A. (2007). Hong Kong: Expansion, reunion with China, and the transformation of academic culture. In W. Locke & U. Tischler (Eds.), *The changing conditions for academic work and careers in selected countries* (pp. 57–76). Kassel: International Centre for Higher Education Research.

Postiglione, G. A. (2011). The rise of research universities: The Hong Kong University of Science and Technology. In P. G. Altbach & J. Salmi (Eds.), *The road to academic excellence: The making of world-class research universities* (pp. 63–100). Washington DC: The World Bank.

Postiglione, G. A. (2013). Anchoring globalization in Hong Kong's research universities: Network agents, institutional arrangements, and brain circulation. *Studies in Higher Education, 38*(3), 345–366.

Postiglione, G. A. (2014). Research universities for national rejuvenation and global influence: China's search for a balanced model. *Higher Education, 70*(2), 235–250.

Postiglione, G. A., & Wang, S. (2011). Governance of the academy in Hong Kong. In W. Locke, W. K. Cummings & D. Fisher (Eds.), *Changing governance and management in higher education* (pp. 343–368). Dordrecht: Springer Press.

Sassen, S. (2004). Local actors in global politics. *Current Sociology, 52*(4), 649–670.

Saxenian, A. (2005). From brain drain to brain circulation: Transnational communities and regional upgrading in India and China. *Studies in Comparative International Development, 40*(2), 35–61.

Schleicher, A. (2012). Hong Kong's success in PISA—One system, many actors. Retrieved from http://oecdeducationtoday.blogspot.hk/2012/05/hong-kongs-success-in-and-pisa-one.html

Sharma, Y. (2016). Appointment raises new fears for academic freedom. *University World News*. Retrieved from www.universityworldnews.com/article.php?story=20160105183710592

Universities Grants Committee (1996). *Higher education in Hong Kong*. Hong Kong: Government Printer.

Universities Grants Committee (2002). *Higher education in Hong Kong (Sutherland Report)*. Hong Kong: Government Printer.

Universities Grants Committee (2004). *Hong Kong higher education: To make a difference, to move with the times*. Hong Kong: Government Printer.

Universities Grants Committee (2014). General statistics on UGC-funded institutions/programmes. Retrieved 18 January, 2016, from http://cdcf.ugc.edu.hk/cdcf/statEntry.do?language=EN.

University of Hong Kong (2014). First and foremost. Retrieved 18 January 2016, from www.cpao.hku.hk/publications/firstandforemost/first-and-foremost/en/index.htm

University of Hong Kong (2015). Global admissions profile 2014/15. Retrieved from www.als.hku.hk/pdf/HKU150131.pdf

University of Hong Kong (2016a). State key laboratories. Retrieved from www.hku.hk/research/state_key_lab.html

University of Hong Kong (2016b). The University of Hong Kong scholar hub. Retrieved 18 January 2016, from http://hub.hku.hk/

University of Hong Kong (2016c). The University of Hong Kong strategic research themes. Retrieved 18 January 2016, from www.rss.hku.hk/strategic-research/

Vogel, E. F. (2011). *Deng Xiaoping and the transformation of China*. Cambridge, MA: Belknap Press of Harvard University Press.
Wildavsky, B. (2012). *The great brain race: How global universities are reshaping the world*. Princeton, NJ: Princeton University Press.
World Bank. 2012. Research and development expenditure (as % of GDP). Retrieved 25 September 2012, from http://data.worldbank.org/indicator/GB.XPD.RSDV.GD.ZS
Zhang, J. (2014). Developing excellence: Chinese university reform in three steps. *Nature, 514*(7522), 295–296.
Zhang, J., & Yu, K. (2014). The search for quality at Chinese universities. In L. E. Weber & J. J. Duderstadt (Eds.), *Preparing universities for an era of change* (pp. 201–210). London: Economica.
Zhang, J., & Zhao, W. (2014). *Research on the reform of the university faculty staff's income distribution and incentive mechanism (Gaoxiao jiaoshi shouru fenpei yu jili jizhi gaige yanjiu)*. Beijing: Social Science Academic Press.
Zhang, L. (2009). Policy direction and development trends for Sino-Foreign partnership schools. *Chinese Education & Society, 42*(4), 11–22.
Zhang, M. (2009). New era, new policy: Cross-border education and Sino-Foreign cooperation in running schools in the eyes of a fence-sitter. *Chinese Education & Society, 42*(4), 23–40.

# 6

# INTEGRATING INTERNATIONAL ACADEMIC STAFF INTO THE LOCAL ACADEMIC CONTEXT IN LITHUANIA AND ESTONIA

*Anna-Lena Rose and Liudvika Leišytė*

## Introduction

In recent years, there has been a growing recognition that reliable knowledge in higher education "cannot be produced in local isolation but can only be obtained by an open and honest inquiry that is international in its scope" (Miller, Mateeva & Nekrassova, 2011). The internationalization of higher education does, however, vary significantly between different countries and cultures across the globe. In fact, we witness an emphasis on a "world of (academic) centers and peripheries" (Altbach, 2004) with respect to the globalization and internationalization of higher education, whereby academic centers are usually located in larger and wealthier countries and tend to attract flows of academic talent from the peripheries, while peripheries increasingly struggle in this regard (Altbach, 2004; Scott, 2015). Additionally, we see a dominance of Anglophone institutions in attracting international talent (Hughes, 2008; Scott, 2015). In this context, small countries on the periphery—especially in countries with low levels of English language proficiency—are disadvantaged and need to invest more heavily in internationalization (Loonurm, 2014). Lithuania (with a population of 2.9 million) and Estonia (with 1.3 million inhabitants) and their higher education systems are interesting cases in this regard. Both countries have been members of the European Union (EU) since 2004, but had formerly been part of the Soviet Union for 50 years until the early 1990s, and their higher education systems have undergone significant transitions, including the first attempts to internationalize.

Mobility is a core concept of the European Union policy frameworks. Academic mobility and international attractiveness in higher education are often associated with excellence; the creation of dynamic, international networks; improved scientific performance; improved knowledge and technology transfer;

and improved productivity—all of which ultimately enhance economic and social welfare (Researchers' Report, 2014c).

EU initiatives such as Erasmus+ have provided structural and financial support for (usually short-term) academic mobility. Additionally, supranational developments that have come along with EU membership—such as the full recognition of qualifications and the principle of free movement through many European states—have aimed to remove a number of obstacles to international mobility of academics within the EU. In this regard, both Estonia and Lithuania have benefited from the relevant EU programs, especially when it comes to outgoing mobility. Further, the availability of funding for mobility from the European Union, the Soros Foundation, the Eurofaculty program, and the British Council have strongly facilitated the mobility of students and staff from the Baltic countries after 1990. The Eurofaculty program, created under the initiative of the Nordic Council of Ministers (1993–2005), is especially noteworthy, as it played an important role in contributing to the development of social sciences and humanities in the Baltic states. Within the scope of this program, retraining was offered to academics from these countries by visiting academic staff from Northern European countries, and funding was provided to increase the short-term mobility of Baltic academic staff and students. As such, Eurofaculty initiated the first significant influx of foreign academic staff to visit Lithuania and Estonia from the Western European countries.

In general, Central and Eastern European countries have primarily understood internationalization as an act of traveling to Western countries for educational or academic work opportunities (Renc-Roe, 2011). Thus, long-term/permanent incoming academic mobility has been rather limited in Lithuania and Estonia. The key reasons for the slow dynamics of academic staff mobility into these two countries in the last 20 years lie in the limited English language competencies among older generations of academic staff, protectionism of these small higher education systems, and limited connectedness to 'Western' scientific centers (Leišytė, 2014).

This chapter aims to find out how universities in Lithuania and Estonia try to attract international academic staff, which factors influence the motivations of international academics to work at universities in these countries, and which national and institutional obstacles to mobility can be observed. Our study is based on document and website analysis. To illustrate the main factors at the institutional level, we present a case study of Vilnius University in Lithuania, which is based on interview data and website analysis.

The chapter is organized as follows. First, we present an overview of the two higher education systems and explore the policy rationales used for attracting international academic staff. Next, the general characteristics of our case study university, Vilnius University, are introduced. The main body of the chapter is dedicated to an examination of the integration of international faculty at Vilnius University. We conclude with an overview of our key findings and a comparison of the policies and practices of academic mobility in the two systems, with suggested avenues for future research.

## Internationalization Attempts in Lithuanian Higher Education

In Lithuania, higher education is provided by public and private universities and nonuniversity institutions. Given the size of the country, Lithuania has a comparatively large number of institutions that provide higher education. Currently, the binary higher education system consists of 22 universities (14 public and 8 private), 24 colleges (13 public and 11 private), and 13 state research institutes. Altogether, the higher education sector educated 159,695 students and employed 13,936 researchers in 2013 (Eurostat, 2015c, 2015d).

Since regaining its independence in 1990, the Lithuanian higher education system has undergone significant transformation (Leišytė and Kizniene, 2006; Leišytė, Zelvys & Zenkiene, 2015; MoE, 2016; Renc-Roe, 2011; Želvys, 2004). The latest reforms to the system were brought along by the 2009 Law on Higher Education and Research (2009, 2012). This legislation increased both the autonomy of universities and the competition for research funding and students (Researchers' Report, 2014b). In 2012, around one-third of all research funding was allocated on the basis of a competitive peer-review procedure. Most of the funding is, however, allocated to universities based on a formula, and part of it comes in through the student voucher system (i.e., state funding provided in the form of student vouchers to the best entrants applying to higher education institutions).

With regard to the internationalization of Lithuanian higher education, the country's participation in the Bologna Process since 1999, as well as its EU accession in 2004 and subsequent financial measures for integration into the European Higher Education Area (EHEA), were particularly important. Further, the Research Council of Lithuania has started to attract foreigners to collaborate with Lithuanian researchers through research funding schemes and has initiated the internationalization of peer review by increasing the number of international reviewers involved in their peer-review processes in the past ten years (Interviewee 11).

To a large extent, the current Lithuanian higher education system follows a "state supervision model" (Leišytė, 2002), in which higher education institutions enjoy a large degree of organizational autonomy while facing lower levels of political and especially financial autonomy (Ritzen, 2013). The European University Association (2012) has rated the Lithuanian higher education system "medium low" in financial and academic autonomy, "medium high" in organizational autonomy, and "high" in staffing autonomy. Regarding staffing autonomy, a criterion referring to a university's ability to recruit and manage its human resources as it sees fit, the 2009 higher education law provides general guidelines concerning the selection procedure and criteria for senior academic staff. Universities that have implemented the provisions of the law can decide on salaries for academic staff members autonomously. Staff may be promoted only if funding is available to finance a position at a higher level.

Along with Bulgaria, Hungary, Latvia, and Romania, Lithuania is one of the EU member states that pays the lowest salaries to academic staff—and the dissatisfaction with salary levels among academics is particularly high (MORE2, 2013). Giving an example, a Lithuanian professor can earn an annual base salary of up to EUR 14,578 (MORE2, 2012). In addition to the base salary, universities can pay bonuses of up to 100 percent to their employees based on performance (such as teaching hours, supervision of dissertations, excellent publications, or attracting external funding). Furthermore, it is important to note that within the limits of a 1.5 full-time equivalent position (whereby academics may not work more than 60 hours per week, inside or outside the university), academics also can work in externally funded projects. Under certain circumstances, the total salary of academics at Lithuanian universities can thus be two to three times higher than their base salary. Up to now, policy makers and university managers have not really focused on improving faculty salaries.

The number of incoming academic staff into Lithuania is rather low and remains stable, whereas the number of outgoing students and academic staff is usually much higher and is increasing (European Parliament, 2009; Leišytė, Zavickiene & Zelvys, 2009)—a process that leads to serious brain drain. In terms of concrete policies focused on attracting international academic staff, the *National Action Plan for Promoting the International Dimension of Lithuanian Higher Education 2013–2016* has to be mentioned. This plan set a number of strategic priorities—such as foreseeing the allocation of funding for the development of joint degree programs with foreign universities and new study programs in foreign languages—that aim at attracting foreign students to come and study in Lithuania. With respect to academic mobility, the plan introduces measures that will help send academic staff on short-term visits abroad and envisions the provision of funding for attracting academic staff from abroad. With regard to the latter, the focus lies mainly on attracting academics of Lithuanian descent, especially those who work outside of the EU in Anglo-Saxon countries and Japan. Although the plan acknowledges the existence of certain bureaucratic barriers, such as visas for foreign academic staff to come to Lithuania, it does not provide a budget for further investigation regarding the causes of these barriers, which would help to reduce them, and does not include clear measures or targets to foster the long-term persistence of foreign academic staff in Lithuania.

Other relevant documents in this regard are the *Brain Retain and Gain Strategy* (2008–2013), as well as Lithuanian Research Council funding schemes geared to attract international faculty. The *Brain Retain and Gain Strategy* was aimed at attracting Lithuanian emigrants and foreigners to carry out academic research in Lithuania. Meanwhile, the Lithuanian Research Council introduced the *Global Grants Scheme* in 2009, which provides project funding as an incentive for Lithuanian emigrants and foreigners to come to Lithuania. Additionally, a Short Period Visits Program was introduced for the period 2009–2013 to enable institutions to invite EU and third-country researchers to Lithuania for short-term visits and to send Lithuanian researchers abroad.

Most of these efforts to tackle the challenge of brain drain were, however, primarily oriented toward preventing young Lithuanian researchers from leaving the country and creating incentives for Lithuanian nationals who had previously left the country for education or work opportunities abroad to return. Whereas in the first 20 years of independence enrollment in the higher education sector tripled, Lithuanian universities are currently facing rapid decreases in student numbers due to demographic change (Paliokaitė & Caturianas, 2013), which is caused by increasing emigration rates among young people and a serious decline in birth rates over recent years (Schmidt-Nielsen et al., 2011). Given the large number of higher education institutions in the country, the competition for students is especially tough. This situation is acknowledged by policy makers attempting to merge institutions and institutions trying to attract students from abroad (MoE, 2016).

Thus, even though a brain gain strategy was developed and the creation of more favorable conditions to attract foreign faculty was discussed at governmental and institutional levels in past years, no specific legal requirements or targets for attracting international academic staff were proposed and used (Interviewee 5).

When looking at other immigration-related policies, we find that incoming academic staff mobility has been somewhat facilitated by an amendment to the Law on the Legal Status of Aliens in 2008, which allows foreign academic staff who have a job contract with a Lithuanian higher education institution to reside within the country temporarily for one year without having to apply for a work permit (Paliokaitė, 2014b). Nevertheless, procedures are still rather lengthy and complicated. Furthermore, Lithuania does also participate in the EU Blue Card scheme and issued 92 blue cards to highly qualified non-EU citizens in 2014, while the average of all participating EU countries in the same year amounted to 527 (Eurostat, 2015a).

We have observed that another EU initiative, the Lithuanian EURAXESS portal, is useful for potential foreign faculty, as it presents basic information on the system, visas, and insurance arrangements, but it is not a place that provides information on job vacancies or available fellowships and grants (Paliokaitė, 2014b). In 2013, 43.7 research posts per thousand researchers in the public sector were advertised across the European Union via the EURAXESS Jobs portal. In Lithuania in this year only 1.3 positions per thousand researchers were advertised on the EURAXESS Jobs portal. A legal obligation to publish positions internationally and in the English language exists only for the heads of public research institutes (Researchers' Report, 2014b). This leads us to conclude that the announcements for academic recruitment in Lithuania are not yet very visible internationally.

Overall, the Lithuanian higher education sector sees small successes in attracting international academic staff. In 2012, 2.5 percent of academic staff employed at higher education institutions nationwide held foreign citizenship, with the biggest share (64 percent) constituting citizens of European countries that are not members of the EU. This is an increase compared to the time of the EU accession in 2004, when the share of foreign academic staff working in Lithuania was only 0.3 percent (Eurostat, 2015b). Further, the number of courses and degrees offered in English has substantially risen in Lithuania over the past ten years. Although most courses are still taught in Lithuanian, there are increasing opportunities for foreign staff to teach in English.

In general, the country has been more successful in attracting Lithuanian nationals from abroad than attracting foreign nationals. In 2014, return migration constituted over 80 percent of total immigration, as opposed to about 15 percent in 2001 (EMN, 2015). There is, however, no statistical evidence of how many academics have returned to Lithuanian universities after having worked in academia abroad. Although findings from our case study of Vilnius University (see later) suggest that international experience is increasingly valued and that an increasing share of academic staff at the university has previously worked or studied abroad (Interviewee 2), Barcevičius (2015) has found that Lithuanian universities struggle to accommodate returning researchers.

## Internationalization Attempts in Estonian Higher Education

After the restoration of independence from the Soviet Union in 1990, Estonia's higher education system experienced fast and radical reforms. Higher education in Estonia is provided by universities, professional higher education institutions, and vocational education schools. Given the size of the country, a comparatively large number of institutions operate within the Estonian higher education system. Overall, the system consists of 33 higher education institutions, among which there are 6 public universities and 1 private university (Archimedes, 2015; Kaiser, Faber, Jongbloed, File & van Vught, 2011). The majority of academic research in Estonia is performed at four of the six public universities. In the academic year 2014–2015, Estonian higher education institutions educated 64,806 students and employed 4,638 researchers.

Estonian higher education institutions enjoy large degrees of financial, academic, organizational, and staffing autonomy (European University Association, 2012). Recruitment can be carried out autonomously by higher education institutions, and each institution can freely decide on staff salaries. Salaries are, however, relatively low. A professor in Estonia, for example, can expect to earn an annual base salary of EUR 21,360 (University of Tartu, 2016). Again, academic staff can receive substantial additional remuneration for the performance of other duties.

The Estonian recruitment system is considered open and transparent. One can observe a rising trend to publish information about job openings in English on internationally visible platforms (Researchers' Report, 2014a), although there are no legal requirements for this. In 2013, for example, 51.1 positions per thousand researchers in Estonia were advertised on the EURAXESS Jobs portal. For comparison, within the same time frame, Lithuania only published 1.3 positions, whereas the EU average was 43.7 (Researchers' Report, 2014d).

Although less drastic in numbers, Estonia faces similar problems as Lithuania with regard to demographic change. The Estonian population, consisting of 1.3 million inhabitants in 2015, is projected to decrease to 1.1 million by 2050 (Eurostat, 2014). Recognizing brain drain and the lack of attractiveness of public research careers as constant challenges (Christensen et al., 2012), the Estonian state introduced its first counteracting measures in 2006, with its *Higher Education Internationalisation Strategy* (2006–2015). Besides the internationalization of study programs and the creation of a supporting legal framework—for example, with regard to the recognition of foreign qualifications and the implementation of a more favorable immigration policy for foreign students and academic staff—one of the key objectives of this strategy was to increase the share of international academic staff. An increased involvement of international academic staff at Estonian higher education institutions is expected to contribute to the "quality of research and teaching," to support "teaching in areas where (local) (. . .) competence is limited," to "implement fresh ideas and methods," and to facilitate an expansion of "the number of courses taught in foreign languages." Additionally, international academic staff is considered an "asset in developing international relations and motivating international students to come to study in Estonia."

The strategy set a target of ensuring that at least 3 percent of full-time academic staff in Estonia would be of foreign origin by 2015. The integration of international academic staff and students is regarded as particularly important, and the strategy demands combined efforts of higher education institutions and the national government to ensure the provision of free language courses and information on cultural, legal, and administrative aspects; access to community services; and medical care in English, and help with integration of academics and students into their new professional and personal circumstances in Estonia.

In 2007, the vast majority of Estonian higher education institutions signed the *Agreement on Good Practice in the Internationalisation of Estonia's Higher Education Institutions*, which, among other points, ensures that institutions post their positions internationally; provide information and assistance to international staff in relation to work arrangements, visa, residence permits, and accommodation; and offer international staff the opportunity to learn the Estonian language.

From 2010 to 2015, Estonia ran the Estonian Research Mobility Scheme (ERMOS), an initiative for postdoctoral researchers that was funded by the European Union with the purpose of developing and diversifying Estonian research potential by increasing international mobility. The scheme was primarily designed to reverse brain drain by enabling the reintegration of Estonian researchers who had obtained their PhDs abroad, but was also open to non-Estonian researchers. Within the scope of ERMOS, 46 fellowships were offered across all scientific disciplines for periods of two to five years.

Just like Lithuania, Estonia has been a member of the European Union since 2004. EU citizens and their family members therefore do not face any barriers to immigration when intending to work in higher education in Estonia. Estonia participates in both EU initiatives that intend to facilitate the immigration of highly educated persons and researchers from third countries: the Scientific Visa Package and the Blue Card scheme. In order to attract foreign researchers to the country, the Estonian Alien Act was amended in 2013, making it easier to issue work permits to enable potential top-level specialists and highly qualified employees to enter the Estonian labor market. The Estonian Research Council, which was founded in 2012, offers grants to every individual affiliated with an Estonian institution, regardless of citizenship or residence status. Additionally, nine EURAXESS service centers are located in three cities across the country. These centers are highly active on social media and, in comparison to their Lithuanian counterpart, post more information on their websites and announce more positions. In 2012 alone, EURAXESS Estonia handled 1,572 service and information requests (Ruttas-Küttim, 2014).

Estonian efforts toward internationalization have already proven successful. Although most higher education courses are still taught in the Estonian language, Estonian universities nevertheless offer a considerable number of courses and full degrees in English (Archimedes, 2013; European Commission, 2015). Given of all of the aforementioned policy initiatives, the target of having at least 3 percent of academic staff of foreign origin by 2015 was already exceeded in 2013. While at the time of EU accession in 2004, only about 1 percent of academics within the Estonian higher education sector had a foreign citizenship, this share increased to about 8 percent in 2014. Fifty-three percent of all foreign academics in Estonia were citizens of other EU member states, followed by 25 percent from European countries that do not belong to the EU, and 14 percent from Asian countries (Eurostat, 2015b).

In light of the contrast in rates of incoming academic staff between the two countries, in the following section we present the case study of Vilnius University in Lithuania, as it will help us better understand the institutional experience with incoming academic mobility. Specifically, we focus on existing procedures for academic staff recruitment and integration, and reflect on the key emerging good practices as well as challenges for incoming academic mobility in this institution.

## General Characteristics of Vilnius University

Vilnius University (VU) is the biggest university in Lithuania and is situated in the country's capital. Having been founded in 1579, the university is one of the oldest establishments of higher education in Eastern and Central Europe. Vilnius University is a comprehensive university and has 12 faculties (Vilnius University, 2015).

In 2015, the university employed 1,348 (full-time equivalent) academic staff members and enrolled 21,006 students (11,543 undergraduates and 3,681 graduate students). The graduation rate in 2012–2013 was 70.1 percent for bachelor students and 81.9 percent for master's students. More than 80 percent of all students graduated within the standard period of study (U-Multirank, 2015).

Vilnius University is the most research-productive university in Lithuania. One-third of Lithuanian scientific publications on the Web of Science have been published by VU researchers (Vilnius University, 2013a). Additionally, researchers at Vilnius University actively co-publish with international colleagues: About 50 percent of publications at VU are international joint publications, where at least one author had an affiliation in another country. The adjusted average citation rate of VU publications over the period 2008–2011 was 0.47. The share of VU publications that, compared to other publications in the same field and year, belong to the top-ten cited publications worldwide is 3 percent (U-Multirank, 2015).

In 2012, about half of VU's total funding was allocated from the Lithuanian state budget. The vast share of state funding was for line-item budget items (37.8 percent), while project-based funding represented only 4.7 percent. Furthermore, the university received 30.8 percent of its funding from European Structural Funds (ESF) and from European Economic Area (EAA) grants, 3.6 percent from other international funding, 8.1 percent from tuition fees, 4 percent from economic activity revenue, and 3 percent from other sources (Vilnius University, $2013_a$). Vilnius University has been very successful and is particularly proud of managing to attract large grants from European Structural Funds (Schmidt-Nielsen et al., 2011; Interviewee 5).

## *Recruitment, Performance Assessment, and Salary Structures*

The regulations for recruitment and performance assessment of academic staff at Vilnius University were last amended in 2013, introducing, above all, provisions to ensure open competition for academic positions. The university announces open positions through its own media, the Lithuanian Research Council, and other national channels. The university regulation states that faculty vacancies only have to be posted internationally if it is deemed necessary. Job applications are forwarded directly to the recruiting department, where a recruitment committee chooses the successful candidate. If the position of a professor or leading researcher is to be filled, the recruitment committee should include a foreign expert (Center for Quality Assessment in Higher Education, 2013; Vilnius University, 2013b).

The length of academic work contracts depends on the academic rank of the hire, as Lithuanian higher education does not offer tenure. The shortest periods of employment are provided to lecturers, whose contracts depend heavily on student demand for courses, and last no more than one year. The longest contracts—which are provided, for example, to professors—may not exceed five years. In order to renew their contracts, at the end of each period academic staff members must once again participate in a competition for their post. If a candidate has successfully applied for the same position two times, he or she has the right to apply for a permanent position at the same academic level after the second period has expired. Academics with permanent positions must nevertheless undergo assessment procedures every five years. A person who fails this assessment is dismissed from their position (Vilnius University, 2013b). As such, positions are not permanent in the same sense that this is understood in many other countries, but nevertheless, a high disposition toward hiring people from within the same institution leads to the fact that, until now, it is highly common for Lithuanians to remain at one institution throughout their careers.

In terms of role descriptions and performance requirements for faculty at VU, due to a lack of critical mass of international faculty, neither their formal responsibilities (with regard to research, teaching, and service activities) nor the evaluation of their performance differs from those of their local colleagues.

## *The Role of the English Language at Vilnius University*

As of the academic year 2014–2015, Vilnius University offered 17 degree programs in English, the first such program having been established in 2005. Additionally, more than 500 courses are offered in English in other study programs. Less than 10 years ago, Erasmus students would have been taught separately from domestic students due to a lack of English language proficiency among some staff members and domestic students. Since then, the situation has drastically changed (Interviewee 2). At the moment, a generational change is taking place. The older generation, having grown up in Soviet times, speaks Russian and German, and in many cases is also fluent in French. In contrast, the younger generation is proficient in English. Many study programs have undergone substantial change within recent years. For some programs, English language proficiency is now used as an admission criterion, and courses are offered in English or Lithuanian, depending on the presence of international students and staff.

Although the general language of communication in most faculties still is Lithuanian, especially in the natural sciences, laboratory notes and publications are written and published in English.

## Case Study: Incoming Academic Staff Mobility at Vilnius University

The data on incoming academic staff mobility at Vilnius University come from a literature review, document content analysis, VU website content analysis, 11 semi-structured face-to-face interviews, and 2 semi-structured e-mail interviews carried out in summer 2015. Our sample includes nine interviews with current and former academic staff members at Vilnius University, six of whom are international and three are Lithuanians, who spent significant time in academia abroad before returning to Lithuania. Furthermore, we conducted two additional face-to-face interviews and two e-mail interviews with experts and administrators at both institutional and policy-making levels.

## Rationale and Procedures of International Recruitment

For the academic years 2011–2012 and 2012–2013, Vilnius University reported that 2.61 percent of its academic staff held foreign citizenship. Within the same time frame, only 0.22 percent of doctoral degrees were awarded to candidates with a foreign citizenship (U-Multirank, 2015). The current total number of international staff is unknown, as, technically, all academic staff members who have registered for residence in Lithuania are legally no longer regarded as foreigners. However, university and faculty web pages and interviews have revealed that most international academic staff are employed as language instructors within the Faculty of Philology. Although much fewer in numbers, we found international academic staff at other faculties. They hold positions at different levels within the academic hierarchy and are involved in teaching, research, and, in some cases, administrative duties.

Vilnius University does not yet have a clearly articulated policy with regard to recruitment of academic staff. As in many other universities in Lithuania, human resource management has not yet been professionalized. Until very recently, the various academic departments of the university were highly fragmented and acted with significant degrees of autonomy (Center for Quality Assessment in Higher Education, 2013; Interviewee 10). Until 2015, the importance of attracting more international staff was only discussed internally, and internal working documents were published at the level of the rectorate, articulating such targets as attracting 20 percent foreign PhD candidates and encouraging faculties to invite at least one visiting professor per semester (Interviewee 5). Recently, however, as a result of the change of status of the university from a state budgetary institution to a public enterprise, significant changes have been implemented in the university's management structure. Following the changes introduced in the 2009 higher education law, a university council with five internal and six external members was established, which voted for a new rector for the first time in March 2015. Requirements imposed by amendments to the 2009 higher education law have greatly enhanced the power of university management—especially the council and the rectorate—vis-à-vis faculties, centers, and institutes. Hopes are high, according to our interview data and other sources (Schmidt-Nielsen et al., 2011), that these developments have created the necessary framework conditions for management to lead the university into a new phase of development. Interviewees at Vilnius University were confident that internationalization and strategies to attract international academic staff will take a prominent place in a new university strategy. A first step toward this was the creation of a Human Resources Development Unit, which took up its work at the beginning of the academic year 2015–2016.

Vilnius University has several reasons to engage in the hiring of international academic staff. In the past, VU had high levels of academic inbreeding. Many positions were filled by internal candidates, with academic staff who had been born and raised in Lithuania, studied at VU, and never left the university in the course of their career. Due to this, in recent years, efforts were made to improve the transparency of hiring processes in order to attract new ideas and fresh minds that will help dismantle old structures and change traditional mentalities. Simultaneously, the aging staff structure is a big concern, and a new talent pool is needed. Due to earlier discussed emigration and demographic changes, the university faces increasingly tough competition for students in order to ensure its basic funding. A higher number of international academic staff at the university is expected to serve as a pull factor for students of both local and foreign origin: "First of all you have to have more [international] professors and then students will come" (Interviewee 5).

Additionally, international academic staff is thought to help to ensure the quality of research and increase possibilities of attracting international funding, especially from European projects, where currently the participation of Lithuanian researchers is rather low (Interviewee 11). Furthermore, the international experiences and networks of international academic staff are expected to entail new opportunities for international cooperation (Interviewee 7), and the external expertise that they bring to the university is needed to contribute to areas and topics that are currently underresearched at VU (Interviewee 5).

Attracting international academic staff to Vilnius University has proven very difficult in the past, mainly because of the lack of sufficient financial incentives. Salaries are very low and, even in projects financed by the Lithuanian Research Council and EU Structural Funds, remuneration is pegged to Lithuanian salaries (Petrauskas, 2013, Schmidt-Nielsen et al., 2011). Interviewees note:

> Salary is very unattractive. [Even doctoral candidates] could not live on the grant they get here if they had to live on it on a permanent basis.
> *(Interviewee 11)*

> The salaries are very low and I have almost each week applicants (...), but I start to discuss with some of them and then when it comes to financial conditions, they say that's not—we will not survive on this scholarship.
> *(Interviewee 5)*

Therefore, Vilnius University engages in a number of alternative forms of brain circulation, which primarily take place on a short-term basis. For example, researchers at the university have many long-standing collaborations with institutions and colleagues abroad, and exchanges take place via the Erasmus+ program (Schmidt-Nielsen et al., 2011).

Additionally, the university has been taking measures to increase the international mobility of its own staff and students. Doctoral students from several faculties have noted that they are required to engage in research visits abroad during their studies (Center for Quality Assessment in Higher Education, 2013). Vilnius University also appoints guest professors from foreign universities. These guest professors have formal contracts with the university and are expected to cover a certain amount of teaching and to mention their university affiliation on their publications. However, apart from some travel expenses being covered via exchange program funds, they do not receive remuneration from the university. There are no formal, university-wide support structures for visiting academics and guest professors. Instead, their integration and the degree of support they receive depend heavily on personal contacts within the departments they visit.

At Vilnius University, recruitment procedures for international academic staff do not differ in practical terms from those for Lithuanian academic staff. Contracts for both groups must comply with standards predetermined by national regulations. While technically and within the legally defined boundaries international academic staff could be offered higher salaries than local academics, universities are often unable to do so because of financial constraints. Acknowledging that the comparatively low levels of salary constitute a huge barrier for the recruitment of international staff, alternative ways of providing additional financial incentives to excellent researchers from abroad have been discussed within Vilnius University in recent years. One of the means considered for this purpose is the establishment of a foundation affiliated with the university, which can allocate additional money for excellent researchers who have been recruited from abroad.

Another recent development is the establishment of the Center for Excellence in Finance and Economic Research (CEFER), a joint research center of Vilnius University and the Bank of Lithuania, which started operating at the beginning of the academic year 2015–2016. In order to ensure the excellence of research and obtain an international reach, CEFER has been looking to hire an international research team, including, at the time of writing this chapter, four international academics. The attractiveness of these positions increased due to the partnership and the funding from the Bank of Lithuania. That created a substantially greater monetary incentive, a possibility to concentrate more on research than on teaching, complete freedom to choose research topics, extra funding to attend international conferences, the possibility to invite seminar presenters and co-authors, involvement in policy work, etc. Researchers receive a basic salary from the university and additional remuneration from the Bank of Lithuania.

## Motivations and Barriers to Incoming Academic Staff Mobility

According to our interviewees, salary is the main barrier for international academic staff to come work in higher education institutions in Lithuania and for Lithuanian academics who have spent a substantial amount of time in academia abroad to come back to Lithuania:

> There is a reason why nobody wants to come here from abroad anymore: Salary. Knowing what he or she could earn in academia abroad, who would want to come to such a cheap labor country as Lithuania? Nobody would do this for pride and glory alone.
>
> *(Interviewee 3)*

International academic staff at Vilnius University are not satisfied with their levels of salary but report that they make ends meet by managing to get bonuses, by engagement in additional paid activities (such as consultancies, translation, or private lessons) outside the university, by securing additional remuneration via their embassies, or by having second jobs in the private sector.

The main motivations for international academics to come to Lithuania were personal, especially as they related to family. Important reasons include reuniting with their spouses and parents and wanting their children to grow up in a familiar environment. Motivations for returning Lithuanians were, however, also strongly influenced by a feeling of obligation to contribute to the development of the country:

> [I returned to Lithuania] primarily because I felt that it is my obligation. (...) In 2004, almost nobody was coming back. A lot of people were leaving, (...) and said: "Lithuania is bad" and were running away. And I thought: It's time to go back (...) to give something back to the country.
>
> *(Interviewee 6)*

> I don't want to have more money. I want to be in a prestigious institution, I want to work with prestigious people, and do things (...), which in my mind are important for our country, for my life, from my kind of perspective. (...) If I was [following the money], I would probably be out of this country.
>
> *(Interviewee 2)*

This reasoning is not surprising, as it has been shown that the Lithuanian diaspora is highly patriotic, and they were an important human capital resource for Lithuanian educational institutions (Ciubrinskas, 2013). For example, the re-establishment of Vytautas Magnus University in 1989 was strongly supported by Lithuanians from the United States. However, these feelings of loyalty were used to legitimize not remunerating highly qualified faculty and expecting that patriotism should be enough to motivate faculty. In our view, this was a huge mistake, resulting in unprecedented levels of brain drain and making it quite difficult to attract international faculty.

Other reasons for coming from abroad to work at VU, based on our interviews, include plain curiosity and interest in Lithuanian language, culture, and history. For some international academic staff members who originate from countries where higher education and research systems suffer from unfavorable conditions due to austerity measures, Vilnius University actually provides career opportunities that they would lack at home.

Generally, despite the concerns regarding salary, our interviewees reported a high level of satisfaction with their work situation at Vilnius University. They were especially positive about a certain degree of independence in carrying out tasks in teaching and research:

> One of the advantages is the degree of independence and flexibility concerning hierarchical structures. Those, who want to make a difference—and ideally bring some funding with them—are at the right place [at Vilnius University].
>
> *(Interviewee 1)*

> I have the feeling that when coming here, one can somehow make a difference. Of course everything one does is—well, one does not revolutionize the world that easily. But it is much easier to do things in a dynamic environment. (. . .) It is nice to be able to take on more responsibilities, to finally leave the role as a student or PhD student, to, well, just have more responsibility and be able to do things. That was one of the main reasons to come here.
>
> *(Interviewee 9)*

Additionally, huge improvements in infrastructure, which were made possible by EU Structural Funds, have been praised, especially with regard to laboratory infrastructure in the natural sciences at Vilnius University:

> The science basis some 3–4 years ago was very poor (. . .). Now we have everything (. . .). We can offer top facilities right now (. . .). Even my colleagues from other countries say: At the moment you have even better conditions than we do.
>
> *(Interviewee 5)*

Respondents were less positive about the rather high teaching loads at Vilnius University. Additionally, the availability and complexity of procedures to apply for external research funding have been criticized. Funding is, in general, open to all researchers, including foreigners. Application grants must, however, be submitted in Lithuanian, posing a language and administrative barrier for non-native speakers applying for funding schemes. The Research Council of Lithuania has been trying to introduce changes, but encountered difficulties with legal requirements (e.g., the need to abide by rules about Lithuanian as a state language). Proposals in some fields, especially within the technical and natural sciences, now have to be completed in both English and Lithuanian, which entails an excessive amount of translation procedures and costs for researchers. This language requirement also means that peer review to evaluate research proposals mostly takes place in Lithuanian, which creates various quality- and cronyism-related problems so common in small academic systems isolated from global science networks. Moreover, it has been criticized that funding is very hard to obtain in research fields that are not regarded "top-priority" fields (Interviewee 4).

### Integration and Impact of International Academic Staff

International academic staff at Vilnius University regard themselves as well integrated into university life. Due to the low numbers of internationals in most faculties and departments, internationals are unlikely to constitute an isolated group. Integration occurs mainly on personal levels and through contacts with colleagues within each academic's own department or faculty. Integration into decision-making bodies, such as the university senate, in contrast, rarely occurs and is deemed extraordinarily difficult, primarily because of language barriers:

> It is not so easy to be a member of any decision-making body at the university if you don't know the language because no one will conduct a meeting in English or in another language.
>
> *(Interviewee 5)*

Respondents were very positive about their relationships with their Lithuanian colleagues. None of them has ever felt any personal discrimination because of their origin or felt like an outsider at any point during their stay at Vilnius University. If there are any tensions, these usually occur as a result of generation clashes, attempts by older generations of local faculty to protect their positions within the university, and suspicion among local academic staff toward the still rather novel phenomenon of internationalization:

> So we asked them what they thought was the most important thing that they had learned during their studies. One of my students answered: "He

[the interviewee] taught me how to think independently!" (. . .) Some of my older colleagues stopped talking to me for days. (. . .) Discussions were not desired, students had to take what was offered to them without murmuring and complaining. But now, traditional structures have broken up. Many of my younger colleagues (. . .) have grown up with this new spirit.

*(Interviewee 3)*

Some of our professors do not have international experience at all. Therefore, they look very cautiously at any claim that you say that you should internationalize. Sometimes their [English] language skills are below average. (. . .) So I would say some psychological aspects are still there.

*(Interviewee 5)*

A further concern for the integration of returning expats is suspicion from local Lithuanians. In a recent study, Žvalionytė (2015) found that a majority of employers and almost half of the Lithuanian population think that people who return to Lithuania have failed abroad. Consistent patterns can also be found for local Lithuanian academic staff members' perceptions of their returning colleagues, which also do not help with integration into the local higher education system and department:

So a lot of people who were back were looked at a bit suspiciously: Why are you back? It is so good abroad, why are you back? Inside everybody wants to get bigger salaries (. . .) and when you are back you have to prove that you are not a loser, because when you are a loser you might come back, this could be their thinking.

*(Interviewee 2)*

In terms of support structures for international faculty, language courses have been noted as important. International academics who have come to Vilnius University in recent years report that they have been made aware of the opportunity to take Lithuanian language classes, which are free of charge and are provided by the Faculty of Philology. Otherwise, there are no specific support structures to facilitate the quality of life and integration of international academic staff at Vilnius University. At the same time, international academics enjoy the same rights as local academic staff and can turn to the VU science and innovation unit for help in research matters and to the international office for other inquiries or problems. Most, however, do not use these structures and instead draw upon support provided by personal contacts, such as Lithuanian spouses, friends, and colleagues.

Despite the lack of institutional-level support structures and other unfavorable conditions mentioned earlier, international academic staff members at Vilnius

University report high levels of satisfaction with both their personal and their working life. The large majority of respondents could not imagine leaving Lithuania again, apart from short-term stays or spending a sabbatical year abroad. Most of the interviewees who have come to Lithuania for personal reasons stay at Vilnius University for the same reasons. Those who were motivated to come to Lithuania by other factors reported that they decided to stay because of a general interest in the country; because of a fascination with the Lithuanian language, history and culture; or because they have met a Lithuanian partner or established close ties in other ways with locals while working at Vilnius University.

Again, salary came up as the most common reason for international academics to leave Vilnius University. As expressed by one interviewee: "People come, people stay for some time, but eventually they look for better salaries" (Interviewee 2). Other reasons to leave Vilnius University included lack of funding to continue one's academic position and strain related to long-distance relationships between international academics and their spouses. With regard to the latter, it is important to note that Vilnius University does not (yet) offer dual-career services to the spouses of new and potential academic staff.

The share of international academic staff at Vilnius University is still much too small to draw clear conclusions about their impact within the university. Yet, both local academics and administrators, as well as international academics themselves, report that international academics have an impact on the internationalization of Vilnius University. They use their own resources and personal networks to establish Erasmus+ connections and new scientific collaborations, and promote VU and its research and teaching activities within their networks.

> It is just networking and putting Lithuania into our networking and also helping the old Europe not to be so cold—it is like there is a different bond and it could help to be more open, to have a different view, not just talking about France and Spain and England like it is all there is but opening up a whole new world.
>
> *(Interviewee 7)*

University administrators have high hopes that once VU succeeds in attracting a critical mass of international academic staff, it will benefit from enhanced international visibility within academic circles and among prospective students. However, given the main obstacle of low salaries, clear structural and financial changes are urgently needed, coupled with well-advertised and transparent recruitment procedures that are accessible internationally. Further, a clear strategy for staff internationalization, which is supported by actions that improve support structures for international faculty, are the only way to ensure that VU can eventually be perceived as an international, faculty-friendly university.

## Discussion

Demographic change fueled by high levels of emigration has led to increasing competition for students among a large number of higher education institutions both in Lithuania and Estonia. In both countries, there is an increasing awareness of the need to attract talent from abroad as one part of the solution to deal with the competition in policy and academic circles. However, as we have seen, both countries—even though they use some policy instruments for attracting foreign faculty, like research funding initiatives—in fact fail to clearly articulate this issue as a priority and indeed as one of the main issues to ensure the survival and quality of both higher education systems.

Our case study of Vilnius University in Lithuania has revealed the lack of a clear institutional strategy for attracting, hiring, and integrating international academic staff. Although the importance of international academic staff for helping to ensure the quality of teaching and research, and for enhancing the international cooperation and visibility of the university, have been recognized both by academics and administrators, no specific strategy or policy has yet been articulated. Additionally, salary levels are very low, by any standard, but particularly in comparison with other European countries (for similar findings see Leišytė, 2013; Paliokaitė, 2014a, 2014b).

According to a recent study by INOMICS (2015), the most important motivations for international academic staff mobility in several countries worldwide include the attractiveness of a high-quality research environment; a high degree of professional flexibility; freedom, autonomy, and independence; and lower teaching loads. The most important negative factors inhibiting mobility include low levels of salary and funding, a lack of opportunities for career development, and having to deal with bureaucracy and administrative procedures. These findings contrast partially with our results from Vilnius University. Although a certain degree of academic autonomy was mentioned by some respondents as a positive aspect of working at Vilnius University, it does not figure among the most important motivations to come to Lithuania. Instead, nearly all respondents reported that their decisions to move to Lithuania and work at Vilnius University were motivated by personal factors, such as Lithuanian spouses; Lithuanian roots; a general interest in the country and its language, culture, and history; or the wish to experience and establish something new. Furthermore, some respondents coming from countries with less favorable conditions in academia reported better career opportunities as a motivation. Low levels of salary, research funding limitations (especially from international and European Union sources), and bureaucratic burdens (particularly tied to applications for research funding) were criticized by respondents. However, these factors did not affect their decisions to move to Lithuania. Language barriers were criticized, especially with regard to grant applications, which have to be completed in Lithuanian or, in some cases, in both Lithuanian and in

English. In everyday life situations, on the other hand, language barriers were less existent.

A similar situation can be found in Estonia. According to an academic mobility study in 2006, a high-quality research environment and opportunities for career enhancement ranked among the least important factors that influence the motivation of international academics to move to the country (Murakas et al., 2007). In contrast, establishing and experiencing something new, an interest in Estonia, the Estonian language and culture, or an interest in the Baltics in general, and other personal aspects—such as an Estonian spouse, friends, or Estonian roots—ranked among the most important motivations to work at an Estonian university (Murakas et al., 2007). In the study of Murakas et al. (2007), international academics at Estonian universities criticized difficulties with legal procedures and language barriers, as well as problems in handling bureaucratic and administrative procedures. While at the time of the study (2006) insufficient remuneration was criticized by respondents, salary levels for researchers in Estonia have increased in recent years, although they are still hardly comparable to other European countries.

Although attracting international academic staff has proven a highly difficult task for universities in Lithuania, the Estonian higher education sector has witnessed a more significant increase in the share of international academic staff since its accession to the European Union in 2004. The differences between the two countries might be attributed to the fact that—in contrast to Lithuania, where clear strategies are lacking at both national and institutional levels—Estonia has issued clear national strategies for internationalization and an obligation for all public universities to implement institutional policies for attracting and integrating international students and academic staff. Additionally, in comparison to their Lithuanian counterparts, Estonian universities participate more actively in the European researcher mobility initiative EURAXESS, including the provision of support to foreign researchers interested in working at Estonian universities and by advertising academic posts internationally. International recruitment of faculty thus is more a reality in Estonia than in Lithuania.

It must be underlined that Lithuania and Estonia are far from alone with respect to the challenges they face regarding incoming academic staff mobility. In fact, similar situations prevail across a wide range of other Central and Eastern European countries. The 2011 audit study of the research system of the Czech Republic, for example, revealed remarkable resemblances, especially to the Lithuanian case, with respect to low levels of incoming mobility; lack of transparency and openness of recruitment processes; and salaries that are far below the EU average (Leišytė et al., 2011). While some of these barriers are endemic in peripheral systems in transition, the national framework conditions are crucial for changing this situation. From this study we see that for small countries that are at the periphery, it is extremely difficult to attract top talent with a limited resource base in today's globalized and competitive academic labor market. Although we have witnessed initiatives for internationalization of faculty in both systems—with Estonia being a bit more open to international recruitment than Lithuania—brain drain in these countries seems to be the first problem to be addressed to ensure that talented people do not leave these countries in the first place. For that, salaries must be made at least somewhat comparable to other European countries so that the systems may become more attractive to local as well as to foreign academic talent.

The case study has shown a good practice of what can be done by engaging in public–private partnerships and creating truly international research centers. However, a much more aggressive and strategic reform of internationalization is needed at both policy and institutional levels in both countries we have considered here—not only with respect to the quality of higher education, but also with regard to the sustainability of higher education in these peripheral systems.

## References

Altbach, P. G. (2004). Globalisation and the university: Myths and realities in an unequal world. *Tertiary Education & Management, 10*(1), 3–25.

Archimedes (2013). *Study in Estonia*. Tallinn: Archimedes Foundation.

Archimedes (2015). Higher education institutions. Retrieved from http://archimedes.ee/en/education-system/higher-education-institutions/

Barcevičius, E. (2015). How successful are highly qualified return migrants in the Lithuanian labour market? *International Migration*. Retrieved from http://onlinelibrary.wiley.com/doi/10.1111/imig.12224/full. doi: 10.111/imig.12224

Centre for Quality Assessment in Higher Education (2013). *Institutional review report Vilnius university*. Vilnius: Studijų kokybės vertinimo centras.

Christensen, T. A., Freireich, S., Kolar, J., & Nybergh, P. (2012). *Peer-review of the Estonian research and innovation system—Steady progress towards knowledge society*. Expert Group Report prepared for the European Research Area Committee. Tallinn: Innovation Studies.

Ciubrinskas, V. (2013). Diaspora as a resource of homeland nationalism forged overseas and contested back home—The case of Lithuanian-Americans. In W. Kokot, C. Giordano & M. Gandelsman (Eds.), *Diaspora as a resource. Comparative studies in strategies, networks and urban space* (105–122). Berlin: Lit Verlag.

EMN—European Migration Network (2015). Who is coming to Lithuania? Retrieved from http://123.emn.lt/en/immigration/who-is-coming-to-lithuania

European Commission (2015). Study in Europe: Country profile Estonia. Retrieved from http://ec.europa.eu/education/study-in-europe/country-profiles/estonia_en.htm

European Parliament (2009). *Cross-border mobility of young researchers* [PE 416.244]. Luxembourg: Publications Office of the European Union.

Eurostat (2014). *Main scenario—Population on 1st January by sex and single year* (datafile). Retrieved from http://appsso.eurostat.ec.europa.eu/nui/show.do?dataset=proj_13npms&lang=en

Eurostat (2015a) *EU Blue Cards by type of decision, occupation and citizenship* (datafile). Retrieved from http://appsso.eurostat.ec.europa.eu/nui/show.do?dataset=migr_resbc1&lang=en

Eurostat (2015b). *Researchers (HC) in government and higher education sector by citizenship and sex* (datafile). Retrieved from http://appsso.eurostat.ec.europa.eu/nui/show.do?dataset=rd_p_perscitz&lang=en

Eurostat (2015c). Students enrolled in tertiary education by education level, programme orientation, sex, type of institution and intensity of participation (datafile). Retrieved from http://appsso.eurostat.ec.europa.eu/nui/show.do?dataset=educ_uoe_enrt01&lang=en

Eurostat (2015d). Total researchers by sector of performance (datafile). Retrieved from http://appsso.eurostat.ec.europa.eu/nui/show.do?dataset=educ_uoe_enrt01&lang=en

Hughes, R. (2008). Internationalisation of higher education and language policy: Questions of quality and equity. *Higher Education Management and Policy, 20*(1), 102–119.

Kaiser, F., Faber, M., Jongbloed, B., File, J., & van Vught, F. (2011). *Implementing U-Map in Estonia—2011 case study report*. Enschede: Centre for Higher Education Policy Studies (CHEPS).

Leišytė, L. (2002). *Higher education governance in post-Soviet Lithuania*. Oslo: University of Oslo, Institute for Educational Research.

Leišytė, L. (2013). *Changes in Lithuanian Higher Education and Research: Being at the Crossroads.* Presentation at the *Futura Scientia* International Workshop "Soviet Past and European Future: Endless Transition in Higher Education and Research", 15 November, Vilnius.

Leišytė, L. (2014). The transformation of university governance in central and Eastern Europe: Its antecedents and consequences. *Leadership and Governance of Higher Education, 1*(1–4). Raabe Verlag. Retrieved from www.lg-handbook.info

Leišytė, L., Benneworth, P., File, J., Kottmann, A., & de Weert, E. (2011). Human resources in R&D. *Final Report No. 7 of the International Audit of Research, Development & Innovation in the Czech Republic*. Brighton: Technopolis Group.

Leišytė, L., & Kizniene, D. (2006). New public management in Lithuania's higher education. *Higher Education Policy, 19*(3), 377–396.

Leišytė, L., Navickience, V., Zelvys, R., & Zenkiene, L. (2009). *The Understanding of the Bologna Process in Lithuanian Higher Education*. Paper presented at the 31st Annual EAIR Forum, 23–26 August, 2009, Vilnius.

Leišytė, L., Zelvys, R., & Zenkiene, L. (2015). Re-contextualization of the Bologna process in Lithuania. *European Journal of Higher Education, 5*(1), 49–67.

Loonurm, E. (2014). *The future of higher education in small countries*. Published online on the platform of the European Association for International Education on September 16, 2014. Retrieved from www.eaie.org/blog/higher-education-in-small-countries/

Miller, L., Mateeva, E., & Nekrassova, N. (2011). The internationalization of Estonian higher education: How the Estonian cultural context impacts the experience of foreign students. *Baltic Journal of European Studies, 2*(1), 103–118.

Ministry of Education and Science (MoE) (2016). *The plan for the improvement of higher education quality*. Vilnius: Ministry of Education and Science of the Republic of Lithuania.

MORE2 (2012). Interim report—country profile renumeration Lithuania. Retrieved from http://ec.europa.eu/euraxess/pdf/research_policies/more2/country_files_more2/2013_07_05_country_profile_LT.pdf

MORE2 (2013). Renumeration—cross-country report. Retrieved from http://ec.europa.eu/euraxess/pdf/research_policies/more2/Report%20on%20case%20study%20of%20researchers_%20remuneration.pdf

Murakas, R., Soidla, I., Kasearu, K., Toots, I., Rämmer, A., Lepik, A., Reinomägi, S., Telpt, E., & Suvi, H. (2007). *Researcher mobility in Estonia and factors that influence mobility*. Tallinn: Archimedes Foundation.

Paliokaitė, A. (2014a). ERAWATCH Country Reports 2012: Lithuania. *JRC Science and Policy Reports*. Luxembourg: Publications Office of the European Union.

Paliokaitė, A. (2014b). ERAWATCH Country Reports 2013: Lithuania. *JRC Science and Policy Reports*. Luxembourg: Publications Office of the European Union.

Petrauskas, V. (2013, October 18). *Collaborative EU scientific projects and the salaries in Eastern and Western Europe.* Presentation held at the 3rd One Baltic Sea Region Policy Round Table Discussion, Gdansk.

Renc-Roe, J. (2011). *Academics in transition—Internationalisation of academic professionals in Eastern Europe and the former Soviet Union.* PhD thesis. Staffordshire: Keele University Department of Educational Studies.

Researchers' Report (2014a). *Researchers' Report 2014—Country Profile: Estonia.* Deloitte.

Researchers' Report (2014b). *Researchers' Report 2014—Country Profile: Lithuania.* Deloitte.

Researchers' Report (2014c). *Researchers' Report 2014—Final Report.* Deloitte.

Researchers' Report (2014d). *Researchers' Report 2014—Scorecards.* Deloitte.

Ritzen, J. (2013, October 22). *Challenges for University Policy in Lithuania.* Presentation at the EIB Round Table on the Future of Higher Education, Vilnius.

Ruttas-Küttim, R. (2014). ERAWATCH Country Reports 2013: Estonia. *JRC Science and Policy Reports.* Luxembourg: Publications Office of the European Union.

Schmidt-Nielsen, B., Saglamer, G., Brudermann, G., Brudermann, U., & McQuillan, D. (2011). Brussels: *Vilnius university: Evaluation report.* EUA Institutional Evaluation Programme.

Scott, P. (2015). Dynamics of academic mobility: Hegemonic internationalisation or fluid globalisation. *European Review, 23*(1), 55–69.

U-Multirank (2015). At a glance: Vilnius University. Retrieved from www.umultirank.org/#!/explore?trackType=explore&detailUniversity=124&section=exploreUniversityDetail

University of Tartu (2016). Salary rules. Retrieved from www.ut.ee/en/university/structure-and-staff/employment/documents

Vilnius University (2013a). Facts and figures 2013. Retrieved from www.vu.lt/site_files/InfS/Leidiniai/VU_Facts_Figures_2013.pdf

Vilnius University (2013b). *Regulation on the performance assessment of the pedagogical and research staff and on the order of organizing open competitions at Vilnius University* [17 December 2013, Protocol No. S-2013–8-]. Retrieved from www.vu.lt/site_files/PeD/Regulations-on-Certification-and-Open-Competitions.pdf

Vilnius University (2015). Facts and Figures. Retrieved from www.vu.lt/en/about-us/facts-and-figures

Želvys, R. (2004). Governance of higher education in Lithuania: Challenges of the Soviet past and perspectives of the global future. *Pedagogika, 75,* 7–11.

Žvalionytė, D. (2015). Being a return migrant—Advantage or disadvantage in Lithuanian labour market? *Politologija, 78,* 58–93.

# 7
# RECRUITMENT AND INTEGRATION OF INTERNATIONAL FACULTY AT GERMAN UNIVERSITIES

The Case of the University of Konstanz

*Martin Bruder and C. Giovanni Galizia*

### Germany: An *Einwanderungsland* for the Best Scientists?

Although Germany has been accommodating substantial numbers of refugees and immigrants for some years, Germans have realized—and many have started to embrace the notion—that their country has become an *Einwanderungsland* (land of immigration). In fact, for each year since 2012, Germany has attracted the second largest number of immigrants in the world, after the United States (OECD, 2015a). However, whether Germany is also an attractive destination for the world's top academic talent is not quite as clear.

In this chapter, we first outline four distinctive features of the German research and higher education system that are important for understanding the context of efforts to recruit, support, and integrate international academics. We also provide some facts and figures on German universities. Besides full professors, *mid-career, nontenured academics with independent track records* (which we refer to in this chapter as 'mid-career academics') emerge as the central group of interest when it comes to recruiting, supporting, and integrating international faculty. We highlight legal provisions as well as national strategies, actors, and funding programs relevant to the internationalization of university faculty. We then turn to the University of Konstanz as an example of an internationally visible, research-oriented university that has been active in establishing novel strategies, structures, and regulations to attract and accommodate international faculty. We conclude by summarizing our findings and assessing the prospects for Germany to be an attractive *Einwanderungsland* for international academics.

## Distinctive Features of the German Research and Higher Education System

When analyzing the recruitment, support, and integration of international faculty, four distinctive features of research and higher education in Germany need to be taken into account.

### The Public Funding of the German System

OECD (2015b) data indicate that public expenditure in Germany accounts for 85.9 percent of all expenditure on tertiary education institutions. This is markedly above the Organisation for Economic Co-operation and Development (OECD) average of 69.7 percent. Although 158 of 427 German universities[1] (i.e., 37 percent) are run privately or by churches, these only account for some 8 percent of the student population.[2] Private funding, therefore, plays a rather limited role in German tertiary education; we will thus focus on public universities only.

### The Prominent Role of Nonuniversity Research Institutions

Nonuniversity research institutions successfully attract researchers from abroad because they offer some of the best research conditions in Germany. The Max Planck Society (focusing on basic science), with 34 percent non-German scientific staff; the Helmholtz Association (advancing large-scale science) and the Leibniz Association (combining their own research with research infrastructure functions), with 20 percent non-German academic staff each; and the Fraunhofer-Gesellschaft (specializing in applied science), with 9 percent non-German scientific staff[3]—together consist of about 250 nonuniversity research institutes. In 2014, the total expenditure for research and innovation of these four institutions alone was EUR 9.6 billion, with approximately 73,000 full-time equivalent (FTE) research staff. This compares to EUR 14.3 billion and 131,000 FTE research staff at universities (Federal Statistical Office, 2016a).

Nonuniversity research institutions have, in part, used yearly budget increases of between 3 and 5 percent since 2005, as well as administrative deregulation by the so-called Academic Freedom Act of 2012, to attract "the world's leading researchers" (Max Planck Society, 2015a, p. 6). In fact, as of January 1, 2015, 31.5 percent of the 22,000 employees at Max Planck did not have German citizenship (Max Planck Society, 2015b). However, given our focus on international university faculty, we will not discuss the specific role of nonuniversity institutions in any detail.

### The Federal Nature of the German Higher Education System

The freedoms of nonuniversity research institutions are not matched by those of German universities. Universities are under the budgetary supervision (and constraints) of the federal states (*Länder*), not the federal government. Only in November 2014 did a change of the German constitution allow the federal government to contribute to the university system on a structural (rather than temporary project) basis. The consequences of this change remain yet to be seen.

Public funding and the budget constraints of the federal states also mean that flexibility in terms of salaries for university faculty is limited. International and national faculty are paid on the same public service pay scale, ranging roughly from EUR 50,000 (for junior professors and junior research group leaders) to EUR 85,000 (for the basic salary of a full professor) per year. Additional payments can be made for new appointees, for positions with particular responsibilities, and for academic performance. Although this gives universities limited flexibility in incentivizing top researchers to come to Germany, it still puts German universities at a disadvantage compared to international institutions and nonuniversity research institutions in Germany when it comes to recruiting the very best researchers.

## *German Universities as Professorial Institutions*

Full professors at German public universities are the most powerful stakeholder group. There were about 46,000 full and nontenured junior professors at German universities as of December 2014 (assistant or associate professorships do not exist in the German context). At the same time, 190,000 scientific staff without tenure (with few exceptions) were also employed (Federal Statistical Office, 2015a).[4] Tenure-track options are only now being piloted. Thus, the academic job market in Germany is characterized, on the one hand, by a very flexible situation for nontenured junior and mid-career researchers (including junior professors and independent junior research group leaders). On the other hand, there is a highly regulated job market for full professorships. Although this is true, generally speaking, for most countries, the extent to which these two markets are separated from each other in Germany has been recognized as a challenge to the competitiveness of German universities and as an area requiring action by the federal government, aimed at creating more predictable career opportunities (CDU, CSU & SPD, 2013).

## Some Basic Figures About Germany's University System

The total expenditure of German universities in 2013 amounted to just above EUR 46 billion—including the previously mentioned EUR 14.4 billion for research and innovation activities (Federal Statistical Office, 2015b), 50 percent more than in 2005. However, with 1.2 percent of its gross domestic product spent on tertiary education, Germany still falls short of the OECD average of 1.5 percent (OECD, 2015b).

In the winter semester of 2015–2016, 2.76 million students were studying at German universities (Federal Statistical Office, 2016b) with 339,000 of them of non-German nationality. Although this is the highest absolute number ever enrolled in German higher education, the share of noncitizen students declined slightly from 12.5 percent in 2005 to 12.3 percent in 2016 due to increasing numbers of German students. Still, Germany is well on track to reach its internationalization target of 350,000 noncitizen students by 2020 (CDU, CSU & SPD, 2013).

In 2014, 3,001 (or 6.6 percent) of 45,749 professors at German universities were non-Germans. Of the remaining 190,615 academic staff, 24,986 (13.1 percent) were non-Germans.[5] In addition to international academic staff, in 2013 there were approximately 52,000 visiting international academics spending time in Germany for varying lengths of time (Bruder, Benneworth, File, Kottmann & de Weert, 2015).

In terms of publications, a recent analysis of Thomson Reuters' Web of Science database (Mund, Conchi & Frietsch, 2015) revealed that Germany accounts for 4.9 percent of the global published research output listed in that database. Therefore, Germany ranks third behind the United States (20.8 percent) and China (14.2 percent).

Germany has 20 universities ranked in the top 200 of the *Times Higher Education* World University Rankings 2015–2016. This makes it the third most-represented country in these rankings after the United States and the United Kingdom.

## International Mobility of Academics: Legal Provisions

German legal provisions concerning entry into and residency in Germany have been liberal, when compared internationally, since the Immigration Act of 2005. Through the European Union (EU) Freedom of Movement Act, scientists from other EU member states can take up residence in Germany and work at German universities after registering with the local authorities (providing proof of adequate financial resources and health insurance coverage).

Non-EU nationals moving to Germany for more than three months must apply for a national visa at a German diplomatic mission abroad (this is true even for 'privileged' foreigners allowed to enter Germany for less than three months without a visa). To obtain the visa, applicants must present proof of a concrete job offer, proof of secure financial resources (e.g., an employment contract), and proof of adequate health insurance coverage. The visa is later changed into a residence permit (e.g., for research purposes). Detailed information on relevant legal provisions has been published by the German Academic Exchange Service (commonly known as the DAAD) (2010).

We do not consider legal requirements, in principle, to constitute a major detriment to German universities' ability to recruit international faculty. In particular, the provision that international students can stay on in Germany for 18 months after completing their degree for job search purposes has been a real pull factor to come to Germany. This is notwithstanding the fact that the individual experience of communicating with the relevant German authorities can be less than welcoming for foreigners. In other words, whereas the letter of the law is relatively liberal, the actual experience is sometimes closer to the original full title of the Immigration Act, which is "Act to Control and Restrict Immigration and to Regulate the Residence and Integration of EU Citizens and Foreigners." No mention of *Einwanderungsland* is made here.

## International Mobility of Academics: National Strategies

The general strategy of the federal government concerning internationalization in science and research, dating from 2008 (Federal Ministry of Education and Research, 2008), formulates the basis of the government's activities in this area. It explicitly states that Germany should become "one of the first addresses for the best researchers and students from all over the world" (p. 5). This strategy is steeped in the brain drain/brain gain debate and addresses concerns that Germany may lose its best scientists to competitors—a longstanding worry that has been rekindled by a controversial recent report of a government advisory body (Commission of Experts in Research and Innovation, 2014, p. 86). The 2008 strategy addresses the need for German researchers to gain international experience and cultivate networks with the best peers worldwide. At the same time, the strategy emphasizes that it needs to be attractive both for expatriate researchers to return to Germany and for the best international researchers to come to Germany on a long-term basis.

More specific plans for action were detailed by the Federal Ministry of Education and Research (2014). The action plan on international cooperation adopts a broader perspective on German competitiveness in an interconnected world than the original strategy. It quotes another major government advisory body, the German Council of Science and Humanities (2013):

> As international interconnectedness grows, the world's nations find themselves in a global competition in which they must seek to make their science systems as capable as possible, so that those systems can contribute significantly to their economic and political importance.
>
> *(p. 19)*

Thus, the focus of the action plan is to make Germany attractive for science and research, with large-scale research infrastructures playing a prominent role in this context. However, the action plan also highlights the need to further develop a "culture of welcome" at German institutions and the marketing of Germany's research resources.

Because German universities fall under the responsibility of the federal states, a specific internationalization strategy for higher education institutions was agreed upon by the federal government and all state governments in 2013 (Joint Science

Conference, 2013). It sets out nine areas of action for which shared goals are formulated. One action area (number 7) directly relates to recruiting excellent international (junior) scientists.

## International Mobility of Academics: Actors and Programs

It is beyond the scope of this chapter to outline all actors and funding programs relevant to recruiting and supporting international researchers for work at German universities. We will briefly mention five main actors.

The Federal Ministry of Education and Research (BMBF), together with the state governments, funds the Excellence Initiative (running 2007–2017, with a budget of EUR 2.7 billion between 2011 and 2017 alone). It has enabled some German universities to professionalize their internationalization activities and recruit and better support excellent international researchers. The German Academic Exchange Service (DAAD) and the Alexander von Humboldt Foundation (AvH) are the main German institutions promoting international mobility. The DAAD plays an important role in coordinating recruitment activities and offers some scholarship programs relevant to mid-career researchers. The AvH runs several prestigious funding programs targeting leading international scientists. For long-term recruitment, the Sofja Kovalevskaja Award for outstanding junior research group leaders and the Alexander von Humboldt Professorship for recognized leaders in their field are particularly relevant.

The Emmy Noether Research Groups and the Heisenberg Program, run by the *Deutsche Forschungsgemeinschaft* (German Research Foundation, DFG), target similar groups and are also open to international applicants. Together, the DAAD, AvH, and DFG run the German Academic International Network (GAIN), aimed at recruiting German scientists working abroad for a future career at German institutions. Besides the national agencies, all core funding schemes of the European Research Council (ERC) offer prestigious opportunities for international mobility within Europe.

We now turn to our case example, the University of Konstanz. We chose this university because it has deliberately taken the decision in recent years to strengthen international recruitment and develop a research-based, internationally aspiring academic institution. In discussing the recruitment, selection, and support of international researchers at the University of Konstanz, we address both of the central groups identified earlier: mid-career scientists/academics and full professors.

## Basic Facts about the University of Konstanz

Located on beautiful Lake Constance in southern Germany, the University of Konstanz was founded in 1966 as a "reform university." The university is structured in three faculties, each with several departments: the Faculty of Sciences; the Faculty of Humanities; and the Faculty of Politics, Law, and Economics. The most prominent disciplines not represented include medicine, engineering, and the arts. In addition, a number of institutional structures are funded by the Excellence Initiative. Among these is the *Zukunftskolleg*, an interdisciplinary institution that is home to junior research group leaders (i.e., nontenured mid-career researchers) of all the disciplines represented at the university.

The University of Konstanz is a relatively small university with 11,410 students in the winter semester of 2013–2014.[6] Of these, 1,370 (or 12 percent) were non-German citizens.

In terms of staff, the University of Konstanz has a total of 1,301 academic staff (reference year 2014),[7] of which 260 (or 20 percent) are internationals. In 2014, the university employed 198 professors (including 173 full professors and 25 junior professors), among whom there were 26 (or 13.1 percent) who did not have German citizenship. The percentages of total international scientific staff and international professors compare favorably with the average percentages (in 2014) of these groups at German universities, where 11.8 percent of all academic staff and 6.6 percent of professors are non-Germans.[8]

International professors come predominantly from other European countries. Of the 26 non-German professors, only 1 is from outside Europe and 11 are from neighboring Switzerland (see Figure 7.1), suggesting that the above-average

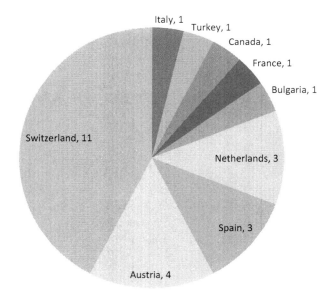

**FIGURE 7.1** International Professors at the University of Konstanz by Country of Origin (2014).

*Source*: German Federal Statistical Office, calculations by DZHW/www.wissenschaft-weltoffen.

number of international professors at Konstanz is partly due to its border location with Switzerland. For other scientific staff, the share of non-Europeans is markedly higher, with just under one-third of all international scientific staff (excluding professors) coming from outside Europe (see Figure 7.2). Also, the number of Swiss scientists in this category (14) suggests that the relatively high share of international nonprofessorial scientific staff is not due to the border location alone.

In 2013, the university had a net budget of approximately EUR 182 million (with EUR 114 million being allocated to personnel expenses). The University of Konstanz has a strong tradition of acquiring third-party funding (which totaled EUR 62 million in 2013). In fact, the university took first place in a recent ranking on funding acquisition (*Deutsche Forschungsgemeinschaft*, 2015, p. 65).

A notable change in the university budget came with its highly successful participation in the Excellence Initiative, as of 2007 (worth EUR 23.5 million, or more than one-third of third-party funding in 2014 alone). In particular, Konstanz was one of 11 universities that successfully applied to become a "University of Excellence." The institutional strategy, called "Modell Konstanz—Towards a Culture of Creativity," prominently includes internationalization activities and the establishment of the *Zukunftskolleg*.

Furthermore, the institution's positions on international rankings attest to the international visibility of the University of Konstanz. Most notably, the university

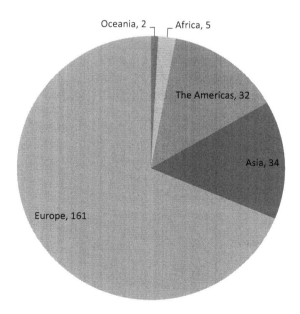

**FIGURE 7.2** International Scientific Staff (Excluding Professors) at the University of Konstanz by Region of Origin (2014).

Source: German Federal Statistical Office, calculations by DZHW/www.wissenschaft-weltoffen.de.

features in the *Times Higher Education* World University Rankings 2015–2016 at rank 175.

The subsequent sections draw heavily on several interviews that we conducted with members of the University of Konstanz. These include Prof. Dr. Winfried Pohlmeier (Vice Rector for Research and Young Researchers), Dr. Nani Clow (Head of International Office), Ms. Julia Wandt (Head of Communications and Marketing), Dr. Christine Abele (Head of Quality Management), and Ms. Sigrid Elmer (Officer of Public Relations and Knowledge Transfer at the *Zukunftskolleg*). Further information was provided by Ms. Michaela Potthast (Head of Controlling).

We will also draw on two recent studies that are particularly relevant for describing the situation of international university faculty in Germany: Wegner (2016) conducted a nationwide study on postdoctoral and mid-career scientists in Germany. Neusel and colleagues (2014) investigated international professors at universities in the federal states of Berlin and Hesse. We believe these studies provide a more complete picture of the situation of international faculty in Germany than we could provide by interviewing a small number of Konstanz faculty.

## Recruiting International Faculty: Motivation, Activities, and Outcomes

The main motivations for international scientists to come to Germany are:

1. Being able to collaborate with experts at the host institution
2. Being able to use attractive research infrastructures/make use of attractive research conditions at the host institution
3. The high reputation of the host institution
4. Germany's scientific reputation (Wegner, 2016)

Abele's evaluation work at the *Zukunftskolleg* shows that, whereas goals related to research and collaboration opportunities and reputation are relevant to all fellows, access to research infrastructure (including laboratories, but also knowledge infrastructures such as libraries) is a particular concern of international scientists. In short, international scientists focus on addressing their own best questions, together with the best scientists, using the best infrastructure at the best institutions in a highly regarded research market. This focus on 'excellence' is mirrored by those at the University of Konstanz responsible for recruiting faculty. The main motive to recruit international faculty clearly is to increase scientific quality. As Pohlmeier put it:

> The goal of our strategy is not to have any particular number of international scientists. We simply want the best scientists that we can get to come

to Konstanz. If these are 90 percent internationals, so be it. Internationalization is not an end in itself; we simply want to get the best we can.

Within this theme, "the best" are defined mainly by their research prowess. They are expected to publish successfully in top international journals and attract external funding. We will follow this 'excellence theme' further and see how it fits with the institutional practices and structures of the university.

Besides scientific excellence, all interviewees mention other motives for recruiting international faculty. These include:

- Internationalization at home. This involves enriching student experience, for example, by exposing them to international teachers who bring their own teaching methods and styles, as well as specific scientific perspectives and intellectual approaches.
- Serving a broader "European project." As Clow put it:

    In order to make the European project work, you need to have intense exchange—both scientific and cultural. For the countries to understand each other, they have to have the experience of 'the other.' Research does not happen just within one country. It happens in a global, but for us, importantly, also in a European environment.

- Advancing international cooperation. Acquiring European funding is seen as a major showcase of a university's qualities (including vis-à-vis the education and research ministries at the state level). International scientists are expected to have closer links to relevant partners abroad—a belief that is well founded in empirical studies (Neusel et al., 2014). These networks are perceived as instrumental for developing successful cooperative grant proposals.
- Increasing international visibility. Internationalization plays a small part in some global university rankings. Improving one's position in these rankings is seen as a positive side effect of internationalization activities.

The internationalization strategy of the University of Konstanz has three goals. First, to create and improve the basis for international cooperation. Second, to foster outward mobility of home students and staff. Third, to recruit highly qualified international undergraduate, graduate, and doctoral students, as well as the best international scientists. Whereas there is a specific target of 30 percent international recruitment for doctoral students, there are no specific targets for nontenured scientists and for professors. Still, the university clearly has committed itself to further efforts in relation to international recruitment.

As Wandt points out, these efforts have received a substantial boost with the success of the institutional strategy that was put forward for the Excellence Initiative in 2007. Today, the Communications and Marketing unit has 17 staff members (although not all of them full-time) and connects external and internal communications, public and media relations (press office), online communications (Internet, intranet, social media), international communications, national and international marketing, corporate design, corporate publishing, event and conference management, and alumni management and fundraising.

As for recruitment, Wandt draws a clear distinction between three groups: undergraduate and graduate students, doctoral students and early postdoctoral researchers, and the two groups of more experienced scientists (mid-career scientists and professors) that are the focus of this chapter. For the third group, recruitment efforts are designed individually and take into account the specific characteristics of the respective university department, the available scientific networks in the relevant research area, and the specifics of the academic job market in the field. As Wandt puts it, there is "no off-the-shelf solution. There are hardly any general ideas and strategies, but we look individually at each department and their existing networks." The only common denominator she identifies is that the main message of any recruitment effort will concern the specific strengths of a research-oriented, dynamic university, which is how the University of Konstanz perceives itself. This individualized approach requires Wandt's unit to be involved in recruitment activities from a very early stage. She explains

> Marketing is not advertisement. Advertisement is only the final step. But we are in touch with the departments already much earlier. We accompany the strategic processes from the beginning. In the end, the details of a position and the structures in which it is situated—what is called the 'product' in marketing—count a lot. We are able to listen in on the meetings and make recommendations. Because in the end you can only support and implement what is there.

Due to its close contact with the target groups of the communication efforts, Wandt believes her unit can act as an early warning system, helping to avoid decisions that fail to adequately consider the needs and concerns of the target audiences.

As for the advertisement itself, both for mid-career scientists and for professors, print and online advertisements go into academic journals, international news journals, and international online platforms, as well as discipline-specific communication channels. The Communications and Marketing unit closely cooperates with regional experts of the International Office to design culturally sensitive advertising. For example, whereas the landmark Imperia statue in Konstanz harbor—referring to a famous prostitute who held legendary powers over both pope and king during the Roman Catholic Council of Constance in 1414–1418—may spark interest in Western European markets, it would not feature in advertisements in Asia.

Notwithstanding the purpose of general marketing activities and advertising, Wandt emphasizes that personal contacts and utilizing existing networks are key to conveying the specific advantages of the university. The university does not make use of head hunters because it is unclear how the personal contact of such agents could be more informative and convincing than the personal contact that internationally connected peers have among each other.

Wandt is relatively skeptical of less targeted marketing activities. In particular, she believes the benefit–cost ratio of academic job fairs and exhibitions is often low. However, she acknowledges that sometimes participation in these events serves a purpose beyond the individual institution.

> Whereas at a national level our focus is on the competitive advantage of our institution, sometimes at the international level the focus is on Baden-Württemberg or Germany as a site for research. Therefore, benefits of these events, which are often supported by state-level foundations or the DAAD, for the university may be less direct.

One of the few international exhibitions the Communications and Marketing team regularly attends is the German Academic International Network (GAIN) meeting, mainly aimed at recruiting German scientists currently working in North America. The GAIN meeting provides a fitting illustration of the fact that recruiting international researchers and recruiting internationally are not the same thing. In other words, German scientists can be recruited from abroad and—due to their international experiences—can contribute to internationalization at home. Meanwhile, Neusel and colleagues (2014) show that only about 20 percent of professors without German citizenship are directly recruited from abroad. Thirty percent came to Germany for a postdoc position or their doctoral studies. And 50 percent of non-German professors were either born and raised in Germany or arrived during their schooling or undergraduate or graduate studies. This finding attests to the importance of the liberal job search opportunities offered to international students completing their studies in Germany. To date, international scientists already living in Germany are not targeted in any specific manner. This is partly because diversity considerations have not been at the forefront of the political agenda in Germany so far.

In sum, both at the level of mid-career researchers and at the level of professors, the University of Konstanz has professionalized its search and advertisement activities in the past five years. Increasing the share of international scientists is an explicit goal of the university and is motivated mainly by a quest for scientific excellence. However, whereas professionalizing international recruitment may already have borne some fruit in the flexible job market for mid-career researchers (both in terms of the share of internationals and the proportion among them from outside Europe), it is slow to leave its mark on the more rigid job market for professors.

One should also consider that recruitment activities of the University of Konstanz take place in an environment that the university is only partly able to influence. This concerns—among other aspects—career paths at German universities and competition from nonuniversity research institutions. There are differing opinions with respect to the effects these factors have on recruitment efforts.

Take the relatively low level of predictability of the German career path up until the point of reaching full professorship. Both Wandt and Pohlmeier consider this to be a severe problem for recruiting top early-to-mid-career scientists. Wandt points out that other German universities—namely the Technical University in Munich—have introduced a tenure system and use it prominently in their marketing activities. Pohlmeier agrees that insecurity is a substantial problem in attracting the best and the brightest. In particular, he points to competition from abroad being able to offer more attractive career perspectives. Still, he cautions that although tenure track may be an attractive selling proposition to any individual, it does not resolve the systemic problem of having too many postdocs in the system. "You put too many people on the motorway. Now it is congested and the exits do not have sufficient capacity. Allowing some to jump the line does not relieve pressure off the exits," he argues. At this stage, the University of Konstanz and many other German universities are experimenting with tenure-track options (Abele). Indeed, tenure-track options may help to address two of the most pressing issues keeping international researchers from staying in Germany (Wegner, 2016): First, they consider it very difficult to obtain a permanent position, and second, they perceive an explicit or implicit expectation to complete a "costly" *Habilitation*.

Having said this, Pohlmeier hints at the fact that insecurity is relative and sometimes also plays into the hands of Germany and the University of Konstanz. He perceives an increase in interest and applications from Southern Europe due to the difficult economic environment in that region.

As for competition by nonuniversity research institutions, Clow and Wandt focus on the fact that nonuniversity research institutions contribute to Germany being considered more attractive both at a general level (i.e., they contribute to Germany's scientific reputation) and at the level of the individual (e.g., when offering joint appointments with the nearby Max Planck Institute for Ornithology). Pohlmeier, in contrast, points out that the better research and career conditions at nonuniversity institutions (including tenured positions below professorships) make it more difficult to recruit and—more importantly—retain outstanding people at the University of Konstanz. 'Defending' a position can be a costly game of offer and counteroffer, which, more often than not, the university has lost.

Still, all in all, those responsible for international recruitment seem convinced that they play the game at their highest level while being aware of what the limits of that level are. With "limited fighting weight" in terms of financial power and flexibility (Pohlmeier), factors such as being research oriented and providing a supportive and international atmosphere, family friendliness, and a beautiful location become relevant additional selling points. Therefore, the support activities described later are not only important for keeping people happy once they arrive, but are also relevant to recruitment. Wandt points out that recent ranking positions have also helped to assure potential candidates that—apart from the quality of their particular research field—Konstanz, more generally, is a dynamic and inspiring place to be.

## Selecting International Faculty

Once mid-career researchers and professors have applied for a position at the University of Konstanz, selection of the best candidate is the next step. Here we ask, what may be the opportunities and obstacles for recruiting international faculty? We will first focus on selection procedures for professors.

The search committee (*Berufungskommission*) is responsible both for generating interest in the vacant professorship and creating a short list of candidates. The relevant university directive[9, 10] explicitly requires the search committee to follow an "active and competition-oriented recruitment strategy," which should strive for "recruitment of the best or best suited." State law outlines some minimal requirements for the composition of the search committee. There is no provision concerning international members of the search committee. However, one expert external to the university must be a member of the committee; also, at least two reviews comparing the different candidates need to be elicited. Only under exceptional circumstances can an internal candidate be appointed. Besides excellent qualifications in teaching and research, leadership ability, interdisciplinary compatibility, and compatibility with overarching university goals (e.g., thematic topics) are relevant selection criteria.

Thus, although there is nothing that prevents international candidates from applying, there are also no specific provisions that make it mandatory to recruit internationally (apart, maybe, from the requirement that the process should be "competition oriented"). Also, there is no requirement to involve international members on the search committee or recruit international reviewers. In addition, the requirement to not appoint people from within the university may both play into the hands of international applicants who face less competition from inside the institution and make it harder for those international researchers who have established themselves at German universities because transaction costs for an intranational move are arguably higher than for Germans.

Given the general appointment framework, the question becomes how search committees work in practice and which process characteristics or criteria may work for or against international scientists being offered a professorship at Konstanz. Two important obstacles Abele identifies are the duration of the selection process and German laws governing public lifetime positions in civil service. Selection processes for professorships are highly regulated and require at least 9 to 12 months. Often, the best international candidates receive alternative offers in the meantime. Civil service law regulates that there is an upper age limit (usually 45 years) for lifetime positions. Thus, if more senior international scientists enter the German system, the financial arrangements both during employment and, in particular, in retirement become markedly less attractive. Another important issue in this context relates to language, namely, the language of the process and the language competencies of the applicant.

The language of the administrative process is German. As Pohlmeier points out, there are different reasons for this. Reviews, for example, are often by German scientists because reviews in Germany are unpaid. International colleagues may expect some form of monetary compensation for providing time-consuming reviews. Also, the ministries of education and research at the state level prefer German-language reviews. Notwithstanding this general picture, in many disciplines (the natural sciences in particular) it is not unusual to have international scientists as reviewers. The general language of the commission meetings will usually also be German—not least because student representatives and administrative staff also play a role in these meetings. However, individual applicants will be able to present themselves in English. Still, in sum, the international outreach in terms of initial advertisement and marketing activities is not matched by the selection process, in which administrative aspects generate a tendency to use the German language and to predominantly involve German reviewers.

Once an international applicant has navigated this difficult selection environment, however, not speaking German does not seem to pose a problem for actual employment. Quite the contrary, Clow explains that the University of Konstanz has the goal to teach 30 percent of its courses in English. Given that less than one out of five of all scientific staff are international, this is an ambitious goal. Recruiting English-speaking applicants helps increase the share of English-language courses. Also, among researchers, English is the lingua franca. "It is not a problem to direct a research group in English," Clow clarifies.

Thus, although non–German-speaking applicants may find it difficult to go through the highly regulated selection process, lack of command of German may not be a hindrance for employment.

Traditionally, professors at German universities have been required to have an *Habilitation* (i.e., in the humanities, to write a *second book* after their PhD thesis, or in the natural sciences, to write an additional thesis). This particularity of university systems in German-speaking countries could pose a problem to international applicants. Indeed, Neusel and colleagues (2014) observed that 48 percent of all international professors held an *Habilitation*. Among German professors, this figure was 78 percent in 2010 (Böhmer, Neufeld, Hinze, Klode & Hornbostel, 2011). Indeed, the *Habilitation* still seems to constitute an additional hurdle (at least in some disciplines) for international scientists (Wegner, 2016).

Selection of mid-career scientists, our second group of interest, is much less regulated and structured than recruitment of professors. Mid-career researchers usually are either hired by a professor, or they gain a position (and the independence that comes with it) through one of the relevant grants (e.g., Sofja Kovalevskaja, Emmy Noether, or ERC Starting Grant). Some universities have dedicated structures for junior research group leaders, which feature their own selection procedures. The *Zukunftskolleg* in Konstanz is one such dedicated structure.

## The *Zukunftskolleg*

Funded by the Excellence Initiative, in 2007 the university transformed its pre-existing Centre for Early-Career Researchers (*Zentrum für den wissenschaftlichen Nachwuchs*) into the *Zukunftskolleg*. It is an institute of advanced studies bringing together postdoctoral researchers, professorial senior fellows, and so-called research fellows. The last group is independent research group leaders—heading a group often composed of doctoral students, postdoctoral researchers, and other scientific staff. In the first seven years of its existence, the *Zukunftskolleg* has had a substantial number of grant holders of the key grants for this target group mentioned earlier: three ERC Starting Grant holders, two Sofja Kovalesvskaja Award holders, and eight Emmy Noether group leaders. In total, 117 fellows have worked at the *Zukunftskolleg* to this point, jointly attracting more than EUR 20 million in third-party funding and generating at least 700 publications. Currently, 24 research fellows are working at the *Zukunftskolleg*, 13 (or 54 percent) of whom are non-German. They are joined by 26 postdoctoral fellows, of whom 16 (or 62 percent) are internationals. In addition, there is a varying number of senior fellows.

The center pursues a '5I-strategy' of early independence, internationality, intergenerationality, intrauniversity cooperation, and interdisciplinarity. Independence is a main attraction for mid-career researchers because it is hard to be found elsewhere in the system. According to David Ganz, a research fellow of the *Zukunftskolleg*,

> Academic freedom is an important precondition for creativity. The research interests of the fellows [at the *Zukunftskolleg*] are not pressed into any set of overarching research topics, as is the case in alternative organizational structures (such as collaborative research centers or clusters of excellence).
> *(Elmer & Galizia, 2013, p. 117)*

All fellows may access relatively generous internal funding schemes (including schemes for interdisciplinary projects), while also being expected to apply for external third-party funding. The positions are focused on research, with no formal teaching requirement. Together, the benefits at the *Zukunftskolleg* outweigh, to some degree, the lack of a tenure-track system for the fellows.

A substantial number of fellowships are supported by a EUR 6.24 million EU Marie Curie COFUND grant for incoming fellowships from abroad (running from 2012 to 2018). Interestingly, although also focusing on recruiting the best, this grant creates a different incentive system. Candidates funded by the Marie Curie COFUND grant have to meet the EU mobility criteria to be eligible for funding. That is, irrespective of whether they are German nationals or not, they must have lived outside the country for two of the past three years. Thus, the same 'excellence theme' in one case (with university professors) results in a share of

13 percent internationals; in another case, (with research fellows at the *Zukunftskolleg*) it results in a share of 54 percent of international fellows. Even just focusing on junior professors, the share is 7 out of 25 (or 28 percent). Given that it is unlikely that the share of excellent internationals suited for the position is nearly twice as high for junior research group leaders (*Zukunftskolleg* Fellows) than for junior professors (which are pretty much equivalent in terms of career level and prestige), one has to ask why "the best" internationals do not seem to apply and succeed as much when it comes to professorships as compared to research fellowships. We believe that this has much to do with the specific character of the *Zukunftskolleg*, in which internationality is structurally ingrained.

Recruitment and selection procedures at the *Zukunftskolleg* are highly structured. Advertisements for each call appear in major international scientific print and online journals and platforms. Administrative staff of the *Zukunftskolleg* also visit major international job fairs. All administrative staff routinely converse in English, and all materials are available in English. The interdisciplinary selection committee consists of members of all 13 departments of the University of Konstanz. In addition, there are 13 external members of the selection committee, many of whom are from abroad—usually from other European countries or the United States. The selection seminar usually lasts for two days, with candidates both presenting their work and being interviewed. The selection procedure is conducted fully in English. All applicants are required to converse in English.

Therefore, the *Zukunftskolleg* provides a "testbed for professionalization in terms of international recruitment and selection," says Pohlmeier. "Even less internationalized disciplines can profit from international recruitment at the *Zukunftskolleg* and benefit from 'internationalization at home' by international research group leaders contributing to research activities and teaching," Clow adds. "If you are looking at the *Zukunftskolleg*, the quality there is very high because the selection process is really competitive."

However, despite implementing a competitive selection process, research fellow positions at the *Zukunftskolleg* are still limited to five years, and the pay scale is fixed. These two features render a position at the *Zukunftskolleg* less attractive for the very top scientists at the international level (at least in some disciplines). Therefore, the *Zukunftskolleg* aims to closely match nonmonetary needs of mid-career scientists. Elmer points out

> ... our key demographic are international scientists in their thirties. These candidates often have to accommodate research and teaching with personal concerns, such as partnership and family. We therefore do our best to support them with dual career arrangements, childcare, personal coaching, and additional funding for research support during pregnancy and childcare. In addition, international researchers receive support in finding housing and in dealing with the relevant government agencies. Some of this we offer ourselves, other things are covered by the Welcome Center.

She also points out that building up a reputation is important:

> The *Zukunftskolleg* has been a model for institutions in Austria, Israel, and England. The career model we offer is being discussed at the national level. Also, it is important to keep the promises made in the appointment procedure in terms of laboratory space, teaching arrangements, and such. In the end, we want to offer an intellectually exciting and well-equipped environment for the very best in their fields.

## Contributions and Experiences of International Faculty

There are no quantitative data on international scientists' experiences, performance, and contributions to university life at the University of Konstanz. This is because the university's controlling mechanisms do not differentiate between German and international scientists. However, the impressions of those concerned with international faculty paint a positive picture. Clow summarizes her experiences: "From my experience in evaluations and different committees, the international scientists are at least on par with their German colleagues." She also points out that the university's quantitative goal to recruit more international scientists demonstrates that the university has no qualms with the quality of those who are present—otherwise, the goal would presumably focus on quality aspects. Pohlmeier and Abele emphasize that international scientists have gone through the same selection procedure as German scientists. In line with the excellence theme, Pohlmeier argues, "In a competitive system you always appoint the best. Our international scientists are just as good as the Germans."

Whether this meritocratic attitude and belief in the 'excellence theme' working its way through the recruitment process sit well with the current percentage of international scientists at Konstanz remains an open question. Indeed, the high percentage of international fellows in the *Zukunftskolleg* (with its high turnover rate), as compared to the percentage of international researchers at the university departments (with a supposedly lower turnover rate), suggests that there is room for future improvement. Importantly, the larger share of international scientists at the *Zukunftskolleg* does not seem to come with diminished career perspectives: Of 65 departing fellows between 2007 and 2015, 38 (or 58 percent) were appointed to professorships or roughly equivalent positions in Germany and internationally.

Clow and Pohlmeier are not aware of widespread difficulties of international faculty at Konstanz. However, they both point to one potential pitfall: language. In particular, they argue that a lack of knowledge of German may decrease the likelihood of mid-career researchers and professors from becoming engaged in university administration. This is because meetings would usually be held in German. Whether less time spent on administration would be a good or bad thing for the individual is open to discussion. On the one hand, spending time on administration usually means spending less time on research. On the other hand, administrative positions sometimes come with power and influence. Unfortunately, there are no data on German language skills of international faculty at Konstanz. Still, it seems that language is less detrimental to administrative involvement than one might think. Neusel and colleagues (2014) find that more than 80 percent of their sample was active in university committees, and approximately 40 to 50 percent were even head of the department at some point. Among mid-career scientists, 62 percent of those employed by the university participate in university meetings and decisions—a percentage higher than that of German academics at a similar career level (Wegner, 2016). This seems to contradict the intuition that a lack of German language skills hinders participation in administration. Still, 31 percent of international scientists indicate that they would be interested in contributing more (Wegner, 2016). Abele's experiences support this picture: At least in some departments, meetings have switched to English when a non–German-speaking person has joined.

Though a limited command of German may not prevent international faculty from engaging in university administration, Wegner (2016) reports problems in other domains. In particular, whereas only 13 percent of those with a fluent command of German report substantial problems in teaching, 40 percent of those without report such difficulties. Similarly, whereas only 18 percent of those with a fluent command of German report substantial problems in conversing with administrative staff, 44 percent of those without report such problems. The effects of fluency in German also concern people's integration in the context of work. For example, whereas 18 percent of those with fluent German skills perceive some problems concerning integration in the working group, 26 percent of those without perceive their integration as lacking. Findings at Konstanz reveal a similar picture: International fellows at the *Zukunftskolleg* report more difficulties integrating within their university department than German fellows; similarly, whereas 81 percent of German fellows consider departmental integration to be *very good*, this is true of only 42 percent of international fellows, according to Abele. Finally, regression models run by Wegner (2016) show that a better command of German is associated with both better social integration into the society outside the university and increased likelihood of wanting to stay in Germany. The study concludes that being or becoming fluent in German is a very important factor to make staying in Germany sustainably successful, even when controlling for other relevant factors, such as personality dispositions, time spent in Germany so far, partner living in Germany, etc.

International university professors spend about one-third of their time teaching. Of international mid-career researchers with university employment, 51 percent teach and 34 percent conduct student exams (Wegner, 2016). These figures are lower than for a comparable group of German researchers in which 74 percent teach and 53 percent conduct student exams. Whether the situation is detrimental to career prospects remains unclear, although the fact that 24 percent of international faculty would like to see more involvement in teaching gives a strong indication that international researchers' lower level of integration into teaching activities may come with serious disadvantages.

Irrespective of their engagement in administration and teaching, the main interest of international faculty (as well as German faculty) at universities[11] is research. Fifty-one percent of international professors say that research is their first priority, with 46 percent claiming a preference for both research and teaching. Only 3 percent have a clear preference for teaching (Neusel et al., 2014). Indeed, international mid-career researchers are more likely than their German comparison group to lead research projects (73 percent versus 44 percent). Detailed analyses of different research performance indicators for international versus German scientists are, unfortunately, lacking for Germany.

A sensitive topic that should not be overlooked is the potential for discrimination due to nationality. Indeed, 24 percent of international professors self-report being discriminated against due to their nationality (Neusel et al., 2014). However, 23 percent also report experiencing advantages due to their nationality. The findings concerning discrimination are corroborated by Wegner (2016): 19 percent of her sample reported experiences of discrimination in the work context, whereas 75 percent do not perceive any substantial discrimination at work.

All in all, international scientists are rather satisfied with their stay in Germany: Neusel et al. (2014) report that about 75 percent of all international professors are *satisfied* or *very satisfied* with their stay. And Wegner (2016) found that 60 percent of more junior scientists employed at a university were *very satisfied* or *satisfied* with their stay.

## Support for International Faculty

Clow points out that "creating a welcoming intercultural environment," as well as "creating optimal conditions for researchers," are central goals of the University of Kostanz's International Office and the Welcome Center. The Welcome Center arranges expert advice on all nonacademic affairs and serves as the central contact point for international faculty. Wegner (2016) found that critical challenges for international scientists include (among other things) the job search for a spouse, learning German, finding accommodations, arranging childcare, visa and resident permit arrangements, and social security matters. For these and many other challenges, the Welcome Center is the first port of call. This includes hands-on support, such as accompanying international faculty to government agencies (e.g., when it comes to securing resident permits), finding childcare and accommodations, all kinds of technical questions (e.g., cell phone contract or opening a bank account), offering guided tours through the town, etc.

Wegner (2016) found that there was a substantial positive correlation between how international scientists perceived the service quality of their university/welcome center and their overall satisfaction with the stay in Germany—even controlling for a number of other influences on overall satisfaction, such as social integration and workplace integration (both with a positive effect on overall satisfaction). Of international professors, 32 percent report using services they perceived as helpful that were offered by the International Office (Neusel et al., 2014).

As far as Konstanz is concerned, University of Konstanz has a relatively small university campus consisting of interconnected buildings. Thus, personal contact is relatively easy to establish. As Clow puts it, "[T]he geography of the university is conducive to interaction." This includes both interaction with other researchers and interaction with the Welcome Center and administrative staff.

Besides the Welcome Center, the Academic Staff Development office offers important services, some of which are of particular relevance to international faculty, including language courses and information on career paths for international researchers. Also, it is possible to book individual coaching sessions. This particular service is clearly distinct from counseling services and provides one-on-one sessions on issues such as strategic career planning (including goal setting), job-related decision making, time management, strategic positioning within the scientific community, and connecting work and family life.

However, despite these professionalized support services, the University of Konstanz has not yet taken the next step—or big leap—that would follow from strictly adhering to the 'excellence theme' described earlier: fully internationalizing all of its services. This would mean offering all administrative and support services (including documents) in both English and German. There is only one part of the university in which this has become a reality: the *Zukunftskolleg*. The experiences there provide strong hints that internationalizing German university laboratories and campuses may still be at its very beginning. When getting serious about creating an environment in which scientific credentials are the only currency that counts, top German institutions in the future may no longer be dominated by home country nationals. However, this step is not yet being considered an option anytime soon by those in charge at the University of Konstanz. As Pohlmeier put it:

> The question of language in academic self-governance is not yet on the table. So far, no department is international to a degree that would make it unavoidable to switch to English. However, there are first examples in continental Europe (namely the Netherlands). It will come . . .

And maybe the beginnings can already be seen. Abele points out that the university now employs a translator who is working her way through all administrative forms and documentation relevant to researchers.

## Conclusion

'Excellence' is a strong theme running through both Germany, in general, and the University of Konstanz, in particular. The Excellence Initiative and the increased pressure on universities to acquire national and EU third-party funding have contributed to a focus on hiring the best and most internationally well-connected scientific staff. Helped by the fact that—at least compared to other countries in continental Europe—the economy has been relatively stable in recent years and all federal governments have shared a commitment to research and innovation—many German universities have been able to increase both the quantitative share of international faculty and the quality of resources and services dedicated to their recruitment and support. However, low shares of international faculty overall indicate that the 'excellence theme' (i.e., recruitment focused on quality alone) does meet severe reality constraints. To soften these constraints, Germany would—in our view—be well advised to take the following steps:

1. Holding on to and consolidating liberal immigration laws. The massive influx of refugees in the wake of the humanitarian catastrophe in Syria and other countries has led to a political climate that is less conducive to further liberalization. Developments in other countries (the United Kingdom, in particular) show that a protectionist backlash is not an outside possibility. At the same time, the crisis situation has also placed adopting an Immigration Act that lives up to its name, both in letter and in spirit, higher on the political agenda.
2. Further professionalizing international marketing services. Much has been achieved, but best practices (pioneered by some universities) still need to spread.
3. Improving career perspectives for mid-career researchers. Positions not offering tenure will remain a hard sell to top researchers, even though places like the *Zukunftskolleg* show that much can be done to offset this disadvantage and still recruit a large percentage of international researchers. German universities should continue to explore tenure-track options. In the long run, such efforts can only be sustainable if the balance between nontenured and tenured positions is readjusted. This would involve shifting more tasks (in particular in the area of teaching) to the professorial level (for recommendations along these lines, see German Council of Science and Humanities, 2008).
4. Internationalizing and debureaucratizing appointment procedures for professors. In a first step, participation of international committee members and reviewers in the process should be strengthened. In a second step, the process needs to become swifter and more easily comprehensible to international researchers.
5. Internationalizing the whole campus and embracing diversity. German universities need to take the next critical step and become truly international institutions, including greatly increasing the use of English throughout the university (in particular in teaching and in administration). Because it is well funded and already highly international (with English as the main working language, both in research and administration), the *Zukunftskolleg* is a test bed

that those interested in getting serious about the internationalization of German universities should watch when analyzing the strengths and potential pitfalls of this approach. This development would be enhanced if diversity considerations move up on the political and institutional agendas.

6   Formulating a coordinated action plan. The activities at the level of each institution need to be matched by a coordinated approach at the policy level. In Germany's federal system, this is notoriously difficult. However, the new constitutional possibilities of the federal government, in conjunction with a renewed commitment of the federal states to strengthen their universities, would allow for the systemic changes necessary to further internationalize university faculty. Actions will need to include implementing programs in the areas of marketing and support, as well as changes in appointment procedures and funding, and legal changes to adjust staff composition in favor of tenured positions and facilitate tenure-track options.

The stakes for Germany to succeed with these changes are high. As a country with few natural resources and a rapidly aging population, future success will critically depend on whether the 'excellence theme' at German universities is more rhetoric or more real (we suppose it will always be a bit of both). In Konstanz and elsewhere, important steps have been taken—but both at the institutional and the policy level, much more needs to be done to really make Germany a highly attractive *Einwanderungsland* for the world's best researchers.

## Notes

1   "Universities" refers to both research universities and universities of applied sciences.
2   Data from the German Federal Statistical Office, calculations by DZHW/www.wissenschaft-weltoffen.de
3   Data from the German Federal Statistical Office, calculations by DZHW/www.wissenschaft-weltoffen.de. This is related to the percentage calculations of non-German staff in the preceding part of the sentence.
4   This only refers to university employees for which university employment is the main occupation (*hauptberufliches Personal*). It excludes, for example, emeriti, visiting lecturers, student assistants, and teaching assistants.
5   Data from the German Federal Statistical Office, calculations by DZHW/www.wissenschaft-weltoffen.de.
6   Data from the German Federal Statistical Office, calculations by DZHW/www.wissenschaft-weltoffen.de.
7   Data from the German Federal Statistical Office, calculations by DZHW/www.wissenschaft-weltoffen.de.
8   Data from the German Federal Statistical Office, calculations by DZHW/www.wissenschaft-weltoffen.de.
9   Whereas the term *international students* refers to nonresident students on temporary study in Germany only (i.e., only to those students who have received their university entry qualifications abroad), the terms *foreign students* and *noncitizen students* refer to all students of non-German citizenship, including those who have received their university entry qualifications in Germany.

10 See www.service.uni-konstanz.de/index.php?eID=tx_nawsecuredl&u=0&g=0&t=1 444141584&hash=4bc4504ceb6d960eaee7aff8421658ed0338090b&file=fileadmin/ informationen/zentral/amtliche/2013/48_13_Richtlinie_Wertschaetzendes Berufungsverfahren.pdf

11 In this case, excluding universities of applied sciences where 56 percent of professors have teaching as their main preference (with the remainder being interested in both research and teaching).

## References

Böhmer, S., Neufeld, J., Hinze, S., Klode, C., & Hornbostel, S. (2011). Wissenschaftler-Befragung 2010: Forschungsbedingungen von Professorinnen und Professoren an deutschen Universitäten. *iFQ Working Paper No. 8*. Retrieved from www.forschungsinfo. de/publikationen/download/working_paper_8_2010.pdf

Bruder, M., Burkhart, S., Franke, B., Heublein, U., & Kercher, J. (2015). *Wissenschaft weltoffen 2015*. Bielefeld: W. Bertelsmann. doi: 10.3278/7004002nw

CDU, CSU & SPD. (2013). *Deutschlands Zukunft gestalten: Koalitionsvertrag zwischen CDU, CSU und SPD* [Shaping Germany's future: Coalition treaty between CDU, CSU and SPD]. Rheinbach: Union Betriebs-GmbH.

Commission of Experts in Research and Innovation (EFI) (Ed.). (2014). International mobility of scientists and inventors and its impact on innovation. In Commission of Experts in Research and Innovation (EFI) (Ed.), *Research, innovation and technological performance in Germany: EFI Report 2014* (pp. 85–105). Berlin: EFI. Retrieved from www.e-fi.de/fileadmin/Gutachten_2014/EFI_Report_2014.pdf

Deutsche Forschungsgemeinschaft (DFG) (2015). *DFG-Förderatlas 2015: Kennzahlen zur öffentlich finanzierten Forschung in Deutschland*. Weinheim: Wiley-VCH. Retrieved from www.dfg.de/download/pdf/dfg_im_profil/zahlen_fakten/foerderatlas/2015/dfg_foerderatlas_2015.pdf

Elmer, S., & Galizia, C. G. (2013). Brücken der Zukunft: Das Zukunftskolleg als Erfolgsmodell in der Postdoc-Phase [Bridges into the future: The Zukunftskolleg as a success model fort he postdoc phase]. In H. Kauhaus (Ed.), *Das deutsche Wissenschaftssystem und seine Postdocs: Perspektiven für die Gestaltung der Qualifizierungsphase nach der Promotion* [The German science system and ist postdocs: Perspectives for shaping the qualification phase after graduation]. Bielefeld: UVW.

Federal Ministry of Education and Research (BMBF) (2008). *Strengthening Germany's role in the global knowledge society: Strategy of the federal government for the internationalization of science and research*. Berlin: BMBF. Retrieved from www.bmbf.de/pubRD/Internationalisierungsstrategie-English.pdf

Federal Ministry of Education and Research (BMBF) (2014). *International cooperation. Action plan of the federal ministry of education and research (BMBF)*. Berlin: BMBF. Retrieved from www.bmbf.de/pub/International_Cooperatin_Action_Plan.pdf

Federal Statistical Office (2015a). *Personal an Hochschulen: 2014* [Personnel at universities: 2014]. Wiesbaden: Statistisches Bundesamt. Retrieved from www.destatis.de/DE/Publikationen/Thematisch/BildungForschungKultur/Hochschulen/PersonalHochschulen2110440147004.pdf?__blob=publicationFile

Federal Statistical Office (2015b). *Finanzen der Hochschulen 2013* [Finances of higher education institutions 2013]. Wiesbaden: Statistisches Bundesamt. Retrieved from www.destatis.de/DE/Publikationen/Thematisch/BildungForschungKultur/BildungKulturFinanzen/FinanzenHochschulen2110450137004.pdf?__blob=publicationFile

Federal Statistical Office (2016a). *Ausgaben, Einnahmen und Personal der öffentlichen und öffentlich geförderten Einrichtungen für Wissenschaft, Forschung und Entwicklung 2014* [Expenditure, income and personnel of public and publicly funded institutions for science, research and innovation 2014]. Wiesbaden: Statistisches Bundesamt. Retrieved from www.destatis.de/DE/Publikationen/Thematisch/BildungForschungKultur/Forschung/AusgabenEinnahmenPersonal2140360147004.pdf?__blob=publicationFile

Federal Statistical Office (2016b). *Studierende an Hochschulen—Vorbericht: Wintersemester 2015/2016* [Students at higher education institutions—preliminary report: Winter semester 2015/2016]. Wiesbaden: Statistisches Bundesamt. Retrieved from www.destatis.de/DE/Publikationen/Thematisch/BildungForschungKultur/Hochschulen/StudierendeHochschulenVorb2110410168004.pdf?__blob=publicationFile

German Academic Exchange Service (DAAD) (2010). *Information on the statutory frameworks applicable to entry and residence by foreign students, academics and scientists.* Bonn: DAAD. Retrieved from www.daad.de/medien/deutschland/stipendien/formulare/info_entry_and_residence.pdf

German Council of Science and Humanities (2008). *Empfehlungen zu einer lehrorientierten Reform der Personalstruktur an Universitäten* [Recommendations concerning a teaching-oriented reform of the staff composition at universities] (Drs. 7721–07). Berlin: German Council of Science and Humanities. Retrieved from www.wissenschaftsrat.de/download/archiv/7721-07.pdf

German Council of Science and Humanities (2013). *Perspektiven des deutschen Wissenschaftssystems* [Perspectives of the German science system] (Drs. 3228–13). Braunschweig: German Council of Science and Humanities. Retrieved from www.wissenschaftsrat.de/download/archiv/3228-13.pdf

Joint Science Conference (GWK) (2013). *Strategie der Wissenschaftsminister/innen von Bund und Ländern für die Internationalisierung der Hochschulen in Deutschland* [Strategy of the ministers of science of the federal government and the federal states for internationalizing the universities in Germany]. Berlin: GWK. Retrieved from www.kmk.org/fileadmin/veroeffentlichungen_beschluesse/2013/2013_Strategiepapier_Internationalisierung_Hochschulen.pdf

Max Planck Society (2015a). *The Max Planck Society.* Munich: Max Planck Society for the Advancement of Science. Retrieved from www.mpg.de/8746421/MPG_Image-flyer_en_2014.pdf

Max Planck Society (2015b). Facts & figures. Retrieved from www.mpg.de/international/facts_figures on 08/27/2015

Mund, C., Conchi, S., & Frietsch, R. (2015). *4. Indikatorbericht: Bibliometrische Indikatoren für den PFI Monitoring Bericht 2015* [4th indicator report: Bibliometric indicators for the PFI monitoring report 2015]. Retrieved from www.bmbf.de/pubRD/4_Indikatorbericht_Bibliometrische_Indikatoren_fuer_den_PFI-Monitoring_Bericht_2015.pdf

Neusel, A., Wolter, A., Engel, O., Kriszio, M., & Weichert, D. (2014). International Mobilität und Professur: Karriereverläufe und Karrierebedingungen von internationalen Professorinnen und Professoren an Hochschulen in Berlin und Hessen [International mobility and professorship: Career trajectories and career conditions of international professors at universities in Berlin and Hesse]. *Final Report for the BMBF.* Humboldt-Universität zu Berlin. Retrieved from www.erziehungswissenschaften.hu-berlin.de/de/mobilitaet/projektergebnisse/abschlussbericht-1/abschlussbericht-internationale-mobilitaet-und-professur.pdf

OECD (2015a). *International migration outlook 2015.* Paris: OECD Publishing. doi: 10.1787/migr_outlook-2015-en

OECD (2015b). *Education at a glance 2015: OECD indicators*. Paris: OECD Publishing. doi: 10.1787/eag-2015-en

Wegner, A. (2016). *Internationale Nachwuchswissenschaftler in Deutschland: Motivation—Integration—Förderung. Ergebnisse einer deutschlandweiten Studie* [International early-career scientists in Germany: Motivation—integration—support. Results of a nation-wide study]. Bonn: GATE-Germany.

# 8

# INTERNATIONAL FACULTY RECRUITMENT IN KAZAKHSTAN

## The Case of Nazarbayev University

*Alan Ruby, Aliya Kuzhabekova, and Jack T. Lee*

### Introduction

Since gaining independence in 1991, Kazakhstan has been reforming and internationalizing its higher education system. It has allowed the growth of private education institutions, encouraged study abroad, and set targets for cross-border institutional partnerships and faculty mobility. It has also fostered and financed the development of internationally oriented universities like Nazarbayev University (NU). Examining NU's first years offers insights into the challenges and opportunities for recruiting and retaining international faculty.

We begin with an overview of the national context, followed by a brief description of the educational policy environment and the government's approach to the internationalization of higher education. We use Nazarbayev University as a case study given its pivotal role in the country's higher education development. Our emphasis is on faculty recruitment because this new university requires a substantial number of academics to reach its goals.

### Context

#### Kazakhstan

Kazakhstan is a landlocked and resource-rich country in Central Asia, whose biggest trading partners are neighboring Russia and China. Kazakhstan's economy has been driven by oil and gas exports, mining, and livestock and grain sales. The government continues to seek ways to diversify the economy, and this is reflected in the country's education policies.

## National Education Policy

Following national independence in 1991, many talented and well-educated people left Kazakhstan, and many sectors of the economy experienced a loss of skilled labor (Hiro, 2009). Another consequence of independence was a decline in the quality of education. The centralized system of education, which had been established during the Soviet era, could not serve the new market economy. In the early years of independence, Kazakhstan started modernizing the educational system to respond to market needs and the government's plans for economic development.

The dissolution of economic and cultural ties following the demise of the Soviet Union also affected Kazakhstan's system of research and innovation, which the government viewed as key drivers of sustainable economic growth. Given these challenges, the State Program for Education Development for 2011–2020 set out three main pillars of higher education policy:

1. Training of professionals to support a more diverse economy
2. Integration into the European Higher Education Area, with greater institutional autonomy, a national qualifications framework, and independent quality assurance
3. Promoting economic development and innovation through closer integration of education, science, and industry

The state program is revised periodically to accommodate economic and political changes such as the articulation of the nation's 2050 Strategy, which has the overarching goal of Kazakhstan becoming one of the world's 30 most developed countries. This requires a significant investment in human capital development and transformation of educational institutions, policies, and processes. Some of the necessary changes are set out in the May 2015 Plan of the Nation: The 100 Concrete Steps, which directs ten higher education institutions to specialize in six key sectors of the economy and proposes increases in academic and managerial autonomy of educational institutions and a gradual shift to English-language instruction in high schools and universities. The stewardship of these changes rests with the Ministry of Education and Science, which is responsible for higher education policy.

## Governance of Education

The national Ministry of Education and Science (MES) directs the higher education system through a framework of 64 legislative acts and accompanying norms and regulations. The governance of public universities is highly centralized, with MES determining personnel policy and compensation rates and appointing, evaluating, and dismissing most university leaders. Rectors of national universities are appointed by the president of Kazakhstan. Rectors report directly to MES and are free from local political control. Within each institution, the rector dominates decision making, and faculty participation in governance is usually limited to offering advice through the academic council, the *Uchenyi Sovet*.

## Financing

While the overall national education budget increased markedly in the last ten years, it has increased less significantly as a proportion of gross domestic product (GDP), moving from 3.2 percent to 3.6 percent. Government spending on higher education is very low in comparison with countries with a similar GDP level. Only 0.3 percent of GDP is allocated annually to higher education. Higher education receives 8.6 percent of the total state budget for education (OECD & World Bank, 2007, pp. 82–83).

The main sources of funding for higher education in Kazakhstan are direct national budget allocations for institutions; state grants, which are effectively tuition vouchers awarded on merit; and tuition fees. Tuition is very important because only 30 percent of students are funded by "state grants," whereas the rest of the students pay tuition.

Currently, there are 126 higher education institutions in Kazakhstan; 71 are public institutions, including 13 that mainly focus on law enforcement. The other public institutions include 9 national universities, 31 regional institutions, 1 autonomous institution (Nazarbayev University), 1 international institution (Kazakh-Turkish University), and 16 institutions that take the form of joint stock companies. There are also 55 private institutions. The number of higher education institutions decreased in last ten years by 30 percent, as the government withdrew the licenses of some small, low-quality, mainly private institutions and merged some public institutions. Many of the private institutions were established in the late 1990s, when Kazakhstan pursued a market approach to higher education and some regional universities opened parallel private entities to generate revenue.

## Faculty

There were around 21,000 higher education faculty members when Kazakhstan became independent. Numbers fluctuated until the late 1990s when they grew in line with the increase in total student enrollment, peaking at the same time. Faculty numbers started to fall as enrollments fell, but after a few years began to grow again, even though enrollments still went down. At the start of the 2014–2015 academic year, there were 40,300 faculty members, a number that includes some part-time academics. Slightly less than half of the higher education faculty holds doctoral degrees or are candidates of science (a qualification broadly equivalent to a PhD). The low salaries for academic posts and the low levels of investment in research in Kazakhstan in the immediate postindependence years deterred talented young specialists from entering doctoral programs, reducing the pool of research-active potential faculty members. In combination, these factors have shaped the demand for international faculty.

Most of the current faculty in Kazakhstan's universities are graduates of either Soviet or postindependence Kazakhstan's universities. They generally lack training in new developments in teaching and research and have few incentives or opportunities for retraining and raising professional qualifications. Students commonly cite frustrations with faculty members' didactic approaches to teaching, low morale, and a predisposition to bribery and plagiarism.

Meanwhile, some universities in Kazakhstan have been quite successful in increasing the quality of education by attracting international faculty. Although these internationally oriented universities like KIMEP (the Kazakhstan Institute of Management, Economics, and Strategic Research) produce good-quality graduates, faculty members struggle to establish or maintain internationally significant research profiles.

## *Internationalization of Higher Education*

The main pillars of the government's current approach to internationalization of education are (Ministry of Education and Science of the Republic of Kazakhstan, 2012):

- Pursuit of trilingualism, with the aim of having all citizens able to communicate in the Kazakh, Russian, and English languages
- The Bolashak Scholarship Program, which supports students in undergraduate and graduate programs at leading international universities and offers a growing number of international fellowships and internships
- A national Strategy for Academic Mobility for 2012–2020 that promotes student and faculty mobility and cross-border institutional partnerships
- Participation in the Bologna process by using the three degree levels (bachelor, master's, and doctoral) and by establishing independent accreditation mechanisms and moving to eliminate state attestation[1]
- Creation of an English-language, research-intensive university, Nazarbayev University, with international partners and internationally competitive faculty

The trilingual education policy is still in its first stages, and higher education institutions use Russian or Kazakh as the main languages of instruction with the exception of KIMEP and Nazarbayev University.

The Bolashak Program has been running for over 20 years and more than 7,000 recipients have returned to Kazakhstan. Half of the recipients earned master's degrees, one-third bachelor degrees, and a much smaller number have earned doctorates. Many have entered the civil service, but over 1,000 Bolashak graduates are working in universities, 200 of them in Nazarbayev University (Nygymetov, 2014); however, few of them hold faculty posts. Some are junior researchers, and some hold posts in administration and policy analysis. Other scholarship programs offer students from Kazakhstan international study and exchange opportunities. Many of these—like the Muskie and Fulbright programs—are funded by other governments.

The Strategy for Academic Mobility for 2012–2020 prioritizes student mobility, particularly within the European Higher Education Area (EHEA). The strategy has a goal of increasing "the number of foreign teachers and staff" by 10 percent annually. This is a more modest goal than those set for growth in foreign students attending universities in Kazakhstan (20 percent annually) and for growth in the number of domestic students traveling to the EHEA for a period of training (50 percent). While the strategy did not include any explicit reference to strategies for recruiting international faculty, the ministry allocated funds for international faculty visits after being advised by the Organisation for Economic Co-operation and Development (OECD) and World Bank 2007 review, which noted that universities lacked "research and innovation opportunities" to attract leading international scholars and suggested that the system overall needed "more emphasis . . . on . . . exchanges with the world's most competitive countries" (pp. 25, 28). This has had some success; over 4,000 foreign scholars and faculty were invited to teach courses in the last five years, but many of the visits were short—under a month, and some even shorter. This was akin to an earlier, more focused initiative that allocated USD 1 million to each of the two national universities, Al-Farabi Kazakh National University and L. Gumilev Euroasian National University, to invite high-profile scientists and teachers to teach and consult with faculty and students for short periods (Tuymebayev, 2009).

There is no specific provision in the 2012–2020 policy to subsidize longer-term international faculty appointments. The limited impact of many short-term visits has led the vice minister to propose concentrating the funds for faculty exchanges on a smaller number of national institutions and, even within those institutions, on programs of economic interest to the government.[2] This is in parallel with a general strategy of concentrating resources on a smaller number of national research universities proposed in the draft 2016–2020 state program.

The State Program for Education Development for 2011–2020 sets an overall student academic mobility goal of 20 percent. This has been successfully attained for graduate students, and even exceeded for doctoral students, where nearly one-third spent a term or semester abroad. But very little progress has been made on achieving the goal for first-degree students. The fifth element in the internationalization policy is the creation of Nazarbayev University, a project that was also conceived as a modernizing strategy for higher education in Kazakhstan.

## Nazarbayev University

Nazarbayev University (NU) is a distinctive feature of the government's 2020 economic and social development strategy. The university's mission is "to be a model for higher education reform and modern research in Kazakhstan and to contribute to the establishment of Astana as an international innovation and knowledge hub" (NU, n.d.). Created through partnerships with leading universities and research institutes in the United States, England, and Singapore, NU is designed to be a research-intensive university that uses English as the medium of instruction.

NU's first cohort of bachelor degree students graduated in May 2015. It graduated master's students in 2014 and 2015, and enrolled its first doctoral students in 2014.

The university's basic goal is to produce graduates who are comparable to those of the best institutions in other countries. It is an elite institution with a highly competitive admissions process. By enrolling approximately 500 new undergraduate students a year, NU is taking in less than 1 percent of the national first-year university cohort. In its first years of operation, NU admitted approximately one out of eight applicants annually.

The NU entrance examinations are designed to identify and select students on the basis of intellect and English-language proficiency. The tests include an initial screening for English proficiency, followed by two subject-specific tests and then an official International English Language Testing System (IELTS) test.

The academic programs and research centers at NU have a strong emphasis on science and engineering and English. This emphasis is a product of the Soviet legacy, which valued science over the humanities (Navoyan, 2011) and the nation's economic priorities, which are skewed toward science-based enterprises.

As well as aiming to become a world-class institution, the government wants NU to serve as a site of innovation, experimentation, and customization. NU is expected to try, test, evaluate, adapt, and customize successful higher education practices from other countries and disseminate these practices to other universities in Kazakhstan. One of the international practices in question is institutional autonomy. NU is legislatively independent of the Ministry of Education and Science. It has a board of trustees that oversees its operation, which includes independent decisions on curriculum design, admission standards, and faculty compensation. The board is responsible for ongoing institutional oversight in partnership with the university president. The president is selected by the board, not the ministry or the government, as is the case with other public universities in Kazakhstan.

In summary, NU aspires to be a globally recognized institution with national and regional impact. It is grounded in a common economic and social vision of society. And it has a marked degree of independence from the ministry and other regulatory bodies in the higher education system.

NU's most notable implementation strategy is its engagement with multiple international strategic partners. NU is neither a branch campus nor a consortium. It has been established by the government of Kazakhstan, and international partners are involved on a contractual basis. Using multiple partners minimizes risks that could come from relying excessively on a single partner. It also has the advantage of enabling the university to select the best provider in support of particular academic programs—for example, a business school—rather than taking bundled services of uneven quality from a single source.

NU is well resourced by international standards and is very well resourced by domestic standards. It pays higher salaries than local institutions for local talent, and pays international recruited faculty at global market rates or better. The infrastructure is notably better than the infrastructure of domestic universities. NU's per capita funding is approximately three times that of funding rates at national research universities. Volatility in commodity prices, especially oil prices, may dampen the level of state support, even though the government has built a sovereign wealth fund to buffer fluctuations in global market prices for oil and gas (International Monetary Fund, 2015).

NU operates under a law that frees it from many regulations and norms expected by the Ministry of Education and the Ministry of Finance. This freedom extends to academic independence and ease of recruitment of international staff. The curricula of the schools and programs at the university are determined by NU, with varying degrees of involvement from the strategic partners, rather than from the ministry, as is largely the case for the nation's public universities. This independence is important to NU's international partners, both in terms of academic programming and faculty recruitment. Furthermore, NU faculty members also participate actively in the university's senate to raise important issues that affect teaching and research. These include traditional topics, such as promotion, as well as measures to enhance health and safety on campus and advocacy of issues that affect local faculty members. This shared governance with the executive leadership of the university is unprecedented in Kazakhstan's higher education system. The press coverage generated recently by a faculty member's claim that he was to be dismissed because he planned to speak critically of Russia's presence in Crimea was substantial. There was print and digital coverage in daily news sources like *The Guardian* and *Eurasia Net* (Leonard, 2015) and 'trade' sources like *University World News* and *The Diplomat* (Putz, 2015), as well as in online blogs. The university's response was that "academic freedom is and always has been a core commitment" embedded in the university charter (Nazarbayev University, 2015).

NU is an avowedly international university. This is obvious in its leadership, which comes from many different nations; its strategic partners; in the recruitment of international scholars and researchers; and the adoption of international academic standards and programs. The deliberate strategy of internationalization has not yet extended to the composition of the student body; there are presently only nine international students.

In summary, after five years of operation, NU has established a high-quality student intake at undergraduate and graduate levels and developed working relationships with a range of international academic partners. How it has gone about attracting and employing high-quality leaders and academic faculty is explored next.

## Focus and Rationale of the Study

Given the early stage of the development of NU, many important faculty-related policies and employment practices are changing to fit the needs of an emerging university. By the time of this study (mid-2015), NU was undergoing the first round of three-year contract renewals for faculty members and finalizing its faculty promotion policy. Most schools are still striving to reach the desired number of faculty overall in order to effectively deliver all their academic programs.[3] While a study of NU faculty's experiences would be more robust when the university is fully staffed, there is still merit in studying these early years. This study captures the diversity of approaches that each school is using in collaboration with different international partners and the perceptions and experiences of some internationally recruited faculty. One can expect the experiences to differ depending on the type of partnership arrangements, the vision of the partner, the availability of local faculty in a given discipline, and the international job market for academics in different fields.

As of September 2015, 339 NU faculty members represent 45 different countries; 21 percent of faculty members are Kazakhstan citizens. Only four nations other than Kazakhstan had more than ten citizens on the faculty: the United States, Canada, Great Britain, and Greece. The second biggest national group was from the United States (70). Citizens from the largely Anglophone nations of Australia, Canada, Great Britain, Ireland, New Zealand, and South Africa make up nearly half the faculty (153). Only nine were Russian citizens, which may seem surprising, given the proximity to Russia and low Russian academic salaries, but this is probably a function of the emphasis on English proficiency and peer-reviewed publications in English language journals, which we discuss later in our survey of recruitment policies and practices.

This study explores the recruitment and hiring processes used by several schools at Nazarbayev University by pursuing three research questions:

1   What approaches are NU schools using to recruit and hire international faculty?
2   What might explain differences in the recruitment experiences among the schools?
3   What lessons can be identified from these experiences with recruitment and hiring?

The study is based on qualitative face-to-face interviews with ten senior faculty members and academic administrators from different schools at NU. These participants were selected for their direct involvement in the recruitment and hiring process (e.g., as a member of a hiring committee or senior leadership team of a school). The schools included in the analysis are the Graduate School of Education (GSE), Graduate School of Public Policy (GSPP), Graduate School of Business (GSB), School of Medicine (SM), School of Humanities and Social Sciences (SHSS), School of Engineering (SE), and School of Science and Technology (SST). It does not include academic staff involved in the Foundation Year program (pre-university).

The interview questionnaire included questions about approaches to determining hiring needs; the venues for, and approaches to, disseminating information about vacancies; characteristics sought for in faculty; characteristics of the applicant pool; successes and challenges in recruitment, as well as changes in approaches over time; and the involvement of the international partners.

## Findings

### *Why Does the University Hire International Faculty?*

From its inception, NU's leadership has pursued the goal of becoming a university comparable to the leading research-intensive universities in the world. It is envisioned as a model university, which disseminates its best practices to the rest of the higher education system. One reason why the government decided to invest heavily in a new university was because prior attempts to modernize the education system by distributing resources among the various existing educational institutions were unsuccessful; poor personnel qualifications and resistance to change among the local faculty presented formidable challenges (Kuzhabekova, Mukhametzhanova, Almukhambetova & Soltanbekova, 2015).

### *How Are Hiring Needs Determined at NU?*

Prior to analyzing the recruitment and hiring process, it was necessary to understand how hiring needs are determined at NU. Our interviews with representatives of hiring teams in several schools revealed that the identification of hiring needs has changed over time. Before accepting the first cohort of students, strategic partner institutions developed blueprints that predicted future annual enrollment rates and the corresponding numbers of faculty at different ranks to support the proposed academic programs. The inaugural dean hired the first batch of faculty members based on these enrollment forecasts.

In subsequent years, as faculty numbers grew, some curricula underwent changes to better reflect the strengths and weaknesses of the student intake and the expertise of faculty members. Some initial programs did not attract sufficient student enrollments, whereas others were very popular and needed larger faculty allocations. These patterns of demand were used to adjust recruitment targets.

Deans now use projected and actual enrollments to determine hiring needs. New targets have to be approved by the university-level executive team based on the available budgets and the competing needs of other schools.

While four out of five NU faculty members are not Kazakhstan citizens, the university's leadership acknowledges that longer-term sustainability depends on increasing the proportion of local staff. Currently most schools do not differentiate between international and local candidates in the recruitment process. Rather, the primary concern is to hire qualified faculty regardless of citizenship. The result is that although most schools are aware of the importance of hiring locals, Kazakhstan citizens are a minority in the total faculty.

The only exception with respect to differential hiring is the case of the NU Medical School. The administration of the medical school has a clear vision regarding the role local faculty should play in comparison with international faculty. Since the school has the goal to train not only medical researchers but also practicing doctors for the country, it needs to hire faculty who have practical experience working in Kazakhstan's health system. It needs people who understand local medical terminology and cultural norms and who can connect Western-trained biomedical researchers and NU students with the realities of health care in Kazakhstan. Hence, the medical school plans to hire a specific number of local clinicians and a specific number of researchers, who may be local or international.

## *What Strategies Are Used to Advertise Faculty Positions?*

Apart from very senior leadership posts in the university, like the provost, there is little reliance on specialized international or domestic search firms. Rather, once hiring needs are identified, schools start to advertise the existing vacancies. The schools take the lead in determining the location and timing of advertisements. Three approaches are commonly used. First, all schools use key conferences in their field as venues to gain visibility for the largely unknown Nazarbayev University. Although many participants mentioned that presence at career fairs, sponsoring social events, and setting up information booths are not directly related to the number of applications for available positions, they raise NU's visibility.

Second, many individuals responsible for recruitment and hiring mentioned that they always post ads on specialized higher education job websites, such as the *Chronicle of Higher Education*, jobs.co.uk, and HigherEdJobs.com. Posting on these websites seems to attract a large number of applications in disciplines that are not in high demand in the international academic job market. This approach is also effective in raising NU's profile.

Third, while the structure and the content of the job ads posted by NU are similar to that posted by Western universities, NU's postings also contain basic information about partner institutions, the city of Astana, and the university. The tone of the postings is often commercial-like, where metaphors describing the reputations of the international partners and the characteristics of the university are intended to attract applicants with an image of a newly created institution that is distinct from anything else in the world. These ads (according to one interviewee) also portray Astana as a modern city undergoing rapid development with promises of an unforgettable adventure:

> ... a little paragraph that explains Astana, that it is a new capital and it is very exciting and everything is modern. We emphasize that this is an ambitious project, which is going to meet the global standard, we talk about the number of students we have ... the fact that they are English-speaking, that the faculty come from many countries, and we talk about the fact that the faculty have PhDs from (recognized) universities. Sometimes we use it for recruiting students; it is very similar to what we put in job ads.

In addition to the common approaches to advertising, there are some differences in how schools make vacancies known to the potential applicants. These seem to be determined by the established practices in a particular discipline and by labor market conditions.

In fields with very strong professional societies, advertising and initial interviewing happens in the specialized annual conferences or via key websites, where the professional societies announce job vacancies. These meetings are attended by many recent graduates, who expect to see all legitimate employers in attendance. In the words of one of the interviewees: "The university does not exist on the map of job seekers unless it sets up a booth at the career fair of this conference."

In some fields, such as sciences and engineering, which have a high level of differentiation, advertisements are posted in key scholarly journals. These journals tend to reach those specializing in specific areas, for example, robotics, and this makes them an effective vehicle to target academics with specific areas of expertise.

Social networks (e.g., Facebook, academia.edu, linkedin.com), as well as special interest groups in larger disciplinary societies, do not seem to play a major role in attracting applicants for vacancies in sciences, engineering, or at the business school. By contrast, in addition to posting in highly specialized journals, these social avenues are more extensively utilized in social sciences and education to attract faculty who conduct research in Central Asia.

Finally, the medical school posts advertisements on its website, which is a tool for attracting and maintaining the interest of job seekers. The dean of the school noted that his school constructs and updates the website so that it contains answers to most of the questions that potential applicants might have about NU. The website portrays NU as an interesting and welcoming place to work. The school puts useful information about its achievements on the website, as well as podcasts from the dean and other faculty members. The dean sees the website as more effective in attracting faculty applicants than other advertising venues.

## What Are the Roles and Procedures in the Process of Selection?

Although multiple approaches are used by NU's schools and departments in attracting and evaluating candidates, a common feature of all processes has been the central role of the provost. For much of the period under review, the provost was very active in the recruitment process, interviewing each recommended candidate and exercising the power to reject a candidate proposed by a dean. While this approach has changed under the current provost, there is still a strong central role in determining final salaries.

Four main approaches are used within NU for selecting and hiring faculty. The choice of the approach seems to be determined by three main factors. First, schools seem to differ in selection procedures depending on whether they offer only professional/graduate programs or both graduate and undergraduate programs. Second, the difference in selection practices also depends on the contractual arrangement with and the extent of involvement of the international partner institution. Third, discipline norms in hiring also create differences among schools.

One approach used at NU places great emphasis on the involvement of existing faculty members. In the Graduate School of Education, for example, the dean appoints faculty members to constitute the hiring committee on an annual basis. The dean also appoints the chair of the committee. This committee includes one of the vice deans and an executive director of the school as ex-officio members. The committee is responsible for initial screening and Skype interviewing of the candidates. The second-round interview is the purview of the international partners (in this case, the University of Pennsylvania and Cambridge University), and these interviews are usually conducted by Skype. The partners offer written advice to the dean, who has the final decision on which candidate(s) to advance to the third and final round of interviews, which is conducted by the dean and the provost. At the end of each round, recommendations are made for proceeding with the next round. While the dean and the partner institution may disagree on who should advance, disagreement is relatively uncommon. The final step is the review of a recommended candidate's case by the NU Salary Committee, which determines the salary level in the job offer.

Another approach followed by most of the multidepartment schools—which, until recently, offered predominantly undergraduate degrees and which had a small number of faculty members in individual departments—involves a process called the International Faculty Assessment Committee (IFAC). In this arrangement, the candidates shortlisted by the chairs of individual departments are interviewed on specific dates in Washington, DC, or in London. The interview team (IFAC) includes the representatives of the hiring department (including the chair) and/or the dean of the school, the provost, and an external expert in the discipline. The latter, in some cases, can be a representative of a partner institution. The candidates are provided round-trip transportation and are interviewed face to face. As long as the interview involves the partner institution, the school representatives, and the provost, the names of the approved candidates may go straight to the salary committee.

A very distinct approach is used by the department of economics, due to a high degree of standardization of the hiring process in the discipline. In this field, universities follow a timeline pegged to the annual meeting of the American Economic Association, where initial interviews are conducted with the candidates. The meeting is very important for the candidate and for the universities, due to the signaling function of the association membership. The representatives of NU's department of economics conduct the first round of interviews at the meeting because this symbolizes for candidates NU's institutional credibility and academic rigor. As one member of the department of economics indicated, if a school does not participate in the interviews at the annual meeting, it sends a message that it is not a serious place of scholarship:

> If you don't do it [go to the annual meeting of the American Economics Association], you are a black sheep. You are sending the wrong signal. So, what happens if you don't go? The candidates consider you as something wrong, something wrong with your university, something is not right here.

Subsequent interviewing is conducted by the department of economics, either at one of the IFAC meetings or by Skype, to make sure that the candidate is approved by the provost and the international partner university.

In the Graduate School of Business (GSB), its partner, Duke University's Fuqua School of Business, is very actively involved in selecting new faculty. All candidates are provided round-trip transportation and two-day accommodation for interviews at Fuqua. During the visit, they give a job talk and meet with Fuqua faculty and students. Duke's active involvement attracts many job applicants, and the interviews are an opportunity to provide the candidates with more information about Astana, NU, and the academic program. In the words of one of the participants, "[T]he interviewees were as much interviewed as they were interviewing."

## *What Characteristics Are Important in Hiring an International Faculty Member?*

One of the questions pursued in the interviews was about the characteristics that distinguished very good candidates in view of hiring team members. Although discipline-specific expectations from the candidates varied between the respondents, five characteristics were noted in many interviews. These were having a degree from a top-ranked university, the ability to conduct high-quality research in the field of specialization, teaching and graduate student supervision experience, stress resilience, and personality fit with the department.

The characteristic considered most important was having a degree from a recognized university, preferably from one of the top-ranked universities in the world. While many interviewees were frustrated with the unwritten requirement, they noted that the reason for this was the desire of the university to project the image of a truly world-class university. As one participant explained:

> The main thing is the PhD from an internationally recognized university. And this university puts a heavy emphasis on ranking of the universities, so actually, there might be an applicant from a top ten university, so I take the advantage of this . . . And one of the reasons for this is because we want to project an image to the world: Yes we are real; we have the best professors. That seems very effective.

Given the global aspirations of the university, a candidate's capacity to produce high-quality research is viewed as the next most important characteristic for faculty positions at NU. In every department represented in the study, hiring committees do not consider applicants without journal publications, regardless of the name recognition of their PhD-awarding institution. Such applicants are encouraged to apply in the future after gaining a basic publication record or are advised to start as instructors. Many participants noted that the lack of publications is one of the reasons why many local applicants with Western PhD degrees do not succeed in the hiring process.

Although research is emphasized more than teaching in the applicants' profiles, many participants in this study valued teaching experience. In many schools, the lack of senior faculty members means that previous experience in teaching and thesis supervision are valued. The ability to teach in English seems to be more critical in sciences and engineering, because these fields tend to attract many applicants from non–English-speaking countries. Even if an international candidate had completed a PhD in an English-speaking country, the person's English writing and speaking skills may still be weak. For social sciences, given the limited research on Central Asia and the post-Soviet region, faculty members are expected to be able to draw on their research in teaching. Even if they do not have experience conducting research in the region or on topics relevant to the region, they are expected to be able to demonstrate how they can adapt their research agenda to local realities and needs. In the words of one participant:

> In economics, number one we are looking for people, who are interested in research in Central Asian-Russian context . . . It does not have to be their prior research field, but it could be a minor research . . . We really want to have research driven teaching . . . because there is not really so much literature here. And we have to develop (the literature) ourselves . . .

Another important feature is the ability of the candidate to cope with the constantly changing, highly unpredictable, and underspecified environment of a new university. One of the ways an applicant can demonstrate this ability is to have prior experience living abroad or working at a new university or academic unit. Many of the interviewed members of the hiring committees are cognizant of the challenges of working in a new institution, and they attempt to avoid recruiting people who would be unhappy in a rapidly changing environment.

Although 'fit' is important in selection of candidates for many hiring committees in the West, the ability to "become an integral part of the family" is even more important for hiring committees at NU. Having like-minded people around is viewed as a prerequisite to building a team that will be able to coexist under the conditions of stress and rapid change. In addition, good interpersonal relations are very important in a small academic community situated in a foreign country where most people do not speak English.

## What Backgrounds Do Applicants Come From?

While NU seeks to hire well-qualified international faculty, the decentralized recruitment processes and the still-emerging central institutional research capability mean that there are no reliable or readily accessible data on the characteristics of applicants. Some generalizations can be drawn from the interviews. Geographically, the majority of applicants come from North America and Europe. Other major sources of applicants include the Middle East (notably, Saudi Arabia) and Southeast Asia (notably, Singapore), Pakistan, and India, especially from universities that have significant numbers of faculty who use English as a language of instruction.

Most applicants hold Western university degrees in the area of specialization. In some fields, such as computer science, there are a great number of underqualified applicants, some of whom hold only a Microsoft training certificate, but still feel qualified to apply.

While there are no centrally held statistics on the number of applications by citizenship, the pool of applicants is likely to reflect the composition of the hired faculty body, which is predominantly Anglophone. Whether this skewed distribution is the result of a bias in the hiring process or a lack of applicants from non-Western countries is difficult to ascertain. Some interviewees said that they exercise more caution when considering applicants with PhDs earned in non-Western institutions:

> [We normally don't hire] people who ... have PhDs from other parts of the world, which are not considered acceptable, you know, unless I know the professor they are working with or I have contacts, or I know they come from really good university in India, and I have people that actually did

their master's degree in India, and PhDs in [the] States, in Canada, and I call them and ask them, "What do you think about this person? This university? And working with this person?"

There seems to be some gender imbalance in appointments, especially in sciences, engineering, and business, which stands in stark contrast to the large number of female students in NU's science and engineering programs. For example, one-third of the School of Engineering's students are female, whereas only 4 out of 35 faculty are women. One potential explanation for the gender imbalance in appointments could be a lower predisposition for international relocation among female academics.

The majority of applicants seem to be early career faculty who are applying for their first position or are currently employed as adjuncts or postdocs. These applicants tend to be of higher quality than the applicants at the more senior levels. The large supply of such applicants benefits Kazakhstan in its effort to build a truly international-level research university. However, attracting high-quality assistant professors is definitely not sufficient for the ambitious goal to be realized. Necessary conditions of employment should be also provided for the faculty to become productive and to stay at the university.

## What Challenges Does NU Face in Attracting International Faculty?

Despite offering a salary and teaching load comparable to US research-intensive universities and good conditions for conducting research, NU faces some difficulties in attracting international faculty, particularly senior-level faculty. Applicant pools at the senior level are relatively weak. A recent senior vacancy in NUGSE attracted no external candidates with experience in leading research programs, and few applicants had solid experience in doctoral supervision. Many vacancies remain at the associate and full professor level. This is a major concern among university administrators since the lack of senior-level faculty presents difficulties in providing proper mentorship for assistant professors, supervision of doctoral students, and leadership in committees that are responsible for developing procedures and policies in an emerging institution. As a result, the quality of teaching, research, and service may all be affected by the lack of more experienced senior-level professors.

Salary and benefits packages are seldom identified as barriers in recruitment. Faculty housing is provided, and there is a modest financial allowance for children's schooling, as well as funds for regular visits to one's home country. The main reasons cited for the inability to attract senior-level faculty include the lack of a tenure system, a poor supply of senior candidates in the labor market, and the remote location of Kazakhstan. Associate professors tend to be middle-aged professionals who are already established and secure in their current places of employment, with an established network of contacts and funding streams. Many have family responsibilities and job security ensured by tenure. These factors, along with the difficulty in reestablishing new funding streams and research networks in a new context, makes relocating to a new university, even at a slightly higher level of salary, unattractive for mid-career academics.

Conversely, pre-retirement academics with fewer family responsibilities and less pressure to publish for tenure or advancement are more interested. However, their age has sometimes been a barrier to being hired. In the past, NU has funded emergency travel for some older faculty so they could receive medical treatments that are not available in Kazakhstan.

Some schools are becoming more strategic in recruiting senior faculty. Different venues are used to post advertisements targeting senior applicants. For example, in economics, whereas job postings on the American Economic Association's website target younger candidates, ads in the *Chronicle of Higher Education* are aimed at individuals already working in the discipline. In other disciplines, job ads are posted in European journals and on job search websites to target early retirement faculty, who are more likely to be found in Europe and Scandinavian countries.

Another challenge seems to be the sheer number of positions that have to be filled as the student population increases with successive intakes and as new schools and programs open. Because many of the schools are starting or scaling up their programs, they have to fill five to ten positions at different ranks per year. All these hiring needs have to be met without sacrificing quality for quantity, and have to be met for several schools simultaneously. Such massive scale hiring requires much coordination and forward thinking, which inexperienced local administrators may still be developing as they grapple with multiple bureaucratic norms and rules.

Many interview participants indicated that the complicated, multistage process of hiring, as well as the inability to negotiate offers, sometimes leads to the loss of highly qualified candidates. Since a variety of different players (IFAC, international partners, university top administration, and the department) are involved in the selection process, the time required for the final decision extends to several months. The layers of review limit effective communication with the preferred candidate. This delay (according to one interviewee) gives the candidate a reason to continue the job search elsewhere:

> Bureaucracy [in] hiring is so slow. It is very debilitating, and we have lost a number of extremely good candidates because they just don't want to deal with that. It takes a long [time] to respond to them, signing the contract, the sort of communication style . . . insulting and aggressive by all these people . . . There are a lot of people, who . . . say: "I am not working here, forget it" and that is the biggest disappointment.

The hiring process at NU generally does not allow contract negotiation, which runs against the expectations of many international applicants. The personnel management system in NU uses a common template for compensation and benefits, much like Kazakhstan's public universities. Nationally, these templates are seen as tools to ensure parity in terms of salary and benefits, between posts of the same rank, and as ways to minimize patronage and favoritism. NU has adopted the same uniform approach. Templates make it difficult to negotiate even small adjustments in terms and conditions. This inflexibility is interpreted by some applicants as a signal that the institution does not care about the differing needs of applicants.

Some participants also commented on the limited involvement of existing faculty members in the hiring process, especially in the schools serving undergraduates and relying on IFAC for hiring. Because the process of interviewing is conducted externally and the final decision on hiring is made by senior NU officials, some faculty members feel that they are not sufficiently consulted on hiring needs or shortages of expertise in a department. The desire to achieve greater efficiency in the process of hiring, as well as the ultimate concern for quality (understood as the involvement of the international partner institutions), has excluded existing faculty members. This is potentially problematic because the feeling of marginalization may undermine the process of integrating a newly hired colleague into a department.

A few schools face the challenge of processing a large number of candidates who are applying merely to improve their employment prospects and salary negotiations at other institutions. These individuals apply to NU without any intention to join the university, even if they receive an offer. Hiring committees became more skilled in identifying and sorting out these applicants. Some interview participants explained that whenever they receive an application from a stellar candidate, they always question why the applicant would like to come to Kazakhstan. They want to hear a clear explanation during the first interview of why the person might be interested in joining NU. If the candidate is unable to provide a clear argument, they do not proceed to the next level of interviewing.

> There are really strong candidates, but we just know they will never come ... They have five publications, already, before they graduated, in top journals. Why would they ever think about applying here? We know these people [are] never going to come here, we just write them: "Thank you, but I don't think that this is a proper university for you to be. But if you really want this interview, we are more than happy to schedule an interview." We do leave the door open, no, we don't close the door.

## *What Are Some of the Successes in the Process of Hiring?*

NU has been successful in attracting qualified faculty. While there are talented local hires among the faculty, the majority of the faculty is international and has contributed to the success of the students in the first graduating class—many of whom have been admitted to top-ranked international graduate schools (Institutional Research, 2015). In terms of research outcomes, NU faculty members have secured institutional, national, and international research grants. In 2015, NU researchers received a significant proportion of Ministry of Education grants. A bibliometric analysis conducted by Kuzhabekova (in press) revealed that NU has made a significant contribution to the number of peer-reviewed contributions produced in Kazakhstan since the first years of its existence and is responsible for a large proportion of peer-reviewed publications in the country.

Many of the participants noted the high quality of assistant professors that have been hired by the university. In the words of one of the interviewees from the School of Humanities and Social Sciences:

> But mostly what we have, our really strong assistant professors, who I think in five years, will be very big names . . . We have the largest concentration of specialists in Eurasia, Kazakhstan, anywhere in the world, which is amazing . . . These people can easily find jobs anywhere else, but they specifically chose to come here.

## *What Is the Role of the International Partner in the Recruitment and the Hiring Processes?*

A distinctive characteristic of NU is its multiple international partnerships. This is a source of differentiation in its recruitment processes. Each school has a different partner or partners, and different terms underlie each relationship. The role of the partner in the recruitment and hiring processes varies depending on the nature of the arrangements. In some schools, partners perform an advisory function, providing feedback during one of the stages of the interview. One example is the Graduate School of Education, where the partners believe that the decision to forward a candidate's file to the provost is the province of the school's hiring committee and its dean. In this case, the role of the GSE partners has changed over time. Initially the partners were very active in the process of hiring the dean and the vice deans, as well as the first group of faculty. They stepped back in subsequent years, as the school's hiring committee has been formed and more senior staff joined the school and were able to take a leading role in faculty governance. The evolving role of the partners in the hiring process mirrors the changing role they play in program design, student admissions, and moderation of student assessments. For example, for the initial intake of master's students, a representative from each partner read the applications and commented on all applicants who met the language requirement. For subsequent intakes, the partners acted as a reference point by reviewing a small selection of applications that represented strong, borderline, and unacceptable candidates. The changed role was based on the premise that the growing faculty body is assuming greater responsibility and the partners' role has shifted to quality assurance and validation.

In some schools, partners actively participated in the process of setting up selection and hiring mechanisms, but were less engaged in the hiring process after the procedures were set up.

In the NU Graduate School of Business, the international partner is actively involved in the process of hiring. As described earlier, candidates are interviewed at Duke to see if there is a match between the applicant's research interests and cultures of Fuqua and NU. Fuqua's active participation in the hiring process is a product of its contract with the Graduate School of Business, whereby it also mentors NUGSB faculty members and co-teaches courses in Astana.

## What Can Be Learned from NU?

There are obvious limits to the power of generalizations from one case, especially when the case is a young, evolving institution. But NU's distinctive characteristics, notably its multiple international partners and its use of devolved and centralized faculty hiring processes, provide a rich set of observations that may be instructive to other emerging institutions. In all, we offer seven points worthy of reflection.

An initial observation is that it is possible for one institution to use multiple models to recruit international faculty. In NU's case, the presence of multiple international partners with different contractual, organizational, and educational relationships has produced different hiring processes. Some partners are directly represented on NU hiring committees, whereas others have taken a benchmarking and quality assurance role after the appointment of the founding dean of a school.

Some of these differences within an institution are discipline based; different disciplines tend to use different recruiting strategies, targeting field-specific forums, journals, and conferences. This aligns with the norms of professional conduct in the subject area with regard to timing of advertisements and interviews.

Similarly, some of the differences are linked to the level of the faculty being recruited. Different strategies have been used to attract junior and senior applicants. New junior staff members have tended to be pursued through the 'job fair' elements of large conferences and professional membership associations. These venues have the benefit of scale, cost effectively reaching many new graduates and postdoctoral fellows. Participation in these discipline-based events has also given a measure of legitimacy to the recruiting process. This is in keeping with the proposition in organizational theory that an institution or agency increases its survival capability when it "incorporates socially legitimated rationalized elements" into its operating environment (Myer & Rowan, 1997, p. 352). This is particularly important for newly established entities. Furthermore, the hiring processes in a developing institution are not static. Policies and procedures evolve as more faculty members are hired to take on the responsibilities of recruiting, screening, and interviewing job applicants.

Pursuing a reputation as a world-class university, NU places a premium on international qualifications, particularly doctorates awarded by high-profile, research-intensive universities. It also values English-language, peer-reviewed publications. These two criteria tend to limit the recruitment of local candidates and favor the recruitment of faculty from English-speaking countries. Several issues arise from this tendency. First is the challenge of building a stable faculty base at a very new university by recruiting in a highly competitive global academic labor market. By opting to offer three-year renewable contracts rather than seven-year pathways to tenure or tenured appointments and an attendant measure of job security, NU is at a comparative market disadvantage.

The consequence of preferring international staff over similarly qualified local citizens also constrains the role NU can, and should, play in "cultural reproduction" (Bourdieu, 1993). As the premier university in the nation, NU has a responsibility to identify, study, critique, conserve, and celebrate important national mores and values. This is more easily and perhaps more appropriately pursued by faculty with a deep affinity for the region, its languages, its peoples, and its identities. This has implications for the university's recruitment, retention, and faculty development strategies.

Overreliance on international faculty has another challenge. Our interviews reveal that while NU is trying to attract faculty interested in conducting research on locally relevant topics, it has actually recruited a relatively small number of faculty with an interest in such topics and an international research profile. Perhaps faculty from the surrounding communities can keep highly internationalized universities in the global South locally relevant in addition to being internationally competitive. This is another area where NU might rebalance its recruitment and retention strategies.

A third issue that arises from a heavy reliance on faculty originating from English-speaking countries is a tendency to conform to organizational modalities prevailing in those countries, without reference to local conditions and circumstances. This "isomorphism" (Levinson, 1989), mimicking other institutions' practices, may constrain organizational innovation and impede the development of a distinctive academic culture aligned to NU's mission and reflecting its historic geographic location and geopolitical interests. For example, NU might incorporate policies and practices from high-performing universities in Singapore, Japan, and Russia and recent initiatives in Europe like Germany's Excellence Initiative (Kehm, 2013). Having a more diverse faculty body in terms of country of origin and PhD training may be very beneficial.

Another challenge revealed through our study is how to successfully recruit and retain senior-level faculty without either long-term contracts or a tenure system. Without debating the costs and benefits of a tenure system, the relative absence of senior faculty within schools and programs impoverishes NU's academic culture. Senior faculty are a source of professional expertise, and they are carriers of organizational traditions and tacit organizational knowledge. Being recognized researchers, they also play a signaling function for the university, helping it to attract new sources of funding and new international partners, faculty, and students.

Our study also suggests that NU has had difficulty in recruiting female international faculty, particularly in some faculties, like engineering. The increasing enrollment of female students in universities around the world (including Kazakhstan) underscores the importance of a representative faculty body. A university reliant on international faculty may need to pay more attention to creating family- and child-friendly employment and living conditions.

NU's case has shown that a variety of recruitment approaches can be used in one institution, particularly when there are multiple academic partners, each with different academic norms. But this may not be relevant for emerging institutions without multiple partners. Nonetheless, some observations may be transferable. For example, involving faculty in the interviewing process has been helpful in ensuring there is a good fit with the personalities of the team and with the pedagogic values and research needs of the department. This is especially pertinent when the faculty are few in number and culturally and linguistically isolated from the surrounding community.

Similarly, the practice of forming a school-specific hiring committee that conducts face-to-face interviews in regions with multiple candidates can be more cost effective than bringing short-listed candidates to the campus. The trade-off is a loss of broader faculty, staff, and student involvement in faculty recruitment.

A third illustrative practice that warrants close consideration is the involvement of an international partner in the hiring process to signal institutional quality and transparency.

NU is in its early stages of development as an institution. The first generation of employment contracts is ending, and issues of retention, continuity, and sustainability are emerging as the university continues to develop. NU's aspirations to be an internationally recognized research university will depend in large measure on the faculty recruited, retained, and promoted.

## Notes

1 Attestation is a process that awards or removes a license to operate as a higher education institution. It usually involves an assessment of how well an institution is following the 'state standards' which specify curriculum content for core courses. (See the OECD and World Bank 2007 review pages 107–123.)
2 Interview with Vice Minister Tahir on June 16, 2015. Strategic Plan of the Ministry of Education and Science RK for 2014–2016.
3 "School" indicates a faculty unit at NU (e.g., School of Humanities and Social Sciences).

## References

Bourdieu, P. (1993). *The field of cultural production: Essays on art and literature*. Cambridge: Polity Press.

Hiro, D. (2009). *Inside central Asia: A political and cultural history of Uzbekistan, Turkmenistan, Kazakhstan, Kyrgyzstan, Tajikistan, Turkey, and Iran*. London: Overlook Press Duckworth.

Institutional Research, Office of the Provost (2015). Undergraduate exist survey: Spring 2015 results.

International Monetary Fund (2015). *Regional economic outlook. Middle East and Central Asia, October 2015*. Washington, DC: Author.

Kehm, B. M. (2013). To be or not to be? The impacts of the excellence initiative on the German system of higher education. In Shin, J.S. & Kehm, B.M., (eds), *Institutionalization of world-class university in global competition* (pp. 81–97). Netherlands: Springer.

Kuzhabekova, A. (in press). The development of university research in Kazakhstan during 1991–2013: A bibliometric view. In I. Silova & S. Niyozov (Eds.), *Globalization on the Margins*. 2nd ed.

Kuzhabekova, A., Mukhametzhanova, A., Almukhambetova, A., & Soltanbekova, A. (2015, March). Can flagships lead Kazakhstani educational system to the desired transformation? Paper presented at the Annual Meeting of the Comparative and International Education Society, Washington, DC.

Leonard, P. (2015). Kazakhstan: Row at President's University Dents claim to academic independence. Eurasianet.org, 24 August. Reprinted in *The Moscow Times*, 25 August.

Levinson, R. M. (1989). The faculty and institutional isomorphism. *Academe*, 75(1), 23–27. Retrieved from http://doi.org/10.2307/40249781

Ministry of Education and Science of the Republic of Kazakhstan (2012). *Academic mobility strategy in Kazakhstan: For 2012–2020*. Astana. http://naric-kazakhstan.kz/ru/akademicheskaya-mobilnost/strategiyamobilnosti-do-2020-goda

Myer, J.W. & Rowan, B. (1997). Institutionalized organizations: Formal structure as myth and ceremony. *American Journal of Sociology*, 83, 340–363.

Navoyan, A. (2011). Tertiary education in Armenia: Between Soviet heritage, transition and the Bologna Process. In M. Martin & M. Bray (Eds.), *Tertiary education in small states* (pp. 193–212). Paris: UNESCO.

Nazarbayev University (2015). Public statement from NU. 26 August & Joint statement by Provost Anne Lonsdale and Professor de Maas, 9 September. Retrieved from www.nu.edu.kz/portal/faces

Nazarbayev University (n.d.). Retrieved from www.nu.edu.kz/portal/faces/main menu/aboutus1

Nygymetov, G. (2014). The role of international "Bolashak" scholarship in quality assurance of education in Kazakhstan. Higher School of Kazakhstan. #1, pp. 24–27.

OECD & The World Bank (2007). *Higher education in Kazakhstan: Reviews of national policies for education*. Paris: OECD.

Putz, C. (2015). Is academic freedom dead in Kazakhstan? *The Diplomat*, 26 August.

Tuymebayev, Z. (2009, February 5). The aims of higher education of the republic of Kazakhstan on the way to the Bologna process. *Speech of Minister of Education & Science of the Republic of Kazakhstan at al-Farabi Kazakh National University* Retrieved from www.edu.gov.kz

# 9

# ATTRACTION, INTEGRATION, AND PRODUCTIVITY OF INTERNATIONAL ACADEMICS IN MEXICO

*Sylvie Didou Aupetit*[1]

## Introduction

Since the 1970s, the National Council for Science and Technology (CONACYT)—the governing body in Mexico for science and technology—has administered overseas scholarship programs and, beginning in the 1980s, programs for attracting international academics. Due to the success of the mechanisms established by such government agencies, few higher education institutions designed their own strategies for linking their faculty recruitment policies with institutional development priorities. Exceptions to this rule include the Colegio de México (COLMEX), as a result of the particular manner of its foundation and because if its nature as an institution devoted to research, as well as the National Autonomous University of Mexico's (UNAM) Institute of Geophysics (IGP), due both to its position in a traditionally internationalized discipline and its connection to UNAM. This institution, the largest and most prestigious in the country, has always acted as a magnet among the international academics settled in the country.

Over the last two decades, there has been an increase in the number of institutions supporting processes for the internationalization of their faculties, due to the progressive installation by the government authorities of a system of guidance and financing of higher education based on quality assurance and extra-budgetary incentive programs; in this system, the percentage of international academics has become proof of competitiveness. For this reason, even newly created institutions, such as the Maya Intercultural University of Quintana Roo (UIMQRoo), have sought to incentivize international scientific mobility in order to legitimize themselves in both their social spheres and their academic fields.

In the majority of cases, however, higher education institutions (HEIs) have practiced a responsive and reactive policy to external opportunities for training through scholarships and the international recruitment programs provided by government agencies. In virtue of this, this chapter presents an overview of relevant public policies and three institutional case studies. We selected these specific institutions because these HEIs sought, with varying degrees of success, to shore up their development projects by recruiting international academics for the purposes of disciplinary consolidation and evidencing a reasoned use of the opportunities provided by the government. Our purpose is to analyze some experiences of institutional choice and schemes for attracting international academics in a very influential framework of governmental action.

## International Academics in Mexico: A Low-Visibility Issue

Although the role of international academics in the reorganization of scientific groups seems a topic of increasing interest worldwide, the sources through which to approach this topic in Mexico are scarce. This is despite the fact that the capacity for postgraduate education and research has been strengthened by historical and ongoing exchanges of ideas, students, and faculty within international scholarly communities (including knowledge transfer and doctoral graduates), plus inverse mobility linked to the return of citizens earning qualifications abroad and the incorporation of foreign academics.

Contemporary studies of this 'brain gain' are few in Mexico and were primarily published during the last decade. Empirical in approach, they analyze programs of inverse migration and invitations, together with networks, chains, and circuits for knowledge transfer and physical mobility. In any case, they show little interest in how international scientists appropriate idiosyncratic codes of professional conduct, integrate themselves into disciplinary cultures, or develop 'glocal' strategies to position themselves within their working fields. Their perspectives and subjects are lacking, particularly in comparison with those explored in the United States (Appelt, van Beuzekom, Galindo-Rueda & Pinho, 2015).

A look at the bibliography on topics related to international academics reveals that in Mexico, the most abundant type of academic production is historical in nature. It concerns foreigners more than those Mexicans with degrees from abroad. In particular, political-intellectual exiles during the 20th century awoke interest among Mexican researchers, with an emphasis on the Spanish during the 1940s and Latin and Central Americans between the 1960s and 1980s. In relation to this group, and focusing specifically on educational sciences, we find biographies of noted international scientists who have contributed to the creation of institutions or the consolidation of disciplinary areas (Guzik, 2009; Queré, 2009). Recently, this literature—classical in style—has been complemented by contributions from the history of science (knowledge transfer networks: Gérard & Maldonado, 2009), sociology (internationalization of the academic profession: Durand, 2013), and political science (attraction and brain gain programs: Didou & Durand, 2013; Góngora, 2015; Morales, 2015; immigration policy: Aragonés, 2012; training elites:

Gérard, 2013). Lastly, some research has examined the repercussions on academic careers of intellectual migration and return (Remedi & Ramírez, 2014).

## Brain Circulation and Public Policies for Reverse Migration and Attraction of International Faculty

With respect to foreign academics, Mexico is less a country that receives highly skilled migrants than one that produces them. Nevertheless, the 2010 population census indicates a rate of increase in the immigrant population greater than that of the population as a whole during the first decade of the millennium. The percentage of people with university degrees in this group is on the rise, although these figures vary according to origin country. In 2010, 187,999 foreigners over the age of 25 and with higher education qualifications had their residence in Mexico (INEGI, 2010), with the most highly educated coming from Europe and the least from Central America and the United States. This was equivalent to between 4 and 5 percent of the Mexican population with similar higher education diplomas living in Mexico (INEGI, 2013), and 20 percent of highly skilled Mexican emigrants located in the Organisation for Economic Co-operation and Development (OECD) zone (National Science Foundation, 2014).

We do not know how many of those foreigners (12,963 of them holding PhDs) work in academia. No government agency publishes this information on a national scale. But, two surveys done by a Mexican research network, one from 1992 and another from 2007, report that the number of foreigners as a percentage of full-time faculty rose from 3.8 percent to 5 percent. The proportion of Mexican academics who earned degrees from non-Mexican institutions increased quickly, from 13.9 percent to 21.8 percent (Galaz et al., 2012, p. 209–210). These percentages indicate that the dynamic of internationalization of the academic profession has depended essentially on the return of Mexican overseas sojourners, irrespective of the slight rise in the percentage of foreigners.

In particular, the research sector concentrates the highest percentages for both groups. In 2009, the National System of Researchers (SNI)[2] registered that 12.8 percent of its 15,561 members were born overseas.[3] It also listed 36 percent of its members, both Mexicans and foreigners, with PhDs from abroad. Many international academics are living in Mexico City, with high clustering in the National Autonomous University of Mexico (UNAM), the Metropolitan Autonomous University (UAM), the Center for Research and Advanced Studies (CINVESTAV), and the National Polytechnic Institute (IPN). The rest are scattered around the country in the autonomous universities of Guadalajara, Puebla, Morelos, and Nuevo León, together with one private institution, the Monterrey Institute of Technology and Higher Education (ITESM). By discipline, they are numerous in physical-mathematical and earth sciences (46.2 percent), whereas the lowest proportion is in health sciences and biotechnology (16.4 percent).

The degrees of 'internationalization' in these areas depend on the educational traditions of each discipline, together with the unbalanced immigration of scientists during the 1990s (Didou & Gérard, 2010, p. 59–61). The largest groups of foreign scientists come from Spain, the United States, Argentina, Cuba, and the Russian Federation (Didou & Durand, 2013), in accordance with schemas of mobility based on proximity, cultural closeness, and contingency. It would be important to know how many of those from the United States are of Mexican origin, but we have not found any statistics concerning this point. Altogether, foreign academics hail from 77 countries, a figure that points to a growing diversification in places of origin—from 56 in 1993, according to Narváez & Rosas (1995).

Mexican PhDs with degrees obtained abroad come essentially from 'mainstream' countries—the United States, Spain, France, Germany, and the United Kingdom, reflecting the geographic trends of overall outgoing student mobility and of CONACYT Scholarship programs at the postgraduate level. These spatial tendencies are also tied to circuits and chains of disciplinary knowledge transmission; of particular importance is the international capacity of certain countries to position themselves during specific periods as international poles for postgraduate education. Their capacity to attract foreign students is a function of the scholarships they offer; the cost of their tuition and fees; their cultural, linguistic, or geographical closeness; or their disciplinary recognition. Such was the case of Spain before the economic crisis.

Most international researchers settled in Mexico show a tendency toward bilateral mobility (i.e., moving between countries of origin and destinations, and, for Mexicans with overseas qualifications, between Mexico and the specific countries where they obtained their PhD degrees). However, some have developed complex mobility patterns, characterized by research activities and study placements in institutions other than those of their birth country or of their professional training. In 2009, approximately 10 percent of the foreigners in the SNI followed this pattern. They were mainly from countries that either were not poles for their disciplines or had only lately consolidated their supply of postgraduate opportunities, or they were young people who had undertaken postgraduate studies in different countries in order to improve their chances of professional advancement. A small proportion of Mexicans with overseas degrees also undertook master's and doctoral study in different locations. A central question for further investigation concerns the concrete referents relating to the formative and professional experiences abroad of international academics with regard to nationality: The proportion of 'endogenous' education acquired in their home country is low among Latin Americans but high among Spaniards, Russians, Americans, the French, and Cubans (SNI database, 2013).

This situation is the result of a policy of educating Mexican postgraduate students abroad, launched in 1975 with the start of the postgraduate scholarship program administered by CONACYT. In 2014, 1,145 of its grantees went to foreign countries: Spain (30 percent), the United States (19.7 percent), Germany (7.1 percent), and France (6.7 percent) (Sánchez, 2015). In the 1990s, CONACYT complemented this 'star program' with others designed to attract returnees and foreign university professors. These programs form part of a policy of in situ internationalization, which unites invitations to scientists from other countries with the repatriation of graduates from abroad.

In fact, in 1992, CONACYT became a pioneer in Latin America by including foreign academics among the beneficiaries of the Program to Support Science in Mexico (PACIME). Jointly funded by the World Bank and the Mexican government, between that year and 2000, the program attracted 2,284 foreign researchers. The most important groups of these academics came from the Soviet Union and the Eastern Bloc. Lately, CONACYT has used its state-funded budget to maintain other programs with similar aims, such as Level II Chair Professorships (i.e., *Cátedras Patrimoniales de Excelencia*) and the Fund for the Consolidation of Research Groups. Unfortunately, the data available are not congruent and do not enable us to calculate how many of the beneficiaries developed their academic careers in Mexico and how many returned to their country of origin or re-emigrated. They only corroborate a distinction between the institutions that knew how to benefit from the programs by attracting international faculty (the universities of Morelos and Baja California and principally UNAM, for instance) and those that, because of their essential makeup and historical traditions, had their own projects predating internationalization policies.

In addition to the program for inviting foreign scientists, CONACYT enhanced its tools for encouraging the return of Mexican PhDs settled overseas—whether recent graduates, postdoctoral students, or senior faculty employed in the labor market of their countries of residence. In 2015, the traditional program for 'repatriation' that formed part of CONACYT's portfolio of complementary support for the consolidation of research groups offered funding totaling USD 36,000 to male researchers, with a bonus of USD 1,800 for mothers of Mexican nationality working at a public institution (50 percent less if the institution is private). In parallel with this, in 2012, CONACYT opened a subprogram of SNI for Mexicans carrying out research activities overseas. The purpose of this subprogram is to provide to its beneficiaries on their return to Mexico, either for the duration of their stay or from the beginning of their contract with a Mexican university, the economic incentive commensurate with their prior classification in the SNI categories, in accordance with evaluation's results of their scientific trajectory.

For its part, the National Association of Universities and Higher Education Institutions (ANUIES) and the Ministry of Higher Education (SEP) fostered mechanisms of overseas study for faculty recruited without PhDs by Mexican universities in order to provide teaching to a growing number of students during the 1980s. Starting in 1993, ANUIES oversaw the program for Improvement of Academic Personnel. In 1998, SEP incorporated this into the Program for the Improvement of Faculty (PROMEP); by 2012, PROMEP had granted 2,529 overseas scholarships. At present, the SEP web page contains no data on the results for the three years from 2013 to 2015 for the Program for Professional Development of Teachers (PRODEP), which replaced PROMEP, but there is no doubt that these programs increased the percentage of doctoral degree holders among faculty, as well as that of Mexican academics with PhDs from abroad.

## Institutional Environments and Individual Dynamics of Acclimation

To gain a deeper understanding of the dynamics of international faculty experiences in Mexico, we structured a sample of respondents, based on the SNI register, which includes foreign scientists' names and birthplaces. We interviewed 17 international academics (7 at the UNAM-IGP, 6 at the COLMEX, and 4 at UIMQRoo). The sample depended on the availability of each individual and the recommendations of the initial interviewees. Consequently, it was not representative of the full range of possible faculty profiles in terms of age, sex, nationality, academic rank or position in the hierarchy, or registration in the SNI. The sample did, however, include representatives of the last three of the four waves of intellectual immigration to Mexico that occurred during the 20th century: Spanish Republicans in the 1940s; Latin Americans during the 1960s and 1980s, as political exiles; 'Russians' during the 1990s; and atypical migrants in the 2000s (Castaños, 2009). The questionnaire we administered dealt with the causes and conditions of emigration to Mexico, landmarks on the career path, working conditions at the host institution, the disciplinary networks of the interviewees, and the way in which the interviewees perceived the academic environments in which they studied compared with those in which they practiced their professions. In three instances, the interviewees occupied positions of responsibility at their institutions and expressed a global vision of institutional strategies, not just individual feelings.

Analysis of the interviews enabled us to see how international academics working in either the social sciences and humanities (linguistics, history, sociology, philosophy, communication, and anthropology) or the hard sciences (seismology, volcanology, physics, geology, biology, and agricultural economics) established professional ties with their host institutions and perceived the working conditions provided in Mexico. Due to the variations in their ages (the oldest was born in 1928; the youngest in 1981), it was possible to glimpse just how government policies on the restructuring of the national research and higher education systems affected the conditions of their recruitment and professional practice.

Because of a lack of resources for fieldwork, we conducted interviews in three institutions selected for their accessibility due to their geographic proximity or the existence of prior contacts that facilitated access to the interviewees. The IGP and the COLMEX are situated in Mexico City and the UIMQRoo is located in the state of Quintana Roo, on the southern border with Guatemala. However, the main reasons for choosing these specific institutions were the differences between their internationalization profiles and the positions they occupy in the higher education sphere. In effect, academics at the IGP, fully respected in their fields, devote themselves to research but usually give classes at other schools across the UNAM. The COLMEX, an institution with a strong reputation for social sciences, has a number of undergraduate, but mostly postgraduate, programs. Although they have used mixed models for the hiring of international academics at both the IGP and COLMEX, the approaches are different: The IGP internationalization model is based on low-level incorporation of foreigners combined with a high rate of Mexicans with overseas qualifications. SNI data on the 184 COLMEX members show that 62 (33.7 percent) are foreign born, 41 (66.1 percent) gained their doctorates abroad, and 68 Mexicans (55.7 percent of the subgroup) have overseas qualifications. International academics thus make up 55.9 percent of the institution's SNI members, if we combine the indicator 'born abroad' with that of 'qualified abroad'; the proportion of international academics reaches 70.2 percent if we take only the country of birth of those who obtained their doctoral qualifications abroad.

IGP and COLMEX, with their high capacity for attracting academics, have been bringing them in for several decades. They provide generous support for attendance at international events and invitations to colleagues from outside, taking care that their eventual academic load should not be an impediment to their outside activities.

The history of the IGP dates back to 1904, when, at a meeting in Paris, representatives from 18 countries founded the International Seismological Association and Mexico decided to create its National Seismological Service (Instituto de Geofísica, 2015). In 2014, the IGP consisted of seven research units (spatial science, geomagnetism and geophysical exploration, solar radiation, natural resources, seismology, volcanology, and the Michoacán Unit). It participates in postgraduate programs in earth sciences and marine sciences. Its academic faculty is made up of 137 members, 71 of whom were recruited as researchers (Instituto de Geofísica, 2013–2017). As a matter of tradition, together with an interest in diversifying its areas of research and the technical demands of team management, it hosts seven foreign researchers (plus two emeritus researchers). The proportion of foreigners in the IGP is higher than the institutional average (5.1 percent versus 1.4 percent) for Mexico (UNAM, 2014). The average age of IGP researchers is 55, though this is lower among the foreigners.

The career histories of the researchers published on the institute's website, though incomplete, indicate that a very high proportion of the faculty was involved in at least one extended placement abroad in connection with obtaining a doctorate. A number began their international mobility at the master's level and, in some cases, studied for this in a location other than where they obtained their doctorates. One group continued along a path of international mobility following their doctorates by means of postdoctoral courses or sabbaticals. Some countries (like the United States, France, Russia, and Japan) and institutions (such as the former USSR Academy of Sciences) have functioned as poles of attraction for education and even ongoing professional development.

Spanish Republicans[4] founded the Casa de España on August 20, 1938. Casa de España later changed its name to COLMEX, which was legally constituted in October 1940. Considered today a 'research university' in the social sciences, it had developed international relationships before these became the object of governmental policy. COLMEX's seven research centers (focused on history, literature and linguistics, economics, sociology, international relations, demographics and urban development, and Asian-African studies) offer seven master's programs, seven doctorates, and three undergraduate degrees, plus a specialization course. Each center has internationalized its faculty in a different way: The Center for Asian-African Studies (CEAA) did so by recruiting both foreigners and nationals who had graduated abroad; the Centers for Economic Studies and International Studies hired more foreigners with overseas qualifications. As a general trend, foreign-born academics come chiefly from the United States, the United Kingdom, France, and Argentina, although, on an individual level, their countries of origin are numerous (28), mainly in the particularly diverse CEAA.

In contrast to both these institutions, UIMQRoo launched its activities on October 30, 2006, as a political-ethnic project to attend to vulnerable populations.[5] In 2012, it enrolled 634 students in undergraduate programs (Language and Culture, Agro-Ecology, Municipal Tourism, Information Technology, Management and Development of the Arts, and Business Development). Its first specialization and master's programs—Intercultural Education—were only created in 2012. It essentially offers teaching aimed at the indigenous population of its region. Since its creation, it has simultaneously fostered an internationalization project (focused on student mobility and the temporary attraction of foreign guest professors) and one with a local focus, involving professors from the community itself with whom it seeks to establish links. It is an institutional scenario in which the attraction of international academics with doctorates is neither as much of a priority nor as easy as in the other two cases, since its central mission is teaching.

Fourteen percent of UIMQRoo's faculty of 52 have an undergraduate degree, 72 percent have a master's, and 14 percent hold PhDs. As a newly opened academic space with an inclusive remit, it has attracted Mexican academics with overseas qualifications but employs only two full-time foreigners. International academics are thus very much a minority on the faculty. Like all their colleagues, they are preoccupied with the strategies of institutional consolidation and teaching duties, which limits their participation in the SNI. Nevertheless, at the urging of the university's founding rector, UIMQRoo has consolidated research capabilities in the area of 'interculturality.' It has run programs focused on student and academic mobility through a network of sister institutions in Canada, the United States, and countries in Central and South America (Rosado, 2014).

This selection of cases made it possible to contrast the experiences of international academics in institutions in two different geographic locations and with two different kinds of profiles. This indicates that the ability of institutions to keep a long-term hold on the international academics on their faculties depends on both their institutional missions and their local settings. IGP and COLMEX constitute environments with established traditions of internationalization, unquestionable prestige in their fields in regard to postgraduate studies, and related integrated routines for international matters. UIMQRoo, situated in a largely unappealing urban context, has pursued international cooperation in order to overcome its limitations, though it has not necessarily sought to internationalize its faculty. The academics interviewed at the first two institutions talked in positive terms about their work environment, particularly those with prior experience at other institutions. Those at UIMQRoo, in contrast, feel themselves to be marginalized and vulnerable, with interests and perceptions regarding the direction the institution should take to be at odds with those of their colleagues.

The institutional context is the main factor that influenced the opinions of respondents: At IGP and COLMEX, the interviewees said they were satisfied with their professional status. At UIMQRoo, they mentioned experiencing adverse situations of isolation and even underlying conflict with the other academics as a consequence of differences, or even incompatibilities, in their professional ethos. These result in disagreements over teaching methods and the definition of their commitments with regard to their work teams, their students, and their institutions.

## Beyond Recruitment: How to Insert Oneself? How to Integrate?

The dissimilarities between the respondents' experiences with regard to matters of recruitment and hiring, productivity on the job, establishing links, and publication made it possible to point to strategic variables that can help us understand practices related to the integration of foreign academics into the case institutions. They enabled an analysis of the relevance of international experience as a constant in the scientific career path (Teichler, 2015). They showed also that the conditions of the foreign academics' arrival and their postmigratory work paths are key success factors in their finding stability and permanence in the host country.

When government or institutional programs assist mobility (e.g., through 'invitation' or recruitment processes), access to financial and logistical supports precede emigration. Such programs are enshrined in agreements and entail mutually agreed-upon obligations before any mobility takes place. When mobility is improvised—that is, based on personal decisions—the migration generally precedes the acquisition of any employment, as this occurs during the actual move to Mexico.

In the first scenario, invitation/recruitment or repatriation programs will enable international academics to defray the costs of moving. IGP and COLMEX leverage both their own resources and those of CONACYT in order to attract researchers on a temporary basis, whom they occasionally recruit for longer-term employment following a trial period. For example, IGP used CONACYT-funded postdoctoral opportunities, or invested either its own institutional resources or those of specific teams, in order to attract young PhDs. A host laboratory could then assess not only the visiting academics' knowledge of their discipline, but also their ability to incorporate themselves into the group, their autonomy with regard to problem solving, their progress in the development of their own lines of research, and their productive capacities. The interviewees considered this way of operating to be effective, but pointed out that the offer of permanent positions did not always correspond chronologically with the conclusion of postdoctoral placements. This time discrepancy forces nonpermanent international faculty to search for alternative solutions, such as seeking a place at a 'friendly' institution—at UNAM itself or in another institution that might provide another postdoc—while they await jobs that are more permanent.

COLMEX, for its part, publishes international job announcements. After selecting a candidate from a short list (based on conferences, courses, and presentations delivered during a visit to Mexico paid for by the institution), it recruits new hires for a maximum probationary period of three years (featuring annual reviews). In the event that the performance is satisfactory, and pending consultation with the faculty *in plenum* and authorization from the office of the general director, COLMEX proposes a permanent position to the academic guest. This procedure makes it possible to renew and diversify the faculty by incorporating colleagues with different profiles in terms of age, career path, and productivity. The investment costs for salaries and the rates of attrition are relatively high, as those selected may opt to accept the appointment temporarily while continuing to look for better positions in other institutions/countries, or—having failed to perform to standard in research, publication, teaching, and/or administrative engagement—are ultimately not taken on by the centers.

Regarding how they heard about the vacancies for which they were ultimately hired, many of the interviewees remarked that they already had had some previous contact, however slight, with a Mexican colleague, who then invited them to put themselves forward for consideration for a position. It was more the specific opportunity of tenure that influenced their move to Mexico than some prior migratory plan, rationalized in terms of a differential analysis of preferences that took into account earnings, logistical support, professional recognition, and residual factors (Oteiza, 1970).

> I'd already done various postdocs in Asia and Latin America and then I started working in international cooperation, in my area, but on temporary contracts. I knew someone in Mexico, here at the University, through my thesis director and, later, I met him at an international conference.

We had interests in common and we stayed in contact. When the post became available, he told me to put myself forward as a candidate. What I wanted was professional stability; I was sick of being part of "Generation Postdoc."

*(male, seismology, 43 years old)*

Spontaneous mobility is the result of choices, whether personal, sentimental, cultural, or professional (i.e., where one's area of research leads, or if there are problems obtaining a permanent job in the country of origin). Integration following arrival in a host country involves mobilization of networks, which may be personal (friends or academic peers) or, when researchers are young, mediated by the thesis director. As the Mexican academic market became more competitive and the number of Mexican PhDs increased in the late 1990s and mainly during the 2000s, this process became more competitive and long: Two of the interviewees mentioned 22 and 25 candidates, respectively, for their posts. As a general trend, the delay between formal and effective hiring lengthened over the past decade to between six and twelve months. The younger interviewees report extremely bureaucratic processes, filtered by competitions involving highly precise job descriptions. The final decision about 'Who is the best candidate available' is subject to collective transactions, both internal and external, that are not always transparent. In contrast, the older respondents describe personal recruitment through vertical, autocratic schemas of institutional management, in which the decisions by those in a position of decision-making power carried the force of law. The differences between these narratives demonstrates the transition from a model of individualized hiring, based on the decision of a direct authority with far-reaching decision-making powers, to one of regulated and collegial—though uncertain—selection. This evolution expresses the normalization that public policies on the evaluation and assessment of teachers and researchers and the reform of institutional management mechanisms have entailed for the academic profession.

Most of the interviewees arrived in the country between the ages of 25 and 30. Might this be due to the fact that Mexican public universities, despite the rhetoric emphasizing their willingness to recruit the best, do not possess the instruments that would enable them to attract illustrious (i.e., mid-career and senior) scientists? Although each autonomous university defines its own pay levels commensurate with the posts occupied, all public institutions have legal barriers to paying foreign academics any more than what local academics are paid, or to grant them specific rewards and incentives aimed at facilitating their professional integration. This is a considerable obstacle for the recruitment of high-prestige scientists, particularly from developed countries. And this situation also gives the most prestigious private institutions (such as ITESM) greater advantages when it comes to attracting and keeping international academics.

Except when the countries of origin/residence of international scientists are wracked by political, economic, or security crises, leading to massive migration and an exodus of professionals involving middle-aged academics (circumstances from which Mexico has profited), Mexico's programs to attract international academic talent mostly focus on recent graduates as promising young scientists. This situation has its positive sides in relation to the easy acclimation and adaptation of these individuals to the new country and institutions, but it hinders the ability to attract scientists with the competencies sufficient to quickly form research groups, such as those created in Mexico by Russians, Poles, and East Germans in the 1990s (Durand, 2013; Izquierdo, 2013).

According to the remarks of the interviewees, their processes of integration—in organizational terms—into their new host institutions in Mexico were conditioned by the culture, the technological resources, and the administrative support mechanisms in place to help them with the immigration process and other matters relating to their installation, or reinstallation, in Mexico. At the same time, their well-being within the institution and their objective possibilities of operating as transnational actors (Bauböck & Faist, 2010), promoters of the circulation of knowledge, and persons depended on the material conditions of day-to-day work provided by the institution and on their acceptance by the local scientific team. Nevertheless, achieving the construction of institutional climates favorable to the insertion of international academics based on empathy and on the granting of responsible personal autonomy has not been an issue of concern in Mexico. This issue is crucial, however, in order for the budgets devoted to the reception of international academics to result in enduring integration. Only then can the system be considered truly beneficial for the individual international academics and the local scientific teams and institutions.

In sum, the 'success' of highly skilled immigrants and returning Mexican academics results from a multifactorial process of cumulative causality. This depends less on the support provided by the federal government to absorb the costs of moving and re(settlement) for international faculty—that is, to facilitate an episode of mobility/the migration process. Rather, more important are the concrete conditions of employment offered by the host institution and the types of integration with, and recognition international faculty receive from, their peers.

Considering that internationalization is a distinguishing mark of the scientific elite (Cornu & Gérard, 2013, p. 3), the respondents were of the opinion that the process in Mexico is influenced by the profiles of international faculty and the prestige of their host institution and cooperative networks of knowledge production. Their positioning within an institution determines the opportunity to obtain extrabudgetary resources and the availability of aid in the form of infrastructure, access to data, or attendance at international conferences. It explains the institution's (or research centers') rhythms of publication and mechanisms for dissemination and scientific engagement. Beyond this consensus, there are differences in the perceptions of the conditions in Mexico for professional practice for those who studied at major disciplinary poles versus those from countries with a lower level of development, and between those who gained concrete professional experience in other countries and those who did not.

In order to overcome eventual obstacles in their professional development, or to optimize their relative advantages, international academics generally participate in networks either as members or as coordinators. The national networks serve as a means to be part of social exchanges, get a topic onto the national research agenda, find students, share resources and infrastructure, carry out discrete parts of a segmented project, and gain legitimacy in the eyes of colleagues at the same institution. International networks, in addition to having these same effects, contribute to the cultivation of prestige and the international dissemination of articles[6]; they enable their members to fulfill the requirements and display the attributes that the Mexican scientific system considers essential for a recognized leader. Moreover, the interviewees link their network activities with having furthered their careers and gained exposure for their areas of research in terms of the strategic addition of resources and means. The networks help them to break out of the isolation caused by working in a semideveloped country and gain professional recognition in top-level disciplinary circuits.

## Intercultural Tensions in Academic Life

Having had work or study experiences overseas leads to the development of a critical approach to the scientific habits and customs in the host country. In general, and aside from any bitterness their comments may have betrayed, all the interviewees emphasized some worrying labor issues, although the assessments of these issues by foreign academics do not always align with those of Mexicans with overseas experience.

First, there is the 'precariousness' of the first few years of professional life. Younger international academics (both those foreign born and trained abroad) express widespread dissatisfaction with the sluggishness of institutions in paying their first salaries and, among those coming to Mexico after training abroad, providing support in sorting out their migratory situations. They denounce also this virtually obligatory passage through professional "purgatory," sometimes stretching to several years, during which they receive low pay and earn "merits" in order to become eligible for programs offering bonuses for productivity at institutional and national levels. They also complain of excessive administrative and academic workloads imposed by the host organization on the weakest (i.e., recently hired) academics.

The second problem area is that of the power of pressure groups in multiple areas of academic life. Incorporation into establishments administered not so much according to regulations as norms and customs deeply destabilizes international academics and marginalizes them or turns them into spectators more than protagonists of internal institutional life. This mainly affects foreigners, but also includes those Mexicans who are not 'indigenous' to their workplace. On occasion, 'outsiderness' limits the possibilities of international faculty to take up positions of responsibility and access resources. Perceptions of the continuously seesawing balance between "malinchismo" [favoring the foreign] and "amiguismo" [endogenous favoritism] vary within a single institution, according to the adaptability, the culture, and the background of the respondents. They explain how individual positions of retrenchment can co-exist with career trajectories on a relatively fast upward path.

The third cause for concern relates to unsatisfactory conditions for retirement. Those foreign faculty from countries with public systems offering generous retirement and health coverage specifically mentioned this problem. Following retirement, they usually lose, as do their Mexican colleagues, any extra payments or productivity incentives, the amounts of which represent a significant percentage of their salaries (as much as 70 percent for those in the higher categories). They go from enjoying private health insurance (normally paid only for active personnel) to having to seek care from the public health system—a step down in medical attention in Mexico. Although all researchers working in Mexico believe that retiring involves a worrying deterioration in their levels of well-being, those of foreign origin are more sensitive to the loss of income and welfare services. In addition, they are reluctant to consider the possibility of not retiring when they reach the statutory age in order to preserve the advantages entailed in professional activity, as their Mexican colleagues frequently choose to do. Considering dignified retirement to be a right, they press their institutions to improve retirement conditions or, on an individual basis, pay for their own retirement and health insurance in their countries of origin, where expatriates are allowed to do so (such as in France, for instance). Some middle-aged foreign academics even think about the possibility of returning to their countries of origin before their age prevents their professional reincorporation there. This does not imply any lack of appreciation for or satisfaction with their current professional situation in Mexico 'for now,' but these individuals see no future in it. COLMEX has implemented a decent retirement system based on resources contributed by the professors' trade union, the institution, and the federal government. It also provides those retirees who wish it access to a collective workspace, but this case is an exception to the rule nationally.

> Here, you're in the "elephants' graveyard." We don't enjoy so much individual space as before, not even a cubicle, but we do have somewhere to receive colleagues, keep a few interesting books, and feel as if we're still part of the institution.
>
> *(male, philosophy, 72 years old)*

Older respondents, generally emeriti, appreciated the fact that educational establishments allowed them to continue to be professionally active, despite having passed the official retirement limit. They liked being able to hang on to the advantages that go with having a job and maintaining their intellectual and social activities.

Regardless of the similarities of opinion in relation to the previously mentioned points, there is a clear difference between international and Mexican faculty with regard to teaching. All the interviewees are involved in teaching tasks, although, due to the profile of the institutions, they work with more postgraduate rather than undergraduate students, with the exception of UIMQRoo. Assessment of the teaching processes aimed at the transmission of knowledge is a delicate subject. The international academics, chiefly those in the social sciences and humanities, criticized the basic education given to the students, the pressure with regard to quantitative graduation criteria applied by CONACYT via the National Register of Postgraduate Quality (PNPC),[7] and the institutional regulations regarding the contents and structure of doctoral theses.

In programs accredited by the PNCP, the admission standards are selective and the rate of acceptance is low. Nevertheless, the interviewees bemoaned the difficulty of attracting good foreign students. The complaints are more scathing still from those respondents in charge of undergraduate programs with more local pools of students and virtually nonexistent selection criteria. They criticize the inadequacy of the knowledge accumulated and the lack of basic skills (e.g., literacy in the social sciences and mathematics in the hard sciences). Identifying good students in a context of 'educational disaster' becomes a question of luck rather than the ability of schools to provide their students with the competencies and specialized knowledge they deserve. In this respect, comparisons between the educational systems in their original and present countries seldom flatter Mexico. Those interviewees with several decades of experience in Mexico also point to an increasing deterioration in the capacities, autonomy, and knowledge acquired by their postgraduate students.

> Here, there is a paternalistic aspect to everything and the students become stressed when you ask them to be autonomous.
>
> *(male, physics, 54 years old)*

Only a few categorize this opinion by making reference to intercultural issues when dealing with indigenous students and to the fact that many of their students are the first in their families to go to university; that is, these students' social and cultural capital is largely incompatible with the university culture. Many foreign faculty complain of overprotective institutional cultures; these individuals believe that their obligation consists of guiding students so that they can gradually gain their independence. They reject the idea of doing this from a position of 'leader' or mandarin intellectual and the notion of lowering their standards under the pretext of 'that's the way it is and nothing can be done.'

With regard to the selection of applicants, the opinion is that preparatory courses serve as a second filter to pick out the most promising students, but these courses do not stop less qualified students from squeezing through the gaps. Here, they believe that the behavior of CONACYT only makes things worse. The obligation, as ruled by CONACYT, to graduate students at the doctoral level in four and a half years and at the master's level in two and a half, all the while under threat of institutions losing their accreditation, leads faculty to be less exigent regarding theses and students to choose 'easy' thesis topics that follow a repetitive logic or to apply matrices that allow them to yield quick results.

> Nearly all the [undergraduate and graduate] theses are very automatic, they're repeated, they apply the same SWOT matrix. They're very easy to do; it's a question of entering slightly different data into the same schema. But the students learn practically nothing. We produce graduates, not thinkers.
> 
> *(male, anthropology, 56 years old)*

Beyond the sometimes vitriolic denunciations of a teaching context that a number of international academics readily describe as "schizophrenic," many of them argue for a redefinition of the regulations on postgrads, a rationalization of the graduation criteria, and the use of better methods of assessment. They judge that current circumstances encourage mediocrity and dissimulation more than the learning of competencies. They do not even correspond to international parameters for measuring the quality of theses.

Consequently, there are profound differences between the professional cultures of the international academics (in the main foreigners) and their national colleagues without living and studying experience in other countries with regard to the training process and evaluation of students. The difficulty in finding suitable solutions nurtures a strong and widespread pessimism among the interviewees. Many of them find that the pressures they are under to grant degrees quickly and in quantity undermine any opportunity to genuinely create a sound system of science and technology and teach research skills to coming generations. They are aware that their demands in relation to their students' performance are greater than those of many of their Mexican colleagues, but boast that their students acquire, often against their will, skills that are essential for the academic profession. Among these, they list the submission of products on time and of the requisite quality; the ability to express ideas in terms of the current standards; and education in collective management skills, task scheduling, and financing. Lastly, they complain bitterly of feeling like voices in the wilderness in relation to both their colleagues and the authorities when it comes to these issues.

Finally, there are differences between foreign and Mexican academics with overseas experience regarding the occupation of positions of authority in their institutions. The former tend to withdraw into academic and scientific fields, the only areas in which they are allowed unfettered competition. Although they point out that in Mexico, the status of foreign migrant is no obstacle to finding work as a scientist in the national academic market, typically, they are unable to compete for posts at the highest level; that is, those of a "political" or even administrative nature. They believe that these are allotted, not according to competence, but rather trustworthiness based on networks of family or political relationships. They point out that, on occasion, due to regulatory stipulations, the fact of not being Mexican by birth prevents them from being a university rector or even the director of a center or an institute.

> I can't be the director. The regulations don't allow foreigners to do that, something that doesn't happen in many developed countries, but, yes, I can be among the best academics and—why not?—be an emeritus when I finish my career.
>
> *(male, geology, 46 years)*

The latter sometimes use their knowledge of the local rules of the game, combined with their international experiences, in order to secure positions of leadership in administrative or decision-making contexts. In their opinion, this enables them to be more sensitive to innovations and good practices, eradicating the old vices such as localism or clientelism, and to establish networks supporting internationalization in their institutions.

## Building a Career in Mexico: A Good Decision?

Many of the interviewees (over 50 years old) had either come or returned to the country several decades earlier. Looking back and reflecting on the advantages and disadvantages of building a career in Mexico, these academics value the efforts made in Mexico to regulate the academic market and channel resources to science and higher education institutions. They appreciate the freedom they enjoyed and indeed still have to develop their lines of research and choose their own topics. Conversely, they believe that the cycle begun 30 years ago of policies for reorganizing the science system based on quality assurance and financing based on objectives and results is defunct and, moreover, that any academic advances achieved are being increasingly rolled back by excessive bureaucratization, irrationality in administrative controls, and the dictatorship of indicators.

They consider Mexico an appropriate choice for developing their career. The migration has allowed them, in disciplinary fields that are still to be fully consolidated in some institutions when they arrived to the country (nano technology/sociology/arts/geophysics), to make substantial contributions that enjoy recognition from their peers, both in Mexico and abroad. They valorize specifically the transfer of knowledge and the inclusion of new topics on research agendas. They mention the introduction of theoretical perspectives, the use of novel ways of approaching scientific issues, or the development of comparative studies as demonstrations of their role as "pioneers" in the advancement of knowledge in their disciplines.

> I gave courses on Friedberg and Crozier's organizational theory, which wasn't used much. I started to work on oil and energy from the perspective of good governance and with an interest in their social, political, cultural and ethnic effects. At that time, no one was doing that. The approaches were highly technical—by engineers and economists.
> 
> *(female, political science, 62 years old)*

Having contributed to the internationalization of their fields by introducing new topics, theoretical perspectives, or instruments, inviting foreign colleagues and promoting outside mobility for their students are other activities the interviewees see as valuable. In this respect, they mention two distinct patterns of second-generation international mobility among their students. One is a transgenerational mobility, in which the students studied in the country of origin or qualification of their director, perhaps even in the same institution. Frequently in the social sciences, this scheme is related at one and the same time to an affective dimension and to decisions that are both intellectual (teacher–pupil transmission) and strategic (consolidation of international networks to support schools of thought, particularly in fields disputed by different generations and groups educated in different countries over the last 30 years). The other is disciplinary mobility, linked with networks and the joint projects of research leaders. All the interviewees agreed that it is essential for their students, especially those at the postgraduate level, to gain international experience, and they proactively help them find the information and resources necessary to obtain placements abroad.

The younger academics—that is, those under 40—are at another stage in the consolidation of their careers (and, therefore, have different degrees of autonomy in their institutions, participation in networks, and levels of recognition). This situation fostered prospective reflections on possible future opportunities for professional insertion in Mexico. The preoccupation with gaining scientific legitimacy, publishing, graduating students, obtaining financing for research, participating in national and international networks, accessing and maintaining themselves within the assessment mechanisms, and rising in the hierarchy leads to career strategies that straddle what is learned in their own educational processes and the demands of the institutions in which they work. They pay close attention to the accreditation of the programs in which they give courses and to the impact factor of the journals in which they publish, and seek early on (and with the support of their former thesis directors) to keep one foot inside and the other outside Mexico. They make an effort to gain legitimacy in a precise research niche and, from here, to earn the label of 'specialist.' In order to cement their reputations, they must join teams and networks, organize events, invite foreign colleagues, and attend international conferences. They enter a race to access resources, build relationships, preserve networks that predate their arrival in Mexico, and strengthen those established following their migration. In order to achieve this, they join disciplinary associations and societies, although they do not always find conditions adequate due to lack of information or recognition of joint academic programs by their receptor institution.

> I have contacts at [***] University. A student of theirs came here to explore his field through a scholarship but the co-tutoring was not recognized and it didn't advance my career. That was a lot of work that has no value for my curriculum vitae and it is a shame because students are a good means for building rewarding collaborations.
>
> *(female, volcanology, 38 years old)*

The younger interviewees, mainly postdocs, are active in alumni and disciplinary associations with a broad geographic radius. They attend international conferences they help organize because this enables them to extend their list of connections, as well as to keep abreast of developments. Their elders, in contrast, prioritize highly specialized and restricted networks and seminars, where "we really learn from and converse with our peers." As one interviewee stated:

> We recently set up the Latin American Association of Translation and Interpretation Studies. I was one of the initiators because it seemed fundamental to me to discuss that problem in the region based on our experiences with different kinds of text.
>
> *(female, linguistics, 69 years old)*

## Conclusion

In order to consolidate an area of research on international academics in Mexico, it would be necessary to assess their working conditions and needs, as well as their contributions to their disciplinary fields and host institutions. This would involve questioning and adjusting the definition of the target population (by deciding, for example, whether to incorporate foreigners with Mexican qualifications). It would necessitate treating their situations comparatively and identifying factors related to failed integration. It would lead to an analysis of how the heads of institutions, departments, and teams evaluate the inclusion of international academics in terms of management, institutional positioning, and the location of the establishment. For now, even in those institutions whose doors are fully open to international academics, the authorities offer no reflection or public data on the contributions of international academics (however defined), and they tend to center their internationalization policies on the outward mobility of their students, rather than on the inward mobility of researchers.

With regard to government action, one question concerns the weight of attraction policies in relation to the "brain drain" dynamic and their efficacy as substantive or reductive means of dealing with the "competencies drain" (Hunger, 2002). It should be noted that in Mexico, the policy of inviting (recruiting) international academics—continuous over the last three decades—continues to be timid, as in the rest of Latin America (Vono, 2006, p. 34). Between 2009 and 2013, these efforts allowed for the attraction of a mere 313 scientists (CONACYT, 2009–2013). The inward mobility of international academics has been perceived as an issue of interest exclusively to scientists and as the responsibility of CONACYT, with no support through any provisions in favor of immigration of highly qualified human resources or through special visas as happens, for example, in Peru.

Finally, the interviews demonstrated that international academics form a very heterogeneous group. It would be useful to categorize them on the basis of meaningful indicators, such as age, degree of progress along career path, nationality of origin, or disciplinary focus, in order to optimize the measurements of which they are the object.

As a general conclusion, the study makes it possible to state that openness of receiving scientific groups in host institutions is the main factor that explains the success of the processes of return and immigration of international scientists. When financial support provided from CONACYT by the way of specific programs ends, and when the team and/or institution has the resources and is sufficiently sensitive to maintaining support for international academics, returnees or foreign-born academics tend to 'stabilize' and to communicate a positive appreciation of migration or return decisions.

However, other issues must be resolved in order to improve the processes of return/immigration, both qualitatively and quantitatively. One solution would consist of articulating a very flat system of incentives to return so as to adapt it to the profile of the people it seeks to attract. Another would be to improve the focus of the international faculty recruitment and support programs: These only take into account the period of transition and accommodation, failing to cover the commencement and consolidation of a scientific career in the foreign academic's new context in Mexico. It would be necessary to develop measures to support international scientists throughout the first three to five years of their stay and channel incentives and resources toward them as needed, if the intention is that they take on the function of mediators and promoters of policies of cooperation.

In summary, the question of what kind of support international academics require in Mexico for their integration into the country/host institution in order to be successful on individual and collective terms remains open and continues to lack an adequate answer.

## Notes

1 This paper was written with the partial support of CONACYT Program Network (Network on Internationalization and Scientific and Academic Mobility—RIMAC).
2 Currently, the SNI registry contains around 20 percent of those academics appointed as researchers (Galaz et al., 2012).
3 In 1993, 544 SNI researchers were born abroad from a total of 3,937 (13.8 percent). These came chiefly from the United States, Argentina, Spain, Chile, and Poland (Narvaez and Rosas, 1995).
4 See www.colmex.mx/archivo-historico/index.php/hisoria
5 See http://transparencia.qroo.gob.mx/portal/Transparencia/DetallesDocumentosDependencias.php?IdUbicacion=93&Inciso=16
6 Among historians at COLMEX, "Publication in those foreign languages seems to be a consequence of the fact that those historians had were native speakers of those languages (English, Italian, German and French) and, in some cases, had done postgraduate studies at institutions where those languages were spoken." (Restrepo, 2011)
7 The PNPC is a list of superior-quality postgraduate courses as assessed by CONACYT based on various indicators, notably graduation on time and a desired number of students per academic.

## References

Appelt, S., van Beuzekom, B., Galindo-Rueda, F., & Pinho, R. (2015). Which factors influence the international mobility of research scientists? *OECD Science, Technology and Industry Working Papers*, 2015/02. Paris: OECD Publishing. doi:10.1787/18151965

Aragonés, A. M. (Ed.). (2012). *Migración internacional. Algunos desafíos*. México: UNAM-IIE.

Bauböck, R., & Faist, T. (Eds.). (2010). *Diaspora and transnationalism: Concepts, theories and methods*. Amsterdam: Amsterdam University Press.

Castaños, H. (2009). Migración internacional de y hacia México: oleadas de migrantes de alta calificación académica. In P. Leite & S. Giorguli (Eds.), *El estado de la migración. Las políticas públicas ante los retos de la migración mexicana a Estados Unidos* (pp. 345–368). México: Consejo Nacional de Población.

Consejo Nacional de Ciencia y Tecnología (CONACYT). (2009–2013). Informe General del Estado de la Ciencia y Tecnología 2002–2013. Retrieved from www.conacyt.mx/siicyt/index.php/estadisticas/publicaciones/informe-general-del-estado-de-la-ciencia-y-tecnologia-2002–2011/informe-general-del-estado-de-la-ciencia-y-la-tecnologia-2002–2011-b?limit=20&limitstart=0

Cornu, J. F., & Gérard, E. (2013). La formación de la elite científica mexicana: un proceso sujeto a las divisiones internacionales del mercado de la formación. In S. Didou & P. Renaud (Eds.), *Circulación internacional de los conocimientos: miradas cruzadas sobre la dinámica Norte-Sur* (pp. 31–52). Venezuela: IESALC-UNESCO.

Didou, S. (Ed.). (2013). *La formación internacional de los científicos en América Latina: debates recientes*. México: ANUIES.

Didou, S., & Durand, J. P. (2013). Extranjeros en el campo científico mexicano: Primeras aproximaciones. *REDIE, Revista Electrónica de Investigación Educativa*, 15(3), 68–84. Retrieved from http://redie.uabc.mx/index.php/redie/article/view/557

Didou, S., & Gérard, E. (2010). *El Sistema Nacional de Investigadores, veinticinco años después. La comunidad científica, entre distinción e internacionalización*. México: ANUIES. Retrieved from http://horizon.documentation.ird.fr/exl-doc/pleins_textes/divers11–11/010052023.pdf

Durand, J. P. (2013). Científicos extranjeros en la Universidad de Sonora: contribuciones e impacto en las comunidades disciplinares locales. Review of Doctoral Thesis. *OBSMAC*. Venezuela: IESALC-UNESCO. Retrieved from www.unesco.org.ve/index.php?option=com_content&view=article&id=3310&Itemid=1383&lang=es

Galaz, J. (2009). The academic profession in Mexico: Changes, continuities and challenges derived from a comparison of two national surveys 15 years apart. *RIHE International Seminar Reports* (pp. 193–212) n. 13. Retrieved from www.rdisa.org.mx/documentos/Productos%20RPAM/The%20Academic%20Profession%20in%20Mexico-%20Changes%20and%20Continuities%202009.pdf

Galaz, J., De la Cruz-Santana, A., Rodríguez-García, R., Cedillo-Nakay, R., & Villaseñor-Amézquita, Ma. G. (2012). El académico mexicano miembro del Sistema Nacional de Investigadores: Una primera exploración con base en los resultados de la encuesta 'La Reconfiguración de la Profesión Académica en México'. In N. Fernández & M. Marquina (Eds.), *El futuro de la profesión académica. Desafíos para los países emergentes* (pp. 344–355). Argentina: EDUNTREF. Retrieved from http://works.bepress.com/cgi/viewcontent.cgi?article=1045&context=galazfontes

Gérard, E. (2013). Dynamiques de formation internationale et production d'élites académiques au Mexique. *Revue d'anthropologie des connaissances, 7*(1), 317–344. Retrieved from www.cairn.info/zen.php?ID_ARTICLE=RAC_018_0317

Gérard, E., & Maldonado, E. (2009). 'Polos de saber' y 'cadenas de saber'. Impactos de la movilidad estudiantil en la estructuración del campo científico mexicano. *Revista de la Educación Superior, 38*(152), 49–62. Retrieved from http://201.161.2.34/servicios/p_anuies/publicaciones/revsup/152/index.html

Góngora, E. (2015). Los investigadores extranjeros en México y sus redes de trabajo: exploración en sociología y biotecnología. In S. Didou & P. Renaud (Eds.), *Circulación internacional de los conocimientos: miradas cruzadas sobre la dinámica Norte-Sur* (pp. 149–170). Venezuela: IESALC-UNESCO.

Guzik, R. (2009). Relaciones de un científico mexicano con el extranjero. El caso de Arturo Rosenblueth. *Revista Mexicana de Investigación Educativa, 14*(40), 43–67. Retrieved from http://scielo.unam.mx/pdf/rmie/v14n40/v14n40a4.pdf

Hunger, U. (2002). *The "Brain Gain" hypothesis: Third-World elites in industrialized countries and socioeconomic development in their home country*. San Diego: University of California, Working Paper 47. Retrieved from www.cctr.ust.hk/materials/library/Brain_Gain_Hypothesis_Third_worlders_in_the_West.pdf

Instituto de Geofísica (2015). *Antecedentes*. México: UNAM. Retrieved from www.geofisica.unam.mx/museo/antecedentes.html

Instituto de Geofísica (2013–2017). *Plan de desarrollo del Instituto de Geofísica 2013–2017*. México: UNAM. Retrieved from www.geofisica.unam.mx/acerca_igf/archivos/planes_desarrollo/plan_IGF.pdf

Instituto Nacional de Estadística y Geografía (INEGI) (2010). Censo de población y vivienda. Retrieved from www.inegi.org.mx/sistemas/olap/proyectos/bd/consulta.asp?p=17118&c=27769&s=est

Instituto Nacional de Estadística y Geografía (INEGI) (2013). Anuario estadístico de los Estados Unidos Mexicanos 2012. Retrieved from www.inegi.org.mx/prod_serv/contenidos/espanol/bvinegi/productos/integracion/pais/aeeum/2012/Aeeum2012.pdf

Izquierdo, I. (2010). Las científicas y los científicos extranjeros que llegaron a México a través del Subprograma de Cátedras Patrimoniales del CONACyT. *Revista de la Educación Superior, 39*(155), 61–79. Retrieved from www.scielo.org.mx/scielo.php?script=sci_arttext&pid=S0185-27602010000300004

# 10

# INTERNATIONAL ACADEMIC RECRUITMENT IN A TURBULENT ENVIRONMENT

The Case of the Higher School of Economics in Russia

*Valentina Kuskova and Maria Yudkevich*

> "Happy families are all alike; every unhappy family is unhappy in its own way."
> *Anna Karenina*, Leo Tolstoy

## Introduction

The National Research University Higher School of Economics (NRU HSE, or simply HSE) was the first public university in Russia to introduce an 'international quality' tenure-track faculty recruiting program across the entire university. The need to internationalize research and teaching became apparent to HSE long before this issue was named as a priority by the Russian Ministry of Education and Science, which suggested this as a key element for the development strategy for Russian universities. Now that the importance of international recruiting is apparent at all levels—from the university to the ministry—HSE is streamlining its policies and procedures in an effort to make its efforts to internationalize both research and teaching even more effective.

Unlike their counterparts in Western countries, Russian universities remained mostly isolated for much of the 20th century, with limited access to new developments in different scientific fields. As a result, many disciplines struggle even today to compete with foreign universities for students and to publish in top journals. In addition to the more obvious reasons for internationalization (such as the globalization of the educational market), there are a number of factors specific to Russia—including the outflow of faculty after the fall of the Soviet Union (Agamova & Allakhverdyan, 2007; Latova & Savinkov, 2012), a decreasing student population as a result of the low birth rates of the 1990s, and an outflow of Russian students to foreign universities—that have caused the higher education

Izquierdo, I. (2013). *Tensiones, distensiones y estrategias identitarias: el caso de los científicos de la ex Unión de Repúblicas Socialistas Soviéticas (URSS) inmigrantes en México en los noventa*. Doctoral Thesis, Universidad Nacional Autónoma de México. Retrieved from http://132.248.9.195/ptd2013/octubre/0704206/Index.html

Morales, J. J. (2015). Canales de reclutamiento, de circulación y de consagración de élites académicas interamericanas alrededor de la Fundación Ford. *OBSMAC*. Venezuela: IESALC-UNESCO. Retrieved from www.unesco.org.ve/index.php?option=com_content&view=featured&Itemid=1146&lang=es

Narváez, N., & Rosas, A. M. (1995). "Brain gain" en la comunidad científica mexicana: una mirada alternativa. In J. B. Meyer et al. (Eds.), *Migraciones científicas internacionales*. París: IRD. Retrieved from http://horizon.documentation.ird.fr/exl-doc/pleins_textes/divers4/010022327-8.pdf

National Science Foundation (2014). Chapter 3. Science and Engineering Labor Force. In *Science and Engineering Indicators 2014*. Arlington: National Science Foundation. Retrieved from www.nsf.gov/statistics/seind14/index.cfm/chapter-3/c3h.htm

Oteiza, E. (1970). Emigración de profesionales, técnicos y obreros calificados argentinos a los Estados Unidos. Análisis de los fluctuaciones de la emigración bruta, julio 1950 a julio 1970. *Desarollo económico*, *10*(39–40), 429–454.

Queré, A. (2009). La cooperación franco-mexicana y el desarrollo de la química analítica en la Facultad de Química de la UNAM. *Boletín de la Sociedad Química de México*, *3*(1), 50–57.

Remedi, E., & Ramírez, R. (2014). La circulación del conocimiento en los procesos de formación, producción y comunicación científica. *Observatorio Nacional Temático del Ecuador*, UTPL/IESALC-UNESCO. Retrieved from http://obnat.utpl.edu.ec/node/166

Restrepo, C. (2011). Producción bibliográfica de los historiadores de El Colegio de México. *Investigación Bibliotecológica*, *25*(54), 111–140. Retrieved from www.scielo.org.mx/scielo.php?script=sci_arttext&pid=S0187-358X2011000200006&lng=es&nrm=iso

Rosado, J. F. (2014). *Reporte anual de actividades*. México: UIMQRoo.

Sánchez, M. D. (2015). *La formación de recursos humanos en México a nivel posgrado: el programa nacional de posgrados de calidad y las becas del CONACYT*. México: SEP/DGESU-UE, 24–25 septiembre. Retrieved from http://dipes.sep.gob.mx/(S(mqnkzx04pycorvnbatxmnuq1))/Europea.asp

Teichler, U. (2015). Academic mobility and migration: What we know and what we do not know. *European Review* 05/2015, 23(S1), S6–S37. doi: http://dx.doi.org/10.1017/S1062798714000787

system in Russia to reevaluate its offerings and attempt to bring its university education more in line with international standards. Attracting foreign faculty and administrators with training and experience necessary to succeed in the international arena has become a large part of this effort.

This chapter describes the Russian education system in general, outlines the perceived benefits of internationalization, and describes how HSE attempts to overcome some of the common problems with international recruiting that the entire university system in Russia is facing. The main focus here is on the benefits of internationalization and the risks inherent in emphasizing this aspect of university development too much, especially with respect to academic culture.

## Key Contextual Information

### The Russian Higher Education System and Internationalization of the Faculty

Whereas some countries, such as the United States, have always attracted international faculty to their higher education institutions (Mamiseishvili & Rosser, 2010), this practice—particularly as a systemic approach—is very new to contemporary Russia. For many years during the Soviet times, the country was closed to all Western influence, including in relation to higher education. Russian research developed in isolation during this period, with availability of international literature severely limited, and publishing only in Russian-language publications was required of faculty. Teaching was also done mostly in Russian, with the exception of some native-language instruction on offer in some of the Soviet Republics. While in the natural sciences such isolation has had very little impact on the quality or scope of research, the social sciences went in a completely different direction from the rest of the world, having been rooted mostly in Marxist-Socialist dogma, largely ignoring other important global trends. As a result, once Russian researchers started to interact freely with their foreign colleagues, many found themselves at a significant disadvantage relative to their international peers. They even lacked some fundamental academic skills and were unable to publish their work in visible international journals, which prevented them from advancing Russian perspectives on the social sciences beyond the country's borders.

The last decade has seen substantial changes in the way that higher education is perceived and structured in Russia, with a deeper understanding of the role that internationalization plays in the advancement of science. Many students are attracted to jobs in international/multinational companies or organizations, both in Russia and abroad, or continue their education in other countries, increasing the demand for world-class programs and better institutional integration into the international academic community. Researchers are able to work with international peers and need to take their own scientific agenda to the international level.

As a result, both the government of the Russian Federation and the individual universities are taking systematic, structured steps to increase research productivity and the presence of Russian universities in the international arena.

Even as this system develops, *internationalization of research* and *internationalization of teaching* are often perceived as distinctly different concepts. That is, teachers from abroad are now welcome, as they provide needed English-language instruction and an international dimension for students, and the presence of foreign students is appreciated as a way to enhance peer-to-peer cross-cultural interaction. However, the internationalization of research remains an elusive concept. Often, administrators are unclear of the steps required to bring research to a world-class level.

Several historical factors contribute heavily to the lack of internationalization of Russian higher education. Historically, the system was rooted in the French and German traditions, quite different from the American and British; this orientation started in tsarist times and was carried first into the Soviet system of education and later into modern Russia (Clark, 1986). Under this system, students enroll in the university with a predetermined major, and—though some cross-disciplinary training is available—they are expected to obtain a degree in the discipline chosen at entry, without the ability to explore other subjects.

There are at least two problems with this system, particularly in relation to internationalization. First, due to the fact that college entry is based on results of the Unified State Exam, students spend a significant share of their time in high school studying a narrow set of subjects needed to perform well on this exam in order to gain entrance to the university. This limits somewhat their exposure to other disciplines (Prakhov & Yudkevich, 2015) and a 'wider world' of information and ideas. Second, while at university, students are usually focused on the practical aspects of their chosen field—namely, acquiring the skills needed to find a job after graduating. However, if job prospects are not considered to be enhanced by having a broader international perspective, then the contributions of an international faculty member, or non-Russian literature, or an overseas experience, are not valued.

More importantly, research and teaching were historically separated. Although this tradition of separation started in the early 1800s with the creation of the Imperial Academy of Sciences, this divided system reached its height during Soviet times, with the creation of the Soviet Academy of Sciences (Graham, 1967). Teaching was not integrated with research; creation of new knowledge was assigned to specialized 'research institutions,' and university faculty were supposed to concentrate on teaching and were assigned heavy teaching loads. Most universities are still focused mostly on teaching, and research institutions, not affiliated with universities, still exist. Moreover, universities focused on teaching may lack the resources necessary to produce researchers; training researchers is still an underdeveloped area in the Russian educational system. Now that the current context calls for internationally competitive universities, training researchers is becoming a high priority for many top Russian higher education institutions.

Though teaching and research are becoming more integrated in the new Russian system and faculty publication requirements are increasing, teaching loads for university professors have not yet been adjusted to account for the time needed to meet research requirements. Moreover, this separation of research and teaching is seen as the main culprit of the lack of understanding of what is involved in internationalization of research and, hence, lack of productivity requirements for international research professors, which will be discussed later in the chapter.

Consistent with the German tradition, the Russian higher education system used to offer the 'specialist' degree, usually requiring five years of university training (more in some disciplines, such as medicine, where university education lasted at least six years). Recently, many universities have switched to the two-tier bachelor-master's approach, which most European universities implemented in the early 2000s under the Bologna Process (Maldonado-Maldonado & Bassett, 2014). However, the specialist programs are still being offered, and higher education statistics in Russia include students of all levels—bachelor, specialist, and master's. The number of students enrolled in these university programs[1] steadily increased in the first decade of the 2000s, from 23 percent of people aged 17 to 25 attending university in the year 2000, to 35.4 percent of the same age group enrolled in the year 2010, when the percentage of registered students reached its peak. By 2013, the number had decreased slightly to 33.7 percent. In absolute numbers, at the beginning of 2013–2014 school year, the number of students reached close to 5,647,000—about 2,592,000 of them men. In 2013, there were 969 higher education institutions in total, 391 of them private. It is worth noting that the higher education reform currently under way in Russia has called for a reduction in the number of educational institutions, with smaller, less efficient universities being absorbed by others or closed altogether; since 2010, the number of institutions has decreased by 13 percent, from a total of 1,115 at the start of the 2010–2011 school year.

The majority of higher education institutions are government funded, though most also have fee-based places for students or entire programs where students have to pay at least a portion of the education cost. In 2011, public institutions were mostly financed from the federal government (53.3 percent of total costs) and state and municipal budgets (1.8 percent); the rest of the operating funds are generated from student fees. Because university entrance into government-sponsored programs is based on merit, higher education is relatively affordable for those students who are part of the "state allocation," though additional financial support is still required to cover living expenses. At the beginning of the 2013–2014 school year, approximately 39 percent of students at all levels were enrolled in government-sponsored slots.

Private universities are fee based and receive very little government funding (e.g., in 2011, government funding accounted for just 0.9 percent of these universities' budgets). However, private universities must also comply with the education requirements of the Russian Federation in order to be able to issue diplomas recognized by the state. These organizations rely mostly on the fees paid by students (which account for 80.8 percent of their budgets) for their operating expenses, and they are mostly for-profit organizations.

Faculty compensation in public universities is heavily dependent on government funding, resulting in relatively low salaries for university professors in comparison to professionals or practitioners in the same fields. In an effort to retain the best talent, some universities provide additional compensation incentives based on performance, with performance criteria and additional compensation structures varying widely from one university to the next. Overall, in 2011, public institutions spent 335.7 billion rubles (at the time, approximately USD 11.2 billion) on salaries (mostly for faculty, though this figure also includes administrative and support personnel). Over 50 percent of this amount—or 174.1 billion rubles (USD 5.8 billion), was paid from nonbudgetary (i.e., the university's own) funds. This number speaks to the efforts that universities make in order to compete for the best faculty on the market. However, these efforts are apparently not sufficient. Many faculty continue to moonlight as professional consultants or have teaching jobs at several universities simultaneously, substantially increasing their teaching loads and leaving even less room for research.

The traditional Russian faculty contract system lacks tenure. Lecturers and researchers are hired via contract, with a one-, three-, or five-year term. Upon initial hiring, a faculty contract is almost always for one year, which is then extended to another one-year or a three-year contract based on performance; three-year contracts could be extended for three years or, with exceptional performance, five years. Recently, some universities started to implement tenure-type contracts based on exceptional performance, but the number of tenured professors remains very low relative to the total number of faculty.

Another important characteristic of the Russian education system is that faculty contracts used to be a formality: When a new faculty member was employed, there was a generally understood set of rights and responsibilities, both on the part of the university and on the part of the faculty; details were left out. With the introduction of international faculty into the Russian education system, employment contracts (at least for internationals) are now very specific, with almost every aspect of employment covered—from working hours to intellectual property matters to insurance coverage. Domestic faculty contracts, for now, remain more general.

In 2013, 9.2 percent of the Russian population was employed in the education sector across all levels, starting from preschool; 16.8 percent of the total were employed in higher education. Women comprised 81.6 percent of higher education employees, and the average age was 42.8. It is also worth noting that in the 2013–2014 academic year, the average student–teacher ratio across all institutions was 9:1, with a 10:1 ratio in public institutions.

Any person with a specialist/master's degree or higher may be employed as a university lecturer, although an advanced 'candidate of science' degree (currently treated as the equivalent of a PhD) or a 'doctor of science' is usually required for career advancement. A 'doctor of science' degree is the highest academic degree in Russia and currently has no equivalent in Western systems. The majority of faculty members employed in Russian universities hold at least some form of an advanced degree: In the 2013–2014 academic year, out of 319,300 full-time faculty employed in Russian higher education institutions, 54.7 percent had the 'candidate of science' degree; 14.1 percent held the 'doctor of science' degree.

The degree itself does not guarantee an academic title. Unlike the tiered system of professorships in the West—with 'assistant,' 'associate,' and 'full' professor levels, which reflect both educational accomplishments and professional productivity—the Russian system, though tiered, is not necessarily tied to these criteria. Someone with a 'doctor of science' degree may also only hold the title of 'docent' and be promoted to a position of a 'professor' only after a certain number of years at the same university, in addition to generally high professional accomplishments. Moreover, administrative positions—such as head of a department or dean of a school—are also given to faculty with long service at the institution; these positions are highly prestigious and are not subject to frequent turnover. Therefore, low mobility and loyalty to one institution is appreciated and rewarded with higher-level positions.

Faculty teaching loads are high and are relatively standard, based on a lecturer's level. For example, faculty with the job title 'lecturer' have a total teaching workload of 900 to 1,000 hours per year. These hours include lectures, preparatory time, consultations with students, supervising diploma and thesis papers, etc.—all teaching related, but not activities related to research or administration.

With a standard 40-week academic year, the weekly workload of a lecturer consists almost entirely of teaching, leaving little or no room for research, yet research activity is required for promotion to a higher-level position, such as that of a 'docent.' With the latest push for Russian universities to become competitive on an international level, most institutions now require serious research output in the form of peer-reviewed academic articles published in indexed international journals. However, as anecdotal evidence suggests, such research productivity is not always easily attainable (Pavlyutkin & Yudkevich, forthcoming).

Perhaps the low level of competition in Russian higher education has created the situation of extensive academic inbreeding, where new faculty members can rarely publish in ways that are considered to be 'better' than their mentors, and hardly ever have a higher level of internationalization (Sivak & Yudkevich, 2015). In some disciplines, the national academic market is practically nonexistent, due to the fact that old educational standards were designed to produce instructors, not researchers. All of these factors have created a situation whereby many universities, in their efforts to become more internationally competitive, must hire professionals from the international job market.

Perhaps, for these (among many other) reasons, some universities began hiring professionals from the international job market in the early 2000s. As of the

2013–2014 academic year, approximately 2,000 international educators were employed at all levels across the Russian higher education system. This is a sizable number, given how recently universities began to recruit and hire internationally, but non-Russians still comprise only 0.6 percent of total faculty in Russia. A number of government programs—including those targeted at attracting internationally renowned faculty into state-sponsored research laboratories with large grants—have been implemented, beginning in the mid-2000s. PhD degrees from top universities worldwide are automatically recognized as equivalent to Russian 'candidate of science' degrees by the Ministry for General and Professional Education of the Russian Federation, making international faculty members eligible for higher-level faculty positions. Immigration policies allow education institutions to attract international hires on special 'highly-qualified specialist' work visas, providing both the university and the employees with more flexibility around work schedules, fewer restrictions with respect to mobility, and lower taxation levels, currently equivalent to that of Russian residents. Overall, it appears that both the government agencies and the education institutions are taking serious steps toward educational internationalization.

## General Characteristics of the Case Study University

The National Research University Higher School of Economics (HSE) is a unique Russian success story in higher education. Created less than 25 years ago as a small alternative program in economics, HSE now has over 25,000 students, 35,000 alumni, 2,500 academic staff, and 22 international research laboratories in four different locations in Russia—Moscow (main campus), St. Petersburg, Nizhniy Novgorod, and Perm. In 2015, for the first time ever, the university was ranked in the top 100 of the QS Global rankings in developmental studies, and the top 200 globally in the fields of economics and econometrics, sociology, and philosophy. It is ranked first in economics in Russia.

In 2009, the university was awarded National Research University status—the first social sciences university to achieve that distinction—allowing it to introduce its own educational standards, many of which are much more rigorous than the current ministry-approved standards. In 2013, HSE became part of an elite group of 15 universities receiving additional funding to promote research and visibility in order to rise in global university rankings.

In 1996, HSE was one of the first public universities in Russia to introduce a tenure-based system for its faculty; by 2015, the total number of tenured professors was 106, out of more than 2,500 faculty members. Tenure for domestic faculty is a highly coveted status, and currently is very competitive to obtain. HSE was also the first university in Russia to introduce tenure-track hiring from the international job market; it therefore represents the only Russian university with close to ten years of experience of faculty internationalization. HSE hires for domestic faculty positions in an open market, meaning all available positions are advertised nationwide, and procedures for hiring at HSE are highly competitive. In streamlining these three areas, the university is striving to achieve the most diverse and highly qualified faculty body possible, with the aim of improving the student experience and increasing research productivity.

Currently, domestic faculty are hired on a competitive basis, with one- or three-year contracts to start; these contracts, based on performance, may be extended to additional one-year, three-year, or five-year contracts. The basic faculty salary is rather low when compared to performance incentives: faculty publishing in the top quartiles of leading international journals are eligible for up to three times their salary in monthly bonuses (subject to a certain cap), paid for up to two years for each high-quality publication. Publications in international, peer-reviewed, indexed journals are considered the gold standard in selecting and retaining faculty; top performers are granted five-year contracts or tenure at the university.

## Rationale for International Recruitment

With an understanding of the important role that international faculty play in the university's development, some international faculty were employed at HSE from its earliest days, with the systematic approach to international recruitment first introduced by HSE's International College of Economics and Finance (ICEF) through a double-degree program with the London School of Economics (LSE). The ICEF requirement to have all courses in this program taught in English by faculty trained at international research universities precipitated the need to hire international faculty. Using the LSE standards for screening and selection, the first international faculty member was recruited at ICEF in 2007, followed by five more hires in 2008.

On the heels of ICEF's success, HSE's faculty of economics hired several faculty members jointly with ICEF in 2009 and 2010. It became apparent very quickly that international faculty, having had different kinds of training and coming from different academic cultures, can have an impact on the educational environment in which they operate. In 2011, based on the success of the early recruitment efforts in economics and using the procedures they had developed, the university made the strategic decision to expand international recruitment to five more faculties, considered to be priority areas in terms of advancement into the international educational market. Since 2011, when 14 new international faculty were recruited in several disciplines, the number of faculty hired from the international market has been steadily increasing up to the 2014–2015 academic year.

At first, international recruiting, with the exception of ICEF, was done on an ad hoc basis. But as the number of faculty from the international job market increased, it became clear that some recruitment and hiring activities needed to be streamlined, not only to fit with the university's strategic intent, but in order to be carried out consistently across all faculties. The Center for Advanced Studies (CAS)—a special department that coordinates the university's entire recruiting effort and later provides research and travel support to international hires—was created in 2009 in an attempt to systematize all recruitment-related activities. Moreover, a university-wide International Recruiting Committee, consisting of academics and high-level administrators, oversees the strategic direction of international recruiting, setting targets, approving budgets, and creating recommendations based on current international job market trends.

After several years of refinement and with substantial input from ICEF, CAS has developed a set of general guidelines and procedures for international recruitment, performance evaluation and promotion, and academic mobility and research support for international faculty. These procedures limit the involvement of administration—leaving hiring decisions to committees consisting of academics (including those recruited from the international market)—and take into account the idiosyncrasies of different disciplines. For example, ICEF procedures are largely guided by the requirements of the University of London. However, the faculty of law endeavors to deal with the reality of substantial (international) differences in jurisprudence practices and low applicability of international research to the realities of the Russian environment, whereas the school of business administration struggles to compete for faculty in the international arena, as the available jobs far outnumber the quality candidates.

At the end of the 2014–2015 academic year, the university employed 71 faculty recruited on the international job market for tenure-track faculty positions. Twenty-four of these faculty are Russian nationals, with all but one educated abroad (i.e., holding a foreign PhD degree). The rest come from the United States, Britain, Germany, China, Greece, South Korea, and elsewhere, representing 21 different countries in total. Because the rank of the university where the PhD was obtained is an important consideration, most of the recruited faculty come from the best schools around the world: Harvard University, University of Pennsylvania, University of Michigan, London School of Economics, University of California–Berkeley, Cornell University, Indiana University, City University London, and similar excellent institutions.

Most were recruited at the assistant professor level, having little to no previous professional experience, though a small number of professors have worked elsewhere before applying to HSE. Given that the majority have been at HSE only for three to four years and started as assistant professors straight out of PhD programs, evaluating their productivity in terms of top-tier international publications is a difficult task, as the publication cycle in the best journals is rather long. But it is worth mentioning that, as of mid-2015, HSE's international faculty have produced very few high-quality publications.

Moreover, some deans perceive newly hired international faculty as being of lower quality than the domestic faculty. The realities of the job market are such that, currently, HSE has very little to offer faculty from abroad in terms of professional development and international reputation. As a result, as one of the deans has pointed out,

> [O]nly those who can't find jobs at top research schools are attracted to HSE: even those who come from better schools are not always successful on the job market. They may not be bad professionals, but they are not better than the domestic faculty; international hires often have lower starting qualities in terms of research organization, subject matter knowledge, or applicability of such knowledge to the local Russian market.

So, perhaps it is unreasonable to expect that these faculty members would produce world-class research and change the academic environment around them for the better.

If one lesson can be learned from HSE's experience, it is that the quick production of many high-quality international publications through international hiring is not possible. But that is not to say that the international faculty at HSE have not played a larger, more important role in the university's overall internationalization efforts, as described later in the chapter.

## Stages of Recruitment Efforts: From 'Courtship' to 'Marriage'

As the first public university in Russia to recognize that systematic recruitment—rather than ad hoc recruitment—was necessary in order to achieve success, HSE has gone through several distinct periods in the development of its internationalization program. In the initial stage, recruiting was hardly strategic. With no external pressure and only a limited understanding of the role that international faculty could play in the university's development, the first faculty members were brought in with the goal of creating "islands of excellence"; as one of the deans stated it, "[I]t was thought that they have some special skills." They were expected to come with their own academic culture, increase standards of publication and teaching, and gradually change the environment around them. The need for students to get some experience in learning entirely in English was a secondary, and far less important, motive for attracting international faculty. In order to entice foreign graduates from top universities to HSE, the salaries were internationally competitive, and the financial burden of supporting the foreign faculty members was carried entirely by the faculties that wanted to recruit such academic staff.

The second stage, understood as a stage of expansion, was better formulated strategically, as the university administration recognized the role that international faculty played in the university's internationalization. Though their productivity was hardly visible early on, their presence had allowed the university to unearth a number of problems that could stifle its internationalization efforts. It became quickly apparent that additional support structures were required in order to accommodate the needs of international faculty, and later, international students. For example, marketing outreach and other efforts to increase HSE's visibility needed to be reevaluated, and more faculties needed to be included in the recruitment process. The apparent need for a special recruiting department resulted in the creation of the Center for Advanced Studies (CAS)—an administrative structure that is rather unique to HSE, as few other universities in Russia have anything similar.

The focus was on attracting select faculty from top universities to continue the expansion of the "islands of excellence" at HSE; quality was more important than quantity. There was still no external pressure to recruit internationally; it was only the commitment of the university administration to take HSE to the next level that fueled the process. In general, this initiative failed. It was a good idea in theory, but in practice, hired faculty were not able to create such "islands of excellence" without dedicated teams around them. So, as a next step, HSE began to create small research centers to allow these individuals to work with young faculty and therefore to provide positive spillover effects within the departments.

Perhaps the university would have continued its recruitment efforts on its own, but in 2013, the government implemented the "5–100" program, which provided additional funding on a competitive basis to a small number of Russian universities, with a goal of enabling at least five of these institutions to reach a top-100 rank in one of the globally recognized university ranking systems. Though there is no specific government policy with respect to employment of international academics, the number of international faculty employed is one of the key performance indicators on which the participant universities must report. In joining this developmental program, HSE took on some externally driven obligations to attract and integrate international faculty and students (Altbach, 2014). These obligations come with a high number of required recruits—as a result, an immediate conflict between internal requirements and external commitments became apparent. If HSE's own strategy was to attract only the top candidates, the externally imposed numbers clashed with the realities of the job market, where top-quality candidates were not available in large numbers. How the aspiration for numbers relates to the overall research productivity of international faculty remains to be seen, as this process is still very new.

At the initial stage of the international recruiting effort undertaken by HSE, expectations for research productivity were vague and uncertain. Simply put, nobody knew what to expect: There were no solid reference points. Informally, the university administration had assumed that newly recruited international faculty would change the university relatively quickly by creating and introducing the patterns of a 'healthy' high-quality academic culture. In reality, it also became apparent that it is rather difficult, if not impossible, to acquire the critical mass of such faculty who are able and willing to change the very atmosphere around them. The HSE administration saw that, instead of bravely changing the world, new recruits, in most cases, stayed isolated and hardly engaged with their environment at all. To some extent, this was due to the fact that the environment itself was rather hostile: As one of the administrators pointed out, it was difficult for many professors and administrators alike to accept new faculty who were perceived to work much less (with lower teaching loads) while getting paid a great deal more (i.e., receiving internationally competitive salaries) than the 'local' faculty.

Reasons for the initial conflicts between the central administration and the deans differed. First, the idea was to hire faculty without giving deans much decision-making authority: They could neither bring forward their 'own' candidates (someone they had hand-picked), nor stop the university from recruiting top candidates they may not have liked. But, as time progressed, a few deans pointed out that their expectations for international faculty were rather low—they could see even at the stage of the job interviews that the quality of attracted candidates was not as high as the administration was expecting. Second, in some cases, the deans were very resistant to the idea of bringing in internationally recruited faculty. They were afraid that the new recruits would take the best courses away from domestic faculty, while getting better salaries, better office space, and all other benefits, and would soon expunge domestic faculty from their positions. Tensions between foreign and domestic faculty also became apparent, as—instead of promoting an environment of academic excellence around them—foreign faculty were generating envy for their international publications.

Having gone through these several stages, the university has developed a much better formulated internationalization strategy, which also relates to faculty recruitment. This strategy consists of several integrated parts: commitment to high quality, better administrative procedures, internationalization of the university's administrative staff (including requirements for dual-language procedures and support structures), increasing other forms of international collaboration (i.e., with visiting professors and international research laboratories), and systematic integration of foreign faculty into university life.

There is also a good understanding of what is required to attract international faculty to Russia. Given the current geopolitical situation, with several countries imposing economic sanctions on Russia and a much weaker ruble, the economic incentives of working in Russia are rather low. Even if the salary is competitive internationally, there is always fear on the part of international hires that the financial situation could change very quickly, as happened in December 2014, with a sharp decline in the value of the ruble. Therefore, in addition to competing on salaries, HSE is offering a much lower teaching load than is the norm internationally (currently equivalent to a 1–1 load in the US system), generous research support and travel funds (consistent with the best international research universities), and an extended yearly mini-sabbatical leave (at least a month at any time throughout the year, in addition to a two-month period of paid vacation and business trips). The university administration is also actively seeking feedback from international faculty on areas of improvement, and a number of substantive administrative changes have been made as a result.

The university administration now realizes that its recruitment strategy needs to be adjusted, not only from one faculty to another, but also from one year to the next. The job market needs to be carefully monitored and hiring targets changed throughout the year, with performance expectations and resulting compensation modified for each individual candidate. Instead of hiring at all faculties every year, the recruiting strategy should be consistent with realities of the job market: For example, if in one discipline the job market is especially tight for candidates, perhaps more need to be hired there at the expense of other fields, where the year is much more generous to the candidates in terms of the number of available jobs. If selected candidates do not meet the bar in terms of publication expectations, maybe they should be given an increased teaching load, with lower research requirements—instead of the blanket contract, where every international hire works under the same conditions. Such fine-tuning must be done several times throughout the year by both the central administration and the recruiting faculties, dictating both the quantity and quality of selected candidates.

Despite the fact that the university's international recruitment strategy is now much better formulated, there is still the 'pressure of indicators': According to the 5–100 roadmap, the share of international faculty should grow much more quickly than is possible, if the university wants to remain on its strategic path to excellence. Current recruiting targets are not realistic, not only from the standpoint of applicant availability, but also financially—given the sharp decline of the ruble against major currencies in 2014–2015, the university is struggling to stay competitive in relation to salaries, because university financing of its recruiting efforts did not increase proportionately to the ruble's depreciation. As one of the deans has stated, what we currently pay to one international faculty for two to three publications a year could financially support several domestic faculty members who would publish even more.

Originally, nobody had thought that an active monitoring of international faculty productivity would be necessary. Administrators assumed, perhaps naïvely, that foreign hires would quickly produce many high-quality journal publications. Over time, it became apparent that the production of high-quality publications requires longer periods; quick publications are not of high quality. So now, only by adjusting individual workloads can the university ensure that the money paid to international faculty is not wasted. So, implementing the active performance monitoring and adjustment system is the next tactical step to take by CAS.

Having realized that recruiting the critical mass of international faculty necessary to change the environment at the university is not something that is possible to attain quickly, HSE has looked into alternative ways of increasing its levels of internationalization. As a result, several new initiatives were developed: International research laboratories were created, along with part-time positions, with or without dual affiliation with HSE, and postdoctoral research positions. All of these initiatives are already being launched, with various degrees of initial success.

## Recruiting Initiatives

The most successful program, by far, is the international research laboratories program, sponsored both by the university itself and Russian Federation government grants. The essence of the program is to assemble a research group, consisting mostly of domestic faculty and students, which is supervised and directed by a leading international scientist with a proven record of high-quality publications and faculty development. Currently, the university has 22 such laboratories. These research groups have clearly articulated performance targets, not limited to publications—they are also required to organize seminars, summer schools, and other educational experiences for domestic faculty; work on developing the research skills of students; and promote the HSE name through organization of, and participation in, high-level international conferences, etc. Each laboratory's scientific supervisor is expected to set up the research agenda for the lab and support all of its efforts, including educational initiatives. The cost of the program for each laboratory includes the salaries of laboratory members and mobility/research funds. Currently, one such laboratory may employ up to 30 people of different ranks, but still only costs the equivalent of three to four international faculty members' salaries. So in terms of productivity and knowledge transfer, this program is more efficient than the standard international recruitment procedure.

The second avenue for attracting international faculty for which HSE holds high hopes is the postdoctoral program. Three postdocs were first hired in the 2013–2014 academic year; two of these were retained a year later, based on productivity, as tenure-track faculty. The program was launched full-scale in 2014; in its second year of existence it attracted five to six applications, on average, for each available position. Some applicants come from the best universities worldwide and have ambitious research agendas. Perhaps they are not ready to commit for three years to HSE, given the uncertainty of the current geopolitical situation, but they are willing to try it out on a limited one-year basis. So far, both the university and the researchers brought in through the postdoctoral program have been quite satisfied with the outcome, with several postdocs applying (and successfully being hired) a year later into tenure-track positions.

Part-time international faculty employment, with or without a second affiliation with HSE, is a program that has recently been rolled out on a limited basis and is still being refined. The idea is to bring an international faculty member, employed full-time elsewhere, to HSE for one to four months a year, depending on the contract with the main employer. So far, only a few faculty members have been hired on this basis, but there is a great deal of interest in expanding the program, both by the faculties and the international hires with whom they have established an ongoing working relationship.

At present, HSE has a well-developed set of procedures for international recruiting, consistent with the best international recruiting practices, which are being implemented at all four HSE campuses. These procedures have been formulated with input from world-renowned faculty, who have become contract-based members of the HSE recruiting staff. The system is two tiered, with a screening committee that reviews the initial set of applications, and a selection committee that works with long-listed candidates. The committees are specific and unique for each discipline.

No international 'head hunters' are involved in the process for the faculty selection, though the university has used the services of such agencies in the past in an effort to hire high-level administrators. The screening committee consists of at least two external members who have tenure at top international research universities and a proven track record of international recruiting. They have been hired to work on a part-time basis through the personal contacts of university faculty and administrators or by the recommendation of other international faculty. Some HSE faculty members, especially those hired on the international job market themselves, could be members of the screening committee. The selection committee consists of at least one external member, the dean of the faculty where the new hire will work, and several faculty members with either international experience or a proven record of international publications. Actual recruiting procedures are rather consistent with international norms and involve several stages of pre-interview evaluation by screening and selection committees and an on-campus interview with the presentation of a paper (often referred to as a 'job talk').

The only substantive difference with the recruiting procedure, when compared with other schools, is that HSE has developed a practice of bringing several job candidates for an interview at the same time. First, unlike at other schools, multiple candidates do not compete for one available faculty position: With high recruiting targets, HSE usually has more slots available than quality candidates, even with a constrained budget. Second, some international hires may feel apprehensive about being employed and living in Russia; interacting with other candidates during the interview could potentially help them establish a professional circle even before they accept the offer.

From the time the offer is extended, the recruiting process is, again, rather consistent with international standards. After the offer is made, the candidate is given a relatively reasonable window of time to think over and negotiate the offer, if there is a need to do so. Whether the offer is further negotiated or accepted/declined with no further communications depends heavily on each candidate's preferences, expectations, and the job market realities. No absolutes or conclusions can be drawn from this experience. Because salary figures are usually competitive internationally, few offers have been declined because compensation terms have not been met; usually, the candidates list other reasons for declining the HSE offer: An offer from a higher-ranked school by far outnumbers any other reasons provided.

From the formal point of view, there is almost no difference between hiring procedures for domestic and international faculty. Indeed, both procedures include an open call for applications, initial screening of applications, selection procedures (with job market interviews, seminars, and public lectures, in certain cases), and final voting. At the same time, in reality, there are substantial differences. While usually about 20 international faculty members are hired each year, in the case of domestic faculty, more than 500 positions are vacated each year—this is due to the fact that the majority of faculty contracts are for one or three years in duration and are not longer than five years. These positions are vacated only technically, because quite often, they are refilled by the same people who most recently held them. But the essence of the program is that domestic faculty are subject to competitive reevaluation on a regular basis. As a result, many procedures in the case of domestic faculty are simply formalities and quite often end in the selection of the same faculty members who vacated the corresponding position at the conclusion of the most recent contract term.

Also, in the case of international hires, selection is done by committees with substantial external representation to exclude potential subjective biases toward particular candidates. For domestic faculty, such precautions are not necessary, as they are evaluated much more often than international hires (who are quite often evaluated on the basis of their potential, not actual, research results).

## International Faculty Obligations, Performance, and Integration

Contracts with international faculty take a rather standard form (again, according to international standards). Their obligations include teaching, research, and service.

Teaching loads are rather low, as mentioned already, since HSE considers low teaching loads to be a significant comparative advantage. Research output is not implicitly specified in the contract; the contract terms state that the international faculty member's performance must be at the "level that warrants granting tenure at an international research university." Initially, when the international recruitment effort had just started at HSE, required research output was clearly delineated in the contract as "at least three publications in acceptable outlets in three years," but was later excluded, because there were many discussions and complaints both by the international faculty and individual departments, as publication quantities and qualities differ widely between disciplines.

Service to the university is assumed, but in many cases, international faculty do not have any service responsibilities assigned to them. This is partly explained by the fact that most administrative processes at HSE are conducted in Russian, and for non-Russian (and therefore often non–Russian-speaking) faculty, it is impossible to take an active part in these processes.

International faculty evaluations were designed according to generally accepted international standards, with an interim review after three years of employment, and a major (tenure) review after six years. The idea was to allow each faculty member sufficient time to develop his or her research agenda in order to publish in the best international, peer-reviewed, indexed outlets. For some disciplines, the publication process is several years long, so, originally, evaluating faculty performance more often seemed unnecessary. Because the first group of international hires has already undergone tenure review, the university currently employs six international faculty members who have tenure or hold the title of full professor.

Overall, the system appears to be fair and in line with the best international practices. However, it is important to note that, despite the university's ambition to hire and retain the best international-quality researchers, tenure standards are still somewhat lower than is seen at comparable universities abroad.

As a result, as the first reviews started to come in, it became apparent that the system may have backfired. First, having an almost-assured pass at the interim review, many faculty members did not produce any results after three years. Second, only a few have passed tenure review so far, and some have been granted tenure based on their teaching and administrative performance, but with only a few (less than five) international-quality publications. While in each case, granting tenure was the result of an individualized consideration, the remaining international faculty received the signal that HSE may extend tenure with just two publications in six years. Finally, even if the performance evaluation is relatively low, deans fight to keep the international hire under consideration, because with the new 5–100 program requirements, the number of internationally hired faculty is a key performance indicator for deans. Therefore, administrators are now tasked with potentially creating a different set of guidelines for retaining international faculty to avoid the situation where an underperforming international hire is being retained in an effort to meet the numbers.

Aside from interim and tenure review, until recently, the university had never taken steps to evaluate the performance of its international hires. In the spring of 2015, however, such an evaluation was performed for the first time, university-wide, for all international hires, with individual publication, teaching, and service records taken into account. Overall, the results were disappointing. When individual faculty were evaluated one by one, the discrepancy between the desired and actual outcomes was not so apparent. But when all international faculty were evaluated simultaneously, it was determined that—relative to domestic faculty—they have a lower number of publications (some have none and would not have passed the review process assumed for domestic faculty), their teaching hours are substantially lower (as well as teaching quality, as judged by student evaluations), and their service was practically nonexistent. Out of 70 evaluated faculty members, 34 were deemed to have not met par on at least one—and for some, all—of the evaluated dimensions. Despite the obvious lack of productivity, these faculty members are protected by international contracts and remain employed at HSE.

Although it may be too early to say that this is a systematic result indicating the failure of the recruiting system, the university administrators have taken the low performance of international faculty to heart, and a new, more structured approach to performance evaluation is currently being developed. International hires will be given a higher level of accountability and will have performance targets better specified in each individual discipline.

An important point in evaluating how the international faculty *feel* at the university relates to their individual efforts to integrate. As an administrator has pointed out, the university controls only some aspects of an international hire's "happiness" with their jobs—namely, the job itself. But even here, "integration is possible if the faculty become a part of some organized—formally or structurally—research group, such as laboratories and research centers. Without such integration, problems arise." But, just as important is the life outside the job; according to a dean,

> [T]hey are not just faculty members. Outside the university, they are fathers, mothers, wives, or husbands. They are just people and they need to have a normal life. Unfortunately, they often feel choked in the situation they find themselves, as the life in the USA or Netherlands, for example, is very different from Russia.

In that regard, how international faculty feel about their lives in Russia largely depends on how well they are integrated into the life outside of the university. This integration process is simpler for those who speak Russian; they usually are much less dissatisfied with their experience than those who do not.

Quite a few are happy with the job itself; fewer are happy with the administrative processes at the university and are not shy about pointing out what HSE could do differently. Even fewer are happy with their lives outside the university, relating to matters over which HSE has no control—medical clinics, availability of daycare, quality of school education for their children, cultural and finer things in life, and others. As one of the deans said, the level of a person's happiness also depends on how serious they are about staying in Russia long-term. Those who accepted the job only to ride the market for a few years generally attempt to integrate less, and as a result, are unhappy. So perhaps, some of the dissatisfaction that people experience is actually due to the fact that people were never serious about being at HSE long-term.

An important integration aspect is international faculty's interactions with each other. Over the years, they have formed a well-structured, cohesive group, akin to a labor union; officially, there is no such union, but unofficially, they act as a group on all aspects of university-related (and unrelated) life. Because academic cultures are different, such a 'union' is certainly not unexpected: International faculty clearly feel more accepted by each other than by domestic faculty. Also, because many do not speak Russian, their ability to form a social circle inside the university is limited to those who are fluent in English and willing to speak the language on a regular basis. But, most importantly, as a group, they face similar problems and feel stronger as a group when negotiating with university administration on all aspects of performance and compensation.

On one hand, such a 'union' is a positive development. Just by its sheer existence, it brings to the administrators' attention the problems that the university is forced to solve. If one person complains about an unsatisfactory matter, this complaint may be overlooked; when a group complains, the administration is forced to act. As a result, many positive changes have taken place at the university, starting with the transition to offering many bilingual systems and services. In addition, an Office of International Integration has been created, with administrative coordinators for international hires present in almost every faculty; these coordinators are tasked with assisting international faculty members with a variety of aspects, some even involving life outside the university—such as making appointments at medical clinics.

On the other hand, this same 'union' gives a significant voice to international faculty where there should not be so much. For example, contractual teaching obligations for most hires were originally specified as "no more than 6 academic hours per week." The idea was to indicate that international faculty would be protected from excessive teaching. However, the differences in contract specifications have created some confusion: Contracts for domestic faculty specified the 'floor' of the teaching load, whereas contracts for international faculty articulated the 'ceiling' of the teaching load. As a result, many international faculty refused to teach the contractually specified number of hours. Because teaching is an integral part of a professor's workload, demands for too low of a teaching load are clearly unreasonable, but came to the forefront as a result of just one international faculty member interpreting the obligation this way, then spreading this information to others. So, further work on integrating international faculty into the HSE academic community has to address such negative aspects of their experience so that they can remain productive members of the academic community.

It would have been naïve to expect no tensions between internationally hired and domestic faculty, as their contractual obligations and respective compensation differ widely. The most apparent tensions arise out of differences in teaching load: Domestic faculty are wary of foreigners who might 'take away' their teaching loads with resulting elimination of their positions altogether. Moreover, not just the administrators, but also the domestic faculty are noticing the lack of impressive research productivity from international hires and feel shortchanged because they have to teach substantially more. Domestic faculty members also notice the numerous complaints from the international faculty, some of which are seen as excessive, and the perceived lack of loyalty to HSE that many foreigners apparently exhibit as they look for other employment opportunities. Finally, being able to obtain tenure in just six years, whereas domestic faculty may never have such a chance, is seen as unfair because publication requirements for domestic faculty often exceed those of international faculty. Combined with higher teaching loads, more administrative duties, and ongoing service requirements, domestic faculty feel that they receive far fewer benefits for a lot more effort.

Of course, there are some tensions within the international faculty group, as well. Some of them are Russian repatriates who have obtained their education abroad or have substantial international experience; they are perceived as 'outsiders' by domestic faculty, but not seen quite as 'international' by the foreign hires. Many have returned to Russia with an idea to 'help' the university, but feel as if their talents are not needed or appreciated. Another source of tension in this group is compensation, whereby newly hired faculty may be getting paid more than those hired in prior years. But the most important issue is the fact that international faculty are constantly comparing themselves to their peers, looking to teach less, publish less, and perform less service—so that their workload is 'fair' relative to others. Of course, this kind of attitude in no way serves the university, and this is something that the university administration needs to carefully address in the near future.

The task of integrating international faculty into the life of the university has always been one of the top priorities for the HSE administration. Not only are international faculty expensive, but they are less productive when not fully integrated into the academic community. Several large-scale initiatives were implemented at HSE in recent years to increase the integration level of foreign faculty. One such effort was the creation of the Office for International Integration, which is tasked with all issues related to international faculty adjustment to HSE, starting from obtaining their work visas. It introduces international faculty to HSE and explains to them how HSE life is structured. It also publishes the international bulletin, "HSE Look" (a monthly English-language circular), with updates on events and changes at the university. However, it seems that more substantial, systematic efforts—and a clearly articulated policy—are still needed.

There is little effort on the part of the central administration to involve international faculty more. Some of this is due to the fact that there is little service that non–Russian speaking faculty could provide; in the words of one of the deans,

> [I]t's close to impossible to involve international hires in the administrative structure for the obvious reasons. Of course, any faculty and almost all administrators are ready to communicate with international hires in English. But we are not quite ready yet to conduct meetings of the Scientific Council, HR committee, some other service functions in English.

Some of the disconnect between international faculty and the administration is also due to the fact that international hires expect to be paid for any additional effort they expend. At the faculty level, the efforts to draw international faculty in are diverse—some actively involve international hires in the life of the university by including them in various committees, whereas others do not bother.

Originally, the idea was to separate international hires from domestic faculty in order to create a less hostile working environment, free of envy and tensions. Since the university could not provide services and salaries at the level of international standards for the whole university, it was important to create "oases of well-being." Such separation included, among other tactics, individual offices, which domestic faculty are not afforded, but now all of these structural accommodations make integration more complicated.

An important aspect of integration is assuring a high quality of life, which international faculty could expect to find elsewhere, and would include medical services, pensions and other social benefits, language lessons for faculty members and their families, etc. The university only has control over a small number of these quality-of-life aspects, unfortunately. One of these is language instruction: Both faculty and their families are offered free Russian language instruction by the university's best "Russian as a second language" teachers. Another service relates to assisting with life outside of work, which faculty coordinators are tasked with, as mentioned earlier. But other issues are entangled with local rules, laws, and regulations, and are largely outside the university's control.

For example, the university provides international hires with private medical insurance at one of the best international clinics in Moscow. However, this insurance does not extend outside of Russia, does not cover cancer and other similar illnesses, and does not insure pregnancy and related expenses. Medical insurance services as an institutional benefit are still underdeveloped in Russia, so there is very little that the university can do in order to provide its international hires with better-quality medical care. Another point of tension is pension benefits: They do not exist for foreigners, only for Russian citizens and permanent residents. However, the university is working on establishing its own pension plan—something that it might later extend to even its domestic faculty to supplement government-sponsored programs. Although it requires a great deal of administrative effort to ensure that all laws are followed and a lot of financial investment, it could actually become one of the positive outcomes of the challenges experienced by international faculty at HSE.

Perhaps because the program is relatively new, only a few faculty members have departed HSE in the last few years. Those were the best performers— academics who were able to obtain employment elsewhere, for example, as a result of their publication activity. It is difficult to say how many will have departed Russia (or opted not to come to begin with) as a result of the sharp depreciation of the ruble at the end of 2014, as the results of the first recruiting season post-crisis are not yet available. However, it is clear already that the university does not have a strategy for dealing with situations where international hires with competitive publication records demand higher compensation as a result of currency devaluation, under a threat of losing that faculty member. Although some mobility is expected, the university has invested a substantial amount of resources into this program, so administrators feel inclined to negotiate to keep the international faculty, even when the benefit of such retention is questionable. It is also unclear at what point such negotiations are just an escalation of commitment on the part of the university without a justified business need.

Because there are no clearly articulated expectations, it is hard to say whether these expectations are met. However, there is a widespread feeling that international faculty do not play the role that they are supposed to play at the university.

This attitude is also supported by the fact that there is growing pressure on domestic faculty in terms of research productivity and teaching, and domestic faculty feel that international academics are in a far better position with respect to publication prospects and have significantly fewer burdens. Domestic faculty interpret this situation as clearly unfair.

The university administration also feels that internationally recruited staff do not produce what is expected from them. The administration has no clear commitment to continue contracts with those who are not good enough for tenure, but is under pressure from the faculty deans, as described earlier, to keep them. Indeed, the deans and the administration understand that huge costs have already been invested and still hope that at, some moment, 'everything will change.' Such lack of credibility also gives a negative signal to domestic faculty, who become increasingly unhappy about the unfairness of the situation.

Whether the university meets the expectations of international faculty is a hotly disputed issue. International faculty, at any given point, might have a long list of complaints against the university. But some of those complaints are generated by the fact that they are already a privileged group, are treated as such, and the more they are given, the more they expect, without any consideration of whether they provide enough in return. Some expectations are clearly unreasonable: For example, many have voiced the desire to live in their native countries full-time, while remaining employed by HSE, and are clearly upset when they are told that such arrangements are not possible. It is difficult to imagine a university elsewhere where such an expectation would be considered reasonable. Other, less drastic, expectations include being paid for work considered as 'service'—for example, serving on committees and performing peer reviews. So, in some instances, international faculty expectations can never be met, simply because they are impossible to meet.

Other unmet expectations clearly have merit, and to the extent possible, the university is working to address them. Even when these expectations cannot be addressed, as is the case with medical insurance in Russia currently, it allows the university to clearly see the areas for improvement if it is to become a leading research university with a recognized name worldwide. So, despite the fact that international faculty may not perform as well as was expected, they certainly serve a greater purpose in terms of pushing HSE to a higher level of internationalization.

## Conclusion

The case of HSE shows that, given enough resources and commitment from central administration, the university can start from ground zero and quickly advance its international recruiting efforts. HSE is quite different from other universities in Russia, as it was the first to implement systematic international faculty recruiting efforts. Other Russian universities were forced to start recruiting by their participation in the 5–100 program or other ministry programs and are still doing it on an ad hoc basis. Over time, however, a more systematic approach should be implemented everywhere. As the HSE case shows, it is rather difficult, if not impossible, to attract high-quality faculty without a clear understanding that recruiting affects the university on every level.

These effects are both explicit and implicit, and the changes that the university is forced to undergo are not limited to the academic environment. International faculty bring their own culture and their own understanding of how things should be done; as such, they create problems that university administrators have to solve, changing the university as a result. Many problems are related to differences in academic cultures, and the absence of clear and well-established rules, perceived as legitimate, lead to reduced levels of international faculty integration and, as a result, lower job satisfaction on their part.

Another important lesson is that it is important to not excessively speed up the recruiting process, due to the clear trade-off between quantity and quality. It is not enough to attract many strong candidates; it is important to create an environment that facilitates the continuous professional development of these candidates in order to reap the full benefits of international recruiting.

Perhaps rather unique to Russia, performance evaluation clearly differs for domestic and international faculty. International faculty are often evaluated by their 'potential,' whereas domestic faculty are only evaluated by actual results. So part of the tension in international recruiting arises from the fact that pressure on the domestic faculty is much heavier, whereas international faculty are blamed for a situation in which "they first get money for nothing and then leave as soon as they get some good results."

Nonetheless, international recruitment is an important strategic initiative in the development of the Russian higher education system. It allows universities to become more aligned, both academically and culturally, with their international counterparts. As such recruiting is still in its infancy, it is difficult to talk about large-scale developments; but it is already clear that introducing differences results in a shock that creates an overall healthier academic environment.

## Note

1 All data in this section obtained from the statistical publication "Education in the Russian Federation: 2014: Statistical Compilation" [in Russian], edited by G. Andruchshak et al., and published by NRU Higher School of Economics Press.

## References

[Agamova, N. & Allakhverdyan, A.] Агамова, Н. С., & Аллахвердян, А. Г. (2007) Утечка мозгов из России: причины и масштабы. *Российский химический журнал*, т. LI, №3. [Russian brain-drain: Reasons and scope. *Russian Chemistry Journal* (in Russian)] 51(3): 108–115.

Altbach, P. (2014). The value of the "top 100" program. *Higher in Russia Education and Beyond*, 1, 7–8.

[Andruchshak et al.]. Андрущак, Г. В., Л.М. Гохберг, А. Л. Кевеш, Н. В. Ковалева, Я. И. Кузьминов, А. Е., & Суринов (Ред.) (2014). Образование в Российской Федерации: *2014:* статистический сборник.—Москва: Национальный исследовательский университет «Высшая школа экономики».

Clark, B. R. (1986). *The higher education system: Academic organization in cross-national perspective*. Oakland: University of California Press.

Graham, L. R. (1967). *The Soviet Academy of Sciences and the Communist Party: 1927–1932*. Princeton, NJ: Princeton University Press.

Latova, N. V., & Savinkov, V. I. (2012). The influence of academic migration on the intellectual potential of Russia. *European Journal of Education, 47*(1), 64–76.

Maldonado-Maldonado, A., & Bassett, R. M. (2014). *The forefront of international higher education*, Dordrecht, Netherlands: Springer.

Mamiseishvili, K., & Rosser, V. J. (2010). International and citizen faculty in the United States: An examination of their productivity at research universities. *Research in Higher Education, 51*(1), 88–107.

Pavlyutkin, I. A., & Yudkevich, M. (2016). The ranking game on the Russian battlefield: The case of the higher school of economics. In M. Yudkevich, P. Altbach & L. Rumbley (Eds.), *The global academics rankings game. Changing institutional policy, practice and academic life* (pp. 171–194). New York and London: Routledge.

Prakhov, I. A., & Yudkevich, M. (2015). Admission policy in contemporary Russia: Recent changes, expected outcomes, and potential winners. In V. Stead (Ed.), *International perspectives on higher education admission policy: A reader* (pp. 83–100). New York: Peter Lang Publishing Inc.

Sivak, E., & Yudkevich, M. (2015). Academic immobility and inbreeding in Russian universities. In M. Yudkevich, P. G. Altbach & L. E. Rumbley (Eds.), *Academic inbreeding and mobility in higher education: Global perspectives* (pp. 130–155). New York: Palgrave Macmillan.

# 11
# INTERNATIONAL FACULTY IN SAUDI ARABIA'S UNIVERSITIES

*Mohammad A. AlOhali*

## Introduction

International faculty provide much-needed competencies to higher education institutions throughout the world and particularly in fields required by today's developing nations. Only a few developing countries have an adequate number of locally available academics, and many countries continually look outward to attract and recruit highly skilled and trained faculty. With increasingly diverse student enrollments as well, international faculty members are becoming ". . . highly visible symbols of the changing face of the population in higher education" (Manrique & Manrique, 1999, p. 103).

This chapter focuses on the general practices adopted by Saudi universities, using the King Fahd University of Petroleum & Minerals (KFUPM) as a case study to illustrate specific policies, practices, opportunities, and challenges. The rationale for hiring teaching and research faculty from other countries varies. These differences could be due to matters of affluence, strategic plans, or simply economic need. The Kingdom of Saudi Arabia (KSA) has a rapidly growing population, and this—together with the economic progress it has witnessed in recent decades—has resulted in a sharp increase in the number of students seeking higher education. The government has responded by increasing the number of higher education institutions and universities. In only the last decade, the number of universities has grown from 20 in 2005 to 39 in 2015. This has consequently led to an increase in demand for highly qualified faculty at Saudi universities. Also, Saudi Arabia aspires to invest in knowledge-based industries to reflect its shift toward the emergence of a 'knowledge-based society.' That goal is highly dependent on knowledge products and highly educated personnel, the key ingredients for economic growth.

The dearth of competencies required for university teaching among the local populace has been a key factor driving Saudi Arabia to hire international faculty since the establishment of the very first university in the country, which was founded in 1957. In 1977, the highest percentage of Saudi national faculty was at the University of Riyadh (now known as King Saud University), at only 16.2 percent. By 2014, 58.4 percent of the total teaching staff at Saudi Arabia's higher education institutions were Saudi nationals. Student enrollments have also grown—from 2009 to 2015, the number of freshman-year students increased by 62.4 percent, and the number of graduate students increased by 35.4 percent. Meanwhile, over the same period, the number of teaching faculty increased by 55.5 percent, which caused the student–teacher ratio to increase from 18 to 21 students per teacher. Universities have seen the number of Saudi teaching faculty increase, while the demand for international faculty is also constantly increasing.

Saudi Arabia has tried to address the need for international faculty recruitment by carefully designing policies and procedures to attract the best available candidates. The prime areas of concern and development in relation to the effort to attract and hire international faculty have been diversification, flexibility in reacting to each university's needs, building on international experience, and developing competitive university support structures. Attention to these matters has been carried out through the establishment of international partnerships with universities and organizations, the expansion of funding sources for teaching and research, and the sharing of valuable information about the universities through various means, including web-based resources.

In this chapter, we discuss how Saudi universities attract international faculty, the policies and procedures that govern their hiring and careers, and their impact on the higher education landscape in Saudi Arabia. The chapter also presents insights gathered from international faculty at 24 universities in Saudi Arabia.

## Policies and Regulations

### Saudi Government Policies

The rapid expansion of higher education in Saudi Arabia over the last three decades has made the tasks of building national capacity in terms of qualified faculty members and attracting world-class expatriate faculty very challenging. Whereas universities may compete for similar personnel from abroad, movement across universities within the kingdom is not common (Altbach, 2003). The government has been working hard with public universities to ensure that human resources policies are in place. Universities must be able to have competitive incentives and pay scales to attract well-qualified faculty from other countries.

Normally, an expatriate faculty member is appointed on a contractual basis. Local faculty are governed by the Ministry of Civil Services and their appointment is permanent. After the age of retirement, which is 60 to 65 years, local faculty may continue on a contractual basis. Apparently, there is no conflict in this regard, as the foreign faculty understand that they are contract employees. The evaluation of the faculty is performed before the end of the contract period and is uniformly based on performance criteria, which include research productivity, teaching load, and performance of community service. The contract period for international faculty is invariably for two years. The contracting procedures are designed to obtain a pool of highly qualified applicants in order to maintain the excellence and high standards of the recruiting university. Foreign faculty contracts are executed between the recruiting university and the international faculty hire, who is considered a foreign 'contractor,' and all such employees are subject to the general laws of the kingdom. Standard contracts for regular faculty members are normally for two years (sometimes four years, for outstanding faculty) with open-ended renewal normally up to the age of 60 years (although renewals can extend to the age of 70).

Employing expatriate faculty members is considered a point of strength and contributes to diversifying the educational and cultural experiences offered by Saudi Arabia's higher education institutions. In some disciplines—such as religion and general studies, where Arabic-language proficiency is required—the foreign faculty is expected to teach in Arabic. In August 2015, there were approximately 28,015 expatriate faculty members in the Saudi higher education system, which accounted for 41 percent of total faculty members distributed in all universities and colleges in the kingdom. These international faculty represent 89 different nationalities from around the world. These data are obtained from the report of the Higher Education Statistics Center, Ministry of Education, KSA.

In addition to the renewable contracts mentioned earlier, expatriate faculty members enjoy negotiable salaries and incremental salary increases based on their area of specialization and market demand. Those with distinguished performance records have been given long-term contracts. Higher education institutions in the kingdom have some autonomy that allows them to compete for expatriate faculty members, offering them different benefits and incentives.

All regulations have been set by the government and updated as needed to attract the best faculty/staff to meet the needs of higher education in the kingdom. Each university develops its human resources policies and procedures in accordance with these regulations, and it is the university that signs the contracts with the faculty it hires. Foreign academics make up around 42 percent of the total faculty members in Saudi Arabia's public universities. In the public sector, all international faculty members are appointed on renewable term contracts—and though there are no tenured posts, many spend their entire careers in the kingdom.

The incentives for foreign faculty to perform adequately are high, given that performance is tied to contract renewal opportunities (Altbach, Reisberg & Rumbley, 2009). Foreign faculty appointments are, to a large extent, decoupled from the Civil Service Ministry. This provides universities autonomy in making appointments, evaluating academic staff, and, within guidelines, setting terms of promotion and even dismissal, as well as salaries. As such, setting the terms of appointment, executing contracts, and conducting evaluations of foreign faculty are tasks performed independently by the university.

The former Higher Education Council established regulations for the recruiting of Saudi and non-Saudi staff, including faculty members, their salaries, and allowances. Subsequent to the merging of the two ministries, a new organizational structure is being put in place. Among the rules for hiring non-Saudi faculty members, each university council can increase by up to 50 percent the designated salaries for those who offer expertise in highly demanded specialties. Furthermore, the university council can give a 100 percent increase to physicians and medical faculty, or for academics who can provide support for rare majors or those with high academic reputations, outstanding skills from a reputable university, extensive experience, or those with particularly excellent qualifications. In addition, the university rector, upon agreement with the chairman of the Public Civil Services Ministry, can apply this same salary increase benefit to other expatriates. Based on the approval of the university council and recommendation of the university scientific council, it is possible to exclude faculty members of high academic reputation, qualification, and experience from certain conditions and prerequisites designated in the regulations for recruiting.

The university council can assign up to 30 percent of basic salary as a special professional allowance for faculty and similar staff with qualifications or expertise in highly sought-after fields. These fields and the allowances that can be offered to such highly qualified faculty members are designated by the council. If the expatriate completes two years of work in the university, he or she earns half a month salary as an end-of-service bonus per every year of service. If the faculty member, lecturer, teaching assistant, and technician or a similar staff person related to teaching completes five years of work in the university, he or she qualifies for a month's worth of salary as an end-of-service bonus per every year of service.

The former Council of Higher Education approved a number of benefits, compensations, allowances, and supplementary incentives for faculty members (some to both domestic and international) at Saudi universities. The set of benefits is meant to represent a developed concept of salary incentives that are effectively and directly correlated with the quality and level of performance and that would constitute a substantial reward, technically and financially. The system grants a faculty member preference based on several factors, which include the scarcity of his or her specialty and the quality of his or her research—notably, privileging that which is of a standard to compete with local, regional, and international prizes in several fields, most importantly science and technology. To attract foreign researchers, the higher education sector focuses on quality when making decisions to hire faculty members. Universities offer incentives for expatriates in an effort to promote the quality of research. Indeed, Saudi universities are attracting distinguished researchers and faculty members to teach and supervise postgraduate students.

## King Fahd University of Petroleum & Minerals (KFUPM)

We will look at the hiring procedure and university regulations at universities in the KSA in general and at King Fahd University of Petroleum & Minerals (KFUPM), in particular, which is a leading educational organization for science and technology. Since its inception, the university enrollment has grown to more than 10,000 students. KFUPM was officially established by royal decree on 5 Jumada 1, 1383 (September 23, 1963). The first students were admitted a year later, on September 23, 1964, when 67 young men enrolled in what was then named the College of Petroleum and Minerals (CPM). KFUPM follows a similar procedure as most of the public universities in the kingdom. It has been consistently ranked among the top universities in Saudi Arabia and the Middle East by international ranking organizations, for example, Quacquarelli Symonds (QS) and the Academic Ranking of World Universities (ARWU).

## Hiring Procedures

Universities in Saudi Arabia advertise for faculty positions in various media in an effort to hire international faculty. Advertisements are handled by the Faculty and Personnel Affairs (FPA) departments of individual universities, in consultation with the specific department seeking to make the hire. These advertisements are usually placed on websites and in international academic magazines, such as the *Chronicle of Higher Education*. Faculty attending conferences are also encouraged to carry brochures about their departments and meet potential candidates and talk to them about possible openings at the university.

Recruitment visits and networking are utilized to 'head hunt' potential candidates. The FPA at KFUPM has a recruitment website, which advertises all current available faculty positions. The university also establishes relationships with overseas recruiting offices and publishers to facilitate faculty recruitment, placement of ads, and settlement of invoices. The university's local publication, "Partners in Excellence," and individual department brochures are sent out to interested applicants and overseas recruiting agencies. The university normally begins to receive applications in September of the current year for potential employment in the succeeding year—that is, to commence work in the following September—providing ample time for visa processing.

The specific requirements regarding teaching and research responsibilities of the prospective faculty members are outlined in the advertising and recruitment materials. The application process is supported online, where interested candidates are guided at each step to accurately complete the job application and initiate the processing of the application. The applicant's material is forwarded to the department seeking to make the hire for preliminary review and evaluation. The application requires a cover letter, a current curriculum vitae or resume, scanned copies of degrees/certificates and academic transcripts, reference letters, a teaching statement (indicating the courses the applicant would prefer to teach, the teaching philosophy, and how technology will be adopted in making teaching/learning effective), and a research statement (whose ingredients may include the areas of research interest and those of research strength, the potential to work in a group, develop research laboratories, etc.). The FPA develops files of potential candidates for further review. Interviews are arranged by the academic department and the deanship of faculty affairs.

The way interviews are conducted varies. In most cases a video call is made, and a group of current faculty members observe the candidate's potential for the position. In addition, other aspects such as communication skills, attitude, and confidence are observed. On an annual basis, members from the deanship of faculty affairs and other faculty in higher administration visit the United States and Europe to meet candidates. Interviews are scheduled in different cities. Faculty who travel abroad for conferences are sometimes requested to meet and report on a candidate. In case of positions such as chair professors, etc., potential candidates are invited to visit the university, along with their spouse, where they deliver a seminar and meet the department head and selected faculty. Briefly, a wide range of methods is adopted to meet and select potential candidates. Preference is given to faculty who can report at the beginning of the academic year.

The entire hiring process can take between four and eight months. Interviews usually take place several months ahead of the September start date to allow plenty of time for other recruitment steps. The main factor contributing to the recruitment time is the visa approval process, which can take between two and six months, and is initiated after the candidate is selected and recommended for hiring, and then approved by the rector. The department also conducts an online interview in the presence of the chairman of the department and some faculty members from the faculty search committee. This interview is mainly to assess the candidate's teaching capability, accent (the individual should be excellent in English), attitude, communication skills, etc. In some cases, faculty are invited to the KFUPM campus to give seminars and be interviewed.

The criteria for selection are primarily based on the qualifications held by the applicant. Candidates with degrees from the United States and Canada are generally preferred because the system at KFUPM, as well as in most of the universities in Saudi Arabia, is based on the North American system of education. In some disciplines, candidates with qualifications from other world regions are also hired, provided they have an exceptional record and can deliver when it comes to the university's expectations and quality.

The specific employment offer varies according to rank, discipline, and the demand from faculty. It also depends on the applicant's past performance in research and, to some extent, the international status and ranking of the university from where the candidate has graduated or where he or she is currently working. Basic salary is normally calculated on the KFUPM salary scale, which is based on the academic qualifications held by the candidate and the relevant years of work experience. However, the basic salary is also very flexible, ad hoc, and negotiable.

Although offers seem modest, according to one study (Altbach, 2003), the total cost to the university is higher than in most other places. Repatriation air tickets for faculty members and three members of family are given for each year of service. Campus life also provides multifarious benefits to faculty and their family, including facilities such as schools, free access to recreational facilities, a community recreation center, and a clinic, to name a few. Security and safety on the whole campus is well maintained, and is the responsibility of the KFUPM Security & Safety Departments.

The basic salary for international faculty is highly competitive, tax free, and boosted by the excellent package of benefits discussed earlier. In addition, there are financial benefits to be accrued when applying for funded projects (local and national). The university research committee, national funding agencies, and industries, etc., that award projects to KFUPM researchers also include line items for faculty to augment their current earnings. For example, faculty enjoy a respectable sum of pocket money in addition to their salary, depending on the funding agency. The faculty member can apply for a travel grant when they attend conferences, provided the specific activity meets the required criteria, per KFUPM regulations and subject to approval. KFUPM support normally covers per diem (including time required for traveling) and conference registration fees. Unlike many institutions globally, foreign and Saudi faculty at KFUPM and other Saudi universities can apply for support to attend more than one international conference during an academic year (with compensation provided for up to three per year).

KFUPM hires international faculty for the following main reasons: to support high-quality teaching and research in areas where local faculty are not available, to have diversity in the faculty body, and to promote competitiveness in faculty work. Faculty with experience in countries with advanced economic and educational systems are preferred, specifically those who studied in the United States or Canada. All professorial-rank faculty members hold PhD degrees. The ages range from early 30s to late 50s or 60s. Currently, KFUPM has 294 professorial-rank international faculty (representing 37 nationalities), with an average age of 49.

The selection/hiring criteria include the following:

- Teaching, which is measured by a number of factors, including student satisfaction, lecture delivery, course management (all done via student evaluation of faculty, department chairman assessment, dean's input)
- Research outcomes, measured mainly through publication in refereed journals and the production of patents
- Community service through projects

KFUPM hires, on average, 30 new expatriate faculty members every year. The acceptance rate of offers is more than 50 percent.

The main reasons international faculty decline offers of employment are mismatches between offered and expected compensation and benefits. The average duration of stay is eight years. The full range of reasons international faculty leave the university includes age, family relocation, termination due to unsatisfactory performance, resignation, and death. However, the *primary* reasons for leaving the university include the following:

- Family issues (such as dependent students wishing to complete their higher education abroad)
- Better compensation offered elsewhere
- Other (better) benefits offered elsewhere
- Termination by the university

With regard to the matter of international faculty leaving so that their children can complete higher education abroad, it should be noted that there are thousands of scholarships for non-Saudi students; however, access to some college disciplines (mainly in the health fields) is highly competitive in public universities. Recently, much better opportunities are found in the private higher education institutes. Other reasons for international faculty to leave include better compensation offered in the region and elsewhere. And, depending on their performance, some faculty members' contracts are terminated by the university.

Annual surveys are conducted by the Office of Planning and Quality to measure the satisfaction of faculty members. Focus group meetings are also organized from time to time to understand satisfaction issues and levels. Performance discussions also take place to improve the productivity and quality of work. High-performing faculty are rewarded financially and through other research support incentives.

In addition to regular full-time faculty, KFUPM and other universities in the KSA attract nonconventional and part-time international faculty. These include chair professors, joint professors, adjunct professors, postdoctoral fellows, etc. While full-time chair professors and postdoctoral fellows are engaged throughout the year, other categories visit the university for a period of just one to two months. Chair professors, both for full-time and part-time positions, are generally selected from a list of Nobel Laureates, Nobel Laureate nominees, Fields medalists, and the list of highly cited researchers identified by Thomson Reuters. These nontraditional faculty have contributed to knowledge transfer and capacity building, etc. A separate office, under the Office of the Vice Rector for Research, assists in their recruitment and appropriates funds for their compensation to facilitate their employment as KFUPM faculty in order to raise the levels of research and research productivity, while tracking return on investment via evaluations, performance, and achievement. In such cases, every contract is carefully tailored in coordination with the FPA to meet the demands and expectations of the researcher in terms of the number of visits to be made to the kingdom, the duration of stay,

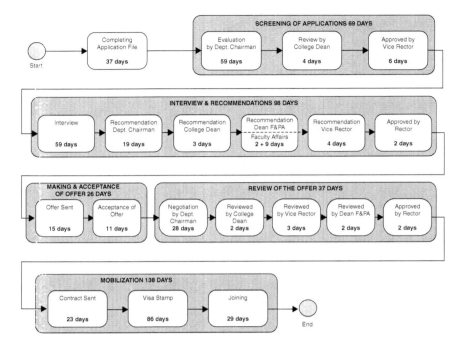

**FIGURE 11.1** Non-Saudi Faculty Recruitment Process at KFUPM.

*Source:* Deanship of Faculty and Personnel Affairs (KFUPM, n.d.).

*Note:* The 116 days includes 105 days of employment visa processing for international faculty. The visa processing requires securing visas through the concerned ministries, legalization of various academic and other documents, medical testing and other formalities prior to granting the visa by Saudi missions abroad.

reimbursement of tickets, activities that will be undertaken while not at the host Saudi institution, renewal criteria, etc. The terms of the contract are agreed upon, and the text of such contracts is approved by the office before being sent by the FPA to the candidate.

Academics at KFUPM have access to some of the world's most highly funded research programs in various science and engineering disciplines. The university encourages its faculty members to develop research projects that could potentially lead to groundbreaking innovations, especially in the energy and high-tech sectors.

## University Regulations

To maintain a level of high-quality instruction, research, and service, a faculty member is expected to spend up to 40 hours per week executing university duties. However, he or she has the freedom to distribute these hours across teaching duties, research development and creative work, office hours, and committee service. In addition, a professorial-rank faculty member is expected to accept a reasonable instructional load during the regular semesters, which is typically two courses per semester.

The teaching load for a full-time professor may vary from semester to semester, depending upon the requirements of the department, the number of students enrolled, and the number of teaching staff available. However, the expectations and workload are the same for both domestic and international faculty members. Also, the evaluation criteria and promotion guidelines are the same for both. The workload may be reduced when a faculty member has other administrative responsibilities; special assignments; approved research; lab development; development of new course materials; and supervision of theses, senior projects, summer training, and co-op students (internships). Promotion of faculty members is linked to their research productivity, teaching load, and performance in community service.

More elaboration of faculty development programs, as well as evaluation, is needed. To improve and support the professional development and growth of faculty members in the university, well-established evaluation procedures are strictly practiced. An annual performance self-evaluation form is completed by the faculty member. The elements of the form indicate that the objective of a faculty career is the building of a highly professional, stable, and competent scholar. The major activities reviewed in the evaluation process include teaching, research, and community service.

It is the intention of the university to encourage the faculty to maintain continuity of service. Therefore, the appointment and contract are usually renewed automatically on a two-year basis, depending on departmental evaluation and recommendations. Otherwise, either party should notify the other in writing of the desire to terminate the contract six months before the expiration date of the contract. In the event of termination, all accrued salary is paid on departure from the university. If either party requests otherwise, a contract termination may be effective at an agreed-upon date. Reasons for contract termination are acceptance of resignation, cancellation of the academic position, unjustified absences, involvement in a crime or severe rule violation, disciplinary dismissal, permanent sickness, reaching the retirement age threshold, or death.

## Current State of International Faculty

### Demographics

In August 2015, the number of teaching staff in the kingdom's higher education institutions was 6,627, with a growth rate of 58.7 percent from 2009. Non-Saudi teaching staff comprise around 41 percent of total teaching staff in the kingdom, and 42 percent of the total teaching staff is female.

The number of teaching staff at all academic ranks has also increased in recent years—the number of teaching staff at the rank of lecturer evidenced the highest increase, with a growth rate of 160 percent from 2009 to 2015. The data from 2009 to 2015 show that more Saudis than non-Saudis were employed as teaching staff; however, the growth rate of non-Saudi teaching staff was 74.5 percent, versus the 44.3 percent growth rate of Saudi teaching staff over the same period. It is worth mentioning here that, recently, two additional efforts were made to increase the number of qualified local faculty members. First, the government supported the universities with new faculty positions (to be filled by qualified Saudi candidates). Second, many Saudi PhD holders returning from their scholarship abroad (those who graduated from reputable international universities) were also hired.

Among Saudi teaching staff, the percentage of females rapidly increased, with an average annual growth rate of 12.7 percent and a total growth rate of 61.3 percent. This was greater than the percentage of male teaching staff, which increased with an average annual growth rate of 7.6 percent and a total growth rate of 33.9 percent. The same pattern applies to the non-Saudi teaching staff; the percentage of females increased with a total growth rate of 124 percent from 2009 to 2015, greater than the male percentage, which increased by a total growth rate of 57.7 percent. In 2015, female teaching staff comprised 47.8 percent of total Saudi teaching staff and 34.8 percent of total non-Saudi teaching staff. These figures indicate growth in the rate of participation of women in the higher education sector in Saudi Arabia.

Some Saudi universities have a higher share of international faculty than others. The international faculty ratio ranges between 72 percent and 9 percent among the universities, and the retention rate (defined as completion of the first contract period of two years) varies between 79 percent and 100 percent.

The efforts of higher education institutions in Saudi Arabia to improve quality and efficiency resulted in a decrease in the number of students per teaching staff (i.e., the student–teacher ratio) to 18:1 from 21:1, which is still higher than the global average of 17:1, and lower than the average of the group of Arab countries of 23:1.

The diversity of international faculty is important, and 89 different nationalities are currently represented in Saudi Arabian universities. These include 18 Arab-speaking countries of the Middle East and North Africa, 18 countries from elsewhere in Africa, 21 Asian countries, and 6 countries in the Americas. Furthermore, 26 countries from the rest of the world are also represented, including Australia, New Zealand, and various European nations.

The distribution of international faculty at the government universities in Saudi Arabia shows that nearly 69 percent of these are from Middle East and Arabic-speaking African countries. Other Asian countries account for around 22 percent, while the Americas, Europe, Australia, New Zealand, and the Pacific account for about 9 percent. International faculty from non–Arabic-speaking African countries make up 0.5 percent of all international faculty at Saudi government universities.

## Motivation and Integration at Local Universities

According to Mamiseishvili and Rosser (2010),

> . . . international faculty members can bring diverse perspectives to the classrooms and can serve as role models to the growing number of international students. Furthermore, with more inclusion of international academics in professional and peer networks and in institutional leadership, they will develop more loyalty and commitment to the institution.

A major role has to be played by the institution with respect to providing an inclusive climate that recognizes the academic advantages and contribution of international faculty members in all aspects of their work, and not only with respect to their research. There are several motivational factors for international faculty to be associated with universities in Saudi Arabia. These include, but are not limited to, the academic environment, research infrastructures, local culture and values, competitive compensation and other benefits, and potential career growth. Several faculty development programs provide the opportunity to faculty members to enhance their skills.

Saudi universities typically hire international faculty members based on the performance records of the academics and the needs of the hiring institutions themselves. Competitive packages for newly recruited faculty are based on applicants' qualifications, experience, the needs of the university, and the academic field. The salary offered at the point of hiring can be doubled based on these criteria. In addition, international faculty are entitled to an annual increment of 5 percent in their basic salaries and in certain cases may earn salaries that exceed those of Saudi faculty.

The universities in Saudi Arabia give importance to the integration of international faculty and their dependents. The use of English as the means of instruction and communication at the universities plays a key role in this effort.

## Utilization of International Faculty and Their Impact on the University

The workload for all faculty members is similar—irrespective of their nationality—and, in general, is 40 hours per five-day week. Faculty in some universities are heavily involved in research work, and interested faculty members are encouraged to form research groups and to apply for both internal university funding and external national funding for their research. National funding may come from sources such as the King Abdul-Aziz City for Science and Technology (KACST), which is KSA's national research funding agency. Some faculty, especially those in sciences and engineering, have a wide pool of both graduate and undergraduate students to engage in their labs and research projects. The universities in

Saudi Arabia strongly promote the publication of research in high-quality, peer-reviewed academic journals and participation of faculty members in well-known international conferences. The universities support such activities through various means, without any discrimination between Saudi and international faculty.

International faculty in Saudi universities bring diversity. The exchange of ideas among the faculty and researchers coming from various parts of the world and the knowledge they bring from different universities play an important role in the development of new ideas, as well as spurring research activities. The affiliation of international faculty members with their previous institutions provides a great opportunity for international collaboration in both academic and research areas. There are several cases of students benefitting from such collaborations through research projects, internship visits, and interaction among students across universities. Moreover, international faculty with industrial experience provide invaluable insight and enrich student learning, while also helping to bridge the gap between universities and industry. This bottom-up approach promises to deliver far-reaching results in the development of Saudi universities and contribute toward the evolution of a Saudi knowledge-based economy.

The impact of international faculty on KFUPM can be highlighted by the increase in the number of published papers by faculty affiliated with Saudi universities in high-quality journals—and their citations. The per-head contribution of both Saudi and international faculty is comparable, but the number of single-author publications of international faculty members is higher. Furthermore, the number of papers co-authored by both Saudi and international faculty members has greatly increased. This is a long-term impact, as the knowledge transfer to and skill development achieved by local faculty members from their interactions with international colleagues will have a continuous positive impact.

Saudi Arabia's plans to build a knowledge-based economy will require collaboration with multinational companies (Al-Ohali & Burdon, 2013). Industrial research parks have been set up at universities—such as Dhahran Techno-Valley at KFUPM in Dhahran, Riyadh Techno-Valley at King Saud University in Riyadh, and Jeddah Techno-Valley in Jeddah—which attract international tenants setting up research and development facilities. The international faculty members at Saudi universities—with their international industrial experience and past affiliations—have proven very instrumental in the development and operation of such initiatives. Recently, commercialization of research, in the form of licensing international patents and developing prototypes of research ideas, has also resulted from such efforts.

## *Assessment and Challenges*

International faculty members are evaluated for the period of their contract. The evaluation includes a student evaluation score as well as a self-evaluation. The faculty members are evaluated based on the feedback received from students, supervision of student projects, supervision of co-op students, and other academic activities. They are also evaluated based on research output in terms of publication of research in high-quality journals, patent production, participation in international conferences, graduate-level thesis supervision, technical seminar presentations and talks, professional consultation activities, and participation on university committees and other activities.

There are several challenges when hiring international faculty in the kingdom. Globally, there is increasing demand for university faculty due the huge increase in higher education accessibility and expansion. This common challenge results in strong competition for hiring a quality faculty member.

Another challenge is identifying the right candidate—someone who will not only match the academic requirements, possess the needed competencies, and is of high caliber, but who also has the will and ability to adapt to a new environment. Although there are clear variations among universities, the academic environment in most major Saudi universities is fairly comparable to that in the Western world. Other newly established universities in Saudi Arabia are currently working hard to complete their modern and comprehensive campuses; there are 11 huge new campuses in the kingdom. Research facilities are developing and funding is available. However, distance between Saudi universities and industry active in state-of-art technologies and innovative research still exists. This is being overcome to some extent by inviting international companies into Saudi science parks aligned with the mission of the university and where such companies can operate physically close to the campus.

Convincing potential candidates that a conducive and secure environment exists in Saudi Arabia is a formidable task, especially in the current climate, when the perception of the entire region is shaped by news of conflicts and dangerous conditions. Among many prospective international faculty there is reluctance to even consider the possibility of relocating to the kingdom.

There are other constraints. Promising doctoral graduates who have received their degrees in Western countries often prefer to remain in the West to pursue longer-term immigration opportunities. Meanwhile, senior faculty who would be attractive to Saudi universities are well rooted in established laboratories with a large number of graduate advisees; hence, they cannot move without giving up their research program. This leaves only a small segment of qualified candidates available to be recruited.

Other concerns from applicants may range from special facilities for their children's education, differences in culture and norms, opportunities for career growth, opportunities for spousal careers, etc.

## National Survey of International Faculty

A survey of international faculty members at Saudi universities was conducted by the Ministry of Education in the last quarter of 2015, where more than 4,000 responses were collected. The survey measured the major reasons faculty join universities in Saudi Arabia, their expectations prior to joining, and current satisfaction level with respect to various aspects of university life. Faculty from all universities in the kingdom were invited to participate in the online survey.

The survey covered both male and female faculty, with a gender distribution across the responses of 42 percent female and 58 percent male. Faculty of various nationalities responded, including individuals from Canada, Egypt, India, Jordan, Yemen, Pakistan, Sudan, Tunisia, the United Kingdom, and the United States. The sampling covered all the public universities of Saudi Arabia. Around 31.4 percent of the respondents had a master's degree as their highest qualification, and 68.6 percent held PhD degrees. With respect to the number of years spent at the university, 12 percent had spent less than a year, 38.5 percent between 1 and 3 years, 44.9 percent between 4 and 10 years, 3 percent between 10 and 15 years, and more than 2 percent had spent more than 16 years.

The questionnaire aimed to statistically measure satisfaction with respect to university administration and management, and satisfaction with the university facilities and infrastructure. Subquestions were presented in the survey to gain more details regarding respondents' opinions. A 5-point scale was used, where 1 represented "strongly agree," 2 "agree," 3 represented "neither agree nor disagree," 4 "disagree," and 5 represented "strongly disagree."

Respondents were asked to indicate which reasons—on a scale of 1 to 5, with 5 being the most preferred—were most important in their decision to join a Saudi university. The main reasons that led faculty to join the university included research, academic environment, family, culture, and compensation package.

Prior to joining the university, respondents were also asked to indicate their expectation level—on a scale of 1 to 5, with 5 being the highest level of expectation— around several key issues relating to their personal and professional lives. The survey indicates that international faculty have high expectations with respect to culture before joining universities in Saudi Arabia. Their expectations are also higher regarding prospective career growth, integration within the university community, and the environment for their families.

Figure 11.2 shows the average score for the overall satisfaction level of the international faculty at Saudi universities, according to their nationalities. These data show that those from India and Pakistan have the highest levels of satisfaction.

Figure 11.3 shows the average score by nationality for international faculty's level of expectation prior to joining a Saudi university, against the overall current satisfaction level of international faculty at Saudi universities. It shows an overall reduction in level of actual satisfaction, as compared to the level of expected satisfaction prior to joining the university.

Despite the indications of unmet expectations presented in Figure 11.3, the survey data also indicate that there are international faculty who are as satisfied, or are more satisfied, after joining a Saudi university, compared to what they had expected prior to being hired. According to the survey data, the areas most likely to exceed international faculty's pre-hire expectations have to do with family and integration with the university community (which 24 percent and 20 percent, respectively, indicated as having exceeded their pre-hire expectations), followed by research (where 19 percent of respondents felt more satisfied than what

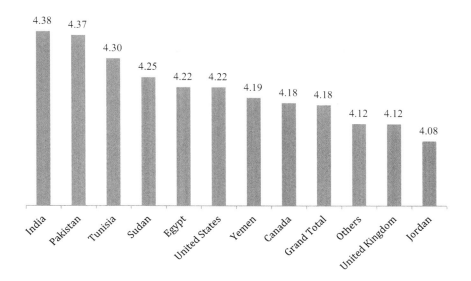

**FIGURE 11.2** Overall Satisfaction among Faculty from Different Countries.

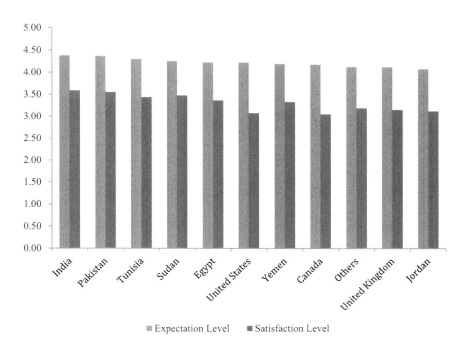

**FIGURE 11.3** Faculty's Level of Expectation Prior to Joining a Saudi University Versus Satisfaction Level after Joining a Saudi University by Nationality.

they had expected prior to joining the university), compensation (which also exceeded expectations for 19 percent of respondents), and career growth (which was deemed more satisfying than expected by 14 percent of respondents).

The data also provide insights into how satisfied international faculty are with respect to factors that may or may not have motivated them to join a Saudi university in the first place. For example, even though family, compensation, and research were not among their prime reasons to join the university, their satisfaction levels in these areas are higher than what they expected.

Saudi Arabia's strategy for university education (AAFAQ, 2011) introduced two programs for faculty recruitment and retention. The two programs call for planning and building capacity, while emphasizing the importance of recruiting excellent international faculty members, developing them, and retaining them. In addition, the programs stressed the role of each university in facing the challenge of international competition for recruiting the best faculty members.

With some improvements, the policies related to higher education in Saudi Arabia are stable and the continuity promises to provide a conducive environment for the active participation of international faculty at the country's universities.

## Conclusion

In this chapter, a range of information about the role of international faculty in universities in the Kingdom of Saudi Arabia was presented. In addition, some aspects about the situation at King Fahd University of Petroleum & Minerals were discussed in detail to provide specific examples and insights. The main reasons Saudi universities seek to hire international faculty include a dearth of competencies among domestic faculty, the simple need to fill enough faculty positions to meet the demands of a growing system, and the desire to bring in diverse perspectives and expertise. General regulations and policies for hiring international faculty are set by the Higher Education Council to provide overall guidance and harmony among all public institutions. However, individual institutions can draw from these unified regulations and craft their own specific policies and procedures. The current profile of international faculty (e.g., in terms of numbers for both genders), their benefits, expectations from universities in terms of deliverables and performance, and other expectations are elaborated. The chapter highlights the positive impact of international faculty in terms of knowledge transfer, assistance in collaboration, and commercialization of research, and it also highlights the challenges faced by international faculty and the available opportunities at the universities in Saudi Arabia.

Saudi Arabia will continue its effort and investment to develop qualified university faculty members, both locally and internationally. Selecting the best local students to be future faculty members and sending them to the best universities abroad to finish their graduate degrees is a continuous effort. At the same time, providing huge funds and activities for intense training and professional development are widely applied to both local and international faculty members in many Saudi universities.

# APPENDIX 11.1

1.  How long have you been at the university?
    - Less than a year
    - Between 1 and 3 years
    - Between 4 and 10 years
    - Between 11 and 15 years
    - Between 16 and 20 years
    - More than 20 years

*2. Please indicate the primary college you are affiliated with.
    - College of Sciences
    - College of Engineering Sciences and Applied Engineering
    - College of Applied & Supporting Studies
    - College of Computer Sciences and Engineering
    - College of Industrial Management (CIM)
    - College of Environmental Design
    - College of Petroleum Engineering & Geosciences
    - Community College

*3. Please rank your main reasons which led you to join the university.

    (Please drag the options and arrange in order with the most important reason on top and so on.)

    - Research
    - Academic environment
    - Family

- Culture
- Compensation package

*4. Please rate the expectation level you had before joining the university with respect to the following:

|  | Very High | High | Neutral | Low | Very Low |
|---|---|---|---|---|---|
| Research | O | O | O | O | O |
| Academic Environment | O | O | O | O | O |
| Family | O | O | O | O | O |
| Culture | O | O | O | O | O |
| Career Growth | O | O | O | O | O |
| Compensation (Salary, Allowances, Benefits, etc.) | O | O | O | O | O |
| Integration with the University Community | O | O | O | O | O |

*5. How have your views about the university changed after joining and working at the university?

- The views have become more favorable (positive change)
- The views have remained similar (no change)
- The views have become less favorable (negative change)

*6. Please rate the overall satisfaction level with the university.

- Very Satisfied
- Satisfied
- Neutral
- Unsatisfied
- Very Unsatisfied

*7. Please rate the satisfaction level with respect to the following:

|  | Very Satisfied | Satisfied | Neutral | Unsatisfied | Very Satisfied |
|---|---|---|---|---|---|
| Hiring Procedure and Process | O | O | O | O | O |
| Relocation to the University | O | O | O | O | O |
| Family Life and Support | O | O | O | O | O |
| Teaching Duties and Responsibilities | O | O | O | O | O |
| Research Work | O | O | O | O | O |
| Career Growth | O | O | O | O | O |
| Compensation (Salary, Allowances, Benefits, etc.) | O | O | O | O | O |

(Continued)

|  | Very Satisfied | Satisfied | Neutral | Unsatisfied | Very Satisfied |
|---|---|---|---|---|---|
| Govt. Policies and University Rules Related to Your Employment at the University | ○ | ○ | ○ | ○ | ○ |
| Integration with the University Community | ○ | ○ | ○ | ○ | ○ |
| Integration with the Local Environment | ○ | ○ | ○ | ○ | ○ |

8. Any comments or suggestions related to the following:
   - Satisfaction level with the university
   - Challenges faced at the university

*Note:* Starred (★) questions indicate that these questions are obligatory.

## Acknowledgments

The author would like to acknowledge with deep thanks and gratitude the review of this chapter and valuable comments received from Dr. Sadiq M. Sait and Dr. Omar A. Al Swailem from King Fahd University of Petroleum & Minerals (KFUPM). Special thanks and appreciation for the data provided by the Deanship of Faculty and Personnel Affairs at KFUPM.

## References

AAFAQ. (2011). *AAFAQ project booklet*. Riyadh: Saudi Ministry of Higher Education.
Al-Ohali, M., & Burdon, S. (2013). International collaboration. In L. Smith & A. Abouammoh (Eds.), *Higher Education in Saudi Arabia* (159–166). Dordrecht, the Netherlands: Springer.
Altbach, P. G. (2003). *Centers and peripheries in the academic profession: The special challenges of developing countries*. New York: Palgrave.
Altbach, P. G., Reisberg, L., & Rumbley, L. E. (2009). *Trends in global higher education: Tracking an academic revolution*. Paris: UNESCO.
Mamiseishvili, K., & Rosser, V. J. (2010). International and citizen faculty in the United States: An examination of their productivity at research universities. *Research in Higher Education, 51*(1), 88–107.
Manrique, C. G., & Manrique, G. G. (1999). *The multicultural or immigrant faculty in American society*. Lewiston, NY: The Edwin Mellen Press.

# 12

# INTERNATIONAL ACADEMICS IN AFRICA

The South African Experience

*Damtew Teferra*

### Introduction: The Scene

South Africa arguably has the most advanced higher education system in Africa. It has a well-developed, well-endowed, and well-established higher education system envied across the continent. If the controversial rankings are used as the gold standard of quality, the only country whose universities feature in most of these growing global rankings is South Africa—albeit in the lower echelons of the rankings. When South African universities are, however, compared against their sister institutions on the continent, they dominate the top of the list.

Overall, Africa's knowledge-producing capacity is probably the lowest in the world: According to numerous sources and authorities, African scholars produce less than 1 percent of the annual global output of knowledge products. Still, half of that 1 percent actually originates from South Africa, making the country the research and knowledge powerhouse of the continent.

The academic and research prowess of South Africa emerges from its ability to attract academics and researchers from around the world—typically from the rest of Africa. The need to attract foreign talent is heightened by the massive urge to increase the number of PhD holders in the country's institutions, up from the current level of 40 percent of all academic staff to 70 percent (NDP, 2012); it is also prompted by the challenges of an aging academic workforce (especially among PhD holders) and a general drive to raise human capital in the country.

This chapter examines the situation of foreign academics in South African higher education institutions by first presenting the general profile of the state of the sector in the country—including enrollment and funding patterns—followed by a critical review of the underlying issues that influence the mobility of foreign academics into the country. The chapter further illustrates the profile of foreign academics in the country by drawing from the experience of a case, the University of KwaZulu-Natal (UKZN), an institution that has been recognized by the Department of Higher Education and Training as the top research producer in South Africa for the last three years. The national case of Botswana is also presented to add more perspectives.

## Higher Education in South Africa: Highlights

Higher education in South Africa goes back to when the first university in South Africa, the University of the Cape of Good Hope (UCGH)—which later became the University of Cape Town—was established in 1873. Since the establishment of the universities of Cape Town, Stellenbosch, and the University of South Africa (UNISA) by the University Act in 1916, the South African higher education system has witnessed numerous shifts and transformations (Subotzky, 2003).

At the end of the apartheid era (in the early 1990s), South Africa had 36 higher education institutions, composed of 21 universities and 15 technikons. After 1994, higher education in post-apartheid South Africa faced a dual transformation challenge: The first challenge emanated from the historical context, particularly the apartheid legacy, and had to do with achieving social equity and building and consolidating democracy; the second challenge was related to economic growth and development, as well as contemporary global developments, such as enabling South Africa to participate in, and engage with, the global order in a proactive way (Badat, 2009).

Following the unveiling of the National Plan for Higher Education (2001), which articulated, among other details, the size and shape of the higher education system through mergers and incorporations, the South African higher education landscape shrank from 36 to 25 higher education institutions, which fell into the three broad categories: traditional universities, universities of technology, and comprehensive institutions. By 2013, the country had added two new public universities. Currently, the private institutions enroll between 10 and 15 percent of the student population.

## Enrollments

On the continent, Egypt, Nigeria, and South Africa—in that order—claim the largest number of students. In post-1994 South Africa, student enrollments have sharply increased. The country now enrolls around one million students in its higher education system, and claims a nearly 20 percent enrollment rate—though major discrepancies by race, among other factors, persist. Unlike most other countries in Africa, the gender discrepancy, however, is in favor of female students. For instance, nearly 70 percent of the University of KwaZulu-Natal students who graduated in 2014 were female. The gender discrepancy in enrollment diminishes, however, as the level of the program increases: 49 percent of UKZN graduating

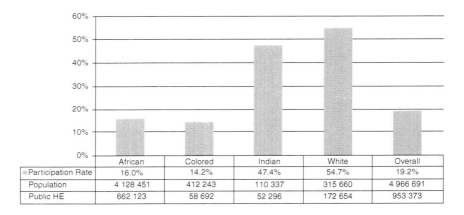

**FIGURE 12.1** Participation Rates (in Public Higher Education) by Race, 2013.
*Source*: Council on Higher Education, 2014.

students in 2014 at the master's level were women, as were 44 percent at doctoral level.

## Funding

The main source of funding for South African public higher education institutions emanates from the government, and this support makes up as little as 30 percent to as much as 65 percent of the total budget per institution (Botha & Fourie-Malherbe, 2015). The second major source of income comes from tuition fees, followed by a third source, composed of income from activities, such as short courses, commissioned research, and endowments, among other sources.

Over the years, although the amount dedicated by the government to higher education has dramatically increased, it has also declined in proportion from 49 percent to 41 percent of institutional subvention, as noted in Tables 12.1 and 12.2. At the same time, the contributions from students have increased from 24 percent to 30 percent of total national spending on higher education.

Recently, the universities in South Africa have been going through turbulent times, triggered principally by resistance to a hike in the annual student fee. As the protest grew bigger, it coalesced around a popular hashtag called #FeesMustFall (Teferra, 2016). The #FeesMustFall slogan has further expanded into other issues, including race and political activism, compounding the problem (Friedman, 2016; Makgoba, 2015).

## International Profile: Students

Ninety-three percent of students enrolled in South African public higher education in 2013 were South African. The overall proportion of foreign students

**TABLE 12.1** Funding Trend: 2004–2005 to 2012–2013

| Year | Block Grant (R' million) | Earmarked Grant (including NSFAS and infrastructure funding) (R' million) | Total Grant (R' million) | % Increase Year on Year (nominal terms) |
|---|---|---|---|---|
| 2004–05 | 8,568 | 1,311 | 9,879 | |
| 2005–06 | 9,145 | 1,635 | 10,780 | 9.1 |
| 2006–07 | 9,956 | 1,799 | 11,755 | 9.0 |
| 2007–08 | 10,234 | 2,823 | 13,057 | 11.1 |
| 2008–09 | 11,550 | 3,570 | 15,120 | 15.8 |
| 2009–10★ | 12,767 | 3,975 | 16,742 | 10.7 |
| 2010–11★ | 14,533 | 4,575 | 19,108 | 14.1 |
| 2011–12★ | 16,387 | 5,610 | 21,997 | 15.1 |
| 2012–13★ | 17,434 | 6,847 | 24,281 | 10.4 |

Notes: Amounts are expressed in 'nominal terms.' In economics, nominal value refers to a value expressed in money of the day (year, etc.), as opposed to real value, which adjusts for the effect of inflation on the nominal value. ★Excluding Funza Lushaka Bursary Programme (DHET, 2012).

**TABLE 12.2** Comparative Funding Streams (in Percentages)

| Source | 2000 | 2002 | 2004 | 2006 | 2008 | 2010 |
|---|---|---|---|---|---|---|
| Government funds | 49 | 46 | 43 | 40 | 40 | 41 |
| Student fees | 24 | 26 | 29 | 28 | 28 | 30 |
| Income generated | 27 | 28 | 28 | 32 | 32 | 30 |

Source: Ministerial Committee for the Review of the Funding of Universities (2014).

in public higher education has averaged 7 percent from 2002 to 2013, with absolute numbers increasing from 48,197 in 2003 to 73,859 in 2013. The proportion of foreign students enrolled in postgraduate programs (15 percent) is higher than those in undergraduate programs (HEMIS, 2012, in Council on Higher Education 2016).

There has been a significant change in the proportion of postgraduate foreign students to local students over the last decade. The foreign postgraduate students increased from 10 percent of the overall postgraduate student population in 2002 to 14 percent in 2012. Most foreign students (73 percent) come from the Southern African Development Community (SADC) region, composed of 15 countries, including Angola, Botswana, Congo (DR), Lesotho, Madagascar, Malawi, Mauritius, Mozambique, Namibia, Seychelles, South Africa, Swaziland, Tanzania, Zambia, and Zimbabwe. South Africa also attracts a small number of students from the rest of Africa (which make up 16 percent of all international students in the country) and from other parts of the world (9 percent). However, the overall proportions of these students have remained basically unchanged through the years (HEMIS, 2012, in Council on Higher Education, 2016).

244  Damtew Teferra

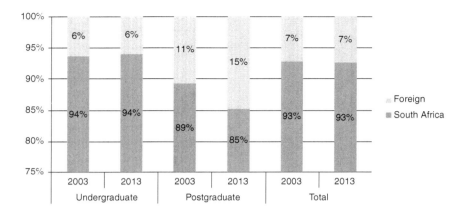

**FIGURE 12.2**  Percentages of Foreign Students in South African Institutions by Qualification Level, Comparative Figures: 2003 and 2013.

*Source*: Hemis (2012) in Council on Higher Education (2016).

## Emigration and Immigration: Academics on the Move

South African institutions are well known for attracting and retaining academics from the continent as well as beyond. However, the exodus of the intelligentsia from the country at the culmination of the apartheid era, which ended with considerable internal strife, is also well recorded. Following the dispensation of the democratic process, South Africa has witnessed both an influx and an outflow of the intelligentsia in measurable numbers. In terms of the outflow, white South Africans largely emigrated to Australia, Britain, and Canada. Grant (2006) notes that more than half the physicians practicing in Saskatchewan, a province of Canada, were foreign trained, of which 17 to 20 percent graduated from South African medical schools.

An influx of mostly (black) Africans from the rest of the continent occurred quickly after the emigration of predominantly white South Africans. The foreign academics from Africa took up the vacant academic and professional positions, largely pushed by prevailing difficult states of affairs in their home countries in the 1990s and driven by economic and financial incentives, as well as better academic and research opportunities in the country. This migration phenomenon from the rest of Africa to Southern Africa, including to Botswana and to some extent Namibia, has been a subject of conversation in the context of brain drain and brain circulation.

One of the factors that draws many to the South African academic space has been the attractive salaries and the associated benefits that come with academic employment. According to Sehoole (2004), because South Africa has a strong economy and a highly developed higher education system compared to other African countries, it has become a destination of choice for most African students and scholars wanting to further their studies and career opportunities.

In further confirmation of its potential appeal, South Africa ranked near the top in an international comparative study on academic salaries, outpacing Japan, France, Norway, Germany, the Netherlands, the United States, Australia, and the United Kingdom, among others (Altbach et al., 2012, p. 11). The remunerative factor has thus played a central role in attracting academics to South Africa from around the world, especially from the African continent.

However, some of these attractive factors and incentives have been slowly chipped away due to prevailing social, political, and financial upheavals the country has witnessed in recent years. Disruptive strikes and political actions on campuses, globally publicized brutal xenophobic attacks, and a sharp decline of the South African rand (in relation to major currencies) have had a chilling effect on the otherwise attractive landscape.

## Academic Staff: Continental Realities

Academic staff are at the heart of a higher education institution, and their abundance and number thus have implications for the quality of education and research. Altbach (2004) stresses that without a strong, committed academic profession, higher education cannot provide effective teaching or top-quality research. In knowledge-based economies, universities must have academic staff who are well qualified, well trained, and committed to academic work. The sub-Saharan region has the lowest researcher-to-population ratio in the world, with fewer than 100 researchers per million inhabitants compared to about 700 per million in North Africa, 300 per million in Latin America, and 1,600 per million in Central and Eastern Europe (World Bank, 2012).

In 2012, Makerere University in Uganda had 1,340 academic staff, of whom only 73 (5 percent) were professors and 115 were associate professors (8.5 percent) (Bisaso, in press). This was a decline from 1,500 in 2011. In Kenya, there were a total of 5,000 academics in the country's public higher education system in 2011. At the University of Nairobi, only 7.7 percent of the academics were full professors (Sifuna, in press). In Tanzania, of about 3,100 academics in the higher education system in 2015, less than 15 percent held a PhD and only 4.7 percent were professors (Ishengoma, in press). The academic staff at the University of Rwanda in 2015 stood at 1,450, composed of only 18 percent PhD holders (University of Rwanda, 2016).

The expansion of enrollment in the entire sector has meant that the need for academics has grown precipitously, both in public and private institutions. This demand has forced academics to take on heavier teaching loads, leaving little room for research activity. It has also opened an opportunity for academics to moonlight pervasively—both in the teaching and management arenas—further thinning the numbers of senior academics and PhD holders who are fully engaged with their respective institutions. Furthermore, a new phenomenon has emerged whereby more senior academics are participating in the national political process. In Tanzania, for example, over 50 percent of Members of Parliament (MPs) had a university credential—about 15 percent of the 171 MPs held PhDs (Ishengoma, 2007).

What is an increasingly worrying reality in the African academic profession is the fast aging of the senior academic ranks. This is a looming threat to the revitalization of African higher education and the building of research capacity. Even the most advanced African country in terms of higher education, South Africa (as described elsewhere in this chapter), is concerned about this problem and is taking steps to extend working age limits as a form of temporary relief from this problem, while it is also recruiting foreign academics.

The stated challenges—stemming from an aging faculty, massive expansion, and moonlighting—are, however, strategically managed, at least so far in the South African context. The country draws heavily on the mobility of international academics into South Africa, largely from African (particularly SADC) countries to address these current and future challenges.

## Foreign Academic Employment: Governing Acts and Regimes

The Department of Home Affairs, Immigration Act 2002 (Act No. 13 of 2002) [Sections 19(4), read with Regulation 19(5)], exhaustively stipulates the skills or qualifications deemed critical for the Republic of South Africa in relation to an application for a critical skills visa or permanent residence permit, where international academic recruitment falls. Under the section for academics and researchers, the act provides two categories: doctoral graduates (where the doctoral degree has been acquired abroad) and research expertise in around 50 diverse and comprehensive specialties. These range from galaxy formation and evolution to deep observations of the earliest radio galaxies, from natural sciences to nanotechnology, from antenna foundation design to ICT (information and communication technologies).

Regarding researchers and academics, the Immigration Act stipulates that applicants must demonstrate the following: confirmation of skills qualification, proof of evaluation of qualification, and letter of recommendation by recognized and accredited bodies, as well as proof of employment and financial means for sustaining oneself and one's family in South Africa. In the postgraduate category, the act stipulates that applicants must have acquired their doctoral credentials in South Africa, with similar provisions as noted earlier for researchers and academics, but also proof, in the form of a sworn affidavit, that the applicant does not have any contractual obligations to return to their country of origin.

The act identifies nearly 50 professional accreditation bodies and councils that assist in the review of applications with respect to specific critical skills. These range from the Council for Scientific and Industrial Research to the South African Qualifications Authority, from the Jewellery Council of South Africa to the

Indlela National Artisan Moderating Body, from several professional education and training authorities in agriculture, banking, fiber processing manufacturing, and the safety and security sector, to the peculiar South African Board for People Practices.

According to the Department of Higher Education and Technology (DHET, 2015), there were a total of 2,060 permanent and 4,332 temporary instructional/research foreign professionals in South Africa in 2014. Table 12.3 provides the trends related to academic employment and enrollment of South African citizens versus noncitizens for the four years from 2010 to 2013.

The recent massive xenophobic attacks exclusively on foreign traders and hawkers targeting individuals of African descent have also caused concern among those in academic circles. Although there is no widespread evidence to support this, the author points to these events as a possible explanation for the uneasiness of his current employing institution to release certain (possibly identifying) data relating to the foreign academics it employs. It was pointed out by the university that some foreign academics may be reluctant to be identified as foreigners—largely driven by underlying fear. According to the university's key custodian of information, there is a plausible risk of litigation by some foreign academics should the university release such information.

In 2014, South Africa introduced new visa guidelines with some immediate effects on travel and mobility to South Africa. According to Hagenmeier, Quinlan, and Lansink (2015), the consequence of the 2014 changes in immigration law six months into the academic year of 2015 was rather disturbing in that the South African higher education sector experienced a sharp drop in international student numbers. At one university, international student numbers dropped by 600 in 2015, and, at another, international student numbers declined by more than 25 percent compared with the previous year. Visiting scholars, postdoctoral fellows, international staff, and university guests are also affected by the new immigration law. The recent spate of high-profile attacks on foreigners and internationally documented news of xenophobia in the country may have some

**TABLE 12.3** South African and International Staff and Post- and Undergraduate Student Profile, 2010–2013

| Year | Permanent Instruction and Research Staff | Foreign Academics | Students in Public Higher Education Institutions | International Students | Postgraduate Students | Postgraduate Students (International Students) |
| --- | --- | --- | --- | --- | --- | --- |
| 2010 | 16,684 | 1,490 | 892,943 | 66,181 | 138,610 | 18,845 |
| 2011 | 16,935 | 1,723 | 938,200 | 70,060 | 147,893 | 20,046 |
| 2012 | 17,451 | 2,137 | 953,373 | 72,857 | 149,027 | 20,770 |
| 2013 | 17,838 | 2,281 | 983,698 | 73,859 | 159,750 | 23,364 |

*Source*: Habib, Price and Mabelebele (2014).

chilling effect on academic mobility, albeit for a short time, if matters—social, economic and political developments—do not deteriorate further.

## Beyond Recruitment and Entry

It is one thing to attract and recruit foreign academics and another to create a conducive working and living environment for them to reach their full potential. Let's first start with the visa acquisition process of foreign academics. Due to incompetence and insufficient understanding of the different categories of the visa process in the respective embassies, academics often find it difficult to acquire the right visa at the right time.

When foreign academics join institutions, they are provided support through a settling-in allowance and other provisions, such as short-stay housing (as is the case at UKZN). However, inherent discrepancies unduly limit foreigners from drawing on existing institutional benefits and provisions. For instance, in the case of UKZN, a staff member must be employed by the university for at least two years before being eligible for a car loan scheme, in effect depriving the academics of the opportunity for two years.

This problem is further compounded because South African banks are also reluctant to grant loans to foreigners who do not have a financial history in the country or have permanent residency or citizenship. Even if one has a financial history somewhere else, this is not relevant or applicable in South Africa. Therefore, foreign academics face a two-pronged challenge: internal (i.e., limitations on benefits at the institutional level) and external (i.e., limitations on access to resources in the broader society).

Another unfavorable policy toward foreigners, which directly affects academics, is the directive that stipulates that banks grant foreigners only partial (20 percent) home loans; that is, a foreigner can only receive a loan in the amount equal to 20 percent of the property value. It is daunting (if not prohibitive) for foreigners, especially those from Africa, to come up with 80 percent of the property value for a home purchase, especially in light of housing costs in a major city.

With the consolidation of the visa process in 2014, the Department of Home Affairs centralized its operation, making it increasingly complicated to address specific issues directly. Communication with the department, and even the visa application process itself, takes place via a third-party company called VFS, which acts as a buffer between applicants and the department. So far, no marked positive change has been noticed since the new visa processing program was introduced—and anecdotal evidence indicates an opposite outcome of the intent of recent adjustments in the visa administration process, including a very high backlog of applications, among other issues.

The South African higher education system functions almost exclusively in English, though the historically "Afrikaans" universities still operate in Afrikaans. As of late, the issue of language has become a matter of contentious conversation, with some institutions, such as the University of KwaZulu-Natal, embracing the Zulu language in the university, whereas others are rejecting Afrikaans. The international staff does not seem to be affected by the internal developments, though the outcome of these issues may have some implications for them, albeit minor and unpredictable.

As noted in this chapter, quite a large number of the African academic staff in South Africa hail from the Southern African Development Community, especially Zimbabwe. Because of the strong historical, linguistic, and cultural ties between the SADC countries and South Africa, the international academic staff from these countries navigate South African social and cultural dynamics with considerable ease and certainty. The largely cosmopolitan and ethnically, linguistically, and racially diverse South African landscape, which prides itself on being the Rainbow Nation, provides rich settings to its diverse international academics.

## International Academic Mobility: "Ambivalence" and "Vigilantism"

Academic mobility is not a new phenomenon. To assert this, it is not necessary to invoke sentimental memories of scholars wandering around the universities of medieval Europe or Islamic philosophers migrating from Cordoba to Cairo—or even to remember the Puritan ministers who crossed the Atlantic to found Harvard College in colonial Massachusetts (and their many successors who traveled from London or Paris to establish new universities in Africa or Asia) (Scott, 2015).

International academic mobility refers here to the movement of foreign academics who are recruited to an academic position in South African institutions on a permanent or long-term basis. Academic positions in South African institutions are typically open to foreign academics, though preferences tend to be given to nationals, as long as they meet the basic minimum requirements for the specified positions. When foreign academics are hired (per the requirements stated elsewhere), they often acquire a visa that lasts between three and five years, though inconsistencies are apparent in the visas issued at different South African embassies.

Once an academic is hired on a five-year contract and stays the full term, the option for permanent residency becomes available. This is particularly vital in facilitating a long-term stay in the South African context, where the distinction between residency holders and citizens is subtle. For instance, unlike most African countries, South Africa allows a permanent resident to apply for automatic citizenship for their newborn children, for siblings, and for themselves.

The new visa rules that became effective in 2015 have, however, made it more difficult for any university entities from getting directly involved in helping secure visas for their foreign academics, other than submitting relevant official documents. This lack of ability to advocate or intervene, even when this is called for, has created considerable problems and anxieties for foreign academics in a number of cases. This is further compounded by the threat of the Department of Home Affairs to penalize institutions if their foreign academics fail to comply with visa regulations, despite the largely recognized incompetence of the department (Mashaba, 2015; South African Legal Information Institute, 2010).

A recruited foreign academic is tied to the hiring institution, and this is reflected explicitly on the visa issued to the foreign academic by being affixed in the passport. Should the academic leave the institution or default on his or her contract, the university is obliged to report the situation to the Department of Home Affairs. For that matter, an institution needs to consent to take the responsibility of informing the department on the status of a foreign academic and his or her family if a situation arises.

In South Africa, to achieve the objectives of programs such as the National Development Plan (NDP), the Industrial Policy Action Plan (IPAP), and the New Growth Plan (NGP), the Critical Skills Work Visa has been systematically promulgated by the government. The Department of Home Affairs has amended the immigration legislation that came with various changes, including the introduction of the Critical Skills Work Visa (CSWV) in 2014—the most important policy program relevant to international academic mobility to the country.

The Critical Skills Work Visa resulted from the merger of the former Exceptional Skills and Quota Work visas. The latter was issued in line with the Quota List of 2009, which had skills categories, requirements, and the quota of skills targeted in the country. The Critical Skills Work Visa is issued in accordance with the critical skills list, which was developed in conjunction with the occupations in high demand and the scarce skills lists of the Department of Higher Education and Training (DHET). The main objective of the Critical Skills Work Visa is to assist the government to realize the achievement of the National Infrastructure Project, the Strategic Infrastructure Projects, and Key National Strategic Projects, in support of the Department of Trade and Industry (DHET, 2016).

Jonathan Jansen, a vice chancellor of a South African university and prominent educational and social critic, in a chapter co-authored with colleagues, unambiguously noted the policy "ambivalence" related to South Africa's role as an African student hub for higher education (Jansen, McLellan & Greene, 2008). While Jansen et al. intimated this view from the student mobility perspective (from surrounding countries), it is this author's observation that the identified ambivalence also pertains, implicitly and explicitly, to academics.

That said, the provision of the policies for attracting foreign academics—earlier in the exceptional skills category, now renamed critical skills—explicitly recognizes the importance of highly skilled labor for the country to build its national economy and raise its global competitiveness. The guidelines further stipulate a priority in processing applications and fast-tracking visa issuance for such applicants with the relevant critical skills. But the practices are far from this stipulation.

Some of the statements in relation to foreigners that come from government offices, either officially or in leaked memos, appear rather confusing. For example, in a recent leaked intelligence report (Joubert, 2016), the dominance of foreigners in the universities and government offices was bemoaned.

In his 2016 State of the Union address, the president of South Africa, Jacob Zuma, made official and unfavorable statements toward foreigners, saying:

> I also announced the Regulation of Land Holdings Bill, which would place a ceiling on land ownership at a maximum of 12,000 hectares and would prohibit foreign nationals from owning land. They would be eligible for long term leases.
>
> *(South African Government, 2016)*

So, although officially the country seeks to import talent to advance its economic agenda, there is a parallel discourse that appears less than welcoming to foreigners.

Beyond the matter of contradictions in the arena of public discourse, the issue of attracting skilled labor for the critical skills category is, according to some, actually mired in far more sinister sentiments than ambivalence—but actual vigilantism, as described by a vice president of the Academic Staff Association at Wits University, Prof. David Hornsby. Hornsby states:

> There seems to be a real disconnect between what is enshrined in the law and the policies and what is being interpreted by Home Affairs officers. If I understand correctly, it's that the Home Affairs officers are unhappy with the current regulations [governing critical skills] and think they're problematic so are therefore not enforcing them.

Hornsby referred to this as "vigilantism which is going on" and said it is concerning for all foreign employees (Naidoo, 2015).

An underlying tension—triggered by the alleged designation of foreign African academics as black South Africans by some institutions as a matter of compliance with the equity and transformation agenda in the country—is also palpable. According to Nkosi (2015), the transformation agenda of the nation to promote social, political, and economic advancement among the majority of black South Africans, and the alleged "trickery" of institutions to count other Africans as black South Africans, have been vehemently attacked. Nkosi (2015). A published and seasoned authority in the trade unions, who described the situation as unsettling to him and fellow academics, reported a trade unionist as saying,

> Something common [across universities] is a cop-out where international scholars, who just happen to be black, are counted as equity candidates. It's the most dishonest, most hypocritical and cynical thing you find. I've said to them that, as far as I'm concerned, there are three categories of academics:

white South African academics, black South African academics and international scholars. You must have balance across the categories. That's all.

*(n.p.)*

Lamenting the continued decline and stagnation of black South African academic staff over the years at various universities and the increased representation of white (especially women) South African academics and African international scholars, the trade union academic noted,

> There's something not right here ...we take a person from Ghana, which, as you know, became independent in 1957, and we say again: "That colleague, competent in his or her own right, is a redress candidate." It cannot be like that. Whether they have permanent residency in South Africa [or not], they cannot count as redress candidates.

He went on to state that

> What irks me is that universities receive public funding, which they use not only to maintain these processes of racial exclusion but also to fund foreign academics. No doubt we need these individuals if we are going to remain academically competitive in the world. But surely those who pay the taxes also deserve a foot in the door? No, at the head table.

In 2013–2014, South Africa had around 16,000 academics in all institutions of higher education, and there had been an increase in the number of foreign academics. According to Higher Education South Africa (HESA, now renamed Universities South Africa, 2014), which briefed the Parliamentary Portfolio Committee on Higher Education and Training, internationalization needs to be construed as "improving the quality of learning and teaching, global awareness, deeper engagement with global challenges, better preparation of students as national and global citizens, access to opportunities that are not available in South Africa" (n.p.).

It was further noted that foreign academics benefited the economy of South Africa, as 7.5 percent of students in higher education were international students. HESA (2014) went on to state that

> [t]here was a need to open the Higher Education [sic] to be internationally competitive. There had to be a balance between local and international students as this will help shift global perceptions about Africa and making it a destination of learning for international students.

*(n.p.)*

According to the report, the chairperson of the committee, a member of the ruling African National Congress (ANC), was concerned about the impact of xenophobia and asked "what could be done about the xenophobic attacks on high level appointments and tensions to foreign academic staff by locals?" It was noted that "[t]he question on how to ensure equitable distribution of the transformation agenda in South Africa was asked" (Parliamentary Monetary Group, 2014, n.p.).

The general notion is that African migrants are here to take only and not to give, a belief that is also shared by professionals (Neocosmos in Singh, 2013). Although xenophobia presents itself mainly in socioeconomically deprived communities, it is found everywhere—"even in institutions of higher learning where one expects a higher level of broadmindedness" (Mogekwu, 2005, p. 10 in Singh, 2013, p. 89). Here, xenophobia may not be expressed in the same manner as in poor communities, where outbreaks of physical violence and attacks on businesses occur, but in "more subtle forms of making the non-national feel so unwelcome and despised in an environment that is psychologically hostile" (Mogekwu, 2005 in Singh, 2013).

A National Immigration Policy Survey study that compared attitudes of South African citizens with those of several other SADC countries—Botswana, Mozambique, Namibia, Swaziland, and Zimbabwe—found that citizens across the region consistently tend to exaggerate the numbers of noncitizens in their countries, to view the migration of people within the region as a 'problem' rather than an opportunity, and to scapegoat noncitizens. The intensity of these feelings, with implications for foreign academics, especially of African origin, varies significantly from country to country. The harshest sentiments are expressed by the citizens of South Africa, Namibia, and, to a lesser extent, Botswana. The citizens of Swaziland, Mozambique, and Zimbabwe are considerably more relaxed about the presence of noncitizens in their countries. In 1997, the Southern African Migration Project (SAMP) set out to document the character and extent of xenophobic sentiment in South Africa. Two national surveys confirmed that South Africans were indeed highly xenophobic. The findings were reported in a joint publication with the South African Human Rights Commission in 2002 (Crush & Pendleton, 2004).

The 2014 study on international students undertaken by Chika Sehoole, an expert in higher education at a major South African university, and his colleague, Jenny Lee, based in the United States, further corroborates this underlying trend. They found out that lack of local friends and xenophobia are among the major challenges international students face (MacGregor, 2014).

## Growing Our Own Timber: Inbreeding or Transformation?

There has been a visible effort to build institutional and national capacity in postgraduate studies in the country by expanding opportunities, as well as demanding that junior and young faculty earn a PhD. This phenomenon is quite widespread in the major institutions, including the universities of KwaZulu-Natal, Rhodes,

Nelson Mandela Metropolitan, Stellenbosch, and Witwatersrand, among others. Indeed, such an effort would be commendable only if it were not projected, explicitly or implicitly, as a concealed attempt to edge out foreign academics and researchers, particularly given that foreign academic staff play a central role in the internationalization of the higher education system in the country and in fostering its global competitiveness.

It is established that the country needs quite a large number of highly qualified individuals to advance its economy and its global competitiveness. In the realization of this objective, the statistics for doctoral output over the past years have shown a steady increase: 977 in 2004; 1,100 in 2006; 1,182 in 2008; 1,421 in 2010; and 1,878 in 2012 (Mouton, Boshoff & James, 2015). The universities are called upon—and expected—to undertake a major effort in ensuring and advancing progress on this front. As important and relevant as the reaction and the efforts to grow 'our own timber' for self-sustenance may be, they may also carry a danger of inbreeding, whereas the presence of nonlocal faculty ameliorates these effects.

The motto of 'producing our own timber' seems to be further reinforced by stringent institutional guidelines that attempt to advance equity and institutional transformation. This is ensured in some institutions, such as the University of KwaZulu-Natal, through a motivated, at times starkly discriminatory, recruitment drive in search of attracting and recruiting 'marginalized' groups to academic posts, over and above foreign academics. Such approaches, as strategic as they may be, have had some chilling effects on the success of international academic recruitment.

## Aging: Pull Factor for Foreign Academics?

The phenomenon of a rapidly aging cohort of senior academics has emerged as a serious concern in the African academic profession and is described as a gathering threat to the revitalization of the continent's higher education system. Even the most advanced African country, South Africa, is seriously concerned about this problem and is expanding retirement age limits as a temporary relief measure (Teferra, in press). The University of KwaZulu-Natal, for instance, has one of the youngest retirement age policies, with professors eligible to retire at 60. With nearly one-third of the academics in the 51 to 60 age bracket, there is, understandably, grave concern about the future staffing of the professoriate at this institution and elsewhere.

The South African academic retirement crisis is clearly evident by virtue of the fact that—as seen in Table 12.4—more than 1,430 professors and associate professors from 13 leading institutions will reach retirement age in the next ten years (Govender, 2014). This growing and impending threat may continue to advance the need to build capacity at home, as well as trigger a drive to recruit more foreign academics.

**TABLE 12.4** South African Professors and Associate Professors Retiring by 2024

| University | Number |
| --- | --- |
| University of Witwatersrand | 309 |
| University of South Africa | 241 |
| University of Cape Town | 179 |
| North-West University | 158 |
| University of Stellenbosch | 157 |
| University of Pretoria | 165 |
| University of the Western Cape | 79 |
| Rhodes University | 55 |
| University of Limpopo | 45 |
| Walter Sisulu University | 28 |
| University of KwaZulu-Natal | 10* |

*Source*: Govender, 2014.

*This figure includes five expected retirements in 2020 and five in 2024. (Information sourced through communication with responsible staff at UKZN.)

South Africa has embarked on a national plan to produce a large number of PhD holders in its national universities in recognition of higher education's critical role in fostering social and economic development. The drive to produce more PhDs is guided by the National Planning Commission, which, in 2012, proposed boosting the production of doctoral graduates to more than 5,000 per year by 2030 (NPC, 2012). Higher Education South Africa (2014), however, challenges this goal as "too ambitious," presumably because South Africa's current capacity to produce doctoral graduates hovers at around a little more than one-third of that number—about 2,000 per year (HESA, 2014).

The need for foreign academics, therefore, will likely increase, both as senior academics assisting in the production of the doctorates to meet these numbers and occupying those academic positions for which there are currently no South African PhD holders. The 'critical' skills category to attract academics directly speaks to these national needs—and imminent challenges.

## Excellence and Mediocrity

South Africa has probably one of the largest, if not the largest, international academic collaboration network in Africa. International institutional agreements and contracts, usually involving international scientific and research collaboration, seem to be the most significant aspect of internationalization in South African higher education, both nationally and at the institutional level (Jansen, McLellan & Greene, 2008). Bawa (2008, p. 130) also acknowledges "excellent examples of partnerships between institutions in the building of graduate programs" and attributes to this phenomenon much of the improvement of the state of PhD studies in the country. Much could be attributed to the contributions of the international academic staff.

South Africa serves as a regional and subregional hub for postgraduate training in Africa. The SADC countries in particular are highly represented in the system. According to UNESCO-UIS, South Africa ranks as the eleventh top host country worldwide, with 61,000 international students studying in the country in 2011. However, according to Nwogu (2012), 75,000 students from Nigeria alone study in Ghana, a finding that severely challenges the accuracy of the UNESCO findings. A survey conducted on 1,700 international students in seven universities in South Africa in 2014 found that nearly 80 percent came from Africa, 23 percent of whom studied at the master's level, 19 percent at the PhD level, and 1 percent as postdoctoral researchers (MacGregor, 2014).

Compared to the countries from which the African students hail, the South African academic institutions enjoy a comparatively much bigger and more competitive pool from which to draw academic staff—both nationally and internationally. They also maintain better mechanisms for weeding out mediocrity and promoting excellence. Yet, the countries from which these students come—and to which they return—are not in that same state of academic maturity. Therefore, upon their return, those trained in South Africa are expected to play a more robust role in their home countries than what is expected of their counterpart students who will remain in South Africa.

These returnee 'foreign' students are expected to provide a high level of academic and institutional leadership (for instance, research supervision, management), teaching, and learning. However, there are considerable weaknesses and gaps in South African doctoral training—the subject of a special issue of the *South African Journal of Higher Education* (2015)—which means graduates of doctoral education in South Africa are often insufficiently prepared to contribute meaningfully to the academic communities in their home countries. On the basis of this and further analysis, this author declares South Africa as arguably an exporter to Africa of excellence as well as mediocrity (Teferra, 2015). It is important to indicate, however, that the significance, role, and implications of the large number of foreign students who have studied in South African universities, who serve as academics in their respective countries, have yet to be fully investigated.

## Academic Mobility Schemes: Potential Conduits of Recruitment

Several academic mobility schemes are mediated through international cooperation on the continent. These mobility schemes have a considerable effect on the recruitment and retention of foreign academics largely in South Africa, but also elsewhere in Africa.

These schemes open opportunities for mobile academics and also (PhD) students to experience and gauge firsthand the academic, social, and political environment in which a foreign academic is recruited and retained. Although it is true that most, if not all, mobile academics and graduates may return to their home institution at the end of these mobility schemes, these opportunities may also create an open door for permanent mobility and an enlarged possibility for network development, which in turn fosters more mobility. Some of these schemes are described next.

## Strengthening African Higher Education through Academic Mobility

### Intra-ACP

The Intra-ACP mobility scheme aims at a broad academic and cultural, as well as geographically diverse, exchange network between higher education institutions in African countries, building on the results of the outcomes and recommendations of "Access to Success: Fostering Trust and Exchange between Europe and Africa (2008–2010)." The overall objective is to promote high-quality education for students and young academics and to increase access to higher education in general.

The consortium comprises eight African higher education institutions: Makerere University, Uganda; University of Buea, Cameroon; Namibia University of Science and Technology, Namibia; Ardhi University, Tanzania; Kwame Nkrumah University of Science and Technology, Ghana; University of the Free State, South Africa; North-West University, South Africa; and Hawassa University, Ethiopia (Intra-ACP, 2016).

### AAU Staff Exchange Programme

The AAU Staff Exchange Programme is designed to foster interuniversity cooperation through the exchange of staff between African universities. The academic staff who participate in the program undertake a range of assignments in their host institutions, including teaching, special lectures, demonstrations, and research.

The program aims at promoting interuniversity cooperation through academic mobility in the form of exchange of staff for teaching assignments; to serve as external examiners; participation in seminars, workshops, and conferences; undertaking collaborative research assignments; facilitating the utilization of sabbatical leave appointments; and enhancing the quality of teaching and research in African universities.

### Africa for Innovation, Mobility, Exchange, Globalization, and Quality

The Africa for Innovation, Mobility, Exchange, Globalization, and Quality (AFIMEGQ) program is a cooperation and mobility program in the area of higher education implemented by the European Commission's Education, Audiovisual and Culture Executive Agency (EACEA). The project is designed to facilitate the movement of master's and PhD students and staff between selected national universities in the African regions as a means of building capacity and encouraging socioeconomic development in each region.

### The Southern African-Nordic Centre

The Southern African-Nordic Centre (SANORD) is a partnership of higher education institutions from all of the Nordic countries and southern Africa. The primary aim of this body, with over 40 members, is to promote multilateral research cooperation on matters of importance to the development of both regions. SANORD intends to advance strategic, multilateral academic collaboration between institutions in the two regions, as they seek to address new local and global challenges of innovation and development.

### EUROSA+ Project

The EUROSA+ project is an Erasmus Mundus Action 2 Partnerships scholarship program funded by the European Commission. It is coordinated by the University of Antwerp, Belgium, and it promotes mobility for South African and European students, researchers, academics, and administrative staff. The partnership offers mobility grants to about 70 South African and 30 European master's students, doctoral researchers, and staff to spend a period abroad at one of the partner institutions.

### SADC Protocol on Education and Training

South Africa is a member of the Southern African Development Community (SADC) and a signatory of the SADC Protocol on Education and Training. Concluded by SADC member states in 1997, the protocol paves the way for educational institutions in southern Africa to cooperate with one another and to ensure the admission of students from the SADC region, in addition to local students. The SADC Protocol encourages institutions in southern Africa to, among other actions:

- Reserve at least 5 percent of admissions for students from SADC nations
- Facilitate the mobility of staff and students within the region for purposes of study, research, teaching, and other pursuits relating to education and training
- Treat SADC students as local students for purposes of fees and accommodation
- Establish institutional partnerships with other institutions of higher learning in the SADC and encourage the establishment of collaboration agreements between their components

This protocol is instrumental in facilitating the mobility of academics within the subregion and, according to some, allows certain foreign nationals, such as Zimbabweans, to readily move to comparatively more stable and developed South Africa with greater ease.

## Foreign Academics: The Case of the University of KwaZulu-Natal

The University of KwaZulu-Natal (UKZN) was formed on January 1, 2004, as a result of the merger between the University of Durban-Westville (established in the 1960s) and the University of Natal (founded in 1910 as Natal University College, which later became the University of Natal in 1949). With one of the largest student populations in the country, at close to 44,000 students, UKZN is spread across five campuses.

The University of KwaZulu-Natal is one of the leading educational institutions in South Africa, with 19 schools offering approximately 2,000 academic programs with bachelor, honors, PGDip (postgraduate diploma), master's, and doctoral degrees. The university stands out for its unique mission "to be a premier University of African scholarship" (UKZN, 2016).

The university strives to enhance the quality of its work and the experience of its students and staff through international partnerships, which it maintains with a number of universities across the world. UKZN is rated among the top 500 universities of the world and one of the top 10 universities in Africa, and has been the most productive university in South Africa in terms of research output for the last three years (UKZN, 2016).

The university maintains international links with over 250 institutions, which facilitate ongoing collaborative academic partnerships. UKZN has 1,238 permanent and 104 contract (i.e., holding contracts of one year and longer) employees. There is approximate gender parity in the population of the academics, with males comprising about 51 percent of this group (see Figure 12.3).

The figure for foreign academics at the university hovers around 14 percent, with the single largest population of foreign academics (40 percent of the total at UKZN) hailing from Zimbabwe, South Africa's restive next-door neighbor. This is followed by India (14 percent), Nigeria (13 percent), and Kenya (10 percent). The large number of Indian academics could be attributed to the predominance of

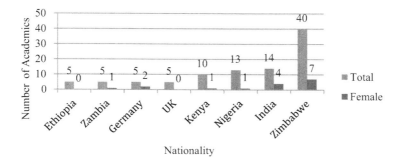

**FIGURE 12.3** Nationality and Gender of Foreign Academics at UKZN.

*Source*: Extrapolated from data provided by Institutional Intelligence unit of UKZN (2016). (Only nationalities with at least 5 academics or more are presented.)

Indian South Africans in the academic profile of the institution (Durban is home to a large Indian population whose presence in the city dates back more than a century and a half) and natural close ties that might develop between these groups.

The population of foreign academics at the university is heavily male. The total percentage of female foreign academics stands at around 18 percent. In terms of academic rank, 18 percent of the foreign academics (in permanent employment) occupy full professorship positions. When contractual employment (i.e., contracts of more than one year) is considered, we see that 28.9 percent of such positions at UKZN are occupied by foreign faculty—a relatively high proportion, when considering that the national average for foreign academics in contractual employment at South African universities stands at around 13 percent.

Foreign academics (in permanent positions) occupy associate professor, senior lecturer, and lecturer positions at the rate of 21.8 percent, 17.84 percent, and 12 percent, respectively. The increasing motivation and directives to recruit local academics, even when these are not readily available, will probably shift this profile, though this trend may be countered by the institution's growing interest in being more internationally engaged.

UKZN, for its size and expressed goals, however, has a 'low-key' international office, which largely caters to foreign students and reports to the Corporate Relations Office. Foreign recruitment and administration fall entirely under the purview of the university's human resources office. Yet, it is often the respective departments and schools that help facilitate the integration and acclimatization of newly recruited foreigners.

## Foreign Academics: The Case of Botswana

This section provides a brief comparative perspective of foreign academic mobility between South Africa and a small country next door, Botswana, an upper-middle-income country like South Africa. The choice of an examination of Botswana is due to its comparable practice of (like South Africa) recruiting international academics—including former vice chancellors. Indeed, it is commonplace to see international recruitment drives for positions in higher education in Botswana in major newspapers in South Africa.

Botswana is a landlocked country in the center of southern Africa with a population of 2 million. It became independent from Britain in 1966 after 90 years of colonial rule. At that time it was one of the ten poorest countries in the world, with a gross domestic product (GDP) per capita income of USD 70 per year. However, in the period from 1966 to 2006, it experienced rapid economic growth of 9 percent per annum on average, and it is now an upper-middle-income country with a per capita annual income of USD 15,705. This economic growth has been based primarily on the mining and export of diamonds, which contribute around 35 percent of the GDP. The state has invested heavily in infrastructure, services, and social protection programs (Tabulawa & Youngman, in press).

Several stages in the development of the University of Botswana (UB) have been recorded. The first stage was the establishment of the University of Basutoland, Bechuanaland, and Swaziland (UBBS), which grew out of negotiations in 1962 that approved the transformation of a Catholic institution at Roma in Lesotho into UBBS. With a collapse of the partnership in 1975, after the independence of Lesotho and Botswana in 1966, the country made considerable strides to build a major public university, the University of Botswana (Weeks, 2003).

Until 2005, the country's only university was the University of Botswana. The Tertiary Education Council estimated in 2013 that 60,000 spaces were available in both public and private tertiary education institutions. During 2011–2012, 46,613 students were enrolled compared to 20,011 during the 2003–2004 academic year. This is a change of 132.9 percent (Tabulawa & Youngman, in press).

In Botswana, policy responses to the high demand for tertiary education have been to build more universities and technical colleges, to sponsor students at recognized private tertiary education institutions, and to continue to place students in higher education institutions outside the country (Damane & Molutsi, 2013). The very capability that the country has to send students out for international study allows it to be an attractive destination for foreign academic employment. Botswana is known to provide competitive salaries and benefits. It is also known to provide good working conditions, as well as safer and more secure living environments (particularly when compared to its larger neighbor, South Africa).

Table 12.5 indicates that nearly one in five academics and researchers in Botswana comes from the SADC economic zone and more than one in three from elsewhere. As a major African magnet for academics, it is relevant to showcase the extent of foreign academic mobility in Botswana.

In terms of staffing, international staff are concentrated in academic and research units. Whereas one in five academic and research staff are international, the ratio is much smaller for management and administrative staff, where we see only one foreigner for every 15 staff members.

**TABLE 12.5** Number of Staff by Nationality and Type—Botswana

| Staffing Categories | Nationality | Staff Number |
| --- | --- | --- |
| Academic and research staff | National citizens | 514 |
|  | SADC citizens | 102 |
|  | Other international | 190 |
| Management and administrative staff | National citizens | 1,400 |
|  | SADC citizens | 25 |
|  | Other international | 40 |

*Source*: SARUA University Questionnaires (2011).

## Conclusion

South African higher education institutions arguably attract the largest number of foreign academics in Africa. Although the academics in the nation's institutions come from around the world, the landscape of international faculty in South Africa is dominated by those from other parts of Africa.

South African institutions stand at the apex of the African academic hierarchy. Despite the steadily declining resource base from the government (not by volume, but by proportion), the institutions still remain relatively well endowed, well managed, and well run. For instance, there are multiple entry points for public and private research funding, and development partners are known to treat South Africa differently than other African countries in terms of developing dedicated programs and resources.

Furthermore, the manner in which research productivity is directly and prominently rewarded in monetary terms in the South African higher education system adds to its appeal. For every publication in a recognized journal, the Department of Higher Education pays a subsidy to institutions of around 120,000 South African rands (an amount ranging between USD 8,250 and 10,000, depending on the currency conversion trends), whereby the institutions then disburse these subsidies at their discretion, at times directly to academics' private bank accounts, as a bonus. All of these realities are subjects of attraction to foreign academics, especially from other less well-resourced African countries.

The South African government fully recognizes the importance of attracting foreign academics to its academic and research institutions. Around 13 percent of academics in South African higher education institutions are foreigners. The government provides preferential treatment of such foreigners in facilitating their entrance to the country, for instance, via the critical skills visa category. However, it appears that despite the declared policies of the government to attract foreign academics to the country, the practice is undermined by ambivalence and red tape. The recent, widely publicized violent xenophobic attacks also undercut the effort.

As the country strives to produce a large number of PhDs—5,000 a year, ideally—and aspires to intensify its global competitiveness, it may continue to expand the opportunities to attract foreign academics, while at the same time driving home the 'growing our own timber' motto as part of its national transformation agenda. The tension between growing one's own timber and attracting foreign academics in the midst of heightened social (read: xenophobia), economic (read: high unemployment), and political (read: leadership crisis) upheavals may not be easy. However, the political and social rhetoric may unravel when the reality hits that mature 'timbers' are known to prefer working in more highly remunerative (and less demanding) jobs outside academia, further creating more demand for foreign academics in the expanding higher education landscape in South Africa.

This chapter was initially planned as an in-depth and critical case study of the UKZN, but this plan was dropped as the approval process for data collection—gate keeper and ethical clearance—was massively delayed. Even after the approval was granted, it became impossible to identify foreign subjects for the study simply because the institution was concerned about legal ramifications; that is, that the foreign academics may not wish to be identified as such out of fear—an outcome of the recent xenophobic attacks, according to a person with knowledge of the situation.

Mired in intense internal competition that stifles institutional differentiation, constrained by overstretched resources, dominated by populist views on 'growing our own timber,' limited by ambivalence in hiring and maintaining foreign academics, and hampered by weak production capacities of doctorates, it is difficult to imagine how the international standing of South African institutions could be easily fostered—and even more difficult to envision how the country's institutions would be deployed in the service of raising its competitiveness at the global level (Teferra, 2015).

The Minister of Home Affairs recently declared another major—and rather favorable and far-reaching—policy move on foreign student visas, with implications for the foreign academic landscape in South Africa. He announced that foreign students in critical areas will soon be allowed to apply for permanent residence upon graduation from a South African university (Hartley, 2016). In the waxing and waning interplay between ambivalence and conviction to attract and retain foreign academics, now the matter of graduating foreign students, another interesting dynamic in foreign academic mobility, appears to emerge in South Africa. This phenomenon is certainly not unique to South Africa, but mirrors experiences of many other countries—in comparable, and even better, social, economic and political conditions—which are grappling with issues of migration and mobility.

## References

Altbach, P. G (2004). The deteriorating guru: The crisis of the professoriate. *International Higher Education*, No 36.

Altbach, P. G., Reisberg, L., Yudkevich, M., Androushchak, G., & Pacheco, Iván F. (Eds.). (2012). *Paying the professoriate: A global comparison of compensation and contracts.* New York: Routledge.

Badat, S. (2009). Theorising institutional change: Post-1994 South African higher education. *Studies in Higher Education*, 34(4), 455–467.

Bawa, A. 2008. South Africa. In: M. Neradi and M. Heggelund (Eds.), *Toward a global PhD? Forces and forms in doctoral education worldwide* (pp. 117–130). Seattle, WA: University of Washington.

Bisaso, R. (in press). Makerere University as a flagship institution: Sustaining the quest for relevance. In D. Teferra (Ed.). *Flagship Universities in Africa.* Palgrave MacMillan.

Botha, J., & Fourie-Malherbe, M. (2015). Priorities for transforming African higher education into the 21st century: Country case study: South Africa. A study presented in the run up to the African Higher Education Summit, Dakar, Senegal.

Council on Higher Education (2014). Annual report of the council on higher education 2013/2014. Pretoria, South Africa.

Crush, J., & Pendleton, W. (2004). Immigration and refugee policy in Southern Africa. Southern African Migration Project. *Migration Policy Series* No. 30. Idasa, Cape Town, and Queen's University, Canada.

Damane, V., & Molutsi, P. (2013). Botswana. In D. Teferra & Knight (Eds.), *Higher education in Africa: The international dimension* (pp. 100–127). CIHE and AAU: Boston and Accra.

Department of Home Affairs (2002). Immigration Act 2002 (Act No. 13). Retrieved from www.dha.gov.za/

Department of Higher Education and Training (DHET). (2012). Retrieved from www.dhet.gov.za/SiteAssets/Latest%20News/Report%20of%20the%20Ministerial%20Committee%20for%20the%20Review%20of%20the%20Funding%20of%20Universities.pdf

Department of Higher Education and Training (DHET). (2015). Retrieved from www.dhet.gov.za/

Department of Higher Education and Training (DHET). (2016). Retrieved from www.dha.gov.za/index.php/immigration-services/scarce-skills-work-permits

Friedman, Steven (2016). The past speaks to the present: The newness of an old education debate. *Chronicle of African Higher Education*, May 2016.

Govender, P. (2014, April 6). Fear of brain drain as profs retire en masse. *Sunday Times*. Retirement. Retrieved from http://academic.sun.ac.za/Health/Media_Review/2014/7Apr14/files/brain.pdf

Government of South Africa (2012). National Development Plan 2030. Pretoria, South Africa: Government of South Africa.

Grant, H. M. (2006). From the Transvaal to the Prairies: The migration of South African physicians to Canada. *Journal of Ethnic and Migration Studies, 32*(4), 681–695. Retrieved from www.safpj.co.za/index.php/safpj/article/download/1152/1546

Habib, A., Price, M., & Mabelebele, J. (2014, September 3). *Internationalisation: Research & innovation in South Africa's universities*. Presentation to the Portfolio Committee on Higher Education and Training, Cape Town. Retrieved from http://pmg-assets.s3-website-eu-west-1.amazonaws.com/140903hesa.pdf

Hagenmeier, C., Quinlan, O., & Lansink, A. (2015). New laws sour SA for foreign students. Retrieved from http://mg.co.za/article/2015-09-11-new-laws-sour-sa-for-foreign-students

Hartley, Wyndham (2016, April 22). Foreign graduates of SA's universities can soon apply for permanent residence. *Business Day*. Retrieved from www.bdlive.co.za/national/education/2016/04/22/foreign-graduates-of-sas-universities-can-soon-apply-for-permanent-residence

HEMIS (2012) in Council on Higher Education (2016). Retrieved from www.che.ac.za/focus_areas/higher_education_data/2013/participation

Higher Education South Africa (2014). South African higher education in the 20th year of democracy: Context, achievements, and key challenges. Higher Education South Africa presentation to the Portfolo Committee on Higher Education and Training in Parliament, Cape Town, 5 March. Retrieved from www.hesa.org.za/hesa-presentation-portfolio-committee-higher-education-and-training

INTRA-ACP. (2016). Strengthening African Higher Education through Academic Mobility INTRA-ACP. Retrieved from http://intra-acp.nust.na/

Ishengoma, J. (2007, October 21–25). Internal brain drain and its impact on higher education institutions' capacity building and human resource development in Sub-Saharan Africa: The case of Tanzania. Conference of Rectors and Presidents of African Universities (COREVIP), Tripoli, Libya.

Ishengoma, J. (in press). The role of African flagship universities in higher education and national development: The case of the university of Dar es Salaam. In D. Teferra (Ed.), *Flagship Universities in Africa*. Palgrave MacMillan.

Jansen, J., McLellan, C., & Greene, R. (2008). South Africa. In D. Teferra & J. Knight (Eds.), *Higher education in Africa: The international dimension* (pp. 100–127, 387–420). CIHE and AAU: Boston and Accra.

Joubert, Jan-Jan (2016, January 31). Shambles in security services laid bare. *Sunday Times*. Retrieved from www.timeslive.co.za/sundaytimes/stnews/2016/01/31/Shambles-in-security-services-laid-bare

MacGregor, K. (2014, September 6). Major survey of international students in South Africa. *University World News No: 333*. Retrieved from www.universityworldnews.com/article.php?story=20140905134914811

Makgoba, W. Malegapuru (2015, November). A country of crises, contrasts and hope. *Chronicle of African Higher Education*.

Mashaba, Sibongile (2015, February 28). Home affairs loses millions in courts. *The Sowetan*. Retrieved from www.sowetanlive.co.za/news/2015/02/28/home-affairs-loses-millions-in-courts

Ministerial Committee for the Review of the Funding of Universities (2014). *Report of the ministerial committee for the review of the funding of universities, October 2013*. Pretoria: Department of Higher Education and Training.

Mouton, J., Boshoff, N., & James, M. (2015). A Survey of doctoral supervisors in South Africa. *South African Journal of Higher Education, 29*(2), 1–22.

Naidoo, R. (2015). Wits' foreign academics struggle to renew visas. *Wits Vuvuzela: A Publication of Wits Journalism*. Retrieved from http://witsvuvuzela.com/2015/04/24/wits-foreign-academics-struggle-to-renew-visas/

Nkosi, B. (2015, March 6). Brazen "trickery" in transformation. *Mail and Guardian*. Retrieved from http://mg.co.za/article/2015-03-06-brazen-trickery-in-transformation

Nwogu, S. (2012). Nigerians spend N160bn annually on education in Ghana—Babalakin. Retrieved from www.punchng.com/news/nigerians-spend-n160bn-annually-in-education-in-ghana-babalakin/

Parliamentary Monetary Group (2014). Retrieved from https://pmg.org.za/committee-meeting/17472/

Scott, P. (2015). Dynamics of academic mobility: Hegemonic internationalisation or Fluid globalisation. *European Review*, 23, S55–S69. doi:10.1017/S1062798714000775

Sehoole, C. T. (2004). Trade in educational services: Reflections on the African and South African higher education system. *Journal of Studies in International Education, 8*, 297–316.

Sifuna, D. (in press). University of Nairobi: Review of the flagship role in higher education in Kenya. In D. Teferra (Ed.), *Flagship Universities in Africa*. Palgrave MacMillan.

Singh, R. Jesika (2013). Examining xenophobic practices amongst university students—A case study from Limpopo Province. *Alternation* Special Edition, 7, 88–108.

South African Government (2016). President Jacob Zuma: State of the Nation Address 2016. Retrieved from www.gov.za/speeches/president-jacob-zuma-state-nation-address-2016-11-feb-2016-0000

South African Legal Information Institute (2010). In the KwaZulu-Natal High Court Pietermaritzburg, Republic of South Africa, Case No. 7802/09 and 71 Other Cases. In the Matter between Maxwell Xoxa Thusi and the Minister of Home Affairs, the Director General: Home Affairs. Retrieved from www.saflii.org/za/cases/ZAKZPHC/2010/87.html

Subotzky, G. (2003). South Africa. In D. Teferra & P. G. Altbach (Eds.), *African higher education: An international reference handbook* (pp. 545–562). Bloomington, IN: Indiana University Press.

Tabulawa, R. and Youngman, F. (in press). University of Botswana: A national university in decline? In D. Teferra (Ed.). *Flagship universities in Africa*. Hampshire: Palgrave MacMillan.

Teferra, D. (2015). Manufacturing—and exporting—excellence and 'mediocrity': Doctoral education in South Africa. *South African Journal of Higher Education, 29*(5): 8–19.

Teferra, D. (2016). Conclusion: the era of mass early career academics and aging faculty—Africa's paradox. *Studies in Higher Education*, 41(10): 1869-1881.

Teferra, D. (2016, February 11). Why free education is a folly in an unequal society. *The Conversation*. Retrieved from https://theconversation.com/why-free-education-is-a-folly-in-an-unequal-society-54515

University of KwaZulu-Natal (2016). Retrieved from www.ukzn.ac.za/about-ukzn/vision-and-mission

University of Rwanda (2016). Retrieved from http://www.ur.ac.rw/

Weeks, S. G. (2003). Botswana. In Teferra, D. & Altbach, P. G. (Eds.). *African higher education: An international reference handbook* (pp. 182–194). Bloomington, IN: Indiana University Press.

World Bank (2012). *Strengthening tertiary education in Africa through Africa centers of excellence*. Washington, DC: World Bank.

# 13

# INTERNATIONAL FACULTY IN HIGHER EDUCATION

Common Motivations, Disparate Realities, and Many Unknowns

*Laura E. Rumbley and Hans de Wit*

## Introduction

The presence of international faculty within higher education institutions and systems around the world is an important dimension of higher education in the global knowledge society of today. The increased global competition for talent, research, funding, and reputation/profile/branding implies that universities compete not only for the best and brightest of undergraduate and graduate students, but also for talented researchers and teachers on a world scale. Indeed, the ratio of international faculty to domestic faculty is one of the indicators in the international rankings of universities, an illustration of the importance of—as well as the strong driving forces motivating—international faculty mobility. But while there is much research on international student mobility, we know little about faculty mobility, which provides the central rationale for this study.

The individual country and institutional case studies that form the heart of this volume present a wide-ranging picture of the international faculty experience across 11 countries and five continents. Our task in this final chapter is to draw out—to the degree this is possible—a set of insights and lessons emerging from the diverse realities of Brazil, Canada, mainland China and Hong Kong, Estonia, Lithuania, Germany, Kazakhstan, Mexico, the Russian Federation, Saudi Arabia, and South Africa. This is no simple assignment, given that precisely one of the clearest themes arising from the case study data is the significance of unique national, institutional, and individual contexts in relation to the international faculty experience. Furthermore, these contextual frameworks cut across a complex set of additional dimensions, namely the academic cultures and communities in which international faculty members find themselves, the practical matters that characterize international faculty mobility and integration, and the political realities that can exert an enormous influence over a range of policies and practices affecting international faculty prospects and experiences. These contextual and frame-of-reference matters—the individual, the institutional, the national or systemic, the practical, the political, and the academic—intersect in myriad ways. These elements are sometimes interlocking, sometimes conflicting and complicating; but in all cases, their manifestations and the pressures they exert seem to have some level of impact on the international faculty experience itself. Further, our understanding and awareness of these pressures provide us with a deeper understanding of the many dynamics affecting the international faculty population in different environments of the world. We also become more aware of the gaps in what we currently know about the fundamentals of international faculty mobility, including who, how, why, and with what impact over the short and long term.

Our exploration of the collective findings of the case studies in this volume is organized around three fundamental units of analysis: the individual, the institutional, and the national/systemic perspective. The goal of this analysis is to highlight key similarities and differences in the ways that the different countries, institutions, and individuals covered in this study understand and relate to the international faculty phenomenon, as well as how they define its contours, experience its dynamics, and understand its consequences and possibilities. First, however, a word about how international faculty are defined around the world.

## What's in a Name? Defining 'International Faculty'

From the outset, the organizers of this study were keen to focus attention on the phenomenon of faculty recruitment and employment in the context of an international academic marketplace. That is, the starting point for understanding the term 'international faculty' was to consider the experience of higher education institutions that formally *hire* faculty from another country, not just extend invitations for temporary 'visits' to teach or conduct research in a more short-term or collegial capacity. It is important to make this distinction, because both the policies for and the implications of those two types of faculty mobility, and the variations within them, are quite different. One can compare them with the differences inherent in definitions of 'international students,' where mobility for credit and degree mobility, and the variations within these phenomena, also vary substantively.

Beyond this fundamental notion as set forward by the editors of this volume, the idea of how to define 'international faculty' for this study was left, to some extent, to the contributing authors to articulate, in light of the realities of the specific country and institution at the heart of their respective cases.

In doing so, this study presents a kaleidoscope of profiles for, and definitions of, international faculty, which provides a fascinating indication of how the status of internationally mobile academics (with more than short-term appointments) can be variously recognized and categorized, depending on the host nation (or institution's) situation and perspective. In the chapter devoted to Brazil, for example, where the country has focused minimal attention on directly importing academic talent from abroad, the notion of international faculty is explored through a consideration of two categories of faculty employed in Brazil: non-Brazilians who obtained their PhD in Brazil and Brazilians who obtained their doctoral degree outside of Brazil.

Meanwhile, in the Estonia and Lithuania chapter, we note that Lithuania's efforts to internationalize its higher education system include providing resources to attract international faculty with a particular interest in recruiting individuals of 'Lithuanian descent' who are now working outside the country. China, too, looks at international faculty recruitment, to a great extent, through a lens of reattraction of Chinese who have been educated or who have developed academic careers abroad. The South Africa, Canada, Kazakhstan, Russia, and Saudi Arabia chapters seem to coalesce most overtly around the idea of international faculty as individuals who do not hold the citizenship of the respective receiving country and are hired largely from some point geographically 'outside.' Indeed, the Saudi Arabia chapter refers consistently to 'expatriate' faculty as a way of articulating how these individuals are distinguished from 'noninternational' academics in that particular national setting. Similarly, the South Africa chapter provides significant detail about visa regulations and procedures, providing a bureaucratic and legalistic insight into what it means to be an international faculty member in that context.

To be sure, the lack of a single definition for international faculty—both in this study and more broadly—is problematic. In addition to the aforementioned distinction between visiting faculty and hired faculty, it is important to note there is great variation within these two categories of mobile faculty. As seen in the literature review chapter in this volume, there has been more research focused on visiting faculty than on international faculty as longer-term hires, which adds to the complexity of defining international faculty for this study. In this sense, the use by international rankings of the percentage of international faculty as a quantitative factor in rankings analysis is problematic. Without a clear definition for this indicator, it is difficult to effectively understand the data, which undermines the reliability of this indicator.

Global and comparative analyses are exceedingly difficult to carry out without a standardized understanding of the term, which in turn can affect our ability to theorize and to generalize to any significant degree. However, the range of definitions is also useful at this, arguably preliminary, stage of making greater sense of the evolving global academic mobility scene. The various approaches to defining and characterizing the international faculty population in different parts of the world begin to expose the wide array of national, institutional, and individual experiences with the phenomenon, and ultimately may help researchers to further refine their parameters for, and approaches to, exploring this issue moving forward. For the purpose of this study, we define international faculty as those

**270** Laura E. Rumbley and Hans de Wit

academics who are hired from abroad by an institution as an employee. They can be either returning nationals or foreigners (noncitizens); they can be teachers and/or researchers.

With some sense of the general outlines of our topic from a definitional perspective, we move to consider questions relevant to the international faculty at the national level.

## The Big Picture: National Perspectives on International Faculty

The countries in this study represent a wide geographic range, reflecting realities in 11 different countries on five continents. They also present some degree of diversity in terms of wealth, economic development, and societal health and well-being (although no countries considered to be in the categories of "low" or "very low development" are included), and an even wider panorama in relation to population size, as indicated in Table 13.1.

Geography, demographics, resource availability, historical realities, and the current national vision and general sense of a national 'trajectory' are key factors in understanding different countries' orientations toward international faculty, their level of interest in recruiting them, and their success in attracting and retaining them. Several key aspects emerge here, including the policy environment—affecting everything from the legal possibility to work, to salary and general working conditions—and fundamental issues of 'place,' such as geographic location, language, and cultural considerations.

**TABLE 13.1** Case Study Countries' Human Development Index (HDI) Ranks and Populations

| Country | HDI Rank* | HDI Category* | Population (2015)** |
|---|---|---|---|
| Germany | 6 | Very high development | 80,689,000 |
| Canada | 9 | Very high development | 35,940,000 |
| Estonia | 30 | Very high development | 1,313,000 |
| Lithuania | 37 | Very high development | 2,878,000 |
| Saudi Arabia | 39 | Very high development | 31,540,000 |
| Russian Federation | 50 | High development | 143,457,000 |
| Kazakhstan | 56 | High development | 17,625,000 |
| Mexico | 74 | High development | 127,017,000 |
| Brazil | 75 | High development | 207,848,00 |
| China | 90 | High development | ***1,383,337,000 |
| South Africa | 116 | Medium development | 54,490,000 |

*Source: United Nations Human Development Programme (2015).
**Source: United Nations Population Division (2015).
***Note: This figure includes mainland China and Hong Kong, but not Macau or Taiwan.

## The Policy Environment

The starting point for this conversation in many of the case studies in this book is whether or not a country has an articulated policy, or an outline of objectives, related to the attraction of foreign talent. In this age of influential global university rankings and the tendency by many policy makers and national leaders to place a premium on 'engaging with the global knowledge economy,' it is increasingly common for countries to put forward national policies for internationalization (Helms, Rumbley, Brajkovic & Mihut, 2015; de Wit, Hunter, Howard & Egron-Polak, 2015). These policies—or programs, initiatives, agendas, visions, and the like—at times include some effort to attract highly skilled individuals from outside the country. The rationale for the focus on attracting international talent is typically expressed as an interest in strengthening local capacity-building efforts and increasing the intellectual output in the host country (Helms et al., 2015). Other factors influencing this process are demographic trends; insufficient local student participation in fields such as science, technology, engineering, and mathematics (STEM); and the increased demands of the knowledge economy (de Wit et al., 2015, p. 284).

Among our case studies, examples of articulated policy positions in this vein can be seen, to varying degrees, in China, Estonia, Lithuania, Russia, and South Africa. But there is enormous variation in terms of what these policy positions look like and how they are expressed. On one end of the spectrum, for example, our China chapter authors provide information on the country's Thousand Talents Program, which is specifically designed to "recruit overseas scientists and returnees by providing attractive salaries as well as research funding and high profile research teams." Estonia's *Higher Education Internationalisation Strategy* (2006–2015) articulates a "target of ensuring that at least 3 percent of full-time academic staff will be of foreign origin by 2015," and—the Estonia chapter authors explain—places emphasis on specific actions to be taken to support the "integration" of international staff (and students), for example, by way of "free language courses" and "access to community services and medical care in English," among other supports.

Meanwhile, South Africa's approach has been to make reference to the need for international talent in public policy documents—such as the *National Development Plan*, the *Industrial Policy Action Plan*, and the *New Growth Plan*—and then to enable the operationalization of international faculty recruitment by introducing a Critical Skills Work Visa regime. And in the Lithuania case study, mention is made of the interest in attracting foreign talent (principally of Lithuanian descent) in the country's *National Action Plan for Promoting the International Dimension of Lithuanian Higher Education 2013–2016*, but neither funding nor clear actions are put forward to reduce visa barriers and other bureaucratic challenges.

We do not see this same sort of clearly defined push (at least on a national or governmental level) for the recruitment of international faculty in all of the countries included in our study, but that does not mean that those not taking such overt positions present national policy environments that are completely disconnected from, or unsupportive of, the international faculty phenomenon. In a variety of cases, immigration policy, for example, sets a very favorable tone for the attraction and retention of academic talent, in a context where such talent is considered to correlate directly with economic development. This is clearly in evidence in the Canadian context, where our Canada chapter authors explain that prospective immigrants are currently evaluated against "three distinct admission categories: economic, family reunification, and humanitarian," with careful consideration of such factors as "educational achievement, language competency, age, and also national labor market needs." In 2015, 65 percent of newly admitted immigrants into Canada were to be classified as economic immigrants, one of two categories (the other being temporary foreign workers) by which international academics may be admitted to Canada. The European Union (EU) countries included in this study—Estonia, Germany, and Lithuania—also intrinsically benefit from the EU's laws related to free movement of the labor force across that particular political collective. Although not included in our study, the EU 'labor mobility effect' is also evident in England—at least pre-Brexit. In that country, according to data from the Higher Education Funding Council for England (HEFCE), the percentage of academics from other EU countries stood at 17 percent in 2014–2015, as opposed to the smaller proportion (12 percent) of academics from outside the EU (Havergal, 2016)—even though the EU academic workforce in England represents only 28 countries, compared to the 140 countries overall from which international faculty in England hail (HEFCE, 2016).

Likewise, we see in Saudi Arabia no articulated national policy or plan for hiring international faculty. However, the national agenda to expand access to higher education in the country, and to attend to issues of quality along the way, has encouraged many Saudi universities to hire internationally, something that has required the responsible Saudi ministry to establish the framework regulations, or 'rules of the game,' by which the universities may hire and retain expatriate academics. This provides a positive policy environment for the attraction of foreign faculty, as did the national Program to Support Science in Mexico (PACIME), which became a "pioneer in Latin America" in 1992 "by including foreign academics" among its beneficiaries.

Brazil stands out in some ways as a unique case—it is a country whose international profile has evolved significantly over the last decade, in light of its dynamic economic growth and its overt commitment to international engagement via such programs as the Science Without Borders initiative, yet little movement has been seen in relation to policy focused on the long-term attraction of foreign academic talent. The authors of our Brazil chapter provide insights into possible reasons for this by noting that the country has long focused on the cultivation of 'home grown' Brazilian academic talent—both domestically and via support for education abroad—and by providing attractive opportunities for international graduate students in Brazil's own quite rigorous and heavily publicly subsidized graduate programs.

Clearly, there is a diverse national policy landscape around the world in relation to international faculty recruitment and overall terms of employment. Where the country has 'come from' historically in relation to the export or import of human capital and what it can offer today in terms of a policy framework (particularly in relation to legal matters, such as immigration and employment status) are all highly relevant factors in this discussion, as evidenced by the case study countries. Complicating matters even more can be the interplay between policy and politics. In the case of South Africa, for example, we are provided with information about an uneasy dynamic between the expressed strategic needs and aspirations of the country in terms of seeking foreign talent in relation to meeting national economic and general development targets, and the realities of a highly unsettled social and political environment on the ground.

## *Location, Location, Location*

Where policy ends, 'real life' begins. And what a country has to offer as a concrete 'experience'—personally and professionally—for internationally mobile faculty also appears to be quite important when undertaking a comparative analysis of foreign faculty experiences. In relation to this matter, the country case studies in this volume point to several important elements. Geography, language, and cultural dimensions of the recruiting country seem to be most salient in this discussion. These matters can be examined discretely, but there is also considerable interplay between location, language, and culture, not to mention historical ties between countries.

The Kazakhstan chapter notes, for example, that the 'remote location' of the country is perceived as a barrier when it comes to international faculty recruitment, as is a general lack of knowledge about the country and daily life there. Indeed, some faculty recruitment ads for Nazarbayev University (NU)—the Kazakh case study institution in this volume—take pains to "portray Astana [the capital of Kazakhstan and where NU is located] as a modern city undergoing rapid development with promises of an unforgettable adventure." Regionalization is another important dimension to consider in relation to geography. South Africa's position as the economic powerhouse of Africa and the leading partner of the Southern African Development Community, or SADC, puts it in a very strong position in relation to its ability to attract academics from the immediate region and, indeed, across the continent. Brazil's relatively small international faculty community also draws significantly from the Latin American 'neighborhood' in which the country is located. And in Canada, 'certain categories of international academics are exempt from all Labor Market Impact Assessments, which assess "the likely impact that hiring a temporary foreign worker (TFW) will have on the Canadian labour market"'—these include (among others) US and Mexican citizens, as a result of the North American Free Trade Agreement, and citizens of Chile, in conjunction with the Canada Chile Free Trade Agreement.

In contradiction to the regionalization argument, however, in the Nazarbayev University case study in Kazakhstan, NU counted just 9 Russians among its 339 international faculty as of September 2015. In this case, the authors suggest that the geographic proximity and other push–pull factors (such as the low salaries in Russian universities and the dynamic working environment offered at NU)—which otherwise might move Russian academics toward Kazakhstan—could be counterbalanced by NU's demanding standards for English-language proficiency (among other professional requirements).

Location also plays a role in the sense that countries and cities with a broad international expatriate community enhance the chance of an international faculty presence by drawing in foreign academics who can combine their academic position with another job, may be motivated to move upon retirement from another position elsewhere, and/or may opt for a change of location in conjunction with a partner or spouse.

## *The Language Factor*

The discussion of location leads easily to a consideration of national realities with respect to language and its effects on international faculty dynamics. The countries and institutions covered in this volume suggest a variety of ways in which language exerts an influence on pathways for international faculty recruitment and possibilities for varying depths of integration for those who are hired. Not surprisingly, 'shared' languages between host country and/or institution and internationally mobile faculty seem to be a significant 'facilitating element,' at the very least. Where English is widely spoken—for example, in Canada, Hong Kong, and South Africa—the possibilities for recruitment of foreign faculty are significantly widened. The same can be said of institutions where the working language is English, wholly or in part, such as at the Higher School of Economics in Russia, Nazarbayev University in Kazakhstan, or King Fahd University of Petroleum & Minerals in Saudi Arabia. Similarly, the case studies in Mexico and Brazil reflect how the use of other widely spoken languages, such as Spanish and Portuguese, affect international faculty recruitment in those contexts. Not surprisingly, international faculty in these two countries are drawn heavily from other Spanish- and Portuguese-speaking countries and regions.

What becomes important to consider, however, is the extent to which non-speakers of the dominant local language can participate fully in the life of their host institutions without those local language skills. The Russian case, for example, notes that

> . . . in many cases, international faculty do not have any service responsibilities assigned to them. It is partly explained by the fact that most of

administrative processes at HSE are conducted in Russian, and for non-Russian (speaking) faculty, it is impossible to take an active part in these processes.

Equally, for those countries featuring a working language that is not widely spoken internationally—for example, Lithuanian and Estonian—the challenge is twofold: how to make a convincing international recruitment case, and how to ensure that recruited academics without local language skills are effectively supported. These two very small countries stand in stark contrast to a very large country like China, which can rely on a comparatively massive internationally educated cohort of young China-born (or ethnically Chinese) academics that it now seeks to integrate into its higher education sector, to maximum effect.

## Culture and Other Considerations

Language is a crucial element when it comes to the national profile presented to internationally mobile faculty, but other elements of the host country reality that may also play a role in relation to its attractiveness to foreign academics. Significant 'cultural differences' of many types may be a matter of concern to some. For example, the author of our Saudi Arabia chapter notes that "differences in culture and norms" may be one of multiple concerns on the minds of applicants for positions in that country; the China chapter also admits that "one challenge for attracting and maintaining high-level foreign talent who are not ethnic Chinese has been the cultural gap." Separately, the Russia chapter alludes to difficulties presented by "the current geopolitical situation, with several countries imposing economic sanctions on Russia and a much weaker ruble," which may plant uncertainties about Russia's economic stability in the minds of some potential recruits. Environmental concerns may even factor in to the international faculty mobility equation—the China chapter authors note that the "noxious air pollution" in some of China's biggest cities represents a "challenge" in terms of attracting talent.

At the national level, a set of tangible and intangible factors together present a 'face' to potential foreign faculty recruits. Whether prospective internationally mobile academics will find this national face attractive or not depends on a multitude of variables. These variables range from the policy framework that actively stimulates (or complicates) their recruitment and legal or professional status in the country, to the aspects of daily life—such as language and cultural norms and practices—that enable their integration (or undermine their effort to fit in), to the broader issues of geopolitics and the environment, which can affect the overall tone and tenor for their own experience and that of any family members who may accompany them. The national context is a crucial dimension of the international faculty story. But, as explored further next, so, too, is the institutional context.

## 'Where the Rubber Meets the Road': International Faculty and Institutional Realities

Although understanding national policies, priorities, and practices with respect to the attraction of foreign academic talent is quite important, the reality is that individual academics are recruited and employed by specific higher education institutions. Without question, the lives of international faculty in a given national setting are colored heavily by the circumstances they face within a particular institutional context; similarly, the host institutions for these individuals represent the 'front lines' of policy implementation when it comes to foreign talent attraction. As such, the institutional level of analysis represents a vital area of concern in terms of making practical sense of the rationale for international faculty recruitment, the ways in which foreign academics are recruited, the terms of their employment, and the extent to which their presence is perceived to exert an impact on their host institutions.

### *Why? Rationale for International Faculty Recruitment*

Across the board, our case study institutions—whether relatively young in age or more longstanding, big or small in size, 'globally recognized,' or less internationally visible as a matter of profile (see Table 13.2)—are all aware of a 'wider world' of higher education, both nationally and internationally. Of course, there is some variation in the levels of such awareness and engagement, and in the stages of development in relation to needs and abilities to attract foreign talent. Some institutions are in full-on 'building mode'; others have already achieved a certain level of global visibility, and—while certainly needing and continuing to actively compete for international talent—seem to sit in a slightly more established position in relation to this work.

For example, on one end of the spectrum, we learn in the Kazakhstan chapter that Nazarbayev University (NU), which graduated its first master's students in 2014 and its first bachelor students in 2015,

> is a distinctive feature of the government's 2020 economic and social development strategy. The university's mission is "to be a model for higher education reform and modern research in Kazakhstan and to contribute to the establishment of Astana as an international innovation and knowledge hub."

NU has committed to operating exclusively in English and has developed a series of unique, strategic international partnerships, which are aimed at elevating the institution to the level of a high-performing, internationally recognized institution. A key part of this strategy involves attracting high-quality faculty from the global academic market. The Higher School of Economics presents something of a similar profile to NU in terms of aiming to stand out on the Russian higher

**TABLE 13.2** Case Study Institutions: Location, Founding Date, and Total Student and Faculty Populations

| Institution | | Founding Date* | Total Student Population (Year) | Total Faculty Population (Year) |
|---|---|---|---|---|
| University of Campinas (Unicamp) | Brazil | 1996 | 34,616 (2014) | 1,900 (2015) |
| University of Toronto | Canada | 1827 | 84,400 (2014–2015) | 13,200 (2014–2015) |
| Shanghai Jiao Tong University (SJTU) | China | 1896 | 35,000 (2014) | 2,900 (2014) |
| University of Hong Kong (HKU) | China | 1911 | 27,933 (2014–2015) | 3,340 (2014–2015) |
| University of Konstanz | Germany | 1966 | 11,410 (2013–2014) | 1,301 (2015) |
| Nazarbayev University (NU) | Kazakhstan | 2010 | | 339 (2015) |
| Vilnius University (VU) | Lithuania | 1579 | 21,006 (2015) | 1,348 (2015) |
| Colegio de México (COLMEX) | Mexico | 1940 | 429 (2016) | 184 (2015) |
| Institute of Geophysics (IGP) | Mexico | 1904 | 245 (2015) | 137 (2013) |
| Maya Intercultural University of Quintana Roo (UIMQRoo) | Mexico | 2006 | 634 (2012) | 52 (2012) |
| National Research University Higher School of Economics (HSE) | Russian Federation | 1992 | 25,000 (2014) | 2,500 (2014) |
| King Fahd University of Petroleum and Minerals (KFUPM) | Saudi Arabia | 1963 | 8,782 (2014/2015) | 970 (2014/2015) |
| University of KwaZulu-Natal (UKZN) | South Africa | 2004 | 44,000 (2016) | 1,342 (2016) |

*Source*: Case study chapters in this volume.

*Note: Some of the founding date information must be qualified by additional details regarding mergers and predecessor institutions. For example, the University of KwaZulu-Natal (South Africa) was established in 2004 as a merger of two institutions. These were the University of Durban-Westville (established in the 1960s) and the University of Natal (founded in 1910 as Natal University College, which later became the University of Natal in 1949). Please see the specific case study chapters in this volume for additional information, where relevant.

education landscape as an innovative and dynamically forward-thinking institution, committed to internationalizing its faculty in order to maximize quality and competitiveness on a global stage. Germany's University of Konstanz, particularly in conjunction with its participation in that country's Excellence Initiative, is also driven to recruit top faculty as a matter of prioritizing quality, regardless of nationality. Quality and competitiveness are also driving factors for South

Africa's University of KwaZulu-Natal and Brazil's University of Campinas, which stand out as nationally and regionally prominent institutions, also with significant international visibility, but with minimal overt focus on international faculty recruitment as a key institutional priority. Indeed, Campinas presents a "lack of a consistent university policy to attract international faculty."

Finally, the two Chinese case study institutions (Shanghai Jiao Tong University and the University of Hong Kong) and the Canadian case of the University of Toronto already enjoy significant global visibility. In some ways, this puts these institutions in a 'comfortable,' highly competitive position to attract international faculty. For example, the University of Hong Kong (HKU) has "no specific strategy for hiring local, national, or international faculty. All searches are worldwide." For this institution, the academic marketplace is intrinsically a global one and, according to HKU's president in 2015, "internationalization 'is an essential component of enhancing our standing in the world.'" Furthermore, HKU's top leadership sees that the ability to foster an "atmosphere of internationalization" will allow HKU to be a place where "the future of global leaders will be born." An interest in continuing to exert a major influence on the production of globally recognized knowledge and expertise is a powerful rationale for seeking out top talent internationally.

Interestingly, although the University of Toronto is also keenly focused on the notion of attracting high-quality academics, it is not as overt in this process (for example, when compared to HKU) with respect to articulating a rationale to recruit specifically 'international' faculty. In alignment with—and in some ways at the forefront of—Canadian orientations toward fostering 'diversity,' our Canada chapter authors suggest that the hiring of internationals at the University of Toronto is part and parcel of that primary interest. Furthermore, the hiring of international faculty at the University of Toronto must situate itself carefully within another key trend in Canada at the moment, that is, a government-imposed 'Canadians first' approach to hiring.

In most cases, we see 'active' orientations toward the hiring of international faculty—although somewhat less obviously so in the Mexican case study institutions, as well as those in Brazil and South Africa. Where there is more organized activity in this area, what motivates institutions to look to international faculty as a source of new academic talent is clearly a function of many factors, but two main trends seem most prominent across the very different institutions in this volume. The first, and perhaps most prevailing, interest is the desire to augment the quality of the institution and its outputs. There may be internal and/or external factors motivating this desire. A general wish to improve one's performance, particularly in relation to research activity, in an increasingly competitive environment is clearly in evidence. There are external factors to take into account as well. The rankings are mentioned in most of the case studies, signaling an awareness of and, to greater and lesser extents, a sensitivity to these global measures of university performance. For some of the case study institutions, programs and policies at the national level are key motivators. Nazarbayev University's very creation by the government was predicated on an interest in seeing that institution stand out on the global higher education landscape, which virtually required the infusion of international academic talent into the ranks of its faculty. The Russian case of the Higher School of Economics (HSE) also demonstrates the push from national policy at the institutional level. The Russian government-sponsored "5–100" program aims to see five Russian universities appear among the top 100 of one of the global university ranking tables by 2020. As the Russia chapter authors note most succinctly: "In joining this developmental program, HSE took on some externally driven obligations to attract and integrate international faculty and students."

Closely related to the overarching interest in improving quality via international faculty recruitment there appears in several of the case study institutions the desire to enhance innovation within the institution itself; that is, through the presence and involvement of 'outsiders,' new ideas and new approaches to teaching, learning, research, and even governance and administration can be considered. The 'diversity' discussion in Canada could be seen as part of this equation, although perhaps the Nazarbayev case in Kazakhstan may be the most obvious example here, given that

> [a]s well as aiming to become a world class institution, the government wants NU to serve as a site of innovation, experimentation and customization. NU is expected to try, test, evaluate, adapt, and customize successful higher education practices from other countries and disseminate these practices to other universities in Kazakhstan.

Motivations are one thing, of course; actually recruiting and hiring international faculty is another.

## *How and Under What Circumstances? International Faculty Recruitment and Terms of Employment*

When it comes to recruiting international faculty, approaches vary significantly, depending on the specific aims and characteristics of the various case study institutions included in our study. These approaches range accordingly:

- A highly targeted and active pursuit of nonlocal talent (as seen at HSE in Russia, and NU in Kazakhstan).
- A more integrated approach of looking at recruitment processes as inherently international by nature (notably at the University of Hong Kong and the University of Toronto).
- An interest in hiring internationally, yet not having particularly consistent or sustained approaches for doing so (as seen in the Vilnius University and University of KwaZulu-Natal cases).

- A seemingly 'passive' orientation to the hiring of foreign academics, which seems to consist mostly of reacting to the candidates who—because of a range of personal and professional developments in the life of the individual scholar, and sometimes policy choices made by the host country over significant periods—materialize for the institution in the course of a faculty search (as in the University of Campinas and Mexican institutional cases). One important element in this discussion may be geography. For example, smaller countries surrounded by larger countries, or institutions that sit in a particularly fertile 'neighborhood' in relation to possible sources of international faculty, such as the University of Konstanz in Germany, may find themselves attracting foreign faculty with a certain degree of ease, simply by virtue of their location.

The approaches taken by the various case study institutions in this volume seem to reflect varying degrees of both urgency or strategic commitment with respect to international faculty recruitment and access to resources to enable recruitment process of different stripes. Nazarbayev University offers a particularly interesting case of an institution that is using a set of very specific partnerships with institutions around the world to advance the development of the university, including in relation to the identification and recruitment of foreign faculty. This stands out as a particularly unique strategy.

Complicating efforts to develop a 'typology' across institutions with respect to approaches to international faculty recruitment is the fact that there is not necessarily uniformity in recruitment processes across individual institutions. That is, some institutions use a variety of recruitment processes simultaneously, tailoring these to different schools, faculties, departments, etc., based on these units' and disciplines' specific cultures, aspirations, and traditions (particularly in an international context) around identifying promising new faculty candidates.

Terms of employment also vary significantly around the world. A number of our case study institutions offer international candidates the same terms of employment as local hires. For example, under Canadian law, "wages and working conditions for foreign academics will be identical to those of domestic hires, including all union or collective-bargaining clauses." In some cases, however, international faculty are offered different terms of employment. At HSE in Russia, international faculty are often excused from service obligations, given that "most of administrative processes at HSE are conducted in Russian." At KFUPM in Saudi Arabia, international faculty are provided highly competitive salaries and are assessed no taxes, offered free schooling on the campus for their children, and given airline tickets each year for the faculty member and three family members to travel round-trip for a visit to the family's home country (among other benefits).

At Shanghai Jiao Tong University, some financial advantages may accrue to international staff who are sufficiently proficient in English to teach in that language, thus advancing the university's interest in offering more English-taught courses. The ability to publish in English also opens doors on rewards that may come with publication in highly cited journals, again offering advantages to some nonlocal faculty. Interestingly, however, the trend to offer higher remuneration packages to international faculty (either foreign born or Chinese returning after obtaining a PhD abroad) seems to have diminished.

Beyond the question of whether terms of employment are equal or similar between international and domestic faculty, there is also the question of the quality of life that can be expected in the host environment on the basis of salary and other conditions. The University of Hong Kong case notes that the salaries on offer to all faculty there are "competitive with top universities overseas." However, property prices in Hong Kong are the "highest of any city in the world," and some nationals—notably Americans—can expect to have their income taxed twice, both by Hong Kong and their home government. At the opposite end of the spectrum, salaries on offer at Vilnius University are "very low"; indeed, "along with Bulgaria, Hungary, Latvia, and Romania, Lithuania is one of the EU member states that pays the lowest salaries to academic staff—and the dissatisfaction with salary levels among academics is particularly high." This presents significant challenges to Vilnius University to cast a wide global net for international recruitment purposes. However, the authors of the Lithuanian case study take pains to note that the "Lithuanian diaspora is highly patriotic," which may motivate some returnees from abroad to integrate into the university regardless of the less-than-ideal terms of employment. The ability to "make ends meet" is also seen as a way of ameliorating the less-than-ideal salary situation in Lithuanian context.

## *To What End? Gauging the Effects of International Faculty*

Assuming institutions are successful in recruiting international faculty, what does this process ultimately deliver to the host institution? Our case study institutions provide a window onto a range of possible benefits and challenges that come with the commitment to hiring and retaining international faculty, although many gaps remain in our understanding of the ultimate effect on host institutions of an international faculty presence.

The interviews conducted by the contributors to this volume speak to a significant amount of positive anecdotal evidence with respect to the impact of international faculty within the respective case study institutions. There is a clear sense that international faculty bring their nonlocal relationships and networks to bear in their work, which is in itself a constructive contribution to the larger efforts of all of the case study institutions to internationalize in meaningful ways.

However, few of the case study institutions have undertaken systematic efforts to measure the performance of international faculty in order to gauge (or attempt to gauge) their impact. Where some comparison has been (even lightly) considered—for example, in the Brazil case study—the international faculty appear to be comparable in their productivity and performance to similarly qualified domestic faculty. Even more revealing, in one case where a specific evaluation of international faculty was conducted at the Higher School of Economics in Russia, the results were not terribly impressive. Indeed, HSE's 2015 evaluation of its international faculty found that "[o]ut of 70 evaluated faculty members, 34 were deemed to have not met par on at least one—and for some, on all—of the evaluated dimensions." When compared with domestic faculty, they had produced fewer publications, had a lighter teaching load, had lower student evaluations, and the service they offered to the university "was practically nonexistent."

Perhaps more than any area touched upon in his volume, the question of 'outcomes' at the institutional level begs for further exploration. Fundamentally, it is crucial to have a better understanding of whether the aspirations institutions have for improved quality, innovation, and competitiveness are realized in some fashion by virtue of the presence of the international faculty. The case studies in this volume begin to point a way forward with respect to understanding this vital level of analysis, both in terms of the experiences of more internationally visible institutions engaged in the 'global race for academic talent' and in the more quotidian realities of potentially lesser-known, yet still aspirational, institutions of varying profiles, working toward greater quality and visibility.

## The Heart of the Matter: International Faculty Are Real People, Too

The story of international faculty mobility is, of course, not complete without a consideration of what this phenomenon means at the most fundamental level—that of the individual. Here, our case studies help us gain some insights into what motivates individuals to be mobile, what attracts them to particular national and institutional settings, and what encourages them to stay or leave after a period of time. This information can be extremely important for institutions and national-level policy makers, as they seek deeper understanding into the motivations of individual academics and the tools that systems and individual institutions of higher education may have at their disposal to attract international talent.

Lessons drawn from the classic literature on push and pull factors in academic mobility (Altbach, 1998, 2007; Cantwell, 2011; Cradden, 2007; Mahroum, 2000) and the dynamics between academic centers and peripheries (Altbach, 2004; Altbach, Reisberg & Rumbley, 2009; Scott, 2015) are very much in evidence in the case studies when attention turns to understanding why academics choose to relocate internationally. In looking at the specifics of our study, two key issues seem to emerge as most prominent when it comes to the motivations of individual faculty to be mobile. The first is the desire to pursue an attractive employment opportunity, where 'attractiveness' may be based on a wide variety of factors, including:

- A sense of the prestige of the hiring institution (the University of Toronto and HKU cases speak to this situation)
- Attractive salary or other employment terms (KFUPM in Saudi Arabia provides insight into this trend)
- Personal ties to the country where the hiring institution is located (the Brazil and Lithuania cases point to a significant influence of personal relationships in particular contexts)
- A conviction that other available opportunities are less satisfactory (the history of Mexico's influx of foreign academic talent shows important examples of this trend, and the Lithuania case study also suggests that national context offers a 'step up' for some in even more underresourced contexts).

Somewhat less common or evident, yet still present in the some of the pictures presented by the case studies, is the motivation for international mobility that is rooted in a sense of contributing to an important project. The Lithuania chapter, for example, talks about the interest among that country's diaspora in returning to contribute to national development, despite low salaries. Mexico's various government-supported returnee programs and China's success in hiring many of its own foreign-educated citizens may point to similar dynamics—that is, the desire to 'make a difference' in a context where the international faculty member feels that his or her contribution would be appreciated. Such rationale can also be found among international faculty who work in universities in developing countries in the framework of capacity building and/or in taking up a faculty position in a developing country upon retirement.

Attention to the very human experience of being appreciated, welcomed, and 'fitting in' is something that arises in several of the case studies. Interestingly, in Estonia's national policy for internationalization, mention is made of the ways that personal, linguistic, and family supports—outside of the immediate purview of an international faculty member's professional life—must be thoughtfully attended to. At the institutional level, we see clearly articulated efforts by the Canadian, Saudi Arabian, and Russian case study universities to provide a fairly extensive menu of support services for international faculty members and their families, ranging from language classes, to cultural orientation programs, to recreational and cultural resources. Interestingly, only one of the case studies—Canada—spoke at any length about services provided specifically in support of spouses/partners seeking employment in the host country after the international faculty member has been contracted. The University of Toronto's willingness to negotiate on issues of academic employment for a spouse/partner, as well as providing a dedicated service—the Dual Career Connection—to assist those spouses/partners seeking nonacademic employment, is notable, in comparison with the relative (or total) lack of attention to this matter at the other case study institutions.

It is important to consider what some of the case study institutions have learned about the levels of satisfaction and dissatisfaction among their international faculty members and the specific issues that give rise to those positive or negative perceptions. General job satisfaction is important to consider, and this study brings a range of perspective on this question to the fore. In Russia, international faculty at HSE find the institution's heavy administrative processes burdensome, whereas more than one interviewee in the Vilnius University case in Lithuania observed that there are significant opportunities inherent in the "independence and flexibility concerning hierarchical structures" and ease of doing things in a "dynamic environment." In Saudi Arabia, faculty surveys indicate that expatriate faculty may opt to leave the kingdom due to a rather standard set of considerations: family issues, better salary and benefits elsewhere, and the expiration of a contract. One of the most dramatic issues related to a faculty sense of belonging is brought forward in the South Africa case, where matters of xenophobia may be affecting the experience of some foreign faculty there.

Ultimately, the Russia case study seems to yield a particularly meaningful insight. According to one HSE dean in that study,

> . . . the level of a person's happiness also depends on how serious they are about staying in Russia long-term. Those who accepted the job only to ride the market for a few years generally attempt to integrate less, and as a result, are unhappy. So perhaps, some of the dissatisfaction that people experience is actually due to the fact that people were never serious about being at HSE long-term.

This point raises our awareness of the fact that the international faculty mobility experience turns heavily on relationships—between institutions and faculty, between faculty and their families, and among faculty members themselves (notably, between domestic and international academics, and within the international academic community itself). In the Hong Kong case, for example, there is a suggestion that there is a fairly seamless set of relationships, given that international faculty members are hired as equals into a university with a formidable international reputation, English is the common university language, foreign academics are easily integrated into the shared governance structure, and there is a high level of academic freedom. At HSE in Russia, where international faculty have not been as uniformly integrated or satisfied with their experience, an informal 'union' of sorts has emerged. Articulating their interests via more of a collective voice has been helpful for foreign academics to feel mutually supported and more effectively 'heard' by the university. For example, the creation of an Office of International Integration is considered to be a result of issues raised collectively by the international faculty. At the same time, the 'voice' of international faculty may be perceived to outweigh their actual number and 'importance' at the university, which can create other, less positive, dynamics, particularly on an interpersonal and political level within the institution.

Without question, the 'human dimension' of the international faculty mobility story is complex and important, and our case studies—both at the national and institutional levels—illustrate the complications involved in the 'people business' that is recruiting and employing foreign academics around the world.

## Missing Links: All We Do Not Know

There is much to explore and to understand about the international faculty mobility phenomenon—both as it is currently playing out and as it will evolve in the future. Our case studies have shone a spotlight on a distinct set of national conditions and institutional experiences, but these are necessarily limited in scope and cannot encompass the wide array of realities against which the full panorama of trends and issues related to international faculty mobility should be analyzed. Some of the issues we have not been able to address more profoundly include:

- The relationship between overall immigration/migration policies and international faculty mobility, an issue that requires more attention in the current political and economic climate
- The differences between international faculty in developed and emerging societies and in the developing world, notably with respect to the phenomenon of brain drain
- Differences in international faculty mobility in the public higher education sector versus the private and for-profit sectors, as our case studies were, with one exception, in the public domain
- Differences by discipline, in particular how international mobility plays out among humanities and social sciences faculty versus those in the STEM fields
- Comparisons between domestic faculty mobility trends and traditions and international faculty mobility policies and dynamics
- If and how gender and age factor in to the international faculty mobility experience
- The impact of online education on international faculty mobility
- The role of political and economic instability (for instance, the current refugee crisis in Europe) and how organizations helping to facility the international movement of academics—such as Scholars at Risk—affect the mobility landscape
- Differences in the realities of faculty mobility across various institutional types, for example in world-class universities, flagship institutions, other research universities, specialized institutions, and universities of applied science, among others

As stated before, surprisingly little study has been done on international faculty mobility. This list provides a guide for further relevant research on this topic.

We have focused on the individual, institutional, and national/systemic perspectives of this phenomenon and have provided a list of potential other relevant issues and factors that merit further investigation. It is useful to remember that there are broader international considerations as well. For example, the South Africa chapter in this volume highlights regional and intercontinental initiatives that offer international mobility opportunities for academics, particularly in relation to the African (and southern African) context. Of course, the mobility fostered in the framework of most of those initiatives is quite temporary in nature, which is not the focus of this study. However, our South Africa case author rightly argues that short-term mobility can stimulate the development of relationships and networks that can pave the way for future long-term mobility. The effect of different types of academic mobility on longer-term faculty mobility merits further exploration.

Notably, all of the case study institutions present stories of evolution. This evolution has been characterized by changing rationales and motivations, and is framed by shifting national and institutional contexts and priorities. Each case study has also alluded, to a greater or lesser extent, to processes of institutional learning and self-awareness about what 'works' in relation to international faculty recruitment and retention, and where further investment and development of resources toward the international faculty recruitment and retention agenda may be necessary. 'Early stage' examples of this work can be seen in our youngest case study institution, Nazarbayev University, which is openly aware of the fact that much of what it is undertaking as an institution is still in its most initial stages. Interestingly, the oldest institution in our study—Vilnius University—is in some ways in an 'early stage' situation in this domain, as well. In 2015–2016, VU opened a new Human Resource Development Unit, and the authors of this case study suggest that a new focus on professionalizing human resources at the university, as well as on strategically prioritizing internationalization, will have an impact on future international academic attraction efforts.

Elsewhere, where there may be longer traditions of welcoming international faculty, the learning curve is still in full swing. In Russia, HSE's experience has led it to conclude that international faculty efforts not only need to be tailored to each school, but also need to be adjusted 'from one year to the next,' in light of changes in particular fields and in the economic outlook, both domestically and internationally.

This study has only been able to establish an outline for comprehending this complex and important topic. More research is needed, as well as the development of a common definition for international faculty mobility and a framework for exploring its key dimensions. In our view, this volume's collective insights and analysis provide a valuable first approach to the understanding of the international mobility of faculty.

# References

Altbach, P. G. (1998). *Comparative higher education: Knowledge, the university, and development.* Hong Kong: Comparative Education Research Centre, The University of Hong Kong.

Altbach, P. G. (2004). Globalisation and the university: Myths and realities in an unequal world. *Tertiary Education & Management, 10*(1), 3–25.

Altbach, P. G. (2007). Globalization and the university: Realities in an unequal world. In P. G. Altbach (Eds.), *Tradition and transition: The international imperative in higher education* (pp. 23–48). Rotterdam, the Netherlands: Sense Publishers.

Altbach, P. G., Reisberg, L., & Rumbley, L. E. (2009). Trends in global higher: Tracking an academic revolution. A report prepared for the UNESCO 2009 World Conference on Higher Education. Retrieved from www.uis.unesco.org/Library/Documents/trends-global-higher-education-2009-world-conference-en.pdf

Cantwell, B. (2011). Transnational mobility and international academic employment: Gate-keeping in an academic competition arena. *Minerva, 49*(4), 425–445.

Cradden, C. (2007). *Constructing paths to staff mobility in the European Higher Education Area: From individual to institutional responsibility.* Brussels, Belgium: Education International.

de Wit, H., Hunter, F., Howard, L., & Egron-Polak, E. (Eds.). (2015). *Internationalisation of higher education.* Brussels: European Parliament.

Havergal, C. (2016, March 10). EU nationals fill four in 10 new university jobs in England. *Times Higher Education.* Retrieved from www.timeshighereducation.com/news/eu-nationals-fill-four-10-new-university-jobs-england

HEFCE. (2016, March 10). English universities reach out to recruit global talent. Retrieved from http://blog.hefce.ac.uk/2016/03/10/english-universities-reach-out-to-recruit-global-talent/

Helms, R. M., Rumbley, L. E., Brajkovic, L., & Mihut, G. (2015). *Internationalizing higher education worldwide: National policies and programs.* Washington, DC: American Council on Education.

Mahroum, S. (2000). Highly skilled globetrotters: Mapping the international migration of human capital. *R&D Management, 30*(1), 23–32.

Scott, P. (2015). Dynamics of academic mobility: Hegemonic internationalisation or fluid globalisation. *European Review, 23*(S1), S55-S69.

United Nations Human Development Programme (2015). *Human development report 2015: Work for human development.* New York: Author.

United Nations Population Division (2015). World population 2015. Retrieved from http://esa.un.org/unpd/wpp/Publications/Files/World_Population_2015_Wallchart.pdf

# CONTRIBUTORS

**Ana Maria F. Almeida** is associate professor at the School of Education, University of Campinas, São Paulo, Brazil. Her research focuses on education and inequality. She is the author of *As Escolas dos Dirigentes Paulistas*, as well as several articles in Brazilian and international journals, and the co-editor of *A Escolarização das Elites* and *Circulação Internacional e Formação Intelectual das Elites Brasileiras*. She has been a visiting professor at the *Ecole des Hautes Etudes en Sciences Sociales* in Paris, at FLACSO in Buenos Aires, and a visiting scholar at the Stanford University Center for Latin American Studies.

**Mohammad A. AlOhali** was appointed Deputy Minister for Educational Affairs at the Ministry of Education, Saudi Arabia, in 2007. He earned his PhD in physics from Duke University. He was the principal manager of the national project "Saudi Arabia Higher Education Strategic Planning." He was Dean of Graduate Studies and Dean of Scientific Research at King Fahd University of Petroleum and Minerals. He chairs and is a member of several universities' boards. He has published over 43 papers in international refereed journals, numerous conference papers, and four book chapters. His research interests include physics structures and reactions, astrophysics, education and science policy and planning, learning strategies, and strategic planning.

**Philip G. Altbach** is research professor and founding director of the Center for International Higher Education in the Lynch School of Education at Boston College. He was the 2004–2006 Distinguished Scholar Leader for the New Century Scholars initiative of the Fulbright program and has been a senior associate of the Carnegie Foundation for the Advancement of Teaching. He is author of *Global Perspective on Higher Education*, *Turmoil and Transition*, and *Student Politics in*

*America,* among other books. He also co-edited *The Road to Academic Excellence,* the *International Handbook of Higher Education, World Class Worldwide: Transforming Research Universities in Asia and Latin America,* and other books. He is a member of the Russian government's "5–100 University Excellence Commission" and other international committees.

**Sylvie Didou Aupetit** is a full-time researcher at the Center for Research and Advanced Studies, Polytechnic National Institute, in Mexico City. She is also the general coordinator of a thematic network on internationalization, academic, and scientific mobility with support of the National Council for Science and Technology in Mexico. Her main areas of interest and research are public and institutional policies in Latin America, with a special focus on transnational providers, institutional diversity in higher education systems in Latin America, and knowledge transfer in comparative perspective. Recently, she has co-authored a book on joint degrees in higher education in Latin America.

**Diane V. Barbarič** is currently undertaking doctoral studies in higher education at the Ontario Institute for Studies in Education (OISE) at the University of Toronto. Her main research interests include jurisdictional-level higher education policy in Canada and Europe and comparative studies. Prior to returning to academia, she worked on bilateral higher education and youth issues at the Canadian Embassy in France. She also taught undergraduate courses and ran Boston College's student exchange program in Paris, France. Diane holds a master's in public policy and management from School of Oriental and African Studies (SOAS), University of London, and is a member of a number of higher education associations.

**Martin Bruder** is head of the Monitoring, Evaluation and Research section of the German Academic Exchange Service (DAAD) in Bonn, Germany. He is responsible for editing compendia on facts and figures about international mobility and cooperation in higher education such as *Wissenschaft weltoffen* and *Profile Data on the Level of Internationalisation of German HEIs.* He is involved in a number of research projects on the situation of international students and scientists in Germany. Prior to his position at the DAAD, he was a junior research group leader in psychology at the *Zukunftskolleg* of the University of Konstanz.

**Ariane de Gayardon** is a research assistant at the Center for International Higher Education and a doctoral candidate in higher education at Boston College. Her research interests include international and comparative higher education, tuition policies, access, and quantitative research models. For her dissertation, she is investigating the effect of tuition policies, especially of free tuition policies, on access in the Latin American context. Ariane holds a master's degree in English linguistics from the Université Paris Ouest-Nanterre and a second master's in engineering from the École Nationale Supérieure des Mines de Saint-Etienne.

**Hans de Wit** is director of the Boston College Center for International Higher Education and a professor in the Lynch School of Education. A native of the Netherlands, where his career as an administrator, researcher, and teacher spanned three decades, de Wit joined the Lynch School in 2015 from the Universita Cattolica Sacro Cuore in Milan, Italy, where he has served as the founding director of the Center for Higher Education Internationalisation. He is also the founding editor of the *Journal of Studies in International Education*, as well as a founding member and past president of the European Association for International Education (EAIE). He has published extensively on various aspects of the internationalization of higher education in local, national, regional, and global contexts and received numerous awards from prominent national and international organizations for his contributions to the field of international education.

**Luciano Antonio Digiampietri** is an associate professor at the University of Sao Paulo (USP). He has an undergraduate degree in computer science from the Universidade Estadual de Campinas (2002) and a PhD in computer science from the same institution (2007). Luciano has experience in computer science, focusing on database, computational biology, and artificial intelligence, working in the areas of bioinformatics, the Internet of Things, and social network analysis.

**Mauricio Érnica** is assistant professor at the School of Education at the University of Campinas, Sao Paulo, Brazil. He obtained a bachelor degree in social sciences from the University of São Paulo and a master's degree in anthropology from the University of Campinas, Sao Paulo, before completing doctoral studies in applied linguistics and language studies at the Pontifical Catholic University of São Paulo and at the University of Geneva. His work has been published in journals in Brazil and Switzerland.

**C. Giovanni Galizia** is professor for neuroscience and zoology in the Department of Biology at the University of Konstanz, Germany, as well as director of the *Zukunftskolleg*, an interdisciplinary institution that supports young postdoctoral researchers in the humanities and natural and social sciences. From 2002 until 2005, he was a founding member of *Die Junge Akademie*, initiated by the *Berlin-Brandenburgische Akademie der Wissenschaften* and the academy *Leopoldina*. He has published several books, including the textbook *Neurosciences*, organized international symposia, and is editor of the *European Journal of Neuroscience* and the *Journal of Comparative Physiology A*.

**Glen A. Jones** is the Ontario Research Chair in Postsecondary Education Policy and Measurement, a professor of higher education, and dean of the Ontario Institute for Studies in Education of the University of Toronto. His research interests focus on higher education governance, systems, policy, and academic work. He is a frequent contributor to the Canadian and international literature in the field of higher education. His most recent book (with Ian Austin) is *Governance of Higher Education: Global Perspectives, Theories and Practices* (Routledge, 2015).

**Marcelo Knobel** is a full professor of the Instituto de Física "Gleb Wataghin" (Gleb Wataghin Physics Institute), of the Universidade Estadual de Campinas (University of Campinas, UNICAMP), Brazil. From 2002 to 2006 he coordinated de Núcleo de Desenvolvimento da Criatividade (Creativity Development Center, NUDECRI), and from 2006 to 2008 he was the executive director of the Science Museum, both at UNICAMP. He was UNICAMP's Vice-President for Undergraduate Programs from 2009 to 2013. Knobel is an Eisenhower Fellow (Multi-Nation Program 2007), a Guggenheim Fellow (2009), and Commander of the Order of Scientific Merit (Brazil), as well as a member of Brazil's *Comissão Nacional de Avaliação da Educação Superior* (National Assessment of Higher Education Commission, CONAES). He has published and spoken widely on topics ranging from the promotion of the popularization of science and technology, to key questions about higher education in Brazil and the world.

**Valentina Kuskova** is deputy first vice rector of the National Research University Higher School of Economics in Moscow, Russia (NRU HSE), an assistant professor at the HSE Faculty of Social Sciences, and a head of the NRU HSE International Laboratory for Applied Network Research. She is interested in a broad range of methodological issues and research design, especially in multidisciplinary studies.

**Aliya Kuzhabekova** is an assistant professor at the Nazarbayev University Graduate School of Education, Kazakhstan. Aliya holds a PhD in higher education policy from the University of Minnesota. Prior to her current appointment, Aliya worked as a postdoctoral fellow at the Center for Science, Technology and Public Policy at the University of Minnesota, where she conducted research on governance of emerging technologies. Aliya's research interests are in international and comparative higher education. Her current work focuses on the analysis of the experiences of international faculty in Kazakhstan, as well as on the barriers and factors contributing to university research capacity building in Kazakhstan.

**Jack T. Lee** is an assistant professor at the Graduate School of Education, Nazarbayev University, Kazakhstan. His research interests focus on comparative higher education, internationalization, and international relations. He completed his PhD at the Ontario Institute for Studies in Education at the University of Toronto under a fellowship from the Social Sciences and Humanities Research Council of Canada. His dissertation on education hubs won the Best Dissertation Award (2015) from the Higher Education Special Interest Group of the Comparative and International Education Society. Prior to his doctoral work, Jack worked at the Centre for Intercultural Communication at the University of British Columbia, Canada.

**Liudvika Leišytė** is a professor of higher education at the Center for Higher Education at the Technical University of Dortmund, Germany. Her research focuses on academic work and organizational transformation in the context of changing institutional environments, with special attention to professional autonomy and the dynamics of governance and management of higher education institutions. She holds a PhD from the Center for Higher Education Policy Studies (CHEPS), University of Twente, and her postdoctoral research was carried out at the Minda de Gunzburg Center for European Studies at Harvard University. Leišytė is an editorial board member of *Higher Education Policy, European Journal of Higher Education*, and *Acta Pedagogica Vilnensis*. She is a co-convener of the higher education section of the European Educational Research Association and a board member of the German Higher Education Research Association.

**Georgiana Mihut** is a research assistant at the Center for International Higher Education and a doctoral student in higher education at Boston College. In addition to international higher education, her primary research interests include the impact of university reputation on graduate employability and quality assurance in higher education. She recently coauthored the report *Sage Advice: International Advisory Councils at Tertiary Education Institutions*. Georgiana is the current chair of the Course Quality Advisory Board of the Erasmus Mundus Students and Alumni Association.

**Gerard A. Postiglione** is recognized as one of the top American researchers studying issues in comparative higher education in Hong Kong, China, and East Asia. He is a pioneer among Western scholars in the field, and his fluency in Chinese has resulted in innovative primary research and fieldwork. He has brought sociological, policy, and comparative perspectives to important educational issues in Asia, such as the establishment of world-class research universities. He is one of the researchers most sought after by international organizations concerned with educational reform in Asia and by major media outlets to inform the public on issues of globalization and higher education.

**Anna-Lena Rose** is research assistant at the Center for Higher Education at the Technical University of Dortmund, Germany. She holds master's degrees in European Studies from the University of Twente (Netherlands) and the University of Münster (German). Her research interests include organizational change in higher education institutions, quality assurance in higher education, and structural change and internationalization within the higher education systems of Central and Eastern European countries.

**Alan Ruby** has a substantial career in government, business, philanthropy, and education. His experience includes being a classroom teacher and serving as the

Australian Deputy Secretary of Education and chair of the Organisation for Economic Co-operation and Development's (OECD) education committee. At the University of Pennsylvania, Mr. Ruby is a senior scholar in the Alliance for Higher Education and Democracy (AHEAD). A highly regarded teacher, he leads graduate seminars on "Globalization and the University." In 2015, he was made a member of the Order of Australia for service to international education through global reform initiatives and his work with philanthropic organizations.

**Yulia Rudt** is a senior lecturer in the law faculties of Novosibirsk State University and Novosibirsk State Technical University. She holds a master's degree in public policy from the Higher School of Economics (Moscow, Russia), and her main areas of research include constitutional law, human rights, and higher education policy in the Russian Federation. She was a visiting fellow at the Uppsala University (Sweden) in 2014 and a fellow at the Central European University in 2015. She has published over 30 articles in national journals and conference papers.

**Laura E. Rumbley** is associate director of the Boston College Center for International Higher Education (CIHE), where she also serves as an associate editor of the quarterly newsletter, *International Higher Education*. She was previously deputy director of the Academic Cooperation Association (ACA), a Brussels-based think tank focused on issues of internationalization and innovation in European higher education. Laura has authored and co-authored a number of publications, including the foundational document for the 2009 UNESCO World Conference on Higher Education, *Trends in Global Higher Education: Tracking an Academic Revolution*. Laura currently serves as a co-editor of the *Journal of Studies in International Education* and as chair of the Publications Committee of the European Association for International Education (EAIE).

**Damtew Teferra** is professor of higher education and leader of Higher Education Training and Development at the University of KwaZulu-Natal (UKZN), Durban, South Africa. He is the founder and director of the International Network for Higher Education in Africa (INHEA). Teferra served previously as director for Africa and the Middle East of the Ford Foundation International Fellowships Program in New York. He was the founding editor-in-chief of the *Journal of African Higher Education* and also founded and currently serves as editor-in-chief of the *International Journal of African Higher Education* and the *Chronicle of African Higher Education*. He has published extensively on African higher education matters, including *Scientific Communication in African Universities: External Assistance and National Needs* (RoutledgeFalmer, 2003), the award-winning *African Higher Education: An International Reference Handbook* (Indiana University Press, 2003), and *Funding Higher Education in Sub-Saharan Africa* (Palgrave Macmillan, 2013).

**Xie Ailei** is a postdoctoral fellow within the Faculty of Education at the University of Hong Kong. His main area of research is on education and social justice, as well as higher education development in China. His work has examined how *guanxi* structures rural parents' choices of school participations (*British Journal of Sociology of Education*, 2015), access to China's higher education (*Chinese Education & Society*, 2015), and university experiences of rural students in China's higher education institutions. He was an assistant professor at Shanghai Jiao Tong University from 2012 to 2013 and a visiting fellow to Cambridge University in 2016.

**Maria Yudkevich** is a vice-rector of the National Research University Higher School of Economics (HSE) in Moscow, Russia, where she is also an associate professor of economics. She chairs HSE's Center for Institutional Studies, which undertakes theoretical and applied economic analysis of institutions. Her research mainly concerns economics and sociology of higher education, particularly faculty contracts, university governance, and higher education markets. Maria Yudkevich has co-edited several books, including *Paying the Professoriate* (2012), *The Future of Higher Education and the Academic Profession* (2013), *Academic Inbreeding and Mobility in Higher Education: Global Perspectives* (2015), and *Young Faculty in the 21st Century: International Perspectives* (2015). She heads the editorial board for *Higher Education and Beyond*, a quarterly bulletin focused on Russia, Eastern Europe, and Central Asia.

# INDEX

Figures and tables are indicated by page numbers in italic type.

2050 Strategy 151
5I-strategy 139
5–100 program 208, 212, 217

AAPM (Academic Administrative Procedures Manual) 60–1
AAU (Association of American Universities) 59
AAU Staff Exchange Programme 257
Abele, C. 132, 137, 141, 142, 144
Aboriginal peoples 54, 56, 61
Academic Administrative Procedures Manual (AAPM) 60–1
academic council (*Uchenyi Sovet*) 152
academic freedom 87, 93, 139, 156
Academic Freedom Act of 2012 125
Academic Ranking of World Universities (ARWU) 59, 82, 224
accents 45, 69, 225
"Access to Success: Fostering Trust and Exchange between Europe and Africa (2008–2010)" (Intra-ACP) 257
acclimation 178–81, 184
accreditation 54, 187–8, 190, 246
Act to Control and Restrict Immigration and to Regulate the Residence and Integration of EU Citizens and Foreigners 128
adjustment processes 37
administrative processes 7, 280
admissions 53, 155, 187, 258, 272

advertising: in Canada 57, 60–4, 71; in China 93; in Estonia 106–7, 120; in Germany 134–5, 138, 140; in Kazakhstan 159–60, 166, 169; in Lithuania 105, 118; in Russia 203; in Saudi Arabia 224
Africa 1, 9, 17, 38; *see also* South Africa
Africa for Innovation, Mobility, Exchange, Globalization and Quality (AFIMEGQ) 257–8
African National Congress (ANC) 252–3
"Afrikaans" universities 248–9
aging 246, 254–5
*Agreement on Good Practice in the Internationalisation of Estonia's Higher Education Institutions* 107
A & HCI (Arts & Humanities Citation Index) 80
Air Force Technology Institute (*Instituto Tecnológico da Aeronáutica—ITA*) 33
Alexander von Humboldt Foundation (AvH) 129
Al-Farabi Kazakh National University 154
Altbach, P.G. 245
American Economic Association 162, 166
*amiguismo* (endogenous favoritism) 185
ANC (African National Congress) 252–3
Angola 243
ANUIES (National Association of Universities and Higher Education Institutions) 177

apartheid era 241, 244
appointment process 2–5, 63, 65–6, 69–70, 137, 141
Arab faculty 56
Ardhi University 257
Argentina 33, 38, 176, 180
Arts & Humanities Citation Index (A & HCI) 80
ARWU (Academic Ranking of World Universities) 59, 82, 224
ASEAN 3+ 25
ASEAN University Network 25
Association of American Universities (AAU) 59
Association of Southeast Asian Nations (ASEAN) 24
Astana 155, 159, 162, 273, 276
Athabasca University 54
attestation 153, 171n1
attrition rate 70, 182
Australia 1, 10, 87–8, 230, 245
autonomy 25, 40, 54–5, 79–80, 88–9, 103, 106, 155, 222–3
AvH (Alexander von Humboldt Foundation) 129

Baltic countries 102
banks 248
Barcevičius, E. 106
Basic Law of the Hong Kong Special Administrative Region of China 89
Beijing 86
Belgium 258
Berlin 132
*Berufungskommission* (search committee) 137
best practices 60, 145
bicultural adaptability 87
bilateral mobility 176
bilingualism 87, 89, 144
birthplace 18, 77, 105, 176, 178–9
birth rates 105, 196
Blue Card Directive 105, 108
BMBF (Federal Ministry of Education and Research) 129
Bolashak Scholarship Program 153–4
Bologna Process 103, 153, 199
bonuses 81, 104, 185, 223, 262
Botswana 243–4, 253, 260–1
brain drain/gain 16–17, 71, 104–5, 107, 128, 174, 192, 244
*Brain Retain and Gain Strategy* 104
Brazil 32–50, 269, 272–3; background 32–5; career-building perceptions in 41–6; higher education system in 35–7; international faculty in 37–41
Brazil, Russia, India and China (BRIC) 78
British Council 102
Buddhism 56
budgets 58–9, 104, 131, 152, 173, 184
Bulgaria 104
bureaucracy 4–5, 11, 33, 40, 104, 119–20, 166, 183
Bureau of Technology and Innovation 88

CAE (Chinese Academy of Engineering) 80–1
Cambridge University 161
Cameroon 257
Campinas 39, 278
campuses 17, 79–80, 226, 233, 245
Canada 10, 51–75, 269, 272, 273; background 51–2, 272–3; citizenship requirements 2; higher education in 53–8; jobs in 9; population of 52–3; *see also* University of Toronto case study
Canada Chile Free Trade Agreement (CCFTA) 58, 274
Canada first policies 5, 62, 64
Canada Research Chairs Program (CRCP) 52, 58
Canadian Association of University Teachers 56–8
Canadian Information Centre for International Credentials, 2015 (TÉLUQ) 54
Canadianization movement 51
"candidate of science" degree 200–2
capitalism 78
career paths 8, 40, 136, 186
careers 46; civil servant faculty (Brazil) 36; considerations regarding 21, 41–6, 189–91; in Mexico 189–91; perceptions of Brazilian academic 41–6
Carnegie Foundation for the Advancement of Teaching and the Changing Academic Profession 95
Carter, Jimmy 78
CAS (Center for Advanced Studies) 204
CAS (Chinese Academy of Sciences) 80–1
Casa de España (later COLMEX) 180
case studies 277; Botswana 260–1; Hong Kong Special Administrative Region 85–90; King Fahd University of Petroleum & Minerals 220; of Mexican universities 174, 178–92; National Research University Higher School of Economics 202–17, 202–18;

Nazarbayev University (NU) 150, 155–71; University of Konstanz 124, 129–44; University of KwaZulu-Natal 259–60; University of Toronto 52, 59–71;Vilnius University 110–19
CCFTA (Canada Chile Free Trade Agreement) 58, 274
Center for Advanced Studies (CAS) 204
Center for Asian-African Studies (CEAA) 180
Center for International Mobility (CIMO) 24
Center for Research and Advanced Studies (CINVESTAV) 175
Centers for Economic Studies and International Studies 180
Central European countries 102
Centre for Early-Career Researchers (*Zentrum für den wissenschaftlichen Nachwuchs*) 139
Changing Academic Profession project 46
Chile 33, 58, 274
China 56, 76–100, 269, 271; background 76–7; faculty in Russia from 204; Hong Kong Special Administrative Region 85–90; international professoriate in 81–5; Mainland 77–80; Shanghai Jiao Tong University 76–7, 79–85, 278, 280–1; University of Hong Kong 90–5, 278
China, People's Republic of (PRC) 76
Chinese Academy of Engineering (CAE) 80–1
Chinese Academy of Sciences (CAS) 80–1
Chinese University of Hong Kong 90
*Chronicle of Higher Education* 93, 159, 166, 224
CIMO (Center for International Mobility) 24
CINVESTAV (Center for Research and Advanced Studies) 175
citizenship 4–5, 8, 18, 51–3, 56–8, 61–3, 125, 164–5, 249, 269
citizenship requirements 2–3
City University London 204
Civil Service Ministry, Saudi Arabia 222
Clow, N. 132, 133, 136, 138, 140, 141, 143
Cold War 91
collaboration 10, 88–9, 94–5
collective-bargaining 57
College of Petroleum and Minerals (CPM) *see* King Fahd University of Petroleum & Minerals (KFUPM)
Colleges and Institutes Canada 53

COLMEX (Colegio de México) 173, 178–82, 186
commercialization 232
communication infrastructure 89
communist bloc nations 77
Communist Party 81
commuter faculty 19
compensation *see* salaries
competencies drain 192
competitiveness index 20
CONACYT (National Council for Science and Technology) 173, 176–7, 182, 188, 192
Congo (DR) 243
Consortium for North American Higher Education Collaboration (CONAHEC) 25
contract arrangements 5–6, 9, 13, 19; in Brazil 33, 35; in China 81, 83; at National Research University Higher School of Economics 211; at Nazarbayev University 157, 166–7, 170; in Russia 200, 208, 211, 214; in Saudi Arabia 221–2; at Shanghai Jiao Tong University 81; at Unicamp 40; at Vilnius University 109–10
cooperation, international 133, 181
cooperation among faculty 17
Cornell University 204
corruption 8
costs: contractual 33; of education 80; hiring 171, 182; living 79; marketing 135; mobility 10; moving 137, 181–2, 184; recruitment 26, 169; tenure systems 170–1; of translations 116; tuition 176
Council for Scientific and Industrial Research 246
Council of Higher Education, Saudi Arabia 223
country characteristics 20
*coups d'état* 33
Cradden, C. 19–20
CRCP (Canada Research Chairs Program) 58
creativity 87
crises, economic 33, 44, 176
Critical Skills Work Visa (CSWV) 250, 271
cross-border partnerships 88
Crozier, M. 189
Cuba 176
Cultural Revolution 77
culture: academic 9–11, 23, 77, 88, 96, 169–71, 187, 197, 203, 205–6, 213, 218; administrative 13, 96; campus 17;

creative 131; differences in 18, 23, 80, 101, 275; integration of 23
"culture of welcome" 128
curricula 7, 34, 51, 79, 87, 155–6, 158
Czech Republic 120

DAAD (German Academic Exchange Service) 24, 127, 129
databases 16, 34, 39–40, 127
DCC (Dual Career Connection) 65–6, 68–9
de Brito Cruz, H. 17
definite migration 19
degrees 35, 79, 82–3, 199, 201
demand forces 16, 17, 20
demographics 23, 97, 105, 107, 112, 119, 140, 229–30, 271
Deng Xiaoping 78
Department of Higher Education and Technology, South Africa 247
Department of Higher Education and Training, South Africa (DHET) 250
Department of Home Affairs, Immigration Act 2002 246
Department of Home Affairs, South Africa 248, 250
Department of Trade and Industry, South Africa 250
Dervin, F. 19
Deutsche Forschungsgemeinschaft (German Research Foundation, DFG) 129
Dhahran Techno-Valley 232
diamond mining 261
diaspora 17, 23, 114, 281, 283
Digiampietri, L. 34
*Diplomat, The* 156
Dirba, M. 19
discrimination 8, 23, 45, 61–2, 116, 132, 143
distance-only universities 54
diversity 11, 55–6, 61, 65, 230, 232
DR (Congo) 243
Dual Career Connection (DCC) 65–6, 68–9
dual-track system 85
Duke University in Kunshan 80, 97
Duke University's Fuqua School of Business 162, 169

EAA (European Economic Area) 109
EACEA (European Commission's Education, Audiovisual and Culture Executive Agency) 257–8

East Asia 96
Eastern European countries 102
economic: considerations 20, 78; development 87, 151; immigration class 53; reforms 87; welfare 102
educational sovereignty of China 79
education gap 54
Education Ministry, Brazil 33
Egypt 1, 234, 241
EHEA (European Higher Education Area) 103, 151, 154
EI (Engineering Index) 80
*Einwanderungsland* (land of immigration) 124, 146
Elmer, S. 132, 140–1
emigration 42, 47, 90, 105, 178, 244–5
Emmy Noether Research Groups 129, 138–9
Employment and Social Development Canada 57
*Employment Equity Policy* (University of Toronto) 61
endogenous favoritism (*amiguismo*) 186
Engineering Index (EI) 80
England 87–8, 118, 141, 155, 272
enrollments 54, 90, 241–2, 245–6
entrepreneurs 86, 88–9
equity statement 61
Erasmus+ 24, 102, 110
Erasmus Mundus Action 2 Partnerships 258
ERC (European Research Council) 129
ERC Starting Grants 138–9
ESF (European Structural Funds) 109
Estonia 106–8, 271–2; *see also* Lithuania and Estonia
Estonian Alien Act 108
Estonian Research Council 108
Estonian Research Mobility Scheme (ERMOS) 107
Ethiopia 12, 257
EU (European Union) 24, 101–2, 107–8, 272
EU (European Union) Freedom of Movement Act 127
*Eurasia Net* 156
EURAXESS 24, 105–8
Eurofaculty program 102
European Commission 24, 258
European Commission's Education, Audiovisual and Culture Executive Agency (EACEA) 257–8
European Economic Area (EAA) 109
European Higher Education Area (EHEA) 103, 151, 154

European project 133
European Research Council (ERC) 129
European Structural Funds (ESF) 109
European Union (EU) 24, 101–2, 107–8, 272
European Union (EU) Freedom of Movement Act 127
European University Association 103
EUROSA+ project 258
evaluations of faculty 282; Brazil 40, 46–7; Canada 69; China 82, 85, 88; Lithuania 110; Russia 204, 210–12, 218; Saudi Arabia 222–4, 229, 232
examinations 40, 155
excellence 61, 133, 139–41, 145–6
Excellence Initiative 129, 131, 133–4, 139, 144–5, 170, 277
Exceptional Skills and Quota Work visas 250
exemptions 57–8
exhibitions, jobs 135
exiles and expatriates 12, 19, 24, 52, 58, 117, 128, 174, 186, 221–3, 227, 269
expectation levels 234–5

faculty: evaluations of 34, 40, 69, 82, 85, 88, 110, 183, 204, 211–12; in Hong Kong 77; in Kazakhstan 152–3, 156; information systems for 105; international distribution of HKU 91; internationalization of Russian 196–202; satisfaction of 84, 85; selection 137–8; at Shanghai Jiao Tong University 81; shortages in 2; *see also* international faculty
Faculty and Personnel Affairs (FPA) 224–5
Faculty Housing Service 67
Faculty Relocation Service 65, 67
family and personal factors 8–9, 22–3, 44, 52–3, 65–6, 140, 213, 226–7, 233
Family Care Office (FCO) 65, 67–8
FAPESP (São Paulo Research Foundation) 46
favoring the foreign (*malinchismo*) 186
favoritism 186
*Federal Contractors Program* (Ministry of Labour, Canada) 61
Federal Ministry of Education and Research (BMBF) 128–9
federal states (*Länder*) 126
fees 57, 242
#FeesMustFall slogan 242
fellowships 105, 107, 139–40, 153
females *see* women

Fields medalists 227
financial considerations 6, 24, 26, 47; *see also* funding
Finland 24
Ford Foundation 33
FPA (Faculty and Personnel Affairs) 224–5
France 38, 176, 180, 245
Fraunhofer- Gesellschaft 125
freedom, academic 8
Friedberg, E. 189
Friedland, M. L. 63
Fulbright program 154
Fund for the Consolidation of Research Groups 177
funding: Canadian secondary education 53, 54–5; Chinese government 79, 81; European Union 107; German system 125–6, 139; for graduate-level degrees 37; and institutional autonomy 54–5; international faculty 104; Kazakhstan 152; for Mexican universities 177, 192; for mobility within the EU 102; Nazarbayev University 156; for research 36, 81, 92, 103–4; for Russian universities 199–200; Saudi Arabia 228, 231; for South African universities 242, *243*, 263; spousal employment 69; for study overseas 78; training programs in Brazil 36; Unicamp 40; University of Konstanz 131; Vilnius University 109, 116, 118
Fuqua School of Business at Duke University 162, 169

Ganz, D. 139
gender distribution 22–3, 52, 97, 105, 107, 112, 119, 165, *259*
generation clashes 116
German Academic Exchange Service (DAAD) 24, 127, 129
German Academic International Network (GAIN) 129, 135
German Center for Research and Innovation 24
German Council of Science and Humanities action plan (2013) 128
German Research Foundation, DFG (*Deutsche Forschungsgemeinschaft*) 129
Germany 24, 38, 272; background 124; contributions of international faculty to 141–3; Excellence Initiative and 139–41, 277; expenditures for 126–7; faculty in Russia from 204; legal provisions for academics in 127–8; and

Mexican scholars 176–7; programs for academics at 129; promotion opportunities in 8–9; recruiting international faculty for 132–7; research and higher education system in 125–6; salaries in 245; selection international faculty for 137–8; strategies for academics 128–9; support for international faculty to 143–4; *see also* University of Konstanz
Ghana 257
global competition 20, 56, 63, 254
*Global Grants Scheme* 104
globalization 1, 5, 89, 95–6, 101; *see also* internationalization
graduate programs in Brazil 36
Graduate School of Business (GSB) 158, 162, 169
Graduate School of Education (GSE) 158, 161, 168–9
Graduate School of Public Policy (GSPP) 158
Grant, H.M. 244
grants 45–6, 55, 81, 108–9, 138–9, 152, 168, 209, 226
Great Leap Forward (China) 77
Greece 91, 157, 204
"Green Passage" system 83
"growing our own timber" motto 253–4, 262–3
Guadalajara 175
Guangzhou 86
*Guardian, The* 156
Gulf Cooperation Council 25
Gulf countries 1, 10

*Habilitation* 136, 138
Hagenmeier, C. 247
Harvard University 4, 79, 204
Hawassa University 257
head hunters 135, 210
health insurance 67, 127, 186
Heisenberg Program (Germany) 129
Helmholtz Association (Germany) 125
heritage, cultural 87
Hesse 132
HigherEdJobs.com 159
Higher Education Council, Saudi Arabia 222
Higher Education Funding Council for England (HEFCE) 272
higher education institutions (HEIs) 173–4

*Higher Education Internationalisation Strategy* 107, 271
Higher Education South Africa (HESA) 252
Higher Education Statistics Center, Ministry of Education, KSA 222
higher education systems 35–7, 53–8
Higher School of Economics (HSE) 274, 276–7, 279, 282
high-tech industries 88
Hinduism 56
hiring 2, 11–13; in Brazil 33; bureaucracy in 166; challenges in 232–4; in China 90, 91, 93; committees for 161; criteria for 57; in Mexico 181; at National Research University Higher School of Economics 203, 211; for Nazarbayev University 157–9, 162–4, 168–9; policies for 51; principles of 61; requirements for 56; in Saudi Arabia 223, 224–8; strategies for 33; Unicamp faculty 40
HKU (University of Hong Kong) 76–7, 90–6, 278
HKUST (Hong Kong University of Science and Technology) 88
Hoffman, D.M. 23
Hong Kong 1, 4, 88, 90; *see also* University of Hong Kong (HKU)
Hong Kong Special Administrative Region case study 85–90
Hong Kong Special Administrative Region of the PRC 76
Hong Kong University of Science and Technology (HKUST) 88
Hornsby, D. 251
Horta, H. 26
housing 65, 67, 140, 165, 248
HSE (Higher School of Economics; Russia) 202–17, 274, 276–7, 279, 282
"HSE Look" bulletin 215
Human Development Index (HDI) Ranks 270
human resources 87, 286
Hungary 104, 281

ICEF (International College of Economics and Finance) 203
IELTS (International English Language Testing System) 155
IES (international education strategy) 55
IFAC (International Faculty Assessment Committee) 161–2

IGP (Institute of Geophysics) 173, 178–9
immigrants 53, 184
immigration: in Germany 124; humanitarian 53; lawyers for 66–7; to Mexico 178, 192; policies 51, 56–8, 272; return 106; rules for 63–4; to South Africa 244–5, 247; status 22
Immigration Act of 2005 127–8, 145
Imperial Academy of Sciences 198
Imperia statue (Konstanz harbor) 134
Improvement of Academic Personnel 177
inbreeding, academic 5, 7, 11, 39, 41, 47, 201, 253–4
India 5, 9–10, 38, 48, 78, 89, 164, 204, 234, 259–60
Indiana University 204
indigenous population 180, 186–7
Indlela National Artisan Moderating Body 247
*Industrial Policy Action Plan* (IPAP) 250, 271
industrial research parks 232
inequality 16, 22, 33
information technology 89
infrastructure 88, 115, 132, 156, 184
innovation 2, 87
INOMICS study 119
insecurity 136
Institute of Geophysics (IGP) 173, 178–9
Institute of International Education: *Open Doors* data 16
Institute of Statistics 16
institutional characteristics 21–2
*Instituto Tecnológico da Aeronáutica— ITA* (Air Force Technology Institute) 33
insurance 67, 105, 127, 186, 200, 216–17
integration 271; challenges to 4, 17, 215; of faculty 85, 94, 181–5, 207, 213, 216, 231; impact of 116–18; of international scholars 10–11, 79, 107; process of 68–9; social 144
intellectual tourists 19
interculturality 180, 185–9
international collaborative research 95
International College of Economics and Finance (ICEF) 203
international education strategy (IES) 55
International English Language Testing System (IELTS) 155
international faculty 267–87; attracting 165–7; background 267–8; in Brazil 37–9; characteristics of 162–4; defined 52, 268–70; as individuals 282–5; institutional realities faced by 276–82; location choices for 273–6; low visibility of 174–5; perspectives on 270; policies regarding 271–3; at Unicamp 39–41, 43
International Faculty Assessment Committee (IFAC) 161–2
internationalization 2–3, 16; of Brazilian universities 32; of Chinese university system 79, 90–1; in Estonian universities 120; and international faculty 3–4; of Kazakhstan higher education 153–4; in Lithuanian higher education 103–6; of Mexican universities 173, 175, 180, 184, 190; at National Research University Higher School of Economics 205–8; policies 271–3; of Russian universities 196–202; in South Africa 254; at University of Toronto 70–1; at Vilnius University 118–19; *see also* globalization
international professors at the University of Konstanz *130*, 131
International Recruiting Committee 204
international scientific staff at the University of Konstanz *131*
Internet access 67, 93
interviews with candidates 62, 160–1, 171, 225
Intra-ACP: "Access to Success: Fostering Trust and Exchange between Europe and Africa (2008–2010)" 257
Inuit 56
inverse discrimination 45
inverse migration 174
IPAP (*Industrial Policy Action Plan*) 250, 271
IPN (National Polytechnic Institute) 175
isomorphism 170
ITESM (Monterrey Institute of Technology and Higher Education) 175

Jacob, M. 17
Janger, J. 20
Jansen, J. 250
Japan 4, 88, 95, 104, 170, 179, 245
Jeddah Techno-Valley 232
Jewellery Council of South Africa 246
Jiao Tong University *see* Shanghai Jiao Tong University (SJTU)
job fairs 135, 140, 159–60, 169
job market 8, 9; in Brazil 36; Estonian 108; in Russia 198, 201–2, 208; stratification of 9–10
job satisfaction 281, 284; in Brazil 46; in China 93–4; in Germany 143–4; levels

of 11; in Lithuania 104, 115, 118; in Mexico 185–6; in Russia 218; salaries and 85; in Saudi Arabia 227, 233–6; at SJTU 84; tenure and 21
jobs.co.uk 159
joint ventures, Chinese law on 79–80
Jones, G.A. 55

KACST (King Abdulaziz City for Science and Technology) 231
Kazakhstan 150–72, 269; background 150; faculty 152–3; financing 152; governance of education 151–2; higher education internationalization 153–4; national education policy 151; *see also* Nazarbayev University (NU)
Kazakhstan Institute of Management, Economics, and Strategic Research (KIMEP) 153
Kazakh-Turkish University 152
Kenya 245, 260
Key National Strategic Projects 250
Kim, D. 18
King Abdul-Aziz City for Science and Technology (KACST) 231
Kingdom of Saudi Arabia (KSA) 220
King Fahd University of Petroleum & Minerals (KFUPM) 224, 236, 274; "Partners in Excellence" 220
King Saud University (University of Riyadh) 221, 232
King's College at York *see* University of Toronto case study
Knobel, M. 17
knowledge-based industries 220, 232, 245
knowledge circulation 17, 101–2, 174, 176
Kunshan 80, 97
Kuzhabekova, A. 168
Kwame Nkrumah University of Science and Technology 257

labor 1–2, 19, 22, 25–6, 67, 104, 127
labor market *see* job market
Labor Market Impact Assessments (LMIAs) 57–8, 273
*Länder* (federal states) 126
land of immigration (*Einwanderungsland*) 124, 146
language 274–5; Arabic 222; barriers 45, 116–17, 119–20; in Canada 54; in China 76, 81–2, 87, 89, 93, 94, 97; competency in Lithuania and Estonia 102, 107–8, 110; differences 23; English 4, 9–10, 76–7, 105–8, 110, 138, 155, 170, 198, 274, 280–1; fluency 12, 33, 46; in Germany 138, 141–2; and the job market 9; in Kazakhstan 153; Russian 9, 197, 216; in South Africa 248–9
Lansink, A. 247
Latin America 9, 38, 56
Latin American Association of Translation and Interpretation Studies 191
Lattes Platform, Brazil 34–5, 37–9, 41, 46, 48n3
Latvia 104
Law on Higher Education and Research (2009) 103
Law on the Legal Status of Aliens (2008) 105
laws: civil service 137; contract 222; educational joint venture 79–80; entry and residency 127–8; higher education 103, 111; hiring 90, 183; immigration and labor 57, 60, 62–3, 145, 247, 272; recruitment 137, 156; search committee 137; status of aliens 105; wages and working conditions 280
Lee, J. 253
Leeman, R.J. 23
legislation 33, 61–2, 103, 151, 155, 250
Leibniz Association 125
Lesotho 243, 261
L. Gumilev Euroasian National University 154
Lithuania and Estonia 101–23, 269, 271, 272; background 101–2; Estonian internationalization 106–8; Lithuanian internationalization 103–6; Vilnius University 108–10, 281; Vilnius University case study 110–18
Lithuanian Research Council 104, 109
Liverpool University in Suzhou 80
LMIAs (Labor Market Impact Assessments) 57–8
London School of Economics (LSE) 203–4
long-term faculty mobility *see* mobility; international faculty
loyalty 114–15, 201, 214, 231

Madagascar 243
Mainland China 77–80
"mainlandization" 94
Makerere University 245, 257
Malawi 243
Malaysia 25, 79, 88, 95

Index **303**

*malinchismo* (favoring the foreign) 186
Mamiseishvili, K. 231
manufacturing transfer 87
Mao Zedong 77
marginalization 15, 17, 23, 167, 181, 186, 254
Marie Curie COFUND 139
market competition 86–7
marketing 22, 128, 133–5, 145
Marxist-Socialist dogma 197
Massachusetts Institute of Technology (MIT) 33
Mauritius 243
Max Planck Society 125
May 2015 Plan of the Nation: The 100 Concrete Steps 151
Maya Intercultural University of Quintana Roo (UIMQRoo) 173, 178, 180–1, 187
media 89, 156
medical education 32
Meek, V. L. 17
mentoring 7, 17
Mercosur 24
MES (Ministry of Education and Science), Kazakhstan 151–2, 151–3, 155–6
Metropolitan Autonomous University (UAM) 175
Mexico 173–95, 177, 183, 188; acclimation in 178–81; attraction policies for 175–8, 272; background 173–4; career-building decisions for 189–91; integration in 181–5; intercultural tensions 185–9; temporary foreign workers in Canada from 58; visibility 174–5
Mexico City 175
Middle East 10, 12, 164, 224, 230, 294
migrants 19, 174–8, 253
Ministers of Finance and International Trade, Canada 55
Ministry for General and Professional Education of the Russian Federation 202
Ministry of Civil Services, Saudi Arabia 221–2
Ministry of Education, China 80
Ministry of Education, Saudi Arabia 233
Ministry of Education and Science (MES), Kazakhstan 151–3, 155–6, 168
Ministry of Finance, Kazakhstan 156
Ministry of Higher Education, Mexico (SEP) 177–8
Ministry of Labour, Canada: *Federal Contractors Program* 61

minorities 23, 55–6, 61
MIT (Massachusetts Institute of Technology) 33
mobility 10, 15–31, 249–53; and attacks on foreigners 247–8; background 15–16; bilateral 176; challenges 22–3; disciplinary 190; EU concept of 101–2; factors contributing to 18–20, 174; funding for 104; importance of studying 16–18; improved 181; incentives for 173; inward 192; legal provisions for 127–8; motivations for 119; national strategies 128–9; policies 23–6, 192; programs for 129, 180; rationales 20–2; schemes for 256–9; spontaneous 183; transgenerational 190
"Modell Konstanz—Towards a Culture of Creativity" strategy 131
modernization 89–90
monetary resources 20
Monterrey Institute of Technology and Higher Education (ITESM) 175
Morelos 175
Moscow 202, 216
motivation 7–9, 63, 132, 231
Mozambique 243, 253
multiculturalism 7, 89
multinational corporations 21
Murakas, R. 119
Muskie program 154

NAFTA (North American Free Trade Agreement) 24, 58, 274
Namibia 243–4, 253, 257
Namibia University of Science and Technology 257
*National Action Plan for Promoting the International Dimension of Lithuanian Higher Education* 104, 271
National Association of Universities and Higher Education Institutions (ANUIES) 177
National Autonomous University of Mexico (UNAM) 173, 175, 178–9
National Council for Science and Technology (CONACYT) 173, 176–7, 182, 188, 192
national development 95
*National Development Plan* (NDP) 250, 271
national educational attainment, Canada 54
National Immigration Policy Survey 253
National Infrastructure Project 250

National Plan for Higher Education (2001) 241
National Planning Commission (South Africa) 255
National Polytechnic Institute (IPN) 175
National Register of Postgraduate Quality (PNPC) 187
National Research University Higher School of Economics (NRU HSE) 196, 202–17
National Research University status 202
National System of Researchers (SNI) 175–7
National University of Singapore 26
Native Indian 56
natural resources 87
*Nature* 82
Nazarbayev University (NU) 150, 155–71, 273–4, 276–8; background 155–8; hiring process at 158–69, 162–9; observations on hiring process at 169–71
Nazarbayev University Graduate School of Education (NUGSE) 165
Nazarbayev University Salary Committee 161
NDP (*National Development Plan*) 250, 271
Nelson Mandela Metropolitan 254
Netherlands 20, 245
networking 17, 42, 46, 118, 185, 191, 224, 255
networks 17, 87–8, 93, 96, 101–2, 133, 160
Neusel, A. 132, 135, 138, 142, 143
*New Growth Plan* (NGP) 250, 271
New York University in Shanghai 80, 97
Nigeria 241, 256, 260
Ningbo 80
Nizhniy Novgorod 202
Nkosi, B. 251
Nobel Laureates 59, 227
noncitizens 5, 127, 247, 253
nondiscrimination 62
non–English-speaking environments 3–4
Nordic Council of Ministers 102
North Africa 230, 245
North American Free Trade Agreement (NAFTA) 24, 58, 274
Northern European countries 102
North-West University 257
Norway 245
Nottingham University in Ningbo 80, 97
Nowotny, K. 20
NRU HSE (National Research University Higher School of Economics) 196, 202–17

NU *see* Nazarbayev University (NU)
Nuevo León 175
Nwogu, S. 256

Office of International Integration 214–15, 284–5
Office of Planning and Quality 227
Office of the Vice Rector for Research 227
Oman 9
online application 65
Ontario Health Insurance Plan (OHIP) 67
open borders 87, 89, 93
Organisation for Economic Co-operation and Development (OECD) 35, 125, 154, 175
orientation program 85

PACIME (Program to Support Science in Mexico) 177, 272
Paganism 56
Pakistan 9–10, 164, 234
Pan, M. 80
Parliamentary Portfolio Committee on Higher Education and Training 252
participation 54, *241–2*
partner employment *see* spousal employment
partnerships 17, 26, 168–9
"Partners in Excellence" (King Fahd University of Petroleum & Minerals) 224
passports 66, 68, 70, 81
paternalism 187
pay scale 140
peer reviews 40, 58, 88, 103, 116, 168, 201, 212
Peking University 79
pensions 216
performance 87, 101–2, 104, 109–10, 200, 212–13, 217–18, 278–9, 281–2
Perm 202
persons with disabilities 61
Peru 192
PhDs, foreign scholars holding 37–9, 48n2
PNPC (National Register of Postgraduate Quality) 187
Pohlmeier, W. 132–3, 136, 141, 144
policies 271–2; domestic labor 57; education 151–4, 261; employment 62; hiring 24, 43, 51, 222, 224–9, 236; immigration 51, 53, 56–8, 70, 202; institutional 6, 25–6, 60–1; integration 18; for international hiring in China

92–6; labor 70; national recruitment
  4–6; regarding science system in
  Mexico 189, 272; regional and national
  23–5; repatriation 17, 177; research leave
  26; retirement 8, 36, 62, 186–7, 254–5;
  for reverse migration in Mexico 175–8;
  Saudi Arabian 221–3, 272; student visa
  263; trade 55; uncertainty of Brazilian
  46–7
politics 246
Portugal 24, 33, 38
Potthast, M. 132
pre-citizenship 2
prestige 12, 22
prizes 223
probation 40, 182
productivity 18, 45, 101–2, 181, 198, 208, 221–2
Program for International Student Assessment (PISA) 77
Program for Professional Development of Teachers (PRODEP) 178
Program for the Improvement of Faculty (PROMEP) 177–8
programming languages 44–5
programs 17–18
Program to Support Science in Mexico (PACIME) 177, 272
promotions 8, 40, 62, 69, 81, 229
protectionism 102
publication 7, 63–4, 77, 80, 92–3, 109, 127, 197, 204, 208, 232
Public Civil Services Ministry, Saudi Arabia 223
public university system in Brazil 35
publishing requirements 24, 40, 45, 47, 81–2, 138, 163, 181, 184, 201, 214, 232
Puebla 175
push and pull factors 7–9, 15–16, 20, *21*, 274, 282–3

QS Global rankings 202
QS World University Rankings (2015) 80–5
Quacquarelli Symonds (QS) 224
quality 53–4, 87, 173
Quebec 9
Quinlan, O. 247
Quintana Roo 178
Quota List (2009) 250
quotas 4, 81

racial studies 32
Rainbow Nation 249

rankings 3–4, 271, 278; Chinese
  universities 97; Germany 127, 131–2,
  136; Hong Kong universities 88–9;
  Kazakhstan 163; mobility and 267, 269;
  Russia 202, 206; Saudi Arabia 224–5;
  Shanghai Jiao Tong University 80, 82;
  South Africa 240; University of Hong
  Kong 93; University of Toronto 59, 63
R&D (research and development) funding 77, 88
recruitment 4–5, 17, 43, 273, 276, 279–81,
  286; for Botswana 260; in Canada 55,
  57–8, 62–4; in China 77, 79, 81–3,
  89, 91, 93; criteria for 60–1; in Estonia
  106–7, 120–1; in Germany 126–7,
  132–7; in Mexico 174, 181–5, 192;
  National Research University Higher
  School of Economics 203–11; at
  Nazarbayev University 157–8, 161–2,
  166, 168–9, 171; processes 12, 52, 57; in
  Russia 196–8, 209–11, 217–18; in Saudi
  Arabia 221, 223–5, *228*; in South Africa
  248–9; training for 68; at University
  of Konstanz 134–5, 140; at Vilnius
  University 109–10
reforms 2; in China and education in
  Hong Kong 86–7; to Lithuanian higher
  education system 103; in Portugal 24
regionalization 273–4
Regulation of Land Holdings Bill 251
religious affiliations 56
repatriation policies 17, 177
reputation 22
research 2–3, 6–7, 17; in Brazil 44–5, 46;
  in China 82, 93, 95; cultural differences
  in 12–13; design for 59–60; funding for
  36–7; in Germany 125–6; and hiring at
  Nazarbayev University 163; institutions
  for 125, 136; opportunities for 93; in
  Russia 197–200, 211; in Saudi Arabia
  224–5; strategies 94–5; structure of 44;
  at Vilnius University 109
research and development (R&D) 77, 88
Research Assessment Exercise 94–5
Research Council of Lithuania 103
Research Grants Council 88
research institutions 198
research networks 89
residency 18, 58, 127, 249
retention 17–18, 55, 58, 70, 281–2, 286
retirement policies 8, 36, 62, 186–7, 221–2, 254–5
reverse migration 175–8
Rhoades 253

Riyadh 232
Riyadh Techno-Valley 232
Rockefeller Foundation 32
Roman Catholic Council of Constance 134
Romania 104
Rosser, V. J. 231
Russell Group 59
Russia 196–220, 269, 271; background 196–202; case study characteristics 202–3; Higher School of Economics 274, 276–7, 279, 282; integration of faculty in 11; international faculty in 211–17; PhD scholars in Brazil from 38; recruitment in 203–11; salary adjustments in 6; scientists in Mexico from 176
Russia, 5–100 programs in 4
Russian Federation 198, 209
Russian Ministry of Education and Science 196

sabbaticals 22, 26, 207
SADC (Southern African Development Community) 243, 249, 253, 256, 258–9, 273
SADC Protocol on Education and Training 258–9
safety and security concerns 4, 156, 226, 247
St. Petersburg 202
salaries 36, 46, 57, 62, 280–1; Brazil 44; China 78–9, 81, 83; in Estonia 106, 120; in Lithuania 104; and living standards 8; in Mexico 183, 185; at National Research University Higher School of Economics 208, 210; at Nazarbayev University 156; relocation relationship to 21; in Russia 200, 214–15; in Saudi Arabia 221–3, 225–6; in South Africa 244–5; Unicamp 40; variations in 5–6, 9, 11; Vilnius University 109–10, 118
Saltmarsh, S. 17
SAMP (Southern African Migration Project) 253
'sandwich' scholarships 36
SANORD (Southern African-Nordic Centre) 258
São Paulo 39–41
São Paulo Research Foundation (FAPESP) 46
Saskatchewan 244
satisfaction survey 233–6; *see also* job satisfaction

Saudi Arabia 1, 220–39, 269, 272, 274; background 220–1; citizenship requirements for 2, 5; faculty in 11–12, 229–33; jobs in 9; national survey 233–6; policies and regulations 221–9
scandals 56
scapegoats 253
scholarships 24, 36–7, 154, 173–4, 176–9, 227, 258
Schoole, C.T. 244, 253
School of Engineering (SE) 158, 165
School of Humanities and Social Sciences (SHSS) 158, 168
School of Medicine (SM) 158–9
School of Science and Technology (SST) 158
Schwarzman Scholars Program 79
science, technology, engineering and mathematics (STEM) 36
Science Citation Index Expanded (SCIE) 80
Science Without Borders 47, 272
Scientific Visa Package 108
screening of applicants 155, 161, 170, 203, 210
search committee (*Berufungskommission*) 137
Second World War 91
selection process *see* recruitment
self-evaluation 229, 232
seniority 8
SEP (Ministry of Higher Education, Mexico) 177–8
service 6–7
sexual minority groups 61
Seychelles 243
Shanghai 80, 86
Shanghai Education Commission 80
Shanghai Jiao Tong Academic Ranking of World Universities 59
Shanghai Jiao Tong University (SJTU) 76–7, 79–85, 280–1
shortages 2
Short Period Visits Program 104
short-term exchanges 19
SHSS (School of Humanities and Social Sciences) 158, 168
Sikhism 56
Simões 17
SIN (social insurance number) 67
Singapore 1, 4, 25–6, 88, 91, 95, 155, 170
Singapore Report of the Committee of the Expansion of the University Sector 25
single-track system 85

Sino-foreign cooperation law (2003) 80
Sino-foreign joint ventures 79–80
SJTU (Shanghai Jiao Tong University) 76–7, 79–85, 280–1
Skype 161–2
SM (School of Medicine) 158–9
SNI (National System of Researchers) 175–7
social development 87
social insurance number (SIN) 67
socialist market economy 86
social networks 160
social sciences 33
Social Sciences Citation Index (SSCI) 80
Sofja Kovalevskaja Award 129, 138–9
Soros Foundation 102
South Africa 240–66, 269, 271–3; academic staff 245–6; and aging academics 254–5; background 240–1; Botswana 260–1; excellence and mediocrity in 255–6; governing acts and regimes 246–7; higher education in 241–5; inbreeding in 253–4; mobility in 249–53, 256–9; recruitment 248–9; University of KwaZulu-Natal (UKZN) 241, 248–249, 253–254, 259–60, 278
South African Board for People Practices 247
South African Human Rights Commission 253
*South African Journal of Higher Education* 256
South African Qualifications Authority 246
South Asia 1, 12, 56
Southeast Asia 25, 89
Southern African Development Community (SADC) 243, 249, 253, 256, 258–9, 273
Southern African Migration Project (SAMP) 253
Southern African-Nordic Centre (SANORD) 258
South Korea 91, 95, 204
South-South cooperation 17, 26
Soviet Academy of Sciences 198
Soviet Union 9, 33, 77, 101, 151, 177, 196
Spain 9, 33, 38, 175–7
Special Administrative Region of China 89
special treatment 64
spousal employment 9, 60, 65–7, 69, 70, 118, 143
spouses 5, 43–4, 66, 118
SSCI (Social Sciences Citation Index) 80

SST (School of Science and Technology) 158
Stanford University 79
State Program for Education Development for 2011–2020 151, 154
Stellenbosch 241, 254
STEM (science, technology, engineering and mathematics) 36
Strategic Infrastructure Projects 250
Strategy for Academic Mobility for 2012–2020 (Kazakhstan) 153, 154, 156
strikes 245
students 16; Chinese international 79; competition for 105; evaluations by 153; foreign born 17; Nazarbayev University 156; non-citizen 127; prejudices of 23; in Russia 199; in Saudi Arabia 221, 230, 232; in South Africa 242–4, 256
student voucher system 103
subsidies for housing 93
supply and demand 16, 20
support services 5, 17, 23–4, 59–60, 65–70, 117–18, 143–4, 184
Suzhou 80
Swaziland 243, 253
Sweden 20
Swirski, T. 17
Switzerland 1, 4, 20, 130–1

Tanzania 243, 245, 257
taxes 93, 281
teaching 6–7, 142; in Brazil 47; in Germany 142–3; in Mexico 186; at Nazarbayev University 163; in Russia 197–201, 213; in Saudi Arabia 224–5, 230; styles of 12–13; at Unicamp 40
Technical University in Munich 136
technology 10, 17, 19, 87, 101–2, 233, 246
TÉLUQ (Canadian Information Centre for International Credentials, 2015) 54
templates, personnel management 166–7
temporary expatriation 19
Temporary Foreign Worker Program (TFWP) 56–7
temporary foreign workers (TFWs) 56–8, 273
tenure 8, 12; Brazilian universities 21, 35–6; Canadian universities 57, 62, 69; Chinese universities 81; funding for 6; German universities 126, 133, 136, 139, 145–6; Mexican universities 182–3; Nazarbayev University 165–6, 170–1; Russian universities 196, 200, 202–4, 209–12, 214, 217; Unicamp 40, 47; Vilnius University 109–10

Tertiary Education Council 261
tests 40, 155
TFWs (temporary foreign workers) 56–8, 273
Thomson Reuters 92–3, 227
Thomson Reuters' Web of Science database 127
Thousand Talents Program 79, 271
*Times Higher Education* World University Rankings 59, 93, 127, 132
"To Make a Difference: To Move with the Times" (University Grants Committee of Hong Kong) 86
traditions 198–9
transition processes 52, 57, 67–8
trilingualism 153
Trilokekar, R.D. 55
Tsinghua University's Schwarzman Scholars Program 79
tuition 37, 54–5, 152, 242
turnover 141
Twombly, S. 18
typologies 15, 18–20, 280

U15 universities 59
UAM (Metropolitan Autonomous University) 175
UB (University of Botswana) 260–1
UBBS (University of Basutoland, Bechuanaland, and Swaziland) 261
UCGH (University of the Cape of Good Hope) 241
*Uchenyi Sovet* (academic council) 152
Uganda 245, 257
UGC *see* University Grants Committee of Hong Kong (UGC)
UIMQRoo (Maya Intercultural University of Quintana Roo) 173, 178, 180–1, 187
UKZN (University of KwaZulu-Natal) 241, 248–9, 253–4, 259–60, 278
UNAM (National Autonomous University of Mexico) 175, 178–9
UNAM (National Autonomous University of Mexico's Institute of Geophysics (IGP)) 173
undergraduate degrees 18, 39–41
underrepresented populations, recruitment of 61
UNESCO (United Nations Educational, Scientific and Cultural Organization) 32
UNESCO-UIS 256
Unesp (*Universidade Estadual Paulista*; University of the State of São Paulo) 39–41

Unicamp (University of Campinas; *Universidade Estadual de Campinas*) 34–5, 39–41, 43, 46–7, 278
Unified State Exam 198
unions 57, 213–14, 251, 284–5
UNISA (University of South Africa) 241
United Kingdom 1, 10, 272; attraction for international faculty to 20; faculty in Russia from 204; jobs in 9; Mexican faculty from 180; Nazarbayev University partnerships in 155; PhD Scholars in Brazil from 38; salaries in 12, 245; scientists in Mexico from the 176
United Nations Educational, Scientific and Cultural Organization (UNESCO) 32
United States 1, 10; attraction for international faculty to 20, 22; China degree programs in the 79; citizenship requirements for 2, 5; definition of international faculty in the 18; faculty in Russia from 204; jobs in 9; Mexican faculty from 174–6, 180; Nazarbayev University partnerships in 155; PhD scholars in Brazil from 38; salaries in 12, 245; teaching styles in 12–13; temporary foreign workers in Canada 58
*Universidade de São Paulo*—USP (University of São Paulo) 32
*Universidade Estadual de Campinas*— Unicamp (University of Campinas) 34–5, 39–41, 43, 46–7, 278
*Universidade Estadual Paulista*—Unesp (University of the State of São Paulo) 39–41
universities, faculty in 21st-century 1–14; background 1–2; definitions of 2–3; hiring 2, 11–13; integration of 10–11; mobility of 10; motivations of 7–9; policies relating to 4–6; recruitment policies for 4; strategies for 3–4; stratification of 9–10; teaching, research, or service by 6–7
Universities Canada 53, 57–8
Universities South Africa 252
University Act (1916) 241
university consolidation period 42
University Grants Committee of Hong Kong (UGC) 88; "To Make a Difference: To Move with the Times" 86
University of Antwerp 258
University of Basutoland, Bechuanaland, and Swaziland (UBBS) 261
University of Botswana (UB) 260–1
University of Buea 257

University of California – Berkeley 204
University of Campinas (*Universidade Estadual de Campinas*—Unicamp) 34–5, 39–41, 43, 46–7, 278
University of Cape Town 241
University of Durban-Westville 259
University of Hong Kong (HKU) 76–7, 90–6, 278
University of Konstanz 124, 129–44, 277; background 129–32; contributions of international faculty to 141–3; recruiting for 132–7; selecting faculty for 137–8; support for faculty 143–4; Zukunftskolleg 139–41
University of Kostanz's International Office and Welcome Center 143–4
University of KwaZulu-Natal (UKZN) 241, 248–9, 253–4, 259–60, 278
University of London 204
University of Michigan 79, 204
University of Nairobi 245
University of Natal 259
University of Pennsylvania 161, 204
University of Riyadh (King Saud University) 221
University of Rwanda 245
University of São Paulo (*Universidade de São Paulo*—USP) 32
University of Science and Technology 88
University of South Africa (UNISA) 241
University of the Cape of Good Hope (UCGH) 241
University of the Free State 257
University of the State of São Paulo (*Universidade Estadual Paulista*—Unesp) 39–41
University of Toronto: *Employment Equity Policy* 61
University of Toronto case study 52, 59–71; appointment process 65–6; background 59; integration process 68–9; interviews for 62; policies 60–2; recruiting international faculty 62–4, 278; research design 59–60; transition process 67–8
University of Toronto Faculty Association 62
University of Toronto Governing Council 62
*University World News* 156
Uruguay 33
USP (*Universidade de São Paulo*; University of São Paulo) 32

value added tax (VAT) 40
values 65, 68, 70, 80
VAT (value added tax) 40
Vilnius University (VU) 102, 106, 108–23, 281; background 108–10; case study 110–19
visas 2, 4–5, 22, 25–6, 67, 104, 127, 202, 246–50
visible minorities 55–6, 61
vouchers 152

wages *see* salaries
Wandt, J. 132, 133–4, 136
Web of Science 36–7, 88, 109
websites 159–60, 166, 224
Wegner, A. 132, 142, 143–4
welfare, social 102
William Solesbury & Associates 19
Wits University 251
Witwatersrand 254
Wolf-Wendel, L. 18
women: in Canada 61; at Nazarbayev University 165, 171; in Russia 200; in Saudi Arabia 230; in South Africa 242; at Unicamp 42, 48n4
"worker bee" faculty 15, 19–20, 26
working conditions 8–9, 20, 43–5, 57, 93, 160, 178, 191, 280
workloads 39–41, 185, 201, 207–8, 211–12, 214–15, 228–9
work permits 4, 66, 67
workplace equity requirements 61
World Bank 154, 177

xenophobia 247, 253, 262–3
Xiamen University 79

Yuanpei College 79

Zambia 243
*Zentrum für den wissenschaftlichen Nachwuchs* (Centre for Early-Career Researchers) 139
Zhang, L. 80
Zhang, M. 80
Zhou Enlai 77
Zimbabwe 243, 249, 253, 260
*Zukunftskolleg* 130–1, 132, 138–41
Zulu language 249
Zuma, J. 251 Žvalionytė, D. 117